The Tomes of Delphi
Win32 Multimedia API

Alan C. Moore, Ph.D.

Wordware Publishing, Inc.

Library of Congress Cataloging-in-Publication Data

Moore, Alan C., 1943-
The tomes of Delphi : Win32 multimedia API / by Alan C. Moore.
      p.   cm.
Includes index.
ISBN 1-55622-666-7 (pbk)
1. Multimedia systems.   2. Microsoft Win32.   3. Delphi (Computer
file).   I. Title.

QA76.575.M663   2000   00-040839
006.7'768--dc21   CIP

ISBN 1-55622-666-7
10 9 8 7 6 5 4 3 2 1
0006

All inquiries for volume purchases of this book should be addressed to Wordware Publishing, Inc., at the
above address. Telephone inquiries may be made by calling:

(972) 423-0090

Contents

Foreword

The book you hold in your hands is the gateway leading into a land of multimedia wonders. By opening these pages you can learn how to add sounds, songs, and movies to your programs. You can transform your computer from a mute, colorless drone into a swinging, swirling, shining multimedia festival of songs, sounds, and colors.

Multimedia is a sleeper in the world of PC technologies. Without anyone ever quite noticing how it happened, all at once multimedia is everywhere. It is a part of the daily computing experience for most people who run Windows or browse the web. It is something that draws in new users, and elevates a program above its competitors.

Today, our computers show us pictures and movies. They beep and burp at us. And, of course, they sing to us. The growth of the MP3 multimedia format has taken the world by storm, and left countless record industry executives tossing and turning in their beds.

Multimedia is everywhere. Our computers play movies for us whenever we copy a file from one place to another using the Windows Explorer. We go on the web and watch video clips from the latest films, and watch famous musicians turn their faces and bodies into so much silly putty as they contort, twist, and shimmy their way through songs aimed at 12-year-olds with sub-par IQs. Even mundane programs such as Word or Excel emit strange grunts and groans by playing wave files in response to certain events.

This book is designed to show you how to bring your own programs to life with the aid of multimedia APIs. Author Alan Moore is a well-known force in the computer industry, and an expert in Delphi software development.

Following in the footsteps of the indispensable *Tomes of Delphi* series, this book will show you the tricks you need to know to write powerful multimedia code. Whether you want to play a simple sound with a minimum of fuss, or plumb the depths of the Windows MIDI programming specification, you have come to the right place. Alan has done all the hard research for you; now you need only put his code to work in your own programs.

So limber up your typing fingers, and get to work having some serious fun with this great book. Spread out before you like glittering rubies are all the deep secrets that Delphi programmers once had to dig long hours to find, plus many more secrets that good programmers have long been hungry to uncover.

And best of all, these wonders are available in Object Pascal. Just boot up your computer, and watch this code run inside Delphi, the world's greatest programming tool! When you are done, get to work creating the next generation of PC programs, bringing them to life, and to wide acceptance, through the wonder of multimedia programming.

Charles Calvert
Borland Developer Relations Manager

Acknowledgments

Writing a book is a major undertaking. Few can complete such an ambitious project without the help and encouragement of family, friends, and colleagues. I'd like to begin by thanking those who were directly involved—my technical editor, Robert Vivrette, and the folks at Wordware, publisher Jim Hill, Wes Beckwith, and editors Beth Kohler and Kellie Henderson. Robert Vivrette's willingness to take time from his busy schedule to tech-edit this work was particularly gratifying. He provided me with important criticisms and wonderful suggestions. I am inspired to nominate Robert for the "Spirit of Delphi Award" for his great service to all of us in the Delphi community.

Without help from colleagues at Kentucky State University, this book would still be a vision in my consciousness. I thank my chairperson, Professor Roosevelt Shelton, for providing support and encouragement, particularly for supporting my application for the sabbatical during which I wrote the majority of this book. I also thank administrators Dean Neville Morgan, Vice President Betty Olinger, and President Mary L. Smith. Two other colleagues at Kentucky State deserve special mention: Professors Charles Bennet and Tucker Landy, both of whom read the early chapters and contributed valuable suggestions.

Had I not already written many technical articles, I doubt I would have even considered writing this book. Two editors in particular helped to shape my development as a technical writer, Tim Gooch (former editor of the COBB Group's *Delphi Developers Journal*) and Jerry Coffey (editor of *Delphi Informant*). Tim published my earliest articles, one of which was the precursor of the Delphi Sound Component Expert presented in Chapter 2. Jerry has been a constant source of encouragement and inspiration. Writing articles, reviews, and the File|New column in *Delphi Informant* has been an absolutely delightful experience, with the side benefit of allowing me to get to know so many wonderful and talented people in the Delphi community.

Several talented developers deserve special thanks for helping me overcome some very frustrating obstacles. When I first started writing experts, two of the top Delphi gurus—Ray Lischner and Mark Miller— helped me unravel some of the mysteries of RTTI, among other complex issues. Turbo Power's master developer, Julian Bucknall, helped me with some tricky C to Pascal conversions and obscure bugs. I would also like to thank one of my favorite people at Borland, Charlie Calvert, for all of his encouragement. Finally, I must express my gratitude to those whose works are included on the CD-ROM—David Churcher, David J. Taylor, and Colin Wilson. These pioneers in Delphi multimedia helped deepen my understanding considerably. I would also like to thank John Ayres for his extraordinary ground breaking as the lead author of *The Tomes of Delphi 3: Win32 Core API* and *The Tomes of Delphi 3: Win32 Graphical API*, and his generous help and encouragement. In his latest book on game programming with Delphi, you will find additional examples of many of the API functions we discuss in this work. John Penman, with whom I am writing a book on Delphi communications programming, read and tested the code for just about every chapter. I cannot thank him enough for taking on the role of first-wave tech advisor.

A book such as this is not written in a vacuum. We should all be thankful to Inprise/Borland for providing the greatest Windows development environment on the planet. And the Microsoft Windows help files (particularly the most recent multimedia ones) that have been included with Delphi are one of the greatest resources available. While I rewrote some of the descriptions to suit my own style, I found the documentation to be very accurate, probably more than 99 percent.

Of course, without the support and understanding of my family, this task would have been much more difficult, if not impossible. I want to thank my daughter, Treenah, for putting up with my irritability as each missed deadline approached and passed. My wife, Ann, was equally understanding and provided tremendous help and encouragement at every stage in the process. Finally, my mother, Mary Lou Moore, deserves so much credit for the advice and encouragement she has given me my entire life. Last but not least, I wish to thank and acknowledge my guru and spiritual teacher, the late Chogyam Trungpa, Rinpoche, for providing me with the meditative discipline without which the completion of this task would have been impossible.

Introduction

The organization of this book follows closely the format of *Tomes of Delphi 3: Win32 Core API* and *Tomes of Delphi 3: Win 32 Graphical API* by John Ayres and his coauthors. The first two chapters provide an introduction to working with multimedia. The rest of the book provides a comprehensive reference to the diverse multimedia APIs. Note that this edition only covers the audio APIs. To simplify your task of exploring the audio APIs, we have created classes that implement many of them. Those classes declare variables of the various types that drive the APIs including device handles, data structures that hold device properties, and much more. They also provide management of multimedia devices and encapsulate all functions within the classes' methods.

The CD-ROM accompanying this book includes all of the sample code introduced in the text. Additionally, it includes a rich collection of freeware and shareware programs and components developed by Delphi pioneers in their exploration of the multimedia APIs. We discuss a few of these in the text.

Getting Started—Intended Audience and Background Information

This book is for intermediate or advanced developers with a sound knowledge of Delphi. Some experience of Windows programming at the API level would be desirable but not essential. Readers who have used either of the first two books in the *Tomes of Delphi* series should find themselves on familiar ground for this volume. In some ways, the multimedia APIs we discuss in this book are less intricate than the core APIs discussed in the earlier books. Nevertheless, they do have interesting and challenging aspects, as we'll discover.

There are certain things you need to know before starting API-level programming. First, you need to know the special types that are used. The language of Windows and the Microsoft APIs is C. The WINDEF.H header file defines a number of special types that have been translated to their Pascal equivalents in the Windows.pas unit. Fortunately, there are fewer of these types in multimedia APIs than in the APIs described in the first two volumes. Some of the most commonly used types are LPSTR and LPCTSTR, both defined as PAnsiChar; PLPSTR, a pointer to a LPSTR (^LPSTR); DWORD, a Double Word; PINT, a pointer to an integer (^Integer); UINT, a Long Word; PUINT, a pointer to a UINT (^UINT); and THandle or HWND, a Long Word used to hold a device's handle. There are other types used but these are the most important ones.

The second aspect of API-level programming you need to know is the Windows messaging system. As you are probably aware, the Windows operating system is an event-driven system. Messages are constantly being sent: from the user to an application, from an application to the operating system, from the operating system to an application, from one application to another application, and so on. Messages trigger events, which in turn also sometimes trigger further messages. Although Delphi does an excellent job of masking many of the details of this messaging system, you still need to understand how messages work before you can work with the APIs.

Most APIs use callback routines to send the message to the application. A callback routine is a procedure or function you include in your code that is never called directly by your application. Instead it is called indirectly when Windows sends a particular message to your application; thus the name callback. With many of the APIs we discuss you have a choice of techniques to handle messages: you can use a callback routine, a callback window, a message handler, etc. In the sample code, we tend to use one or both of the first two approaches. In some sample applications and components on the CD-ROM, you will find examples of other approaches. As in other endeavors, there is more than one way to accomplish a task in Windows programming.

Once you set up a mechanism to send messages you need a corresponding one to receive and respond to them. If you are using a callback function you need to define that function and provide a case statement that includes all of the messages to which it might respond. If you are using a callback window and use the handle of your application's main window as the callback handle (the approach used here), then you need to implement the DefaultHandler() method in the calling application to respond to the various messages. We demonstrate both of these approaches in this book. Now that we have some idea of what is involved in Windows API programming, let us look at the contents of this book.

Chapter One—The Anatomy of Multimedia

Before we embark upon any journey it is helpful to know what route we will be taking and what attractions we might encounter along the way. Chapter 1, The Anatomy of Multimedia, accomplishes that goal. It begins by posing and attempting to answer the question, "What is multimedia?" It explores the meanings of this word outside the realm of computers since there are implications to the use of multimedia in art that also apply to computer programming. Then it provides a brief history of the use of multimedia in computing, particularly in the Windows environment. Next it poses the question, "Why multimedia?" This provides an opportunity to explore multimedia's communicative power in three application-writing areas: educational applications, business applications, and games. Finally, in tackling the question, "How multimedia?" the chapter concludes with a brief overview of the various APIs that form the core of this volume.

Chapter Two—Building a Multimedia Application

The second chapter is a very practical one in which we show you how to build the following artifacts: (1) a multimedia database application; (2) a series of multimedia components with which to build that application; and (3) a Delphi expert to streamline the task of producing components. Those aspects of the code that play sounds are discussed in this chapter. Appendix A discusses the details of writing Delphi experts.

This chapter introduces two of the most commonly used multimedia functions: SndPlaySound(), the venerable sound-producing function from Windows 3.x days, and the more modern PlaySound() function introduced in Windows 95. This is the only chapter that seriously attempts to provide support for Delphi 1 and 16-bit programming. Note that most of the programs in the book should work under Delphi 1 if you remove 32-bit specific code.

Chapter Three—The Wave API

In the third chapter, we begin with the familiar reference format of the *Tomes of Delphi* books. We start with an introduction to waveform audio and the issues related to input and output. Then we explain the identifiers, structures, and functions that comprise the Wave API. We explain Wave input and Wave output, showing how to use the popular double-buffering technique in each. Significantly, we encapsulate this API in several classes, greatly simplifying the task of working with it. These classes include one for memory management, setting up buffers for recording and playing sounds; a WaveIn class that handles all of the details of sound recording; and a WaveOut class that handles sound playing.

All of the constants, types, structures, and functions defined in mmsystem.pas are included. In addition, we discuss the various approaches to using Windows callback routines and Windows messages. The example application in the chapter demonstrates most of the functions discussed. We also discuss certain aspects of a freeware application called SweepGen by David Taylor.

Chapter Four—The MIDI API

In the fourth chapter, we go further by introducing MIDI. First, we provide a general introduction and brief history of MIDI. As with the Wave API, we discuss the identifiers, structures, and functions that make up the MIDI API. Here we explain MIDI input, MIDI output, and MIDI streams. Again, we wrap all material in the API in several classes, greatly simplifying the task of working with it. The classes include a general support class that implements MIDI streams; a MidiIn class that handles all of the details of MIDI input; and a MidiOut class that handles MIDI playing.

As with waveform audio, all MIDI constants, types, structures, and functions defined in mmsystem.pas are included. Similarly, we discuss alternative approaches to using Windows callback routines and Windows messages. The example application in the chapter demonstrates most of the functions discussed.

Chapter 5—The Auxiliary API

One of the shortest chapters in the book, Chapter 5 introduces auxiliary services that provide access to miscellaneous devices like CD-ROMs. As with most of the other multimedia APIs, this one provides a way to determine the number of devices and their capabilities. Beyond that, it is quite limited, mainly providing a means of adjusting the volume of an audio device.

Chapter 6—Multimedia Mixers

Multimedia mixers provide a method of combining various devices and controlling their characteristics. With the mixer services, you can route audio lines to the input or output of a destination device and control various aspects of sound recording or reproduction. This chapter discusses the mixer architecture and its elements including the audio line, audio sources and destinations, and mixer controls.

Various mixer control types are supported including fade controls, list controls, meter controls, number controls, timing controls, sliders, switches, and custom controls.

As with the Wave and MIDI APIs, all mixer constants, types, structures, and functions are defined in mmsystem.pas. The example application in the chapter demonstrates most of the functions discussed. We build a new mixer class to wrap up the types, structures, and functions.

Chapter Seven—Timers and Joysticks

The Windows multimedia system also includes support services for input and output, timing devices, and joysticks. We cover multimedia input and output in Chapter 8. In this chapter, we explore timers and joysticks. As we will see, the low-level timers in the multimedia system are the most powerful in the entire Windows operating system. With these timers, you can schedule timer events with great precision. In our example programs we use these timer services with MIDI and Wave. Timers use system time as a reference point; the system includes two functions to determine it, TimeGetTime() and TimeGetSystemTime(). We demonstrate both approaches in another example program. Timers are powerful and flexible; you can program them to deal with a variety of situations.

An input device popular with computer games, the joystick provides a powerful alternative to using the keyboard or the mouse. As you probably know, a joystick provides both positional information and button messages. As with the other multimedia devices we have discussed, you can determine the capabilities of a joystick and its driver through the joystick functions that we will be discussing. You can also query a joystick's position and button status information.

Chapter Eight—Multimedia Input and Output Support

Delphi provides a great deal of support for the most common Windows file input and output operations. However, Delphi's built-in functions do not provide direct support for some of the special requirements of multimedia files. The special multimedia file I/O services discussed in this chapter provide functionality beyond the standard I/O services provided by Delphi and other programming languages, functionality specific to the Windows multimedia system. This multimedia functionality supports buffered and unbuffered file I/O, Resource Interchange File Format (RIFF) files, and memory files. You can either extend services using custom I/O procedures or share services among applications.

As in previous chapters, all multimedia I/O constants, types, structures, and functions defined in mmsystem.pas are included. The example application in the chapter demonstrates most of the functions discussed, and shows how to record and play back WAV files using functions like MmioRead() and MmioWrite(). Using the MmioSeek() function you can move to a specific location in a file. These and the other functions discussed in this chapter give you a great deal of control in working with multimedia files.

Chapter Nine—The Media Control Interface API

Most multimedia APIs that we examined in previous chapters are rather low level, providing support services for wave audio, MIDI, timing, mixing, multimedia file I/O, and so on. The Media Control Interface (MCI) abstracts many of these services, thus allowing you to work at a higher and more general level. The interface provides a standard set of commands for playing multimedia devices and recording multimedia resource files. Because of this abstraction, these commands are device independent and apply to nearly every kind of multimedia device including waveform audio, MIDI, CD audio, digital-video playback, and similar devices.

In this chapter, we discuss the two ways you can work with the MCI: command strings and command messages. The command string interface is straightforward and provides a simple textual version of the command messages; on the other hand, command messages provide the same functionality but are faster since they require no interpretation. Ideally, you should use command strings during prototyping and use the faster command messages for production software. This chapter provides examples of working with each system.

Time to Explore

In addition to these nine chapters, there are three appendices: Appendix A, A Primer on Delphi Experts, explains the basics of creating a Delphi expert; Appendix B, Other Sources of Information, gives a compendium of books and Internet sites to help you to learn more about multimedia programming; Appendix C, A Glossary of Audio and Multimedia Terms, explains the technical terms used in audio and multimedia.

It is time to start exploring. Most chapters are self-contained and do not depend upon other chapters. For that reason, you can start anywhere. If you prefer to start by learning a bit about the world of multimedia, start with Chapter 1. If you want to dive headfirst into multimedia programming, turn to Chapter 2. To explore a particular API or support service, turn to its particular chapter. You may read the book sequentially from beginning to end, developing a thorough knowledge of the fascinating world of multimedia. On the other hand, you may use the book as a handy reference. Whatever road you choose, enjoy the journey!

Chapter One

The Anatomy of Multimedia

Why Multimedia? How Multimedia?

Multimedia. For the computer user or developer this word could suggest several possibilities: animated images moving across the monitor screen, sounds coming from different directions, or video clips capturing our attention. Interestingly, the word itself did not originate with personal computers. It goes back, in fact, to the beginning of the twentieth century as a term associated with the visual arts for works that use more than one medium. Such media could include oil paint, cloth, metal objects, and so forth—anything which could be drawn on or attached to a canvas. A classic example of a multimedia art genre is the collage, used by Pablo Picasso and others.

In the 1950s, the term was applied to a newly emerging form of performance art where various performance media (visual arts, music, poetry, and dance) were combined to create a new composite vehicle for expression. The "happening" is the best known type of multimedia performance art. In 1952, the American composer and philosopher John Cage, along with other notable artists such as Merce Cunningham and Robert Rauchenberg, presented the first such event, a "happening" at Black Mountain College.

Do these two uses of the word multimedia have anything in common with the use of this word in the world of personal computers? Very much! Whether we're concerned about the visual arts, the performing arts, or (if we dare to use such a phrase) the art of computer programming, the purpose of a multimedia approach is to expand our ability to communicate by allowing us to use more than one expressive medium.

In this first chapter, we'll explore why and how we might use the Windows APIs to do this. We'll begin by reviewing a little history. Then we'll answer the question, "Why multimedia?" Finally we'll provide an overview of these APIs when we answer the question, "How multimedia?"

Multimedia in Windows

In the world of personal computers, multimedia capabilities appeared first on non-PC (non IBM-compatible) computers such as the Amiga and Apple Macintosh, then under DOS on the PC, and finally in the Windows environment. The initial support for sound and video was introduced as Multimedia Extensions under Windows 3.x and became standard with the introduction of Windows 95. The original 16-bit multimedia API was expanded in the 32-bit APIs that support Win32, Windows 95/98, and Windows NT. Interestingly, much of the API is still 16 bit.

Even in Windows 2.x, there were functions for playing sounds, primitive as they were. In Windows 3.0, these functions were expanded considerably; in Windows 3.1, an additional expansion created a full-blown multimedia system. This latter system included the ability to play everything from *.avi files to *.wav files, to use high-speed timers, and to access the sound card's synthesizer through MIDI commands. Before we explore the details of these capabilities, we need to explore why we would want to use multimedia in our applications at all.

Why Multimedia?

As I explained in the opening paragraph, a multimedia approach—whether in the visual arts, the performing arts, or computing—can add power and excitement to our communication. But before considering the most compelling reasons for using multimedia in our applications, let's consider some of the possible reasons Microsoft chose to add multimedia support to its platforms. Certainly, part of the reason was to compete successfully with the other popular computers—to demonstrate that the Windows environment was as rich as that of Apple Macintosh and other platforms. At the same time there must have been a desire to attract more game producers to the Windows environment. From the start, game programmers have pushed the limits of a computer's capabilities. Educational programs, designed to engage students as much as possible, followed closely. Business applications were generally the last to take advantage of the new multimedia features. But as we'll soon see, multimedia has recently begun to invade the domain of business applications.

If you're writing games with Delphi, the APIs we'll be examining in this book might or might not meet your needs. For simple games, these APIs will often be sufficient. On the other hand, if you're writing complex games, you'll probably want to also examine some of the DirectX APIs. These are particularly well suited to game programming. For educational programs, these APIs are very useful. Let's take a look at some examples of multimedia applications in education.

Multimedia and Education

Technology, in general, and multimedia computers, in particular, have revolutionized the field of education. Most educational disciplines sport specialized CD-ROMs that enable a student to learn a great deal of information in an enjoyable way. As a college teacher I use these resources more and more each year. But how do others in the field of education feel about this? When I participated in a seminar on the string quartets of Beethoven at Harvard in the summer of 1992, I recall hearing the seminar leader, Professor Lewis Lockwood, make an interesting prediction. During the final session, he indicated that in the future CD-ROMs would be used in place of books as texts and research sources.

We had a guest presenter that day, Professor Robert Winter of UCLA. In addition to being a Beethoven scholar, he is the author of a popular series of music CD-ROMs on the works of major composers. His works in this medium include *Multimedia Beethoven* (the *Ninth Symphony*) and *Multimedia Stravinsky* (*The Rite of Spring*). At that session, Winter gave us a preview of his latest multimedia production, which inspired Lockwood's prediction. The power of educational CD-ROMs lies in their ease of use and multifaceted approach to their subject matter. In *Multimedia Stravinsky*, Winter introduces students to *The Rite of Spring* from a variety of viewpoints: the cultural setting of Paris at the turn of the century, the ballet for which the music was written, Stravinsky's orchestra, and the structure of the music itself. There are hypertext links between all of these areas and a multimedia glossary in which Winter provides definitions of musical terms. He even pronounces those words. The user can listen to the entire piece, particular sections, or individual instruments. There's even a game on the CD-ROM to help the student learn the material. Needless to say, very little of this would be possible without the multimedia capabilities now available in Windows.

As Delphi developers, we are less concerned with producing CD-ROMs and more concerned with creating tools or frameworks for computer users. While authors like Robert Winter tend to use authoring software to produce their CD-ROMs, I intend to demonstrate how, with Delphi, we have all the tools we need to achieve a similar result. In fact, with Delphi we have much greater flexibility and a higher level of control than with standard authoring applications. The multimedia APIs we'll be working with in this book provide many of the tools and techniques needed to produce such CD-ROMs, especially in the domain of audio recording and playback. Other tools, such as those needed to create hypertext, are available elsewhere in Delphi or through third-party vendors. With Delphi we could even create new authoring applications to compete with those already on the market, providing functionality not available with those tools.

Another important use of multimedia in the field of education is computer-assisted instruction (CAI) programs. CD-ROMs are essentially non-sequential in their construction, so the user can browse them in many different ways. CAI programs, however, tend to be sequential; they generally consist of a series of questions for which the user (student) must provide an answer. Here again, multimedia (particularly sound, but also animation) can add life to such programs.

Multimedia in Business Applications

There's little doubt that multimedia approaches will become even more important in the field of education, but what about business applications? We may have difficulty recognizing the appropriate use of sounds or animation in business computing. But we don't have to look very far to find convincing examples. Popular financial applications such as Quicken make excellent use of multimedia, and for the same reason as educational applications—to communicate more effectively and powerfully with the user. To demonstrate this point, in Chapter 2 we'll develop a multimedia database application which will show convincingly how multimedia can make a subtle but important difference even in such a mundane application. In this chapter, we'll suggest some of the many ways multimedia can be used in the world of business.

I've already outlined some of the uses of multimedia in education. But education or training is important is business too. With Delphi you can just as easily produce a CAI program in business as you can in education.

And the same advantages that apply to CD-ROMs as educational tools are applicable to training in various fields of business. No doubt it would take considerable time to produce a CD-ROM (or an online multimedia/ hypertext system) that served as an encyclopedia for a business' management structure, standard operating procedures, company policies, and so forth, but that time would be well spent since it would increase everyone's productivity. Rather than continuing an environment in which a new employee must ask job-related questions of his or her coworkers or supervisor, a company could create a multimedia repository of policies and procedures in which he or she could simply look up the information.

The potential for multimedia business applications goes much further. With Delphi, a developer could create an interactive, multimedia company report which could even perform calculations with live data. I am not aware of any standard authoring packages or tools that can accomplish that, but Delphi certainly can. For ongoing communication within a company, electronic newsletters can be an attractive and cost-effective means of keeping employees informed. They help to decrease the cost of printing, duplication, and storage and can be a powerful communications vehicle. The same holds true for external communication. Consider electronic brochures and catalogues, for example. While the cost of color printing can be rather high, the cost of making the same information available electronically is much less.

When you consider the addition of sound and animation (or video), the advantages of multimedia escalate considerably. Even in advertising your own software, multimedia can help. When I reviewed a programming tool from Nevrona Designs called Propel, I was quite impressed with a multimedia introduction to the company's product. The "Propel Guided Tour," which you can download from http://www.nevrona.com/ ndfiles.html#protour, includes some of the introductory information in the Propel manual, but in a way that is even easier to understand. This tour gives you a very clear introduction to how the product works.

There's no doubt that multimedia can add a great deal of communicative power to any application, whether it is in the field of entertainment, education, or business. But how do we use Delphi to harness the many multimedia capabilities inherent in today's computer hardware and in the Windows environment? Delphi's built-in capabilities are rather limited, consisting of a media player component that allows you to play a variety of file types such as *.wav files and *.avi files. However, with the

Windows multimedia APIs that we'll be exploring in this book, you can build a wide variety of multimedia applications. In beginning to answer the question, "How multimedia?" let's have a look at those APIs.

How Multimedia?

The Windows operating system is rich with multimedia support. The multimedia API (which we consider as separate, single-purpose APIs) provides device-independent access to a wide variety of hardware including sound cards, CD-ROM drives, MIDI devices, and so on. The APIs also support a variety of multimedia file types. These APIs fall into three general groups: low level, mid level, and high level. Several low-level APIs tend to be more device specific and require more work to use; one high-level API (MCIWnd) is very general and provides an easy means of associating a Windows control with multimedia functionality; and one mid-level API (MCI) can be applied to a variety of devices but requires more programming than the high-level API. In Windows 3.x, the Media Control Interface (MCI) was the highest available API. With Windows 95, an even higher interface was introduced—the MCIWnd class. This class is not available in Delphi. We'll be examining each API in detail in its own chapter, describing the syntax and use of each function and providing example programs. Here we'll briefly showcase each API in order to get an indication of when to use it.

Low-level APIs

As we'll see, the low-level APIs require a bit more work than the MCI. With the low-level APIs, you often must determine the devices available, determine their capabilities, open a device, manipulate it, and finally close it. Some of those steps require several API function calls. Despite these chores, the low-level Wave API, Auxiliary Audio API, the MIDI API, and several others provide more control over the various media devices; they also provide the ability to manipulate various multimedia file types, including *.wav, *.mid, and *.avi. There are additional low-level APIs for implementing audio mixers and working with joysticks. A small API—a collection of a few functions, structures, and identifiers—provides access to the most precise timing functions in the entire Windows API, essential for the time-critical audio functions.

The Wave API provides a powerful, low-level programming interface to audio devices. The functions fall into two general groups: Functions that begin with the word WaveIn provide the ability to record WAV files, while those that begin with the word WaveOut provide the ability to play WAV files. While most of the Waveform API functions are low level and require some work, there's one exception. The PlaySound() function, with which we'll be working in Chapter 2, provides a convenient means of playing WAV files. Closely related to these functions are the auxiliary audio functions, which control auxiliary audio devices. The five functions in this group provide the means to get the number of auxiliary devices, discover the capabilities of a device, work with a device's volume, and send messages to these devices.

Another important group of low-level functions is those related to the Musical Instrument Digital Interface, or MIDI. If you've worked with sound very much, you're probably aware that MIDI is a rather old interface (older than Windows) that was originally created to enable different synthesizers and other electronic music equipment to communicate with each other. While MIDI allows such communication with MIDI through devices, in Windows it has an even more important function: It enables communication with a computer's sound card and its built-in synthesizer. These MIDI functions provide a powerful and effective way to create and play computer music. Since you can work directly with the "instruments" stored in a sound card's synthesizer, you can use data structures, which are much smaller than creating the same music with a WAV file. With the MIDI API you can select and use various patches (specific sounds or instruments), and perform many sound playing operations on the fly through two kinds of MIDI messages: long and short. We'll examine all of these capabilities and more in Chapter 4, The MIDI API.

The low-level multimedia input/output functions provide all of the common file operations with buffered and unbuffered files, files in standard Resource Interchange File Format (RIFF), memory files, and even custom file formats. Operations include creating, deleting, opening, closing, reading, and writing files; they also include testing for a file's existence, working with filenames, and several others. There are also low-level functions for working with AVI files. These include a large number of routines for file input/output, streaming AVI data, and editing AVI streams. If you're using these APIs for writing a Windows action game, you have an API that provides functions for working with joysticks and another that provides a handful of timer functions. Useful as the low-level APIs are, there are situations where you don't need this level of control. In those cases you can work with the higher level, less-demanding API, the Media Control Interface, or MCI.

MCI—The High-level API

The Media Control Interface (MCI) is a higher level API that provides a somewhat easier way to work with multimedia files and devices. Since these functions can work with a variety of file types and devices, you can create a sophisticated multimedia application with less coding. With MCI you have two complementary approaches using two sets of commands for performing these tasks. The first, MciSendString(), is well suited for prototyping applications. The second, MciSendCommand(), is faster and better suited for production software.

The command strings used with MciSendString() consist of strings of words resembling natural language sentences. These command strings have corresponding command messages, making it possible to transform a command string into a command message. As you have probably guessed, the messages are more complicated to use than the strings. They require working with various parameters, not just using an easy-to-recognize string of words. We'll be examining each of these APIs in detail beginning in Chapter 3. But first we're going to get our hands dirty and find out what multimedia can add to our applications. In the next chapter, we'll build a multimedia database application along with tools to help us build other applications.

Chapter Two

Building a Multimedia Application

In this chapter, we're going to accomplish quite a lot. Our main and final task will be to build a multimedia database program. Prior to that we'll build a series of sound-enabled components that we'll use to build our application. To facilitate the easy construction of those components, we'll build a powerful Delphi expert that will give us considerable control over the functionality of the components we build. All of these components will be based upon one of two API functions: PlaySound() in the 32-bit version and SndPlaySound() in the 16-bit (Windows 3.x) version. First, we need to understand these functions and their use.

Playing Sounds

The Windows Multimedia API contains two high-level functions for playing WAV files, standard Windows digital sound files with a *.wav extension. Both are Boolean functions that return true if the operation is successful. PlaySound() is the newer, enhanced function that you should use in Windows 32-bit applications; SndPlaySound() is the older Windows 3.x function provided for backward compatibility.

Table 2-1: High-level WAV functions

Function	Description
PlaySound	32-bit, high-level function for playing WAV files
SndPlaySound	16-bit, high-level function for playing WAV files; provided for backward compatibility with Windows 3.x

PlaySound   *mmsystem.pas*

Syntax

```
function PlaySound(
  pszSound: PChar;          {A string that specifies the sound to play}
  hmod: HMODULE;            {Handle of exe file containing resource to be loaded}
  fdwSound: DWORD           {Sound playing option flags}
): BOOL; stdcall;
```

Description

Plays a sound specified by the given filename, resource, or system event.
(A system event may be associated with a sound in the registry or in the
WIN.INI file.)

Parameters

pszSound: A pointer to a null-terminated string that specifies the sound
to play. Three flags in fdwSound (SND_ALIAS, SND_FILENAME, and
SND_RESOURCE) determine whether the name will be interpreted
as a filename, a resource identifier, or an alias for a system event. If
no flag is specified, PlaySound() searches the registry or the
WIN.INI file for an association with the specified sound name. If
found, the sound event is played. Otherwise, the name is interpreted as a filename. To stop a non-waveform sound, specify
SND_PURGE in the fdwSound parameter.

hmod: Handle of the executable file (DLL or EXE) that contains the
resource to be loaded. This parameter must be null unless
SND_RESOURCE is specified in fdwSound.

fdwSound: Flags for playing the sound. The values are defined in Table
2-2.

Table 2-2: Values for fdwSound flags

Value	**Meaning**
SND_APPLICATION	Sound played using an application-specific association
SND_ALIAS	PszSound parameter is a system event alias in registry or WIN.INI
SND_ALIAS_ID	PszSound parameter is a predefined sound identifier
SND_ASYNC	Sound is played asynchronously with PlaySound returning immediately

Value	Meaning
SND_FILENAME	PszSound parameter is a filename
SND_LOOP	Sound is played repeatedly until PlaySound() is called with PszSound set to null
SND_MEMORY	Sound event's file is loaded in RAM, with its memory location pointed to by pszSound
SND_NODEFAULT	If the sound cannot be found, don't use default sound (returns silently)
SND_NOSTOP	Sound event will yield to (not stop) a sound event that is already playing
SND_NOWAIT	If the sound driver is busy, return immediately without playing the sound
SND_PURGE	Sounds for the calling task are stopped
SND_RESOURCE	PszSound parameter is a resource identifier; hmod identifies its instance
SND_SYNC	Sound is played synchronously; PlaySound() returns after sound completes

When you're using SND_ALIAS, do not use either SND_FILENAME or SND_RESOURCE. The various alias constants are shown in Table 2-3. You can play a sound synchronously or asynchronously. In the latter case, the PlaySound() function returns immediately after beginning the sound; in the former case, it doesn't return until the function has finished playing the sound. To terminate an asynchronously played waveform sound, call PlaySound() with pszSound set to null. Finally and quite obviously, you would never use SND_ASYNC and SND_SYNC together in the same function call.

Table 2-3: Alias constants defined in mmsystem.pas

Name	Meaning
SND_ALIAS_START	Alias base (0)
SND_ALIAS_SYSTEMASTERISK	System asterisk
SND_ALIAS_SYSTEMQUESTION	System question
SND_ALIAS_SYSTEMHAND	System handle
SND_ALIAS_SYSTEMEXIT	System exit
SND_ALIAS_SYSTEMSTART	System start

Name	Meaning
SND_ALIAS_SYSTEMWELCOME	System welcome sound
SND_ALIAS_SYSTEMEXCLAMATION	System exclamation
SND_ALIAS_SYSTEMDEFAULT	System default sound

How do you stop a sound that is in a continuous loop begun by calling this function with the SND_ASYNC flag? Follow this procedure: Call PlaySound() again, setting the pszSound parameter to null and including the SND_ASYNC flag to indicate an asynchronous sound event. If you specify SND_NOSTOP, the indicated sound event will yield to (not interrupt) another sound event that is already playing. If a sound cannot be played because the particular resource needed to generate it is busy playing another sound, the function immediately returns FALSE without playing the sound. If this flag is <u>not</u> specified, PlaySound() will attempt to terminate the currently playing sound. After that the audio device can be used to play the new sound.

When you use SND_PURGE, all sounds for the calling task will be stopped. If pszSound is not null, all instances of the specified sound are stopped. On the other hand, if pszSound is null, all sounds that are playing and that are associated with the calling task will be stopped. Finally, when you want to stop a SND_RESOURCE event, you must specify the instance handle. Any sound specified by pszSound must conform to these two constraints:

- It must fit into available physical memory.
- It must be playable by an installed waveform audio device driver.

PlaySound() searches the following directories for sound files: the current directory, the Windows directory, the Windows system directory, directories listed in the PATH environment variable, and the list of directories mapped in a network. For more information about the directory search order, see the documentation for the OpenFile() function.

If it cannot find the specified sound, PlaySound() uses the default system event sound entry instead. If the function can find neither the system default entry nor the default sound, it plays no sound and returns FALSE. Now let's examine the older function, SndPlaySound().

SndPlaySound   *mmsystem.pas*

Syntax

```
function SndPlaySound(
  lpszSoundName: PChar;
  uFlags: UINT
  ): BOOL; stdcall;
```

Description

Plays a waveform sound specified either by a filename or by an entry in the registry or the WIN.INI file. This function offers a subset of the functionality of the PlaySound() function; SndPlaySound() is maintained for backward compatibility. If the specified sound cannot be found, SndPlaySound() plays the system default sound. If there is no system default entry in the registry (or the WIN.INI file), or if the default sound cannot be found, the function produces no sound and returns with a value of FALSE. The specified sound must not exceed the limits of available physical memory and must be playable by an installed waveform audio device driver. If SndPlaySound() does not find the sound in the current directory, the function searches for it using the standard directory search order.

Parameters

lpszSoundName: A pointer to a null-terminated string that specifies the sound to play. This parameter can be either an entry in the registry, an entry in WIN.INI identifying a system sound, or the name of a waveform audio file. (If the function does not find the entry, the parameter is treated as a filename.) If this parameter is null, any currently playing sound is stopped.

uFlags: Flags for playing the sound. The values are defined in Table 2-4.

2

Chapter

Table 2-4: Values for uFlags flags in SndPlaySound

Value	Meaning
SND_ASYNC	Sound is played asynchronously with SndPlaySound() returning immediately
SND_LOOP	Sound is played repeatedly until SndPlaySound() is called with pszSound at null
SND_MEMORY	Sound event's file is loaded in RAM, with its memory pointed to by pszSound
SND_NODEFAULT	If the sound cannot be found, don't use default sound (returns silently)
SND_NOSTOP	Sound event will yield to (not stop) a sound event that is already playing
SND_SYNC	Sound is played synchronously; SndPlaySound() returns after sound completes

Building a Sound Component Expert

In the sound-enabled database application we'll build in this chapter, we'll need a series of sound-enabled Delphi components. Since we don't want to have to do a lot of cutting and pasting, let alone unnecessary coding, we're going to start by building an expert that will make it easy to create those new components.

For all of these examples we'll support all Delphi versions. In Delphi 1, we'll use the SndPlaySound() function, while in all of the 32-bit versions we'll use the newer PlaySound() function. In both the expert and the components, we'll frequently use conditional definitions so that we can use a single unit instead of separate versions to compile the 16-bit and 32-bit versions.

The project file which we use to create the *.dll that runs this expert is the library file SndExprt.dpr. Like many Delphi experts, most of this project file involves basic expert housekeeping rather than producing sounds. For that reason, we're not going to discuss it in detail here. However, if you're interested in learning more about experts in general or the inner workings of this expert in particular, study Appendix A, A Primer on Delphi Experts. Here we'll simply point out some of the essential features and concentrate on those elements related to producing sounds.

If you simply intend to use the sound playing functions we discussed above in a limited way, it would be best to just add the function to one of the event handlers like this:

```
procedure TForm1.Button1Click(Sender: TObject);
begin
 PlaySound('Tada.wav', 0, (SND_ASYNC or SND_FILENAME));
 { perform other functions here}
end;
```

However, if you're going to be using sound with many events, in many controls, or differently in the same control, this could get tedious. One solution would be to use a component-creation product such as Eagle Software's Component Development Kit (CDK). This author has used that feature-rich product often, even creating a sound generating template to hook into the Click event, just as we're doing here. The code for that template is included in the current version of the CDK. The expert we'll be creating works well in this situation where we are simply adding sound playing capabilities to standard controls. Let's look at the details.

User Interface

As with many experts, the sound component expert consists of notebook pages and dialog boxes. On the first page (Figure 2-1), the user enters the basic information: the name of the new component, its ancestor, and its ancestor's unit.

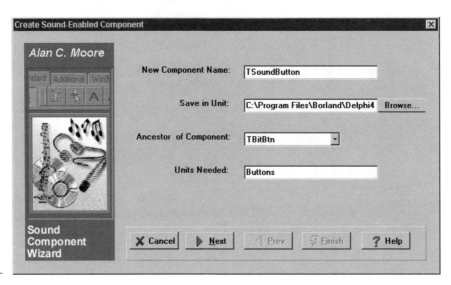

Figure 2-1

On the second page (Figure 2-2), the user checks the events to be sound enabled.

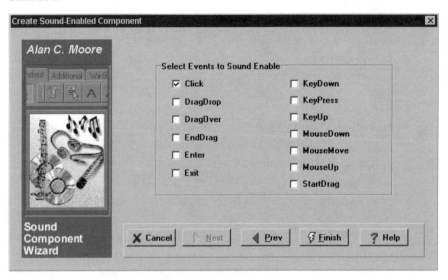

Figure 2-2

Whenever you click on an event (the first time), a dialog box (Figure 2-3) comes up allowing you to enter the properties you want to use: the way(s) in which the sound might be played or stopped, whether the new sound should interrupt or yield to a sound already playing, and a default WAV file (if there is one).

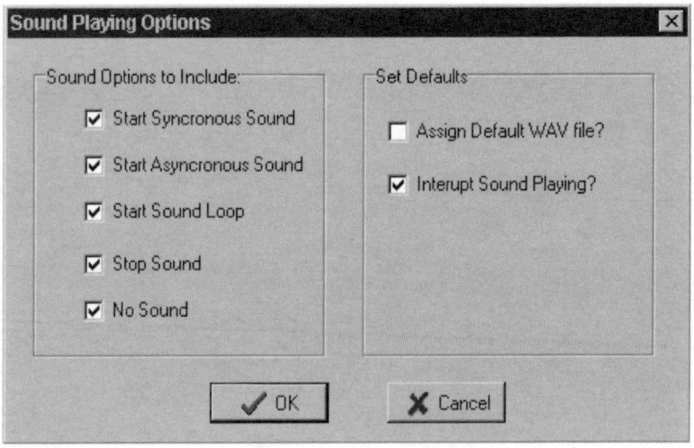

Figure 2-3

Once you've chosen all of the events you plan to implement (which could be just a few), you click Finish and the final form comes up.

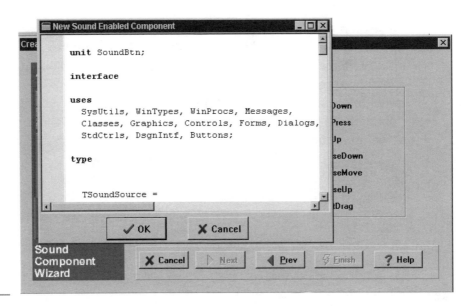

Figure 2-4

The main part of this last form (Figure 2-4) is a memo in which the generated source code is available for viewing and/or editing. Once you click OK, the edited code is saved. How is all of this implemented in the code? Let's find out.

All of the functionality of the expert's user interface is implemented in the Sndexp1.pas unit, included in its entirety on the CD-ROM accompanying this book. This unit and the component-generating unit, CompGen1, both depend upon a third unit, SndTypes.pas (Listing 2-1). This latter unit stores the global variables, types, and constants used in the other units. We'll discuss all of these units presently, but first let's find out how our expert is activated.

When the menu item is clicked, the expert's Execute() procedure is called. In the following code fragment, the method ExecuteExpert() in the Sndexp1.pas unit is called and sent a copy of ToolServices. Note the try/except block. This is good practice in a *.dll expert:

```
try
ExecuteExpert( ToolServices );
except
HandleException;
end;
```

The expert's main dialog box is implemented in Sndexp1.pas. The ExecuteExpert() method brings up this modal dialog box. The implementation is shown below. The {$IFNDEF DEBUG} block facilitates testing by allowing us to run the expert as an *.exe rather than a *.dll. (For additional information on this and other conditional define statements, see Appendix A.) In the former case, we are unable to use the tool services as we do in the *.dll.

```
procedure ExecuteExpert( ToolServices: TIToolServices );
begin
 {$IFNDEF DEBUG}
 iTools := ToolServices; { Keep a local copy of the Tools API instance }
 {$ENDIF}
 SoundCompForm := TSoundCompForm.Create( Application );
 try
 SoundCompForm.ShowModal;
 finally
 SoundCompForm.Free;
 end;
end;
```

When this procedure is run, the first page of the expert (Figure 2-1) comes up and the user enters the basic information.

In the first field, the user enters the name of the new component, which by convention begins with the letter "T." When the user clicks on the second field, he or she can either enter a filename or bring up a File|Save dialog box by clicking on the Browse button. The third field, a combo box, provides a convenient means for the user to choose the ancestor of the new component from all of the available components in the library. This magic is made possible through Delphi's Tool Services. Please see the section, "Using Tool Services to Access Installed Components," in Appendix A.

If you study the unit, you'll notice that the various data elements—the new component name, the filename, its ancestor, and the units needed—are set in the NextBtnClick() method (shown below) before moving to the second page. The variables used are CompName, UnitName, CompAncestor, and AncestorUnit. It's important that all of these except the last one (which may not apply if it's one of the standard units included) be entered. So, the code fragment shown below includes a check for that and gives the user a message if something is missing.

```
If (NoteBook1.PageIndex = 0) then if ((Edit1.Text = '') OR
  (ComboBox1.Text = '') OR (Edit2.Text = '')) then
  begin
  ShowMessage('You need to enter component information!');
  Exit;
  end else
  begin
  CompName := Edit1.Text;
  UnitName := Edit2.Text;
  CompAncestor := ComboBox1.Text;
  AncestorUnit := Edit3.Text;
  FHandlingInternally := False;
  end;
```

Whenever one of these events is checked, a dialog box automatically comes up, asking for the parameters for that sound event. This dialog box always appears with either the default values checked (in this version, none at all) or the previously selected values (if the event had been selected previously). The user must choose at least one event before the Finish button becomes enabled. Again, we check this in the code to make sure.

Sound Playing Options

In the resulting components, we use various properties to control what sounds are played and how those sounds are played. These properties are arranged in a hierarchical manner. The main property added to each component, SoundPlayEvents, contains a series of properties, XSoundPlayEvent, where X is the name of one of the standard events to be sound enabled. These properties—which are classes like ClickSound-PlayEvent, EnterSoundPlayEvent, and ExitSoundPlayEvent—contain the subproperties that control the playing of sounds for these events.

The subproperty SoundSource indicates the type of sound source to which the FileName parameter points. It is of the enumerated type, TSoundSource (ssAlias, ssAlias_ID, ssFilename, ssMemory, ssResource, ssNone). The 16-bit version of this expert uses a subset of this type that works with SndPlaySound: (ssFilename, ssMemory). The Boolean property Yield determines if the requested sound will interrupt a sound already playing. This property is connected with the SND_NOSTOP flag. All of the flags associated with the PlaySound() function (introduced in Windows 95) are shown in Table 2-2.

How do we get our expert to produce a component with this new composite property? To accomplish this we use several types and data structures, all of which are defined in the SndTypes.pas unit, shown in its entirety in Listing 2-1.

Listing 2-1: SndTypes.pas unit contains global types, variables, constants, and structures

```
uses SysUtils;
const
 {$IFNDEF VER80}
 EventMax = 12; { number of events user can sound-enable; 0-based –
     actual number of events is one more }
 {$ELSE}
 EventMax = 11; { number of events user can sound-enable; 0-based –
     actual number of events is one more }
 {$ENDIF}
type
 String80 = String[80];
 String30 = String[30];
 String15 = String[15];
 String2 = String[2];
 TSoundPlayOption = (spPlayReturn,
     spPlayNoReturn,
     spPlayContinuous,
     spEndSoundPlay,
     spPlayNoSound);
 TSoundPlayOptions = set of TSoundPlayOption;
 SoundFactors = packed record
 Yield : boolean;
 WavFileDefault : boolean;
 DefaultWavFile : TFileName;
 SoundPlayOptions : TSoundPlayOptions;
 end;
var
 { storage for properties }
 SoundFactorsArray : Array [0..EventMax] of SoundFactors;
 { used for formatting new types in CompGen1 }
 SoundOptions : Array[0..EventMax] of integer;
 { holds the string value for the 3rd PlaySound parameter from the
 fdwSoundFlags array }
 fdwSoundValue : string15;
const
 BasicEventNames : array [0..EventMax] of String15 = ('Click', 'DragDrop',
 'DragOver', 'EndDrag', 'Enter', 'Exit', 'KeyDown', 'KeyPress',
 'KeyUp', 'MouseDown', 'MouseMove', 'MouseUp'
```

```
{$IFNDEF VER80}
, 'StartDrag'
{$ENDIF}
);
EventNames : array [0..EventMax] of String15 = ('Click', 'DragDrop',
  'DragOver', 'DoEndDrag', 'DoEnter', 'DoExit', 'KeyDown', 'KeyPress',
  'KeyUp', 'MouseDown', 'MouseMove', 'MouseUp'
{$IFNDEF VER80}
, 'DoStartDrag'
{$ENDIF}
);
ParametersArray : array [0..8] of string80 =
('', {used with Click, DoEnter, DoExit }
  'Source: TObject; X, Y: Integer', {used with DragDrop}
  'Source: TObject; X, Y: Integer; State: TDragState; var Accept:
      Boolean',
  {used with DragOver}
  'Target: TObject; X, Y: Integer', {used with EndDrag}
  'var Key: Word; Shift: TShiftState', {used with KeyDown and KeyUp}
  'var Key: Char', {used with KeyPress}
  'Button: TMouseButton; Shift: TShiftState; X, Y: Integer',
  {used with MouseDown and MouseUp}
  'Shift: TShiftState; X, Y: Integer', {used with MouseMove}
  'var DragObject: TDragObject'); {used with StartDrag in 32-bit versions}
  ParamsArray : array [0..8] of string80 = ('',
  {used with Click, DoEnter, DoExit }
  '(Source, X, Y)', {used with DragDrop}
  '(Source, X, Y, State, Accept)',
  {used with DragOver}
  '(Target, X, Y)', {used with EndDrag}
  '(Key, Shift)', {used with KeyDown and KeyUp}
  '(Key)', {used with KeyPress}
  '(Button, Shift, X, Y)',
  {used with MouseDown and MouseUp}
  '(Shift, X, Y)', {used with MouseMove}
  '(DragObject)'); {used with StartDrag in 32-bit versions}
  EventPrefixes : array [0..EventMax] of string2 = ('ck', 'dd', 'do', 'ed',
    'en', 'ex', 'kd', 'kp', 'ku', 'md', 'mm', 'mu'
    {$IFNDEF VER80}
    , 'sd'
    {$ENDIF}
    );
  fdwSoundFlags : array [0..3] of string15 = ('SND_ALIAS', 'SND_FILENAME',
          'SND_RESOURCE', 'NIL');
type
 TSoundSource =
```

```
{$IFDEF VER80}
(ssFilename, ssMemory);
{$ELSE}
(ssAlias, ssAliasID, ssFilename, ssMemory, ssResource);
{$ENDIF}
{Current Event Selected in the Expert}
EventSelected = (esClick, esDragDrop, esDragOver, esEndDrag, esEnter,
    esExit, esKeyDown, esKeyPress, esKeyUp, esMouseDown, esMouseMove,
    esMouseUp
{$IFNDEF VER80}
, esStartDrag
{$ENDIF}
);
EventCheckBoxStatus = (ecbsUndefined, ecbsDefined, ecbsChecked);
var
AnEventSelected : EventSelected;
EventIsEnabled : array [0..12] of boolean;
EventCheckBoxArray : array [0..12] of EventCheckBoxStatus;
implementation
end.
```

We've already examined the enumerated type TSoundSource. As we explained previously, we can sound enable any of the standard events in the new components we produce. When the user clicks on one of the event check boxes, we need to keep track of which one it is so that we can store the data selected in the proper place. We store this data in a series of arrays. To keep track of the current array members, we use the EventSelected enumerated type shown in Listing 2-1.

We need to keep track of the status of each check box (and the possible sound event class it may eventually produce). We use another enumerated type, EventCheckBoxStatus, to accomplish this. There are three possibilities as shown in Table 2-5.

Table 2-5: EventCheckBoxStatus settings and their meanings

Setting	Meaning
ecbsUndefined	The check box has never been checked; default setting at beginning of each run
ecbsDefined	Data entered earlier for the particular check box, but not currently checked
ecbsChecked	Data entered and check box checked

By keeping track of the checked status of each check box, we can inform the component-producing engine which events require new classes and subproperties to be sound-enabled. We use the EventCheckBoxStatus array to store the check box status of each event. Using this approach, if the user enters data, unchecks the box, and then decides to check it again, the original data entered in the pop-up dialog box will appear and can be edited or simply reselected. If the user decides to cancel the operation (entering data for a particular event), the box is automatically unchecked.

In adding this functionality, the author also introduced a rather nasty bug. Whenever the user canceled the dialog box shown in Figure 2-3 or exited without choosing any options, the check box on the expert was unchecked and the status was changed to ecbsDefined.

Unfortunately, the process of unchecking the check box was interpreted by the expert as a click and the dialog box was brought up again. The author's friend, Mark Miller of Eagle Software, suggested an elegant solution to the problem. In the code shown in Listing 2-2, note the private variable FHandlingInternally. This essentially short-circuits the otherwise automatic reshowing of the dialog when the UnCheck method is called.

Listing 2-2: CbClickClick() method handles check box clicks

```
procedure TSoundCompForm.cbClickClick(Sender: TObject);
begin
 if FHandlingInternally then
 exit;
 FHandlingInternally := True;
 try
 if NOT SoundPlayingDataEntered then UnCheck;
 finally { wrap up }
 FHandlingInternally := False;
 end; { try/finally }
end;
```

As you can tell from examining Listing 2-1, EventCheckBoxStatus is by no means the only array we use. Event names are used in constructing the new classes we'll be discussing soon. In order to keep track of them, we use a constant array of strings whose members correspond to the event/check boxes. We use the EventNames array for this purpose. We also need to keep track of the information entered in the dialog box for each sound event. We store that information in a packed record, SoundFactors, declared in SndExp1. That record contains the following fields:

- SoundSource: TSoundSource;
- Yield: boolean;
- WavFileDefault: boolean;
- DefaultWavFile: TFileName;
- SoundPlayOptions: TSoundPlayOptions;

Again, since we must store this information for each event selected, and since there are 13 possible sound events (12 in the Delphi 1 version), we store the data in the following public array in SndExp1:

```
SoundFactorsArray: Array [0..MaxEvents] of SoundFactors;
```

The Expert Engine

Having examined the user interface and some of the data types used to store the information generated, let's discuss the expert's component-creating engine. The easiest way to do this is to take a look at one of the generated components first. In fact, this was the approach we used in writing and later updating the expert. We created a prototype of the kind of component we wanted to produce and then wrote the engine unit, CompGen1.pas, with the goal of generating the prototype we had in mind. As you might guess, the most often used line of code in the WriteALine() method is:

```
Memo1.Lines.Add(StringIn);
```

Since we call this method for every line of code generated, the CompGen1.pas unit is quite large. We'll discuss the main routines here. The entire file is included on the CD-ROM. We begin by calling several routines that write the beginning of a standard component unit: WriteUnitHeader(), WriteInterface(), and WriteUses(). These are so standard that they could probably be applied to your own code generation projects.

The first routine we'll consider in depth, WriteTypes(), writes all of the new types that support sound playing in our component. It creates a specific Sound Options type for each event enabled. That way, we can customize each sound event in a component. First, we declare the

TSoundSource type which we've already discussed (note the conditional define for Delphi 1):

```
WriteALine(' TSoundSource =');
WriteALine(' {$IFDEF VER80}');
WriteALine(' (ssFilename, ssMemory);');
WriteALine(' {$ELSE}');
WriteALine(' (ssAlias, ssAliasID, ssFilename, ssMemory, ssResource);');
WriteALine(' {$ENDIF}');
```

In the same method, we declare the sndFlags type for the 32-bit version only. Then, in the WriteSoundOptions() method, we use lines like the following to access the data collected from running the expert and produce the proper types. You'll notice that we use strings associated with the event to name them, as in:

```
If spPlayReturn in SoundFactorsArray[j].SoundPlayOptions
   then AddSoundOption(EventPrefixes[j] + 'spPlayReturn');
```

We create an enumerated type that contains only those sound playing options (synchronous, asynchronous, loop, etc.) we might want to implement in the particular event of the particular component. Here are two such generated types from our TSoundEdit component:

```
TClickSoundPlayOption = (ckspPlayReturn,
    ckspPlayNoReturn,
    ckspPlayContinuous,
    ckspPlayNoSound,
    ckspEndSoundPlay);
TEnterSoundPlayOption = (enspPlayReturn,
    enspPlayNoReturn,
    enspPlayContinuous,
    enspPlayNoSound,
    enspEndSoundPlay);
```

While we use all five possible sound events in each type, we could just as easily use one or two. It all depends on how many we checked in the dialog box we discussed earlier. As in SndExp1, we use similar arrays in the CompGen1.pas unit to store the strings associated with the events supported. In the above example, we use the prefix "ck" for the Click option type and "en" for the Enter option type.

Now we'll create our classes. And since we are going to create a separate class for each event that is sound enabled, we are going to start by creating the base class for all of those, taking advantage of the inheritance built into an object-oriented language such as Object Pascal. This is the base class from the TSoundEdit component:

```
TSoundPlayEvent = class(TPersistent)
 private
 { Private declarations }
  FSoundFile : String;
  FSoundSource : TSoundSource;
  FYield : boolean;
  FhmodValue : HMODULE;
 public
 { Public declarations }
  constructor Create(AOwner: TComponent);
 published
 { Published declarations }
  property SoundFile : String
    read FSoundFile write FSoundFile;
  property SoundSource : TSoundSource read FSoundSource Write FSoundSource
    default ssFilename;
  property hmodValue : HMODULE read FhmodValue write FhmodValue;
  property Yield : boolean read FYield write FYield default False;
  end;
```

Note that the hmodValue is valid for only the 32-bit version, as it refers to the additional parameter in the PlaySound() function that is not in the older SndPlaySound() function. One of the advantages to creating a base class like this is that we don't have to repeat code in descendent classes. If we enable many sound events, that could involve considerable repetition. Since the code for the above class does not ever change, we do not have to worry about coming up with unique names and prefixes as we do in the descendent classes. This makes the code generation much easier. Here is a descendent class:

```
TClickSoundPlayEvent = class(TSoundPlayEvent)
Private
{ Private declarations }
FClickSoundPlayOption : TClickSoundPlayOption;
Public
{ Public declarations }
constructor Create(AOwner: TComponent);
Published
{ Published declarations }
Property ClickSoundPlayOption : TClickSoundPlayOption read
    FClickSoundPlayOption write  FClickSoundPlayOption;
end;
```

Note that we need to define just one new property here, ClickSoundPlayOption, the property that determines how the sound will be played. We've already defined its type—the enumerated type TClickSoundPlayOption. The reason we must go to all of this trouble is because we want to give the developer the option of using specific sound playing options (from one to five). Listing 2-3 shows the code in CompGen1.pas that produces the above declaration:

Listing 2-3: Code to write new sound classes

```
procedure WriteSoundClasses;
var
j: Integer;
NewClasses : integer;
NewClassArray : array [0..EventMax] of string;
procedure WriteSoundPlayEventsClass;
var
 i: Integer;
begin
 WriteALine(' TSoundPlayEvents = class'
   + '(TPersistent)');
 WriteALine(' Private');
 WriteALine(' { Private declarations }');
 for i := 0 to (NewClasses-1) do { Iterate }
 WriteALine(' F' + NewClassArray[i] + 'SoundPlayEvent : T' +
   NewClassArray[i] + 'SoundPlayEvent;');
 WriteALine(' Public');
 WriteALine(' { Public declarations }');
 WriteALine(' constructor Create(AOwner: TComponent);');
 WriteALine(' Published');
 WriteALine(' { Published declarations }');
 for i := 0 to (NewClasses-1) do { Iterate }
 begin
 WriteALine(' Property ' + NewClassArray[i] + 'SoundPlayEvent : T'
     + NewClassArray[i] + 'SoundPlayEvent read F'
     + NewClassArray[i] +
     'SoundPlayEvent');
 WriteALine('   write F' + NewClassArray[i] +
   'SoundPlayEvent;');
 end;
 WriteALine('end;');
 WriteALine('');
 end; { WriteSoundPlayEventsClass }
 begin { WriteSoundClasses }
NewClasses := 0;
for j := 0 to EventMax do { Iterate }
```

```
if EventCheckBoxArray[j]= ecbsChecked then
begin
NewClassArray[NewClasses] := BasicEventNames[j];
inc(NewClasses);
WriteALine(' T' + BasicEventNames[j] + 'SoundPlayEvent = class'
   + '(TSoundPlayEvent)');
WriteALine(' Private');
WriteALine(' { Private declarations }');
WriteALine(' F' + BasicEventNames[j] + 'SoundPlayOption : T' +
   BasicEventNames[j] + 'SoundPlayOption;');
WriteALine(' Public');
WriteALine(' { Public declarations }');
WriteALine(' constructor Create(AOwner: TComponent);');
WriteALine(' Published');
WriteALine(' { Published declarations }');
WriteALine(' Property ' + BasicEventNames[j] + 'SoundPlayOption : T' +
   BasicEventNames[j] + 'SoundPlayOption read F' +
   BasicEventNames[j] + 'SoundPlayOption write F' +
   BasicEventNames[j] + 'SoundPlayOption;');
WriteALine('end;');
WriteALine('');
end; { for }
WriteSoundPlayEventsClass;
end; { WriteSoundClasses }
```

That may seem like a lot of code to write a series of rather simple classes, but it does more than just write all of these classes, as we'll see. Let's start with the individual classes. First, we need to determine which events will be sound enabled by iterating through the check box flags with the following code:

```
for j := 0 to EventMax do { Iterate }
 if EventCheckBoxArray[j]= ecbsChecked then
```

In our example, there is only one, the Click event. We build an array that contains information on which events are sound enabled. We use the variable NewClasses to keep track of how many are actually used. Here's how we build that array, which contains the basic names of the enabled events:

```
NewClassArray[NewClasses] := BasicEventNames[j];
```

We do not use this array immediately, but we will later. The code that follows simply writes the remainder of the class declaration. When we reach the last line, we call a nested procedure with:

```
WriteSoundPlayEventsClass;
```

That procedure writes yet another class—the main class that contains
all of the individual sound-enabled events and their subproperties.
Now, within this procedure, we are able to make good use of the
NewClassArray, creating a property for each sound-enabled event. Here
is the generated code for this class:

```
TSoundPlayEvents = class(TPersistent)
Private
{ Private declarations }
FClickSoundPlayEvent : TClickSoundPlayEvent;
Public
{ Public declarations }
constructor Create(AOwner: TComponent);
Published
{ Published declarations }
Property ClickSoundPlayEvent : TClickSoundPlayEvent read
      FClickSoundPlayEvent
   write FClickSoundPlayEvent;
end;
```

Again, we have just one event here, the Click event. But we could just as
easily have three or twelve. We have one more class to create, the component class itself. Some of the information for this class comes from the
first page of our expert, namely its ancestor class. Other than that, the
code is identical for any component created with this expert. Here is the
main component's class declaration:

```
TSoundButton = class(TBitBtn)
 private
 { Private declarations }
 FSoundPlayEvents : TSoundPlayEvents;
 protected
 { Protected declarations }
 public
 { Public declarations }
 constructor Create(AOwner: TComponent); override;
 procedure Click; override;
 published
 { Published declarations }
 property SoundPlayEvents : TSoundPlayEvents
   read FSoundPlayEvents write FSoundPlayEvents;
end;
```

It doesn't seem that we have added all that much, but keep in mind that there is a great deal hidden within the SoundPlayEvents property. If you enable many events and then view all of the details, it could take up most of the space in the Object Inspector.

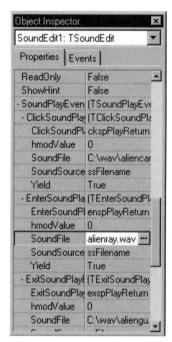

Figure 2-5

Next, we need to create constructors for these classes. That chore is quite straightforward, so we'll skip a detailed discussion of it. One issue that we should mention is that we need a way to handle the options on our pop-up dialog concerning defaults (Wavfile or Yield). In the individual event classes we handle that situation with this code, using data collected in our expert:

```
if SoundFactorsArray[j].WavFileDefault then
  WriteALine(' FSoundFile := ''' + SoundFactorsArray[j].
    DefaultWavFile + ''';') else
  WriteALine(' FSoundFile := ''*.wav'';');
  WriteALine(' FSoundSource := ssFilename;');
if SoundFactorsArray[j].Yield then
  WriteALine(' FYield := True;') else
  WriteALine(' FYield := False;');
```

Even more interesting is the method that actually does the work, in this case the Click method. Listing 2-4 shows that code.

Listing 2-4: An event handler override to play a sound

```
procedure TSoundButton.Click;
var
  fdwSoundValue : DWORD;
  AhmodValue : HMODULE;
  AFileName : array [0..255] of char;
  function GetfdwSoundValue(ASoundPlayEvent : TSoundPlayEvent): DWORD;
begin
  case ASoundPlayEvent.SoundSource of
```

```
 ssFilename: result := SND_FILENAME;
 ssMemory: result := SND_MEMORY;
 ssAlias: result := SND_ALIAS;
 ssAliasID: result := SND_ALIAS_ID;
 ssResource: result := SND_RESOURCE;
 end; { case }
end; {GetfdwSoundValue}
begin
 with SoundPlayEvents do
 begin
 fdwSoundValue := GetfdwSoundValue(ClickSoundPlayEvent);
 If (fdwSoundValue=SND_RESOURCE) then AhmodValue :=
  ClickSoundPlayEvent.hmodValue
 Else AhmodValue := 0;
 StrPCopy(AFileName, ClickSoundPlayEvent.SoundFile);
 If ClickSoundPlayEvent.yield
  then fdwSoundValue := (fdwSoundValue OR SND_NOSTOP);
 case ClickSoundPlayEvent.ClickSoundPlayOption of
 ckspPlayReturn: PlaySound(
    AFileName, AhmodValue, fdwSoundValue or snd_Async or snd_NoDefault);
 ckspPlayNoReturn: PlaySound(
    AFileName, AhmodValue, fdwSoundValue or snd_Sync or snd_NoDefault);
 ckspPlayNoSound: ;
 ckspPlayContinuous: PlaySound(
    AFileName, AhmodValue, fdwSoundValue or snd_Async or snd_Loop or
        snd_NoDefault);
 ckspEndSoundPlay: PlaySound(
    nil, AhmodValue, fdwSoundValue or snd_Async or snd_NoDefault);
  end; {case}
 end;
 inherited Click;
end;
```

First, we use the local function GetfdwSoundValue() to determine the sound source type (SoundSource) and return the corresponding flag. We then plug that flag into the last parameter of the PlaySound() function along with other appropriate flags. Unless we use the SND_RESOURCE flag, AhmodValue is set to 0. One option that we don't enable here concerns default sounds: snd_NoDefault is always set. Of course we could add an additional subproperty. That will have to wait for the next version, perhaps. We've covered many of the details of our expert and have also given some clues about the nature of the components that it can produce. To get a better idea of the layout of the components produced, study the SoundEdt unit which contains four sound-enabled events. Now we're going to leave theory behind and put our expert to work to quickly produce five components.

Expanding the Component Palette

For all of these components we're going to keep things simple and ignore the default Wavfile and Yield options. We'll concern ourselves only with selecting events to sound enable and deciding what kinds of sound playing options we want to enable for those events. So, if you'd like to get some practice using this expert, bring it up and we'll get started. In Delphi, click on the Component|Sound item and enter the information from Table 2-6 on the first page.

Table 2-6: Basic information for TSoundButton

Component Name	Unit	Ancestor	Unit(s) Needed
TSoundButton	SoundBtn.pas	TBitBtnButtons	Buttons

On the second page, select the Click check box and select all of the sound playing options in the left column. Close the dialog box, click Finish, and click OK in the final window. Congratulations! You've just created your first sound-enabled component. Now let's create another one. Bring up the Sound Component Wizard again. This time enter the information from Table 2-7 on the first page.

Table 2-7: Basic information for TSoundEdit

Component Name	Unit	Ancestor	Unit(s) Needed
TSoundEdit	SoundEdt.pas	TEdit	(None)

This time we're going to sound enable four events: Click, Enter, Exit, and KeyPress. On the second page, click on each of these in turn and select all of the sound playing options in the left column for each. Close the dialog box, click Finish, and click OK in the final window. All right! Now you've created your second sound-enabled component. We've got three more to go. Bring up the Sound Component Wizard again. This time enter the information from Table 2-8 on the first page.

Table 2-8: Basic information for TSoundListBox

Component Name	Unit	Ancestor	Unit(s) Needed
TSoundListBox	SoundLB.pas	TListBox	(None)

In our third component we're going to sound enable three events: Click, Enter, and Exit. On the second page, click on each of these in turn and select all of the sound playing options in the left column for Click and Enter. For the Exit event, select just Stop Sound and No Sound. As before, close the dialog box, click Finish, and click OK in the final window. Three down, two to go. Bring up the Sound Component Expert again. This time enter the information from Table 2-9 on the first page.

Table 2-9: Basic information for TSoundDBGrid

Component Name	Unit	Ancestor	Unit(s) Needed
TSoundDBGrid	SoundDBG.pas	TDBGrid	DBGrids

In our fourth component we're going to sound-enable two events, Click and Enter. On the second page, click on each of these in turn and select all of the sound playing options in the left column for each. Again, close the dialog box, click Finish, and click OK in the final window. Bring up the Sound Component Wizard again. This time enter the information from Table 2-10 on the first page.

Table 2-10: Basic information for TSoundDBNavigator

Component Name	Unit	Ancestor	Unit(s) Needed
TSoundDBNavigator	SoundDBN.pas	TDBNavigator	DBCtrls

In our last component we're going to sound enable three events: Click, Enter, and Exit. On the second page, click on each of these in turn and select all of the sound playing options in the left column for Click and Enter. For the Exit event, only select Stop Sound and No Sound. As before, close the dialog box, click Finish, and click OK in the final window. That's it. In a short period of time (I'd be surprised if it took more than five or ten minutes) we've created five new components. Now let's use those components and create a sound-enabled database application.

Adding Sound to a Database Application

The database we're going to create is a video database—a means of
keeping track of your home video library. You can use the sample database on the CD-ROM if you like. However, I doubt that you have the
same videos as this author. So, if you'd like to build it from scratch begin
by creating the folder in which you are going to store the database files.
Create an alias to it called VIDEODB. Now let's create the structure of
the table. Open Database Desktop, create a new Paradox table called
VidTapes.db and enter the field definitions from Table 2-11.

Table 2-11: Structure for VidTapes.db

Field	Name	Type	Size	Key
1	Title	A	30	NA
2	Category	A	20	NA
3	TapeNumber	A	8	NA
4	Length	N	NA	NA
5	Speed	A	3	NA
6	Description	A	30	NA

Now go ahead and enter information about the tapes in your library.
On the other hand, if you'd like a peek at some of the titles in my library,
copy the file VidTapes.db to the folder you've named as the VIDEODB
alias.

Having set up the database, we'll now set up the multimedia database
program that will access it. Create a new project and name it VideoPrj.
Name the main form VideoU.pas. Drop the components on it as shown in
Figure 2-6 and set their properties as shown in Table 2-12.

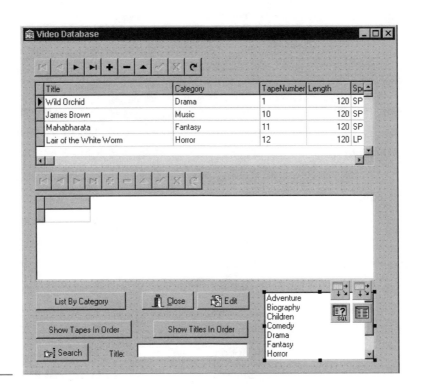

Figure 2-6

Table 2-12: Properties for the video database project

Class	Property	Value
TVideoDatabase	Name	VideoDatabase
(TForm)	Caption	'Video Database'
TSoundDBNavigator	Name	SoundDBNavigator1
	DataSource	DataSource1
TSoundDBGrid	Name	SoundDBGrid1
	DataSource	DataSource1
TSoundDBNavigator	Name	SoundDBNavigator2
	DataSource	DataSource2
TSoundDBGrid	Name	SoundDBGrid2
	DataSource	DataSource2
TSoundListBox	Name	SoundListBox1

Class	Property	Value
	Items.Strings	('Adventure' , 'Biography', 'Children', 'Comedy', 'Drama', 'Fantasy', 'Horror', 'Music', 'SciFi')
TSoundButton	Name	ListByCategoryBtn
	Caption	'List By Category'
TSoundButton	Name	CloseBtn
	Kind	bkClose
TSoundButton	Name	ShowTapesInOrderBtn
	Caption	'Show Tapes In Order'
	OnClick	ShowTapesInOrderBtnClick
TSoundButton	Name	ShowTitlesInOrderBtn
	Caption	'Show Titles In Order'
	OnClick	ShowTitlesInOrderBtnClick
TSoundButton	Name	EditBtn
	Caption	'Edit'
	OnClick	EditBtnClick
	Glyph	/Images/Buttons/Find.bmp
	NumGlyphs	2
TSoundButton	Name	SearchBtn
	Caption	'Search'
	OnClick	SearchBtnClick
	NumGlyphs	2
TLabel	Name	Label1
	Caption	'Title: '
TSoundEdit	Name	SoundEdit1
TDataSource	Name	DataSource1
	DataSet	Table1
TTable	Name	Table1
	Active	True
	DatabaseName	'VideoDB'
	TableName	'VidTapes.DB'
TDataSource	Name	DataSource2

Class	Property	Value
	DataSet	Query1
TQuery	Name	Query1
	DatabaseName	'VideoDB'

We haven't quite finished with the properties yet; we've just dealt with the usual ones. Now we'll set the sound event properties. We've included all of the *.wav files indicated on the CD-ROM accompanying this book. These include many of my favorites collected over the years from various sources—CD-ROM collections, the Internet, friends, and so forth. If you're a sci-fi fan, you'll probably enjoy them. Many are a bit too long to work as effectively as we might wish, so be sure to experiment with other *.wav files until you have the multimedia aspect of this application working to your satisfaction. For all of the sound event subproperties, keep the defaults of:

```
SoundPlayEvents.?SoundPlayEvent.hmodValue = 0
SoundPlayEvents.?SoundPlayEvent.Yield = True
```

The sound events listed in Table 2-13 include *.wav files and SoundPlay options. You can find all of these as subproperties under SoundPlay-Events in the Object Inspector. The specific *.wav files I have chosen are listed below. However, please be creative and try substituting some of your own choices or moving these around to arrive at an effect with which you feel comfortable.

Table 2-13: Properties for sound events (all are under SoundPlayEvents in Object Inspector)

Class	Property	Value
TSoundDBNavigator	Name	SoundDBNavigator1
	ClickSoundPlayEvent. SoundFile	'alienray.wav'
	ClickSoundPlayEvent. ClickSoundPlayOption	CkspPlayReturn
TSoundDBGrid	Name	SoundDBGrid1
	ClickSoundPlayEvent. SoundFile	'alientrn.wav'

Class	Property	Value
	ClickSoundPlayEvent.ClickSoundPlayOption	CkspPlayReturn
	EnterSoundPlayEvent.SoundFile	'basketbl.wav'
	EnterSoundPlayEvent.EnterSoundPlayOption	EnspPlayReturn
TSoundDBNavigator	Name	SoundDBNavigator2
	ClickSoundPlayEvent.SoundFile	'aliencar.wav'
	ClickSoundPlayEvent.ClickSoundPlayOption	CkspPlayReturn
	EnterSoundPlayEvent.SoundFile	'alienca.wav'
	EnterSoundPlayEvent.EnterSoundPlayOption	EnspPlayReturn
	ExitSoundPlayEvent.SoundFile	'african.wav'
	ExitSoundPlayEvent.ExitSoundPlayOption	ExspPlayNoSound
TSoundDBGrid	Name	SoundDBGrid2
	ClickSoundPlayEvent.SoundFile	'aweuuwee.wav'
	ClickSoundPlayEvent.ClickSoundPlayOption	CkspPlayReturn
	EnterSoundPlayEvent.SoundFile	'aliensp.wav'
	EnterSoundPlayEvent.EnterSoundPlayOption	EnspPlayReturn
TSoundListBox	Name	SoundListBox1
	ClickSoundPlayEvent.SoundFile	'alientrn.wav'

Class	Property	Value
	ClickSoundPlayEvent. ClickSoundPlayOption	CkspPlayReturn
	EnterSoundPlayEvent. SoundFile	'aliencar.wav'
	EnterSoundPlayEvent. EnterSoundPlayOption	EnspPlayReturn
	ExitSoundPlayEvent. SoundFile	'alienca.wav'
	ExitSoundPlayEvent. ExitSoundPlayOption	ExspPlayNoSound
TSoundButton	Name	ListByCategoryBtn
	ClickSoundPlayEvent. SoundFile	'alienray.wav'
	ClickSoundPlayEvent. ClickSoundPlayOption	CkspPlayReturn
TSoundButton	Name	CloseBtn
	ClickSoundPlayEvent. SoundFile	'alientrn.wav'
	ClickSoundPlayEvent. ClickSoundPlayOption	CkspPlayReturn
TSoundButton	Name	ShowTapesInOrderBtn
	ClickSoundPlayEvent. SoundFile	'bleenk.wav'
	ClickSoundPlayEvent. ClickSoundPlayOption	CkspPlayReturn
TSoundButton	Name	ShowTitlesInOrderBtn
	ClickSoundPlayEvent. SoundFile	'aliensp.wav'
	ClickSoundPlayEvent. ClickSoundPlayOption	CkspPlayReturn
TSoundButton	Name	EditBtn

2

Chapter

Class	Property	Value
	ClickSoundPlayEvent. SoundFile	'alienray.wav'
	ClickSoundPlayEvent. ClickSoundPlayOption	CkspPlayReturn
TSoundButton	Name	SearchBtn
	ClickSoundPlayEvent. SoundFile	'bombsaw.wav'
	ClickSoundPlayEvent. ClickSoundPlayOption	CkspPlayReturn
TSoundEdit	Name	SoundEdit1
	ClickSoundPlayEvent. SoundFile	'aliencar.wav'
	ClickSoundPlayEvent. ClickSoundPlayOption	CkspPlayReturn
	EnterSoundPlayEvent. SoundFile	'alienray.wav'
	EnterSoundPlayEvent. EnterSoundPlayOption	EnspPlayReturn
	ExitSoundPlayEvent. SoundFile	'aliengu.wav'
	ExitSoundPlayEvent. ExitSoundPlayOption	ExspPlayReturn
	KeyPressSoundPlayEvent. SoundFile	'aliencar.wav'
	KeyPressSoundPlayEvent. KeyPressSoundPlayOption	KpspPlayReturn

In addition to the bitmap for the EditBtn (\Images\Buttons\find.bmp), you'll need two glyphs for the EditBtn, which toggle between two database states: browse (read-only) and edit. In setting the properties, be sure to set OnClick event handlers for the buttons as indicated in Table 2-12. Now enter all of the code in Listing 2-5.

Listing 2-5: Main unit for video database program

```
unit VideoU;
interface
uses
 Windows, Messages, SysUtils, Classes, Graphics, Controls, Forms, Dialogs,
 Grids, DBGrids, SoundDBG, ExtCtrls, DBCtrls, SoundDBN, StdCtrls,
 SoundEdt, Buttons, SoundBtn, SoundLBx, DBTables, Db;
type
 TVideoDatabase = class(TForm)
 SoundDBNavigator1: TSoundDBNavigator;
 SoundDBGrid1: TSoundDBGrid;
 SoundDBNavigator2: TSoundDBNavigator;
 SoundDBGrid2: TSoundDBGrid;
 SoundListBox1: TSoundListBox;
 ListByCategoryBtn: TSoundButton;
 CloseBtn: TSoundButton;
 ShowTapesInOrderBtn: TSoundButton;
 ShowTitlesInOrderBtn: TSoundButton;
 EditBtn: TSoundButton;
 SearchBtn: TSoundButton;
 SoundEdit1: TSoundEdit;
 Label1: TLabel;
 DataSource1: TDataSource;
 Table1: TTable;
 DataSource2: TDataSource;
 Query1: TQuery;
 procedure ListByCategoryBtnClick(Sender: TObject);
 procedure EditBtnClick(Sender: TObject);
 procedure ShowTapesInOrderBtnClick(Sender: TObject);
 procedure ShowTitlesInOrderBtnClick(Sender: TObject);
 procedure SearchBtnClick(Sender: TObject);
 procedure FormActivate(Sender: TObject);
 private
 { Private declarations }
 public
 { Public declarations }
 end;
var
 VideoDatabase: TVideoDatabase;
implementation
{$R *.DFM}
procedure TVideoDatabase.ListByCategoryBtnClick(Sender: TObject);
var
 ACategory : string;
begin
If SoundListBox1.ItemIndex = -1 then
```

2

Chapter

```
begin
 Exit;
end;
case SoundListBox1.ItemIndex of
 0: ACategory := '''Adventure''';
 1: ACategory := '''Biography''';
 2: ACategory := '''Children''';
 3: ACategory := '''Comedy''';
 4: ACategory := '''Drama''';
 5: ACategory := '''Fantasy''';
 6: ACategory := '''Horror''';
 7: ACategory := '''Music''';
 8: ACategory := '''SciFi''';
end; {case}
Query1.Close;
Query1.SQL.Clear;
Query1.SQL.Add('SELECT * FROM VIDEO1 WHERE CATEGORY='+ ACategory);
try
 Query1.Open;
except
 on EDataBaseError do ;{ The dataset could not be opened }
end;
end;
procedure TVideoDatabase.EditBtnClick(Sender: TObject);
begin
if DataSource1.AutoEdit then
 begin
  DataSource1.AutoEdit := False;
  EditBtn.Glyph.LoadFromFile('Edit.bmp') ;
  EditBtn.Caption := 'Edit';
 end
else
 begin
  DataSource1.AutoEdit := True;
  EditBtn.Glyph.LoadFromFile('NoEdit.Bmp');
  EditBtn.Caption := 'Read Only';
 end;
end;
procedure TVideoDatabase.ShowTapesInOrderBtnClick(Sender: TObject);
var
 TapeNumber : string;
begin
TapeNumber := 'TapeNumber';
Query1.SQL.Clear;
Query1.SQL.Add('SELECT * FROM VIDEO2 ORDER BY ' + TapeNumber);
try
```

```
 Query1.Open;
except
 on EDataBaseError do ;{ The dataset could not be opened }
end;
end;
procedure TVideoDatabase.ShowTitlesInOrderBtnClick(Sender: TObject);
begin
Query1.SQL.Clear;
Query1.SQL.Add('SELECT * FROM VIDEO2 ORDER BY TITLE ASCENDING');
try
 Query1.Open;
except
 on EDataBaseError do ;{ The dataset could not be opened }
end;
end;
procedure TVideoDatabase.SearchBtnClick(Sender: TObject);
begin
If SoundEdit1.text='' then Exit;
Query1.Close;
Query1.SQL.Clear;
Query1.SQL.Add('SELECT * FROM VIDEO2 WHERE TITLE='''
    + SoundEdit1.Text + '''');
try
 Query1.Open;
except
 on EDataBaseError do ;{ The dataset could not be opened }
end;
end;
procedure TVideoDatabase.FormActivate(Sender: TObject);
begin
 DataSource1.AutoEdit := False;
 EditBtn.Glyph.LoadFromFile('Edit.Bmp');
 EditBtn.Caption := 'Edit';
end;
end.
```

That's it! We're ready to compile and run the program. We'll be building additional example programs in the remaining chapters, but they will be simpler and more directly related to multimedia issues. In the next chapter, we'll explore waveform audio and build a class that encapsulates all of the low-level functions.

Chapter Three

The Wave API

In the last chapter, we built our first multimedia application. The use of the high-level audio functions PlaySound() and SndPlaySound() made our task relatively simple. Now we're going to explore the lower level Wave audio functions. Although these require more work, they do offer more options. These options are:

- ■ Querying the capabilities of an audio device
- ■ Recording sounds
- ■ Controlling recording and playback conditions
- ■ Working with sounds in memory

Of course, you can also use files with these low-level APIs; however, that task is considerably more complicated than what we experienced in the previous chapter. The functions we'll examine in this chapter do not support file manipulations. We'll use the multimedia input/output routines in order to facilitate that task, a topic we'll cover in Chapter 8, Multimedia Input and Output Support. For now, we'll take an in-depth look at the building blocks that make up the Wave API. We'll begin by discussing waveform audio in general. Then we'll look at some of the structures and routines that apply to both input and output of waveform audio. Finally, we'll examine the use of the input and output functions and how these relate to each other. Throughout the chapter, we'll build several new Delphi Wave classes that encapsulate basic waveform functionality and make it easier to use.

3

Chapter

Waveform Audio—An Introduction

Waveform audio is digital audio. How could it be otherwise? After all, we're working with computers. But what about analog audio? Analog audio is audio in the real world, not the world of computers and other electronic devices like synthesizers or sequencers. Digital audio can be represented in visual form—that's what an oscilloscope does. Sound editors like Sonic Foundry's Sound Forge can also display sound visually. Figures 3-1 and 3-2 show two of the WAV files we used in the last chapter, alienray.wav and aliencar.wav, respectively.

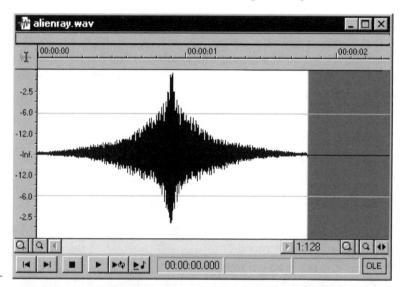

Figure 3-1

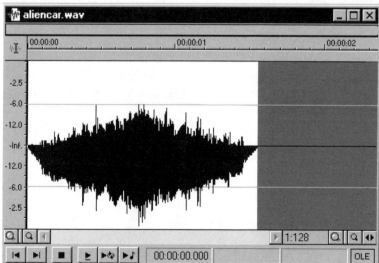

Figure 3-2

Analog sound must communicate with digital sound. Take microphones and speakers, for instance—they are analog devices that respond in an analogous way to sound vibrations. Air pressure is transformed into electronic signals. Those oscillating electronic signals—analogous in nature to the sound waves they represent—can be transformed into digital signals. Otherwise we could not record sound and play it back. The relationship is similar to that of pixels in a digital representation of visual phenomena. In both cases, the more data that we can digitize, the closer we come to having a true representation of the visual or audio phenomena that we are trying to reproduce.

Fortunately, you needn't be too concerned about the transformation process itself. Engineers have worked out most of the nasty details, such as those involved in translating a digital pattern to and from an actual sound sent or received though an analog device. Device drivers accomplish much of that work. If you would like to understand more about the theoretical basis of digital audio, you may want to familiarize yourself with the terms in Appendix C, A Glossary of Audio and Multimedia Terms. For now, our task is simply to deal with the digital audio data. Although we'll continue to discuss related issues, our focus will remain on the multimedia APIs throughout this book.

By understanding how digital data works, you can produce various kinds of audio waves such as sine waves, square waves, or sawtooth waves; using sophisticated algorithms, you can filter waves or manipulate them in countless other ways. These topics, however, are beyond the scope of this book. One sample program on the CD-ROM demonstrates techniques to accomplish these tasks—the freeware application SweepGen. This audio sweep generator written by David J. Taylor is shown in Figure 3-3 on the following page. It provides some wonderful examples of working with digital audio data. This application does some very interesting things with sine waves. You can sweep through sine waves of various frequencies manually or automatically.

We could devote an entire chapter to fully describing the features of this application. Rather, we'll limit our discussion to some of the sound producing code itself.

3

Chapter

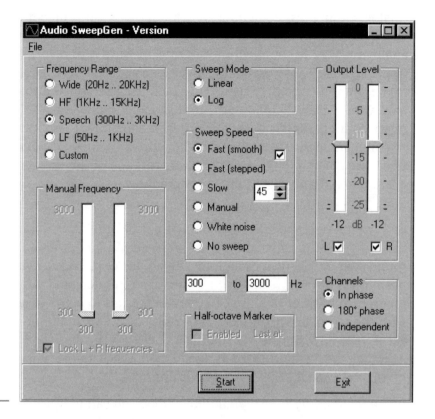

Figure 3-3

In working with waveform audio, you have certain specific choices: You can use various sampling rates, in monaural or stereo, in 8 or 16 bit. SweepGen uses the highest quality sound generally available: a sampling rate of 44,100 kHz, which produces the best CD-quality sound, stereo support, and 16-bit sound. In 16-bit stereo, each discrete element (called a sample) consists of two bytes—one for each channel. The actual values of those elements (their amplitudes) range from −32,768 to 32,767. In SweepGen, the basic audio sample constants are defined as follows:

```
audio_sample = -32767..32767;
sine_table_samples = 1 shl 15;   // number of samples in sine table
```

Here are some of the types that the author uses in building sine tables. Note how the above constants are used:

```
type
 PSineTable = ^TSineTable;         // sine value store
 TSineTable = array [0..sine_table_samples-1] of audio_sample;
 PMonoBuffer = ^TMonoBuffer;       // pink noise buffer type
```

```
TMonoBuffer = array [0..max_buffer_samples-1] of audio_sample;
   // 1-channel
PBuffer = ^TBuffer;              // output buffer type
TBuffer = array [0..2*max_buffer_samples-1] of audio_sample;
   // 2-channels
```

Since SweepGen produces sine waves and not complex sound events, it
does not require a large sound buffer. Variables (of the above types used
to build sine tables) are declared in the main form unit and memory is
allocated for the buffers (more about that later). Listing 3-1 shows the
routine that actually builds the sine table that provides the audio data
used by other routines.

Listing 3-I: The build_sine_table() routine from David Taylor's SweepGen

```
procedure TForm1.build_sine_table (magnitude: extended; table:
PSineTable);
var
 i: integer;
 quarter_table: integer;
 half_table: integer;
 x: integer;
begin
 // Assume 16-bit audio goes from -32767..32767, avoids clipping.
 // There are only 2^15 samples here, this simplifies the subsequent angle
 // calculation but might restrict the dynamic range produced with noise
 // sidebands. However, in the quality of equipment likely to be
 // encountered this won't matter. You've got the source code, so
 // you can alter this if you like.
 half_table := sine_table_samples div 2;
 quarter_table := half_table div 2;
 table^ [0] := 0;
 x := round (magnitude * 32767.0);
 table^ [quarter_table] := x;
 table^ [half_table] := 0;
 table^ [half_table + quarter_table] := -x;
 for i := 1 to quarter_table - 1 do
  begin
  x := round (magnitude * (32767.0 * sin (2.0 * i * Pi /
sine_table_samples)));
  table^ [i] := x;
  table^ [half_table - i] := x;
  table^ [half_table + i] := -x;
  table^ [sine_table_samples - i] := -x;
  end;
end;
```

However, we're dealing with stereo here, two channels left and right. Therefore, Taylor calls this method for each channel. Here is one of those routines:

```
procedure TForm1.build_left_sine_table;
begin
 if left_sine_table_valid then Exit;   // nothing to do
 build_sine_table (left_amplitude, left_sine_table);
 present_left_amplitude := left_amplitude;
 left_sine_table_valid := True;
end;
```

Once a WaveOut device has been properly opened and sound playing has begun, Windows sends an MM_WOM_OPEN message to the application. The Build_left_sine_table() method is called within that message handler as shown in Listing 3-2. It writes two buffers of data to the wave device and performs other housekeeping chores. This listing also provides an excellent example of using a loop in playing sound (something we don't do in the Wave class we'll be building to accompany this chapter).

Listing 3-2: MM_WOM_OPEN() message handler from David Taylor's SweepGen

```
procedure TForm1.MM_WOM_OPEN(var Msg: tMessage);
// This code handles the WaveOutOpen message by
var
 samples: integer;                // max valid sample in the buffer
begin
 btnStart.Caption := '&STOP';  // first, tell user how to stop the sound!
 // build sine-wave tables if required
 if not left_sine_table_valid then build_left_sine_table;
 if not right_sine_table_valid then build_right_sine_table;
 // populate the first wave header
 with p_wave_hdr1^ do
  begin
  lpData := pChar (p_buffer1);  // pointer to the data
  dwBufferLength := 0;          // fill in size later
  dwBytesRecorded := 0;
  dwUser := 0;
  dwFlags := 0;
  dwLoops := 1;                   // just a single loop
  lpNext := nil;
  reserved := 0;
  end;
 // populate the second wave header
 p_wave_hdr2^ := p_wave_hdr1^;   // copy most of the data
 p_wave_hdr2^.lpData := pChar (p_buffer2);  // except the buffer address!
```

```
// fill in a single buffer that is repeated, fast sweep or white/pink
// noise for a slow or single sweep, this sets up the frequencies
samples := fill_buffer (0);
case speed of
 fast_smooth, fast_stepped, white:
  begin
  with p_wave_hdr1^ do
   begin
   dwBufferLength := 4 * samples;          // convert samples to bytes
   dwFlags := whdr_BeginLoop or whdr_EndLoop; // repeating buffer
   dwLoops := $FFFFFFFF;                    // a fair number of loops
   end;
  // prepare both headers but only write the first (infinite loops)
  waveOutPrepareHeader (hWave_out, p_wave_hdr1, SizeOf (TWaveHdr));
  // mm_wom_close will unprepare both headers, so prepare this one anyhow
  waveOutPrepareHeader (hWave_out, p_wave_hdr2, SizeOf (TWaveHdr));
  waveOutWrite (hWave_out, p_wave_hdr1, SizeOf (TWaveHdr));
  end;
 slow, manual, no_sweep:
  begin
  buffers_played := 0;
  buffers_written := 0;
  all_written := False;
  // now write the first two buffers into the wave output
  // this will result in two mm_wom_done messages
  waveOutPrepareHeader (hWave_out, p_wave_hdr1, SizeOf (TWaveHdr));
  write_next_buffer (p_wave_hdr1);
  waveOutPrepareHeader (hWave_out, p_wave_hdr2, SizeOf (TWaveHdr));
  write_next_buffer (p_wave_hdr2);
  end;
 end;
end;
```

Filling the sine wave buffer with proper values to produce a sine wave requires some interesting code as shown in Listing 3-3. In a comment extracted from the code, the author describes his method as follows: "[This method] fills a section of two-channel buffer with a sine wave. The angle parameter is updated so that phase continuity is maintained between calls to this routine. If the right-hand sine table is given as the parameter, the buffer is written with a one-sample offset, i.e., the right channel."

Listing 3-3: The fill_buffer_with_sinewave() method from SweepGen

```
procedure TForm1.fill_buffer_with_sinewave (
        sine_table: PSineTable; bfr: pBuffer;
        f: extended;
        var angle: integer; index, samples: integer);
const
 fract_bits = 15;
var
 sample: integer;      // looping over the required samples
 d_angle: integer;     // 32-bit number with 15 fractional bits, i.e. 17.15
 max_angle: integer;   // maximum number of samples in the sine table
 w: audio_sample;      // one single sample
begin
 // Compute the angular step per sample corresponding to the desired
frequency
 d_angle := round ((sine_table_samples shl fract_bits) * f / sample_rate);
 // This is the maximum number of samples in the sine table
 max_angle := (sine_table_samples shl fract_bits) - 1;
 // point index to right-hand sample if required
 if sine_table = right_sine_table then Inc (index);
 for sample := 0 to samples - 1 do
  begin
  w := sine_table^ [angle shr fract_bits];  // get current sine value
  bfr^ [index] := w;                        // store it in the caller's buffer
  Inc (index, 2);                           // point past next Left or Right
  Inc (angle, d_angle);                     // bump the angle
  angle := angle and max_angle;             // wrap to 360 degrees
  end;
end;
```

This should give you a taste for the kind of code needed to digitally produce different kinds of sounds. Various books described in Appendix B describe powerful techniques to accomplish similar tasks. Now we'll discuss the main topic, Windows built-in support for waveform audio.

General Support for Waveform Audio

The functions, constants, and structures that support waveform audio generally fall into two groups: WaveIn for those involved with recording sounds and WaveOut for those involved with playing sounds. There are a few constants and structures that apply to both input and output, which we'll discuss in this section. We'll begin with some of the general constants used for waveform audio error or informational return values. Table 3-1 shows three general data types and three general constants defined in mmsystem.pas.

Table 3-1: General multimedia types and constants

Value	Meaning
VERSION	An integer (UINT) indicating a version number; major (high byte), minor (low byte).
MMVERSION	An integer (UINT) indicating the multimedia version number; major (high byte), minor (low byte).
MMRESULT	Multimedia error return code used by most functions—0 means no error.
WAVE_FORMAT_QUERY	A flag used in the final parameter of WaveInOpen() or WaveOutOpen(). The function queries the device to determine whether it supports the given format, but it does not open the device.
WAVE_ALLOWSYNC	A flag used in the final parameter of WaveOutOpen(). If this flag is specified, a synchronous waveform audio device can be opened. If this flag is not specified while opening a synchronous driver, the device will fail to open.
WAVE_MAPPED	The uDeviceID parameter specifies a waveform audio device to be mapped to by the wave mapper.

Of these, MMRESULT is particularly important since it is commonly used as the return value for the various multimedia functions we'll be discussing. If it returns a value of 0 (MMSYSERR_NOERROR), the particular function was successful; if not, the error code it returns will often contain information helpful in debugging a program or system. Mmsystem.pas also contains constants for common errors, as shown in Table 3-2.

Table 3-2: Waveform error messages and their meanings

Error Message	Meaning
WAVERR_BASE	Base value for all waveform error messages
WAVERR_BADFORMAT	Waveform format unsupported
WAVERR_STILLPLAYING	A sound is still playing and cannot be interrupted
WAVERR_UNPREPARED	A required header has not been properly prepared
WAVERR_SYNC	The device is synchronous
WAVERR_LASTERROR	The last error in this group

Now we'll take a look at some of the basic waveform audio data types. The most basic one, HWave, refers to any waveform. It does not appear to be used with any of the waveform audio functions. Note that those types that begin with the letter "P" are generally pointers as in the following example:

```
type
  PHWave = ^HWave;
  HWave = Integer;
```

There are similar types for WaveIn and WaveOut:

```
PHWaveIn = ^HWavein;
HWaveIn = Integer;
PHWaveOut = ^HWaveout;
HWaveOut = Integer;
```

The PHWaveIn type is used for the first parameter in most of the WaveIn functions. Likewise, the PHWaveOut type is used for the first parameter in most of the WaveOut functions. Here, the value SomeWaveIn, of type HWaveIn, is used as the first parameter of a callback routine:

```
procedure waveOutProc(SomeWaveIn : HWaveIn; uMsg : UINT;
    dwInstance :DWORD;
                    dwParam1, dwParam2 : DWORD); stdcall;
```

We'll discuss this and other callback routines later in this chapter. We'll see that various callback functions can be used with waveform input and output. However, there is just one standard callback type defined in mmsystem.pas (one I have not used, nor have seen used by others, by the way):

```
type
 TFNWaveCallBack = TFNDrvCallBack;
```

There are several types common to both waveform audio input and output; these are declared in our TWave class, as follows:

```
TWave = class
 private
 { private values }
 FNumDevices : UINT;              // number of input or output devices
 public
 { public values }
 CurrentMMRESULT : MMRESULT;      // used in all functions
 WaveFormat : TWaveFormat;        // used in all formats
 DeviceID : UINT;                 // waveform input or output device
 property NumDevices : UINT read FNumDevices Write FNumDevices;
 function GetNumDevices : UINT; virtual; abstract;
 constructor Create(BufferSize, BlockSize : Cardinal);
 destructor Destroy(CloseBuffers : boolean);
 published
 { published values }
end;
```

Before you can open a waveform device for input, you need to perform certain tasks. One of the first is to create one or more memory buffers for the sounds you'll be recording and playing back. Since it is possible to use the same buffers for both processes, we'll encapsulate the buffer management in a single class, TWaveBuffer. Before we discuss that class in detail, we need to understand WAVEHDR, a structure common to both waveform input and output, and included as a parameter in both the WaveInOpen() and WaveOutOpen() functions. In fact, if WaveHdr is not properly initialized, calling either WaveInOpen() or WaveOutOpen() will certainly fail. We show how to initialize the various WAVEHDR fields under the descriptions of these two functions later in this chapter. If you go back and examine the earlier examples from SweepGen, you'll see examples of the WAVEHDR structure. Both functions include a WaveHdr parameter. Here is the declaration from mmsystem.pas:

```
type
 PWaveHdr = ^TWaveHdr;
 wavehdr_tag = record
  lpData: PChar;
  dwBufferLength: DWORD;          { length of data buffer }
  dwBytesRecorded: DWORD;         { used for input only }
  dwUser: DWORD;                  { for client's use }
```

```
  dwFlags: DWORD;                { assorted flags (see defines) }
  dwLoops: DWORD;                { loop control counter }
  lpNext: PWaveHdr;              { reserved for driver }
  reserved: DWORD;               { reserved for driver }
end;
TWaveHdr = wavehdr_tag;
WAVEHDR = wavehdr_tag;
```

The members of WAVEHDR are explained in Table 3-3.

Table 3-3: WAVEHDR members

Member	Description and Use of Member
lpData	A PChar that points to the data buffer used to transfer blocks of data between an application and its waveform devices. You must designate memory for the buffer to which this points and for the WAVEHDR structure itself (see Listing 3-1).
dwBufferLength	This DWORD member indicates the length of the data buffer to which the lpData member points.
dwBytesRecorded	When the header is used in input, this DWORD member indicates the bytes recorded and ready to be passed to the operating system. This value is not necessarily the same as dwBufferLength. It should be set initially to 0. See the RecordSounds() and ContinueRecording() methods of the TWaveIn class for examples of using this parameter.
dwUser	Like Delphi's tag member, you can use this DWORD member in any way you like. For example, you could initialize it to a particular value to keep track of the specific buffer that was being processed in a multi-buffering scheme.
dwFlags	Flags within a DWORD member that store information about the buffer and its use (see description of specific flags in Table 3-4). This member should be set initially to 0.
dwLoops	This DWORD member indicates the number of times to repeat (loop) a particular sound segment. This member is used only with output buffers.
lpNext	This PWaveHdr member points to the next WAVEHDR structure in the application's queue.
reserved	This DWORD member, used by the driver, should be set to 0.

The dwFlags member is important in sending wave header information back to the application. These flags are described in Table 3-4.

Table 3-4: dwFlags flags member of the WAVEHDR structure

Value	Meaning
WHDR_DONE	Done bit
WHDR_PREPARED	Set if this header has been prepared
WHDR_BEGINLOOP	Loop start block
WHDR_ENDLOOP	Loop end block
WHDR_INQUEUE	Reserved for driver; test this flag to determine if there are still data blocks waiting to be processed. See Listing 3-21.

Double Buffering

The following example shows how to work with the WAVEHDR structure and the various buffers in setting up a double buffering system. Double buffering is one of the most common approaches when playing or recording sounds. While one buffer is being processed by the application, another buffer can be sent to the operating system. The general process for recording is outlined in Figure 3-4. This process of double buffering usually requires the use of callback routines (or at least reacting to messages sent by waveform devices). First, we'll discuss how to set up the

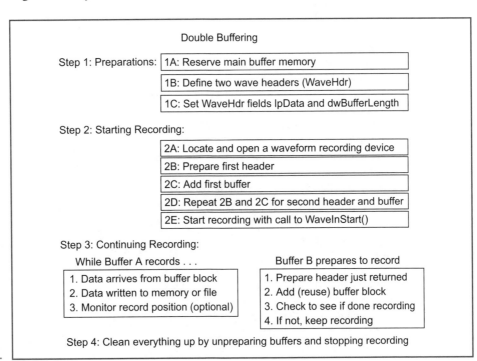

Figure 3-4

buffers. In the rest of this chapter, we'll discuss the other details of double buffering as we discuss the functions involved.

To set up these buffers, you need to determine how much memory to allocate for the main playback buffer and the block buffers. In the WavClass.pas unit, two constants define default values for the buffer:

```
const
DefaultBufferSize = 327680; // if not specified in function calls
DefaultBlockSize = 32768;   // if not specified in function calls
```

When using this class, if you enter zeros in the AllocateBuffers() method (shown in Listing 3-4), these default values will be used. This function first sets buffer sizes, then initializes the memory for the temporary buffer blocks (FBlockBuffers), sets aside memory for the FWaveHeaderArray, and sets initial values for the FWaveHeaderArray members. Finally, MainSoundBuffer is initialized. All of this takes place within a try/except block. If anything goes wrong, the function returns false and the user is encouraged to close the application.

Listing 3-4: Setting up memory buffers for double buffering

```
function TWaveBuffer.AllocateBuffers(var MainBlockSize,
     BufBlockSize : Cardinal): boolean;
var
 j: integer;
begin
 result := True;
 if BufBlockSize=0 then
  SecondaryBufferSize := DefaultBlockSize
 else
  SecondaryBufferSize := BufBlockSize;
 if MainBlockSize=0 then
  MainSoundBufferSize := DefaultBufferSize
 else
  MainSoundBufferSize := MainBlockSize;
 try  // make sure we are able to allocate memory
 for j := 0 to MaxBuffers-1 do // Iterate through the buffers
 begin
 FBlockBuffers[j] := AllocMem(SecondaryBufferSize);
 FWaveHeaderArray[j] := AllocMem(SizeOf(WaveHdr));
 ResetHeader(FWaveHeaderArray[j], j);
 end;
 MainSoundBuffer := TMemoryStream.Create;
 except
  if MainSoundBuffer<>Nil then
```

```
   MainSoundBuffer.Free;
   result := False;
  end;
 end;
end;
```

The ResetHeader() function initializes certain members of the WAVEHDR structure. Of course, we must remember to clean things up after we're done. Cleaning up involves freeing all of the memory we allocated in Listing 3-4. Listing 3-5 shows how we do that in the TWaveBuffer class:

Listing 3-5: Freeing all of the buffers created in Listing 3-4

```
function TWaveBuffer.DeAllocateBuffers: boolean;
var
 j: integer;
begin
 result := True;
 try
  for j := 0 to MaxBuffers-1 do  // Iterate through the buffers
  begin
   with FWaveHeaderArray[j]^ do
    begin
    FreeMem(lpData);
    lpData := Nil;
    end;
   FreeMem(FWaveHeaderArray[j]);
   FWaveHeaderArray[j] := Nil;
   FBlockBuffers[j] := Nil;
  end;
 except
  result := False;
 end;
 MainSoundBuffer.Free;
end;
```

3

Chapter

Messages, Callbacks, and Processing Sound

We've already mentioned the use of callback routines in processing sounds. All of the various wave callback routines have one thing in common: They all work with the various callback messages. Three are used for output and three are used for input as shown in Table 3-5.

Table 3-5: Waveform messages used with WaveOut and WaveIn callback functions:

Value	Meaning
MM_WOM_OPEN	This message is sent to a window or other recipient (callback, thread, etc.) when the given waveform audio output device is opened. The wParam parameter is an hOutputDev value. It is the handle of the device that was opened and is sending this message. The lParam member is reserved and must be set to zero.
MM_WOM_CLOSE	This message is sent to a window or other recipient when the given waveform audio output device is closed. After this message has been sent, the device handle set when the output device was opened is no longer valid. The wParam parameter is the handle of that device. The lParam member is reserved and must be set to zero.
MM_WOM_DONE	This message is sent to a window or other recipient when the given waveform audio output device's output buffer is being returned to the application. Buffers are returned to the application either when they have been played or when the WaveOutReset() function is called. The wParam member is the handle of the output device that played the buffer. The lParam member is the address of a WAVEHDR structure identifying the buffer.
MM_WIM_OPEN	This message is sent to a window or other recipient when the given waveform audio input device is opened. The wParam parameter is an hInputDev value. It is the handle of the device that was opened and is sending this message. The lParam member is reserved and must be set to zero.
MM_WIM_CLOSE	This message is sent to a window or other recipient when the given waveform audio input device is closed. After this message has been sent, the device handle set when the input device was opened is no longer valid. The wParam parameter is the handle of that device. The lParam member is reserved and must be set to zero.

Value	Meaning
MM_WIM_DATA	This message is sent to a window or other recipient when the given waveform audio input device has data in its input buffer and that buffer is being returned to the application. This message can be sent either when the buffer is full or after the WaveInReset() function is called. The wParam member is the handle of the input device that owns the buffer. The lParam member is the address of a WAVEHDR structure identifying the buffer.

Before you open any input or output device you must determine how you will deal with these messages. One simple approach is to write your own event handler, which is what you'd do if you were building a component. The SweepGen application we discussed earlier uses this approach. First, you declare a procedure to handle the message using the standard form:

```
procedure mmWomOpen (var Msg: TMessage); message mm_wom_open;
```

With this approach, you would include all of the processing code within the MmWomOpen() procedure. One example of this approach is shown in Listing 3-2. If you use this approach you'll need to specify the call-back_window flag in the dwFlags parameter of the device-opening function (see the definitions of WaveInOpen() and WaveOutOpen()). You could also write your own low-level callback function to process messages sent by the device driver. We use that approach in building our Waveform classes. In this case, be sure to specify both the callback_function flag in the dwFlags parameter and the address of the callback in the dwCallback parameter of the device-opening function. We'll discuss this in more detail when we discuss opening these devices and processing their messages. First, we need to understand in detail how these callbacks work.

How do the different ways of using callbacks differ from each other? Messages sent to a callback function are quite similar to messages sent to a window. The main difference is that those sent to a callback function have two Double Word parameters instead of one unsigned integer and one Double Word parameter. One of the advantages of using callback functions is that you can call them from another thread running asynchronously from the application's thread. If you do that, you should be sure to use critical sections to protect data that is shared between the callback routine and the rest of the application from accidental corruption.

It is important to remember to avoid calling functions that take too long to return within the waveform callback functions you write. Ignoring this point could lead to your application being deadlocked. This constraint applies to the Wave API functions we'll be discussing in this chapter as well as to the MIDI API functions discussed in the next chapter. According to the Microsoft Windows multimedia documentation, if you write a low-level audio callback that shares data with other code you must use a critical section or comparable mutual exclusion mechanism to protect the integrity of the data. You can use one of the following techniques to pass instance data from an application to a low-level callback routine located in a dynamic link library:

■ Pass the instance data using the dwInstance parameter of the function that opens the device driver.

■ Pass the instance data using the dwUser member of the WAVEHDR (Wave API) or MIDIHDR (MIDI API) structures that identify an audio data block being sent to a device driver.

If you're working with more than 32 bits of instance data, you can pass a pointer to a structure containing the additional information. Now that we have some background information on callback routines, we'll be able to understand their use in communicating with audio devices. We have just one more topic we need to cover before discussing recording and playing sounds—device capabilities.

As you've seen already, the Wave API allows you to work with messages in different ways. There are also several ways to determine a wave device's capabilities. One of these is to tell Windows the capabilities you want and have it find an appropriate device. To achieve this you can specify the capabilities you're looking for in the WAVEFORMAT structure and call WaveInOpen(); or you can call WaveOutOpen() with the WAVE_MAPPER constant in the second parameter, DeviceID. The WAVE_MAPPER constant is defined in mmsystem.pas as:

```
WAVE_MAPPER    = UINT(-1);
```

The WAVEFORMAT structure defines the format for waveform audio data. This structure includes format information common to all waveform audio data formats. Formats that require additional information include this structure as the first member in another structure, along with the additional information. The basic structure, WAVEFORMAT, is defined in mmsystem.pas as follows:

```
type
 PWaveFormat = ^TWaveFormat;
 waveformat_tag = packed record
  wFormatTag: Word;        { format type }
  nChannels: Word;         { number of channels (i.e. mono, stereo, etc.) }
  nSamplesPerSec: DWORD;   { sample rate }
  nAvgBytesPerSec: DWORD;  { for buffer estimation }
  nBlockAlign: Word;       { block size of data }
 end;
 TWaveFormat = waveformat_tag;
 WAVEFORMAT = waveformat_tag;
```

The various members of this structure are described in Table 3-6.

Table 3-6: WAVEFORMAT members and their meanings

Member	Meaning
wFormatTag	Format type. The following commonly used type is defined in mmsystem.pas: WAVE_FORMAT_PCM. PCM (Pulse Code Modulation) is very common in waveform audio.
nChannels	Number of channels in the waveform audio data. Mono data uses one channel and stereo data uses two channels.
nSamplesPerSec	Sample rate, in samples per second.
nAvgBytesPerSec	Required average data transfer rate, in bytes per second. For example, 16-bit stereo at 44.1 kHz has an average data rate of 176,400 bytes per second (two channels, two bytes per sample per channel, 44,100 samples per second).
nBlockAlign	Block alignment, in bytes. The block alignment is the minimum atomic unit of data. For PCM data, the block alignment is the number of bytes used by a single sample, including data for both channels if the data is stereo. For example, the block alignment for 16-bit stereo PCM is 4 bytes (two channels with two bytes per sample).

As mentioned above, formats that require additional information include this structure as a member in another structure along with the additional information. The extended form of this structure, WAVEFORMATEX, is defined as follows in mmsystem.pas:

```
PWaveFormatEx = ^TWaveFormatEx;
tWAVEFORMATEX = packed record
```

3

Chapter

```
wFormatTag: Word;      { format type }
nChannels: Word;       { number of channels (i.e. mono, stereo, etc.) }
nSamplesPerSec: DWORD;    { sample rate }
nAvgBytesPerSec: DWORD;    { for buffer estimation }
nBlockAlign: Word;       { block size of data }
wBitsPerSample: Word;    { number of bits per sample of mono data }
cbSize: Word;            { the count in bytes of the size of }
end;
```

The various members of WAVEFORMATEX are shown in Table 3-7.

Table 3-7: Values for WAVEFORMATEX members

Member	Meaning
wFormatTag	Waveform audio format type. These types are registered with Microsoft Corporation for various compression algorithms. A complete list of format tags is in the MMREG.H header file.
nChannels	Number of channels in the waveform audio data. Monaural data uses one channel and stereo data uses two channels.
nSamplesPerSec	Sample rate (in samples per second or hertz) in which each channel should be played or recorded. Common values for nSamplesPerSec (when wFormatTag is WAVE_FORMAT_PCM) are 8.0 kHz, 11.025 kHz, 22.05 kHz, and 44.1 kHz. For non-PCM formats, this member must be computed according to the manufacturer's specification of the format tag.
nAvgBytesPerSec	Required member. Average data transfer rate, in bytes per second, for the format tag. If wFormatTag is WAVE_FORMAT_PCM, nAvgBytesPerSec should be equal to the product of nSamplesPerSec and nBlockAlign. For non-PCM formats, this member must be computed according to the manufacturer's specification of the format tag. You can use the nAvgBytesPerSec member to estimate buffer sizes.
nBlockAlign	Block alignment, in bytes. The block alignment is the minimum atomic unit of data for the wFormatTag format type. If wFormatTag is WAVE_FORMAT_PCM, nBlockAlign should be equal to the product of nChannels and wBitsPerSample divided by 8 (bits per byte). For non-PCM formats, this member must be computed according to the manufacturer's specification of the format tag. You must process data in multiples of nBlockAlign bytes at a time. Further, data written to or read from a device must always start at the beginning of a block.

Member	Meaning
wBitsPerSample	Bits per sample for the wFormatTag format type. If wFormatTag is WAVE_FORMAT_PCM, then wBitsPerSample should be equal to 8 or 16. For non-PCM formats, this member must be set according to the manufacturer's specification of the format tag. Note that some compression schemes cannot define a value for wBitsPerSample, so this member can be zero.
cbSize	Size, in bytes, of the extra format information appended to the end of the WAVEFORMATEX structure. This information can be used by non-PCM formats to store extra attributes for the wFormatTag. If no extra information is required by the wFormatTag, you must set this member to zero. Note that for WAVE_FORMAT_PCM formats (and only WAVE_FORMAT_PCM formats), this member is ignored.

We mentioned WAVE_FORMAT_PCM above, a type that is referred to several times in Table 3-7. PCM (pulse code modulation) is one of the common ways of storing sampled sound data. Each sample is stored as a series of numbers representing the positive and negative voltages that define a particular sound wave's characteristics. WAVE_FORMAT_PCM is such a popular format that it has its own constant and special format. The latter, however, has now been superceded by the WAVEFORMATEX we discussed above. The declarations of the WAVE_FORMAT_PCM and PCMWAVEFORMAT structure from mmsystem.pas are as follows:

```
const
 WAVE_FORMAT_PCM   = 1;
type
 PPCMWaveFormat = ^TPCMWaveFormat;
 pcmwaveformat_tag = record
   wf: TWaveFormat;
   wBitsPerSample: Word;
  end;
 TPCMWaveFormat = pcmwaveformat_tag;
 PCMWAVEFORMAT = pcmwaveformat_tag;
```

We've discussed the constants and structures common to both waveform audio input and output. Now we'll take a detailed look at waveform audio input (recording) and later output (playback). You'll see that the two processes are quite similar, but do include important differences. In both cases, the process is parallel. First, you must find a suitable input or output audio device. Second, you must open that device and properly prepare the block buffers. Third, you must begin and then continue the

3

Chapter

process of recording or playing sound. Finally, when the recording or playing is finished you must perform certain cleanup chores. Let's see how this general process applies to recording sounds.

Recording Sounds with Waveform Audio

To record sound, you must find a device that can perform the task correctly: monaural or stereo, 8 bit or 16 bit, and at one of three sampling speeds. Although some devices support all of these, others do not. There are two ways to find an appropriate device. You can either use the WaveInGetDevCaps() function to ascertain the capabilities of a given device or use the WaveInOpen() function in a special way to determine if a given device meets your current needs. Using the first approach, you must examine the WAVEINCAPS structure returned by the WaveInGetDevCaps() function to determine if it contains the properties you want. With the latter approach, you must fill a WAVEFORMATEX structure with the properties you want and then call the WaveInOpen() function with the Wave_Mapper parameter. In this case, the system opens the device that comes closest to matching the properties you've specified in WAVEFORMATEX.

To use the first approach to query the capabilities of the audio devices on a computer, you must first determine how many such devices are available. The Windows multimedia system provides the WaveInGetNum-Devs() function to return the number of input devices on a particular computer.

Once you have found a suitable device, you can open it with the WaveInOpen() function. This function returns in its first parameter a handle that is used by all of the other functions. It also sets up the callback mechanism that will take care of WaveIn messages (see discussion above). We'll discuss more of the details of this when we discuss the WaveInOpen() function. If at any point after this you want to get the device number (not the handle) of the input device, you can use the WaveInGetID() function.

If you haven't already done so, you need to get memory for the data buffers as we discussed above. Then you need to prepare the buffer block headers with the WaveInPrepareHeader() function and add those buffers to the system queue with the WaveInAddBuffer() function. As we've discussed already, we use a double buffering system in our wave classes so that while the system is working with one buffer, the application can process the other.

The WaveInStart() function begins the recording process. It continues to return block buffers to the system until the application no longer accepts them, until the WaveInReset() function is called, or until an error occurs in the process of adding block buffers. In the sample application that demonstrates these classes (in the case, the WaveIn class), we stop recording when the large playback buffer is full.

Once the process of recording has been completed, you must close things down in a very specific manner. First, you need to call WaveInStop() and WaveInReset() to ensure that recording is finished. It is a good policy to also call WaveInUnprepareHeader() to clean up the block buffer headers. You must do this, in any case, before freeing the memory associated with those headers and their block buffers. Finally, you must call WaveInClose(), after which the handle for the device becomes invalid.

As stated previously, most of these functions report the result of their operations in MMRESULT, a constant integer. Once you have a MMRESULT value, you can use it to get a string that provides a description of the problem using the WaveInGetErrorText() function. After having taken a general look at the process of recording, let's take a detailed look at all of the functions and structures.

3

Chapter

Tip: When debugging multimedia applications, always check the value returned in a variable of type MMRESULT. If the error is caused by a lack of hardware capabilities, be sure to provide the user with an error message and make certain that you exit from the problem gracefully.

function WaveInGetNumDevs   *mmsystem.pas*

Syntax

```
function WaveInGetNumDevs
  : UINT; stdcall;
```

Description

This function takes no parameters and simply returns the number of input devices found on a particular computer. Once you know the number of devices, you can then query each device to determine its capabilities. Listing 3-6 shows how to do this using this function and TWaveInCaps (Borland's naming of the WAVEINCAPS structure).

function WaveInGetDevCaps   *mmsystem.pas*

Syntax

```
function WaveInGetDevCaps(
hwi: HWAVEIN;
lpCaps: PWaveInCaps;
uSize: UINT
): MMRESULT; stdcall;
```

Description

This function queries the waveform input device, hwi, determines its capabilities, and places them in the LPCAPS structure. The result is returned in MMRESULT. The MMRESULT type is used in most of the functions we'll be discussing in this chapter. See its description in Table 3-1 along with the possible return values.

Parameters

hwi: An integer (UINT) identifying a waveform audio input device. It can be either a device identifier or the handle of an open waveform audio input device. The WAVE_MAPPER constant can also be used as the device identifier.

lpCaps: The address of a WAVEINCAPS structure to be filled with information about the capabilities of the device specified by hwi.

uSize: An integer (UINT) indicating the size of the WAVEINCAPS structure. Use SizeOf(WAVEINCAPS) to get this value.

Return Value

Returns MMSYSERR_NOERROR if successful. Otherwise, it returns one of the following errors: MMSYSERR_BADDEVICEID, indicating the device identifier specified is out of range; MMSYSERR_NODRIVER, indicating that no device driver is present; or MMSYSERR_NOMEM, indicating that memory could not be allocated.

WAVEINCAPS and its related structures, which hold information about a waveform input device's capabilities are defined as follows in mmsystem.pas:

```
type
PWaveInCapsA = ^TWaveInCapsA;
PWaveInCaps = PWaveInCapsA;
tagWAVEINCAPSA = record
 wMid: Word;                                  { manufacturer ID }
 wPid: Word;                                  { product ID }
 vDriverVersion: MMVERSION;                   { version of the driver }
 szPname: array[0..MAXPNAMELEN-1] of AnsiChar; { product name (NULL
                                                   terminated string) }
 dwFormats: DWORD;                            { formats supported }
 wChannels: Word;                             { number of channels supported }
 wReserved1: Word;                            { structure packing }
end;
tagWAVEINCAPS = tagWAVEINCAPSA;
TWaveInCapsA = tagWAVEINCAPSA;
TWaveInCaps = TWaveInCapsA;
WAVEINCAPSA = tagWAVEINCAPSA;
WAVEINCAPS = WAVEINCAPSA;
```

Table 3-8: Values for the main members of WAVEINCAPS

Member	Meaning
wMid	A Word value indicating the manufacturer identifier of the device driver for the waveform audio input device.
wPid	A Word value indicating the product identifier for the waveform audio input device.
vDriverVersion	An MMVERSION value indicating the version number of the device driver for the waveform audio input device. The high-order byte is the major version number, and the low-order byte is the minor version number. See Listing 3-6 for code to display the version as a fixed-point number.
szPname	A null-terminated string holding the product name.

Member	Meaning
dwFormats	A DWORD value holding the constants (bits) that represent the various formats supported. The standard formats are listed in Table 3-9.
wChannels	A Word value specifying whether the device supports monaural (1) or stereo (2) input.

Table 3-9: Values for dwFormats member of WAVEINCAPS and WAVEOUTCAPS

Value	Meaning
WAVE_FORMAT_1M08	11.025 kHz, mono, 8-bit
WAVE_FORMAT_1M16	11.025 kHz, mono, 16-bit
WAVE_FORMAT_1S08	11.025 kHz, stereo, 8-bit
WAVE_FORMAT_1S16	11.025 kHz, stereo, 16-bit
WAVE_FORMAT_2M08	22.05 kHz, mono, 8-bit
WAVE_FORMAT_2M16	22.05 kHz, mono, 16-bit
WAVE_FORMAT_2S08	22.05 kHz, stereo, 8-bit
WAVE_FORMAT_2S16	22.05 kHz, stereo, 16-bit
WAVE_FORMAT_4M08	44.1 kHz, mono, 8-bit
WAVE_FORMAT_4M16	44.1 kHz, mono, 16-bit
WAVE_FORMAT_4S08	44.1 kHz, stereo, 8-bit
WAVE_FORMAT_4S16	44.1 kHz, stereo, 16-bit

Listing 3-6 shows how to find and display the properties of a waveform input device.

Listing 3-6: Finding and displaying properties for all WaveIn devices on a computer

```
procedure TfrmWaveInDevicesProperties.FormCreate(Sender: TObject);
var
 FNumInputDevices : Cardinal;
 FWaveInCaps : TWaveInCaps;
 k: integer;
 j: Integer;
 Node,
 FormatNode: TTreeNode;
begin
 if WaveIn=Nil then
  WaveIn := TWaveIn.Create(0, 0);
```

```
FNumInputDevices := WaveIn.GetNumDevices;
TreeView1.Items.Clear;
for j := (FNumInputDevices-1) downto 0 do  // Iterate
begin
 waveInGetDevCaps(j, @FWaveInCaps, SizeOf(TWaveInCaps));
 Node := TreeView1.Items.AddChildFirst(nil, 'Device '+IntToStr(J+1));
 TreeView1.Items.AddChild(Node, 'Manufacturer ID: ' +
  IntToStr(FWaveInCaps.wMid));
 TreeView1.Items.AddChild(Node, 'Product ID: ' +
  IntToStr(FWaveInCaps.wPid));
 TreeView1.Items.AddChild(Node, 'Driver Version: ' +
  IntToStr(hi(FWaveInCaps.vDriverVersion)) +
  '.' + IntToStr(lo(FWaveInCaps.vDriverVersion)));
 TreeView1.Items.AddChild(Node, 'Product Name: ' +
  FWaveInCaps.szPname);
 FormatNode := TreeView1.Items.AddChild(Node, 'Formats Supported: ');
  for k := 0 to (WaveFormatTotal-1) do
   if (FWaveInCaps.dwFormats and (1 shl (k+1))=(1 shl (k+1))) then
    TreeView1.Items.AddChild(FormatNode, WaveFormatArray[k]);
 TreeView1.Items.AddChild(Node, 'Channels Supported: ' +
  IntToStr(FWaveInCaps.wChannels));
 end;  // for Input Devices
end;
```

function WaveInGetErrorText   *mmsystem.pas*

Syntax

```
function WaveInGetErrorText(
  mmrError: MMRESULT;
  lpText: PChar;
  uSize: UINT
  ): MMRESULT; stdcall;
```

Description

This function returns a textual description of the error identified by the given error number, MMRERROR. The error string is placed in the lpText parameter. See Listing 3-7 for an example of how to set up a general utility routine to return these strings for both input and output return values.

Parameters

MmrError: An MMRESULT error constant returned by one of the WaveIn functions.

lpText: A string explaining the error, MMRERROR.

uSize: An integer (UINT) indicating the size of the PChar buffer that holds the description of the error. In the WavClass unit, the constant MsgLength is set to 128, sufficient for any of the message strings.

Return Value

Returns MMSYSERR_NOERROR if successful. Otherwise, it returns one of the following errors: MMSYSERR_BADERRNUM indicating the specified error number is out of range; MMSYSERR_NODRIVER indicating there is no device driver present; or MMSYSERR_NOMEM, indicating that memory could not be allocated.

Example

Listing 3-7 reports both input and output errors. That's why its first parameter is IO_Direction, indicating input or output. The functions called in this procedure are input- or output-specific.

Listing 3-7: A general utility function to respond to and report audio input and output errors

```
function ReportError(IO_Direction : TIO_Direction;
          AMMRESULT : MMRESULT;
          ErrMessage : string)
        : boolean;
 var
  TempBuffer : Pchar;
  begin
   if ErrMessage='' then
   begin
    TempBuffer := Nil;
    StrNew(TempBuffer);
    if IO_Direction=iodInput then
      waveInGetErrorText(AMMRESULT, PChar(TempBuffer), MsgLength)
    else
      waveOutGetErrorText(AMMRESULT, PChar(TempBuffer), MsgLength);
    ErrMessage := StrPas(TempBuffer);
    StrDispose(TempBuffer);
   end;
   case IO_Direction of      //
```

```
    iodInput: WaveIn.WaveInStatus := wisError;
    iodOutput: WaveOut.WaveOutStatus := wosError;
  end;                          // case
  result := True;               // Always true; always exit on return
 end;
```

function WaveInOpen   *mmsystem.pas*

Syntax

```
function WaveInOpen(
  lphWaveIn: PHWAVEIN;
  uDeviceID: UINT;
  lpFormatEx: PWaveFormatEx;
  dwCallback, dwInstance, dwFlags: DWORD
  ):MMRESULT; stdcall;
```

Description

This function opens the given waveform audio input device for recording with the device identifier. If successful, the parameter lphWaveIn contains a handle for the device that will be used by other WaveIn functions.

Parameters

lphWaveIn: A PHWaveIn value which is the handle identifying the open waveform audio input device. This handle should be saved in a variable visible to other waveform input functions so that they can use it when they are called. This parameter can be NULL if WAVE_FORMAT_QUERY is specified in dwFlags.

uDeviceID: An integer identifying the waveform audio input device to open. It can be a device identifier, the handle of an open waveform audio input device, or the WAVE_MAPPER constant. In the latter case, the function will select a waveform audio input device capable of recording in the specified format.

lpFormatEx: The address of a WAVEFORMATEX structure identifying the desired format for recording waveform audio data. You can free this structure immediately after WaveInOpen() returns.

dwCallback: The address of a fixed callback function, an event handle, or a handle of a window or thread called during waveform audio recording to process messages related to the progress of recording. If no callback function is required, this value can be zero. In the example, two alternate approaches are shown: a callback function and a callback window.

dwInstance: User-instance data passed to the callback mechanism. This parameter is not used with the window callback mechanism and should be set to 0 in that case.

dwFlags: Flags for opening the device. Those flags are given in Table 3-10:

Table 3-10: Values for the dwFlags member of WaveInOpen()

Value	Meaning
CALLBACK_EVENT	The dwCallback parameter is an event handle.
CALLBACK_FUNCTION	The dwCallback parameter is a callback procedure address.
CALLBACK_NULL	No callback mechanism. This is the default setting.
CALLBACK_THREAD	The dwCallback parameter is a thread handle.
CALLBACK_WINDOW	The dwCallback parameter is a window handle.
WAVE_FORMAT_DIRECT	The ACM driver will not perform conversions on the audio data.
WAVE_FORMAT_QUERY	If this flag is specified, WaveInOpen() queries the device to determine if it supports the given format, but the device is not actually opened.
WAVE_MAPPED	If this flag is specified, the uDeviceID parameter specifies a waveform audio device to be mapped to by the wave mapper.

Return Value

Returns MMSYSERR_NOERROR if successful. Otherwise, it returns one of the following errors: MMSYSERR_ALLOCATED, indicating the specified resource is already allocated; MMSYSERR_BADDEVICEID, indicating the specified device identifier is out of range; MMSYSERR_NODRIVER, indicating that there is no device driver present; MMSYSERR_NOMEM, indicating that memory could not be allocated; or WAVERR_BAD-FORMAT, indicating an attempt to open the device with an unsupported waveform audio format.

Example

The following segments of code show how to set up and manage a call-back system for waveform input. In order to accomplish this, and to have these functions return as quickly as possible, you simply post a message as we've done in the example program—a message of your own creation. We define those messages as follows in the WavClass unit:

```
const
 WaveIn_Started = WM_User + 150;    // For waveInOpen callbacks
 WaveIn_Recording = WM_User + 151;  // For waveInOpen callbacks
 WaveIn_Stop = WM_User + 152;       // For waveInOpen callbacks
 WaveOut_Started = WM_User + 153;   // For waveOutOpen callbacks
 WaveOut_Stop = WM_User + 154;      // For waveOutOpen callbacks
 WaveOut_Finished = WM_User + 155;  // For waveOutOpen callbacks
```

In Listing 3-8, we use the first three of these messages (those for input) in our callback routine. These messages are sent back to the application's main window, as we'll see. Listing 3-9 shows the steps involved in opening an audio input device. Note that the OpenRecordWaveDef() method includes a nested function, GetCaps(), which checks for the support of different capabilities.

Listing 3-8: Callback routine for WaveIn

```
procedure waveInProc(SomeWaveIn : HWaveIn; uMsg : UINT; dwInstance :
             DWORD; dwParam1, dwParam2 : DWORD); stdcall;
begin
 case uMsg of    //
  WIM_OPEN: PostMessage(HWND(MainFormHandle), WaveIn_Started, 0,
    dwParam1);
  WIM_CLOSE: PostMessage(HWND(MainFormHandle), WaveIn_Stop, 0, dwParam1);
  WIM_DATA: PostMessage(HWND(MainFormHandle), WaveIn_Recording, 0,
    dwParam1);
 end;          // case
end;
```

Listing 3-9: Function for opening an audio input device

```
function TWaveIn.OpenRecordWaveDev(SaveTo : SoundRecordTo; NumChannels :
    Channels;
       RequestedSamplingRate :SamplingRate; Bit16Use :
       boolean;
       var ReturnErrMsg : string) : boolean;
var
 FormatStruc : tWAVEFORMATEX;
 DevNum : integer;
```

```
function GetCaps(ChannelNum : Channels;
            SampRate : SamplingRate;
            var DeviceToUse : Integer) : boolean;
var
 TotalsDevs : integer;
 j: Integer;
begin
 result := False;
 TotalsDevs := GetNumDevices;
 for j := 0 to (TotalsDevs-1) do              // Iterate
 begin
  CurrentMMRESULT := waveInGetDevCaps(j, @WaveInCaps, SizeOf(WaveInCaps)
    {CapStructSize});
  if CurrentMMRESULT=MMSYSERR_NOERROR then
    DeviceToUse := j;
  if Bit16Use then
  case SampRate of                            // 16 bit only
   sr11_025 : if (((ChannelNum=chOne) and // 16 bit mono at slowest speed
   (WaveInCaps.dwFormats and
   (1 shl WAVE_FORMAT_1M16)=(1 shl WAVE_FORMAT_1M16))
   or ((WaveInCaps.dwFormats and          // 16 bit stereo slowest speed
   (1 shl WAVE_FORMAT_1S16))=(1 shl WAVE_FORMAT_1S16)))) then
    begin
     result := True;
     Break;
    end;
   sr22_05 : if (((ChannelNum=chOne) and  // 16 bit mono at medium speed
   (WaveInCaps.dwFormats and
   (1 shl WAVE_FORMAT_2M16)=(1 shl WAVE_FORMAT_2M16))
   or ((WaveInCaps.dwFormats and          // 16 bit stereo medium speed
   (1 shl WAVE_FORMAT_2S16))=(1 shl WAVE_FORMAT_2S16)))) then
    begin
     result := True;
     Break;
    end;
     sr44_1 : if (((ChannelNum=chOne) and // 16 bit mono fastest speed
   (WaveInCaps.dwFormats and
   (1 shl WAVE_FORMAT_4M16)=(1 shl WAVE_FORMAT_4M16))
   or ((WaveInCaps.dwFormats and          // 16 bit stereo fastest speed
   (1 shl WAVE_FORMAT_4S16))=(1 shl WAVE_FORMAT_4S16)))) then
    begin
     result := True;
     Break;
    end;
  end                                         // case
  else
```

```
   case SampRate of                        // 8 bit only
    sr11_025 : if ((ChannelNum=chOne) // lowest rate *should* be supported
     or ((WaveInCaps.dwFormats and        // 8 bit stereo at slowest speed
      (1 shl WAVE_FORMAT_1S08))=(1 shl WAVE_FORMAT_1S08))) then
      Break;
    sr22_05 : if (((ChannelNum=chOne) and // 8 bit mono at medium speed
      (WaveInCaps.dwFormats and
      (1 shl WAVE_FORMAT_2M08)=(1 shl WAVE_FORMAT_2M08))
     or ((WaveInCaps.dwFormats and        // 8 bit stereo at medium speed
      (1 shl WAVE_FORMAT_2S08))=(1 shl WAVE_FORMAT_2S08)))) then
       begin
        result := True;
        Break;
       end;
        sr44_1 : if (((ChannelNum=chOne) and // 8 bit mono at fastest speed
      (WaveInCaps.dwFormats and
      (1 shl WAVE_FORMAT_4M08)=(1 shl WAVE_FORMAT_4M08))
     or ((WaveInCaps.dwFormats and         // 8 bit stereo at fastest speed
      (1 shl WAVE_FORMAT_4S08))=(1 shl WAVE_FORMAT_4S08)))) then
       begin
        result := True;
        Break;
       end;
     end;
    end;                                    // for
   end;
begin    {OpenRecordWaveDef}
 DevNum := 0;
 AHandle := 0;
 if Not GetCaps(NumChannels, RequestedSamplingRate, DevNum) then
  begin
   FormatStruc.nChannels := WaveInCaps.wChannels;
   FormatStruc.nSamplesPerSec := 22050;
  end
 else
  begin
   FormatStruc.nChannels := 2;
   FormatStruc.nSamplesPerSec := 44100;
  end;
 FormatStruc.wFormatTag := WAVE_FORMAT_PCM;
 FormatStruc.wBitsPerSample := 8;
 FormatStruc.nBlockAlign := Round((FormatStruc.nChannels *
              FormatStruc.wBitsPerSample) / 8);
 FormatStruc.nAvgBytesPerSec := FormatStruc.nSamplesPerSec *
                FormatStruc.nBlockAlign;
 FormatStruc.cbSize := 0;
```

```
CurrentMMRESULT := waveInOpen(@AHandle, DevNum, (@FormatStruc),
   DWORD(@WaveInProc), DWORD(MainFormHandle), DWORD(callback_function));
result := (CurrentMMRESULT = MMSYSERR_NOERROR);
if Not result then
  waveInGetErrorText(CurrentMMRESULT, PChar(ReturnErrMsg), MsgLength)
else
 ReturnErrMsg := WAVE_IN_REC_DEV_OPEN_MSG;
RecordDevAvailable := result;
end;
```

function WaveInClose   *mmsystem.pas*

Syntax

```
function WaveInClose(
  hWaveIn: HWAVEIN
  ): MMRESULT; stdcall;
```

Description

This function closes the given waveform audio input device.

Parameter

hWaveIn: The handle of the waveform audio input device. If the function succeeds, the handle is no longer valid.

Return Value

Returns MMSYSERR_NOERROR if successful. Otherwise, it returns one of the following errors: MMSYSERR_INVALHANDLE, indicating that the specified device handle is invalid; MMSYSERR_NODRIVER, indicating that no device driver is present; MMSYSERR_NOMEM, indicating that memory could not be allocated; or WAVERR_STILLPLAYING, indicating that one or more block buffers are still in the queue.

Example

Listing 3-10 shows how to properly shut down a recording device. First, you need to be certain that all block buffers have been returned by calling WaveInReset(). WaveInStop() is probably not required but doesn't do any harm. Then you need to call WaveInUnprepareHeader() to clean up the buffers. The buffers can then be either disposed (their memory freed) or used again (prepared again). Finally, having done all of this you can call WaveInClose().

Listing 3-l0: A procedure to properly shut down a waveform input device

```
procedure TWaveIn.CloseDownRecording;
var
 j: Integer;
begin
 WaveInStop(AHandle);
 WaveInReset(AHandle);
 for j := 0 to 1 do  // Iterate
  WaveInUnprepareHeader(AHandle, WaveBuffer.FWaveHeaderArray[j],
        SizeOf(WAVEHdr));
 WaveInClose(AHandle);
 RecordDevAvailable := False;
end;
```

function WaveInPrepareHeader   *mmsystem.pas*

Syntax

```
function WaveInPrepareHeader(
hWaveIn: HWAVEIN;
lpWaveInHdr: PWaveHdr;
uSize: UINT
): MMRESULT; stdcall;
```

Description

This function prepares a buffer for waveform audio input. This is a temporary block buffer used to input audio data to be stored in memory or in a file. Before calling this function you must initialize several of the WAVEHDR structure's members, particularly lpData, dwBufferLength, and dwFlags. The lpData member should point to a valid PChar for which memory has been set and dwFlags must be set to zero.

Parameters

hWaveIn: Handle of the waveform audio input device.

lpWaveInHdr: Address of a WAVEHDR structure that identifies the buffer to be prepared.

uSize: Integer indicating the size of the WAVEHDR structure. You can simply use the SizeOf(WAVEHDR) function for this parameter.

3

Chapter

Return Value

Returns MMSYSERR_NOERROR if successful. Otherwise, it returns one of the following errors: MMSYSERR_INVALHANDLE, indicating that the specified device handle is invalid; MMSYSERR_NODRIVER, indicating that no device driver is present; or MMSYSERR_NOMEM, indicating that memory could not be allocated.

Example

Listing 3-11 shows how to properly set up the members for the WAVEHDR structure. Listing 3-12 shows how to continue the recording process once it has begun. This routine is called in response to a MM_WOM_DONE message.

Listing 3-II: How to properly set the initial values of a WAVEHDR structure before preparing it

```
procedure TWaveBuffer.ResetHeader(var AWaveHeaderPtr : PWaveHdr; Buf:
     Integer);
begin
 with AWaveHeaderPtr^ do
 begin
  lpData := PChar(WaveBuffer.FBlockBuffers[Buf]);
  dwBufferLength := WaveBuffer.SecondaryBufferSize;
  dwBytesRecorded := 0;
  dwFlags := 0;
  lpNext := Nil;
 end;  // with AWaveHeaderPtr^
end;
```

Listing 3-I2: Continuing the recording process after it has begun in response to MM_WOM_DONE message

```
function TWaveIn.ContinueRecording(WaveHdrPtr : Integer;
     var ResultMsg : string) : boolean;
var
 TempWavHdr : PWaveHdr;

begin
 TempWavHdr := PWaveHdr(WaveHdrPtr);
 if WaveInStatus <> wisRecording then
  begin
   result := False;
   exit;
  end;
 result := False;
```

```
WaveBuffer.FPlaybackBufferPosition := WaveBuffer.MainSoundBuffer
      .Position;
  if ((TempWavHdr.dwBytesRecorded + WaveBuffer.FPlaybackBufferPosition)
    <= WaveBuffer.MainSoundBufferSize) then
    begin
     try
      WaveBuffer.MainSoundBuffer.WriteBuffer(TempWavHdr.lpData^,
       Cardinal(TempWavHdr.dwBytesRecorded));
      MM_Time.wType := Time_Bytes;
      CurrentMMRESULT := waveInGetPosition(AHandle, @MM_Time,
       SizeOf(MMTime));
      if CurrentMMRESULT<>MMSYSERR_NOERROR then
       begin
       waveInGetErrorText(CurrentMMRESULT, PChar(ResultMsg), MsgLength);
       result := False;
       WaveInStatus := wisError;
       Exit;
       end;
      CurrentTime := MM_Time.cb;
      CurrentMMRESULT := waveInPrepareHeader(AHandle, TempWavHdr,
            SizeOf(WaveHdr));
      if CurrentMMRESULT<>MMSYSERR_NOERROR then
       if ReportError(iodInput, CurrentMMRESULT, ResultMsg) then Exit;
      CurrentMMRESULT := waveInAddBuffer(AHandle, TempWavHdr,
            SizeOf(WaveHdr));
      if CurrentMMRESULT<>MMSYSERR_NOERROR then
       if ReportError(iodInput, CurrentMMRESULT, ResultMsg) then Exit;
     except
      WaveInStatus := wisDoneRecording;
     end;
    end
    else
     begin
      WaveInStatus := wisDoneRecording;
      ResultMsg := 'Recording Completed Successfully';
      exit;
     end;
  result := True;
end;
```

3

Chapter

function WaveInUnprepareHeader   *mmsystem.pas*

Syntax

```
function WaveInUnprepareHeader(
hWaveIn: HWAVEIN;
lpWaveInHdr: PWaveHdr;
uSize: UINT
): MMRESULT; stdcall;
```

Description

This function cleans up the preparation performed by the WaveIn-PrepareHeader() function. After passing a buffer to the device driver with the WaveInAddBuffer() function, you must wait until the driver is finished with the buffer before calling WaveInUnprepareHeader(). Unpreparing a buffer that has not been prepared has no effect, and the function returns zero. You must call this function before freeing the buffer.

Parameters

hWaveIn: The handle of the waveform audio input device.

lpWaveInHdr: The address of a WAVEHDR structure that identifies the buffer to be unprepared.

uSize: An integer indicating the size of the WAVEHDR structure. You can simply use the SizeOf(WAVEHDR) function for this parameter.

Return Value

Returns MMSYSERR_NOERROR if successful. Otherwise, it returns one of the following errors: MMSYSERR_INVALHANDLE, indicating that the specified device handle is invalid; MMSYSERR_NODRIVER, indicating that no device driver is present; MMSYSERR_NOMEM, indicating that memory could not be allocated; or WAVERR_STILLPLAYING, indicating that one or more block buffers are still in the queue.

Example

Listing 3-10 shows how to properly shut down a recording device, including the use of the WaveInUnprepareHeader() function.

function WaveInAddBuffer   *mmsystem.pas*

Syntax

```
function WaveInAddBuffer(
  hWaveIn: HWAVEIN;
  lpWaveInHdr: PWaveHdr;
  uSize: UINT
  ): MMRESULT; stdcall;
```

Description

This function sends an input buffer to the given waveform audio input device identified by hWaveIn. You need to prepare the buffer with the WaveInPrepareHeader() function before you pass it to this function. When the buffer is filled, the application is notified and the WHDR_DONE bit is set in the dwFlags member of the WAVEHDR structure.

Parameters

hWaveIn: The handle of the waveform audio input device.

lpWaveInHdr: The address of a WAVEHDR structure that identifies the buffer to be unprepared.

uSize: An integer indicating the size of the WAVEHDR structure. You can simply use the SizeOf (WAVEHDR) function for this parameter.

Return Value

Returns MMSYSERR_NOERROR if successful. Otherwise, it returns one of the following errors: MMSYSERR_INVALHANDLE, indicating that the specified device handle is invalid; MMSYSERR_NODRIVER, indicating that no device driver is present; MMSYSERR_NOMEM, indicating that memory could not be allocated; or WAVERR_STILLPLAYING, indicating that one or more block buffers are still in the queue.

Example

See Listing 3-12.

3

Chapter

function WaveInStart   ***mmsystem.pas***

Syntax

function WaveInStart(
hWaveIn: HWAVEIN
): MMRESULT; stdcall;

Description

This is the function that actually starts the input process (recording) on the given waveform audio input device, hWaveIn. If you call this function when input has already started, it has no effect and returns with a value of zero. Buffers are returned to the application when they are full or when the WaveInReset() function is called. The dwBytesRecorded member of the header will contain the length of data recorded. If there are no buffers in the queue, the data will be discarded without notifying the application and input continues.

Parameter

hWaveIn: The handle of the waveform audio input device.

Return Value

Returns MMSYSERR_NOERROR if successful. Otherwise, it returns one of the following errors: MMSYSERR_INVALHANDLE, indicating that the specified device handle is invalid; MMSYSERR_NODRIVER, indicating that no device driver is present; or MMSYSERR_NOMEM.

Example

Listing 3-13 shows how to use WaveInStart() to begin the recording process.

Listing 3-13: Initiating the recording process

```
function TWaveIn.RecordSounds(RecordTo : SoundRecordTo;
            var ResultMsg : string)    : boolean;
var
 j: Integer;
begin
 result := False;
 WaveBuffer.MainSoundBuffer.Position := 0;
 WaveBuffer.FPlaybackBufferPosition := 0;
 for j := 0 to (MaxBuffers-1) do  // Iterate
 begin
```

```
WaveBuffer.ResetHeader(WaveBuffer.FWaveHeaderArray[j], j);
CurrentMMRESULT := waveInPrepareHeader(AHandle, WaveBuffer
        .FWaveHeaderArray[j], SizeOf(WAVEHdr));
if CurrentMMRESULT=MMSYSERR_NOERROR then
 begin
  CurrentMMRESULT := waveInAddBuffer(AHandle, WaveBuffer
        .FWaveHeaderArray[j], SizeOf(WAVEHdr));
  if CurrentMMRESULT<>MMSYSERR_NOERROR then
   begin
    waveInGetErrorText(CurrentMMRESULT, PChar(ResultMsg), MsgLength);
    Exit;
   end;
 end
 else
 begin
  ResultMsg := HEADER_PREPARE_ERR_MSG;
  Exit;
 end;
end;  // for
CurrentMMRESULT := waveInStart(AHandle);
if CurrentMMRESULT<>MMSYSERR_NOERROR then
 begin
  WaveInStatus := wisError;
  waveInGetErrorText(CurrentMMRESULT, PChar(ResultMsg), MsgLength);
  Exit;
 end;
WaveInStatus := wisRecording;
result := True;
end;
```

function WaveInStop   *mmsystem.pas*

Syntax

```
function WaveInStop(
  hWaveIn: HWAVEIN
  ): MMRESULT; stdcall;
```

Description

This function stops waveform audio input, or recording. If you call this function when input has already started, it has no effect and returns with a value of zero. If there are any buffers in the queue, the current buffer will be marked as done (the dwBytesRecorded member in the header will contain the length of data), but any empty buffers in the queue will remain there.

Parameter

hWaveIn: The handle of the waveform audio input device. If the function succeeds, the handle is no longer valid.

Return Value

Returns MMSYSERR_NOERROR if successful. Otherwise, it returns one of the following errors: MMSYSERR_INVALHANDLE, indicating that the specified device handle is invalid; MMSYSERR_NODRIVER, indicating that no device driver is present; MMSYSERR_NOMEM, indicating that memory could not be allocated; or WAVERR_STILLPLAYING, indicating that one or more block buffers are still in the queue.

Example

See Listing 3-10.

function WaveInReset   *mmsystem.pas*

Syntax

```
function WaveInReset(
  hWaveIn: HWAVEIN
  ): MMRESULT; stdcall;
```

Description

This function stops input on the given waveform audio input device and resets the current position to zero. Any pending buffers will be marked as done and returned to the application.

Parameter

hWaveIn: Handle of the waveform audio input device.

Return Value

Returns MMSYSERR_NOERROR if successful. Otherwise, it returns one of the following errors: MMSYSERR_INVALHANDLE, indicating that the specified device handle is invalid; MMSYSERR_NODRIVER, indicating that no device driver is present; or MMSYSERR_NOMEM, indicating that memory could not be allocated.

Example

See Listing 3-10.

function WaveInGetPosition   mmsystem.pas

Syntax

```
function WaveInGetPosition(
  hWaveIn: HWAVEIN;
  lpInfo: PMMTime;
  uSize: UINT
  ): MMRESULT; stdcall;
```

Description

This function retrieves the current input position of the given waveform audio input device. The position is set to zero whenever the device is opened or reset. Before calling this function, set the wType member of the MMTIME structure to indicate the time format you want. After calling this function, check wType to determine whether the desired time format is supported. If the format is not supported, the member will specify an alternative format. For additional information on times, see Chapter 7.

Parameters

hWaveIn: The handle of the waveform audio input device.

lpInfo: The address of an MMTIME structure.

uSize: An integer giving the size of the MMTIME structure.

Return Value

Returns MMSYSERR_NOERROR if successful. Otherwise, it returns one of the following errors: MMSYSERR_INVALHANDLE, indicating that the specified device handle is invalid; MMSYSERR_NODRIVER, indicating that no device driver is present; or MMSYSERR_NOMEM, indicating that memory could not be allocated.

Example

See Listing 3-12.

3

Chapter

function WaveInGetID   *mmsystem.pas*

Syntax

```
function WaveInGetID(
hWaveIn: HWAVEIN;
lpuDeviceID: PUINT
): MMRESULT; stdcall;
```

Description

This function gets the device identifier for the given waveform audio input device. Microsoft includes it to support backward compatibility. New applications can cast a handle of the device rather than retrieving the device identifier.

Parameters

hWaveIn: The handle (returned by WaveInOpen()) of the waveform audio input device for which to retrieve a device ID.

lpuDeviceID: A pointer to a UINT (integer) that holds the device ID.

Return Value

Returns MMSYSERR_NOERROR if successful. Otherwise, it returns one of the following errors: MMSYSERR_INVALHANDLE, indicating that the specified device handle is invalid; MMSYSERR_NODRIVER, indicating that no device driver is present; or MMSYSERR_NOMEM, indicating that memory could not be allocated.

Example

See Listing 3-14 under WaveOutGetVolume(), which uses WaveOutGetID(), for an example of how to use this function.

function WaveInMessage   *mmsystem.pas*

Syntax

```
function WaveInMessage(
hWaveIn: HWAVEIN;
uMessage: UINT;
dw1, dw2: DWORD
): MMRESULT; stdcall;
```

Description

This function sends messages to the waveform audio input device drivers.

Parameters

hWaveIn: The handle of the waveform audio input device.

uMessage: An integer indicating message to send.

dw1, dw2: Two DWORD parameters for message parameters.

Return Value

Returns a DWORD indicating the return value of the message.

Example

These messages are driver-specific, so we cannot show an example here that will definitely work on your system. To use this function, you need to know the specific messages that your sound card and its driver(s) will accept. Here is a general example of how you might call this function:

```
procedure TWaveIn.SendMessage(ADriverMessage: UINT; MsgParam1,
    MsgParam2: DWORD);
begin
  waveInMessage(AHandle, ADriverMessage, MsgParam1, MsgParam2);
end;
```

Playing Sounds with Waveform Audio

The process of playing sound is very similar to that of recording sound. As in the recording process, you must first find a device that can perform playback in accord with your specifications: monaural or stereo, 8 bit or 16 bit, and at one of three sampling speeds. As before, there are two ways in which you can find an appropriate device. You can either use the WaveOutGetDevCaps() function to ascertain the capabilities of a given device or you can use the WaveOutOpen() function in a special way to determine if a given device meets your current needs. Using the first approach, you must first examine the WAVEOUTCAPS structure returned by the WaveOutGetDevCaps() function to determine if it contains the properties you want. With the latter approach, you must fill a WAVEFORMATEX structure with the properties you want and then call the WaveOutOpen() function with the Wave_Mapper parameter. In this

3

Chapter

case, the system opens the device that comes closest to matching the properties you've specified in WAVEFORMATEX.

Before you can use the first approach to query the capabilities of the audio devices on a computer, you must first determine the number of such devices. The Windows multimedia system provides the WaveOut-GetNumDevs() function to return the number of output devices on a particular computer.

Once you have found a suitable device you can open it with the WaveOutOpen() function. As with the WaveInOpen() function, this function returns, in its first parameter, a handle that will be used by all of the other functions. It also sets up the callback mechanism that will take care of WaveOut messages. We'll discuss more of the details of this when we discuss the WaveOutOpen() function. If at any point after this you want to get the device number (not the handle) of the output device, you can use the WaveOutGetID() function.

If you haven't already done so, you need to get memory for the data buffers as we discussed above. (Note that in the sample application accompanying this chapter we use the same buffers for input and output.) As before, you must prepare the buffer block headers, this time using the WaveOutPrepareHeader() function. There is no WaveOut-AddBuffer() function. As we did in the recording process, we use a double buffering system in the recording process so that while the system is working with one buffer the application can process the other.

The WaveOutWrite() function begins the playing process. It continues to return block buffers to the system until the application no longer accepts them, until the WaveOutReset() function is called, or until an error occurs in the process of adding block buffers. In the sample application that demonstrates these classes (in this case the WaveOut class), we terminate playing when we reach the end of the large playback buffer. With playing there are additional capabilities, including a WaveOutPause() function that pauses playback and a WaveOutRestart() function that resumes playback. We use these in the example program to pause playback until the two buffers are filled with playback data and then begin playing back. This is a common approach.

Once the process of playing has been completed, you need to close things down in a very specific manner. This is a bit simpler than shutting down a recording device. First, you need to call WaveOutStop() and WaveOutReset() to make certain that playing is finished. Again, you should call WaveOutUnprepareHeader() to clean up the block buffer headers. You must do this, in any case, before freeing the memory associated with those headers and their associated block buffers. Finally, you must call WaveOutClose(). After this the handle for the device is no longer valid.

As with WaveIn functions, most WaveOut functions also report their result in MMRESULT. Once we have a MMRESULT value, we can use it to get a string that provides a description of the problem using the WaveOutGetErrorText() function. Now that we have taken a general look at the process of playing sounds, let's take a detailed look at all of the functions and structures.

function WaveOutGetNumDevs   *mmsystem.pas*

Syntax

function WaveOutGetNumDevs
  : UINT; stdcall;

Description

This function takes no parameters and simply returns the number of output devices found on a machine. Once you determine the number of devices, you can then query each device to determine its capabilities.

Example

The following code from the WavClass.pas unit wraps this function in a method of the WaveOut class:

```
function TWaveOut.GetNumDevices : UINT;
begin
 result := waveOutGetNumDevs;
end;
```

function WaveOutGetDevCaps   *mmsystem.pas*

Syntax

```
function WaveOutGetDevCaps(
  hwi: HWaveOut;
  lpCaps: PWaveOutCaps;
  uSize: UINT
  ): MMRESULT; stdcall;
```

Description

This function queries the waveform output device, hwi, determines its capabilities, and places that information in the lpCaps structure. The result is returned in MMRESULT. The MMRESULT type is used in most of the functions we'll be discussing in this chapter. See the possible return values below for more information.

Parameters

hwi: An integer (UINT) identifying a waveform audio output device. It can be either a device identifier or the handle of an open waveform audio output device. The WAVE_MAPPER constant can also be used as the device identifier.

lpCaps: The address of a WAVEOUTCAPS structure to be filled with information about the capabilities of the device specified by hwi.

uSize: An integer (UINT) indicating the size of the WAVEOUTCAPS structure. Use SizeOf(WAVEOUTCAPS) to get this value.

Return Value

Returns MMSYSERR_NOERROR if successful. Otherwise, it returns one of the following errors: MMSYSERR_BADDEVICEID, indicating that the device identifier specified is out of range; MMSYSERR_NODRIVER, indicating that no device driver is present; or MMSYSERR_NOMEM, indicating that memory could not be allocated.

Example

See Listing 3-14.

The following structure defined in mmsystem.pas, WAVEOUTCAPS, holds information about a waveform output device's capabilities:

```
type
PWaveOutCapsA = ^TWaveOutCapsA;
PWaveOutCapsW = ^TWaveOutCapsW;
PWaveOutCaps = PWaveOutCapsA;
tagWAVEOUTCAPSA = record
  wMid: Word;              { manufacturer ID }
  wPid: Word;              { product ID }
  vDriverVersion: MMVERSION;    { version of the driver }
  szPname: array[0..MAXPNAMELEN-1] of AnsiChar; { product name (NULL
                                               terminated string) }
  dwFormats: DWORD;        { formats supported }
  wChannels: Word;         { number of sources supported }
  dwSupport: DWORD;        { functionality supported by driver }
end;
tagWAVEOUTCAPSW = record
  wMid: Word;              { manufacturer ID }
  wPid: Word;              { product ID }
  vDriverVersion: MMVERSION;    { version of the driver }
  szPname: array[0..MAXPNAMELEN-1] of WideChar; { product name (NULL
                                               terminated string) }
  dwFormats: DWORD;        { formats supported }
  wChannels: Word;         { number of sources supported }
  dwSupport: DWORD;        { functionality supported by driver }
end;
tagWAVEOUTCAPS = tagWAVEOUTCAPSA;
TWaveOutCapsA = tagWAVEOUTCAPSA;
TWaveOutCapsW = tagWAVEOUTCAPSW;
TWaveOutCaps = TWaveOutCapsA;
WAVEOUTCAPSA = tagWAVEOUTCAPSA;
WAVEOUTCAPSW = tagWAVEOUTCAPSW;
WAVEOUTCAPS = WAVEOUTCAPSA;
```

Table 3-11: Values for the dwSupport member of WAVEOUTCAPS

Member	Meaning
WAVECAPS_PITCH	Supports pitch control.
WAVECAPS_PLAYBACKRATE	Supports playback rate control.
WAVECAPS_VOLUME	Supports volume control.
WAVECAPS_LRVOLUME	Supports separate left and right volume control.
WAVECAPS_SYNC	The driver is synchronous and will block while playing a buffer.
WAVECAPS_SAMPLEACCURATE	Returns sample-accurate position information.
WAVECAPS_DIRECTSOUND	Supports DirectSound.

Table 3-12: Values for the main members of WAVEOUTCAPS

Member	Meaning
wMidWord	A value indicating the manufacturer identifier for the device driver for the waveform audio output device.
wPidWord	A value indicating the product identifier for the waveform audio output device.
vDriverVersion	An MMVERSION value indicating the version number of the device driver for the waveform audio output device. The high-order byte is the major version number, and the low-order byte is the minor version number. See Listing 3-6 for code to display the version as a fixed-point number.
szPname	A null-terminated string holding the product name.
dwFormats	A DWORD value holding the constants (bits) that represent the various formats supported. The standard formats are listed in Table 3-9.
wChannels	A WORD value specifying whether the device supports monaural (1) or stereo (2) output.

function WaveOutGetVolume   *mmsystem.pas*

Syntax

    function WaveOutGetVolume(
    hwo: HWAVEOUT;
    lpdwVolume: PDWORD
    ): MMRESULT; stdcall;

Description

This function retrieves the current volume level of the specified wave-form audio output device. Volume settings are interpreted logarithmically—the perceived increase in volume is the same when increasing the volume level from $5000 to $6000 as it is from $4000 to $5000. Since not all devices support volume changes, it is important to determine whether a particular device supports volume control. To do this, use the WAVECAPS_VOLUME flag to test the dwSupport member of the WAVEOUTCAPS structure (filled by the WaveOutGetDevCaps() function). To determine whether the device supports left- and right-channel volume control, use the WAVECAPS_LRVOLUME flag to test the

dwSupport member of the WAVEOUTCAPS structure (filled by
WaveOutGetDevCaps()).

Parameters

hwo: The handle of the waveform audio output device.

lpdwVolume: The address of a variable to be filled with the current volume setting. The low-order word of this location contains the
left-channel volume setting, and the high-order word contains the
right-channel setting. A value of $FFFF represents full volume, and
a value of $0000 is silence. If a device does not support both left
and right volume control, the low-order word of the specified location contains the mono volume level. The full 16-bit setting(s) set
with the WaveOutSetVolume() function is returned, regardless of
whether the device supports the full 16 bits of volume level control.

Return Value

Returns MMSYSERR_NOERROR if successful. Otherwise, it returns one
of the following errors: MMSYSERR_INVALHANDLE, indicating that the
specified device handle is invalid; MMSYSERR_NODRIVER, indicating
that no device driver is present; MMSYSERR_NOMEM, indicating that
memory could not be allocated; or MMSYSERR_NOTSUPPORTED, indicating that the function is not supported.

Example

In the WavClass unit, the following type is defined for different volume
levels:

```
VolumePlaybackValue = (vpvSilent, vpvSoft, vpvMedium, vpvLoud,
    rpvFull);
```

Note how this is used in Listing 3-14. Also note how we check to make
sure that the system supports this feature and how we exit gracefully if it
doesn't provide that support.

Listing 3-14: Using the WaveOutGetVolume() function

```
procedure TWaveOut.AdjustVolume(VolumeLevel : VolumePlaybackValue;
        ChannelsNum : Channels;
        SamplingRateRequested :SamplingRate;
        UseBit16 : boolean);
var
 ADeviceID : UINT;
```

3

Chapter

```
AVolLevel : DWORD;
WOutCaps : TWaveOutCaps;
ResultMsg : string;
begin
if Not OpenSoundPlayDev(ChannelsNum, SamplingRateRequested, UseBit16)
then
 begin
  ShowMessage('Could not open Sound Playing Device');
  Exit;
 end;
WaveOutGetID(AHandle, @ADeviceID);
WaveOutGetDevCaps(ADeviceID, @WOutCaps, SizeOf(WOutCaps));
if ((WOutCaps.dwSupport and (1 shl WAVECAPS_VOLUME))=
  (1 shl WAVECAPS_VOLUME)) then
 begin
  WaveOutGetVolume(AHandle, @AVolLevel);
  case VolumeLevel of  //
   vpvSilent: AVolLevel := MakeLong(0, $0000);
   vpvSoft: AVolLevel := MakeLong(0, $4000);
   vpvMedium: AVolLevel := MakeLong(0, $9000);
   vpvLoud: AVolLevel := MakeLong(0, $CCCC);
   rpvFull: AVolLevel := MakeLong(0, $FFFF);
  end; // case
  WaveOutSetVolume(AHandle, AVolLevel);
 if Not PlaySounds(ResultMsg) then
  begin
   ShowMessage(ResultMsg);
   exit;
  end;
 end
else
 begin
  ShowMessage('This system does not support Volume control');
  CloseDownPlayback;
 end;
end;
```

function WaveOutSetVolume   *mmsystem.pas*

Syntax

```
function WaveOutSetVolume(
  hwo: HWAVEOUT;
  dwVolume: DWORD
  ): MMRESULT; stdcall;
```

Description

This function sets the volume level of the specified waveform audio output device for the current instance. Changing the volume on a handle changes it for an instance of the device, rather than changing the default volume for the device (and affecting all instances of the device). Not all devices support volume changes. To determine whether the device supports volume control, use the WAVECAPS_VOLUME flag to test the dwSupport member of the WAVEOUTCAPS structure (filled by the WaveOutGetDevCaps() function). To determine whether the device supports volume control on both the left and right channels, use the WAVECAPS_LRVOLUME flag. Most devices do not support the full 16 bits of volume level control and will not use the high-order bits of the requested volume setting. For example, if a given device supports 4 bits of volume control, requested volume level values of $4000, $4FFF, and $43BE will all produce the same physical volume setting: $4000. The WaveOutGetVolume() function returns the full 16-bit setting set with the WaveOutSetVolume() function. Volume settings are interpreted logarithmically—the perceived increase in volume is the same when increasing the volume level from $5000 to $6000 as it is from $4000 to $5000.

Parameters

hwo: The handle of the waveform audio output device.

dwVolume: A DWORD indicating the new volume setting. The low-order word contains the left-channel volume setting, and the high-order word contains the right-channel setting. A value of $FFFF represents full volume, and a value of $0000 is silence. If a device does not support both left and right volume control, the low-order word of dwVolume specifies the volume level, and the high-order word is ignored.

Return Value

Returns MMSYSERR_NOERROR if successful. Otherwise, it returns one of the following errors: MMSYSERR_INVALHANDLE, indicating that the specified device handle is invalid; MMSYSERR_NODRIVER, indicating that no device driver is present; MMSYSERR_NOMEM, indicating that memory could not be allocated; or MMSYSERR_NOTSUPPORTED, indicating that the function is not supported.

Example

See Listing 3-14.

function WaveOutGetErrorText   *mmsystem.pas*

Syntax

```
function WaveOutGetErrorText(
  mmrError: MMRESULT;
  lpText: PChar;
  uSize: UINT
  ): MMRESULT; stdcall;
```

Description

This function returns a textual description of the error identified by the given error number, MmrError. The error string is placed in the lpText parameter. See Listing 3-7 for how to set up a general utility routine to return these strings for both output and output return values.

Parameters

MmrError: An MMRESULT error constant returned by one of the WaveOut functions.

lpText: The string explaining the error, MmrError.

uSize: An integer (UINT) indicating the size of the PChar buffer that holds the description of the error. In the WavClass unit, the constant MsgLength is set to 128, which should be sufficient for any of the message strings.

Return Value

Returns MMSYSERR_NOERROR if successful. Otherwise, it returns one of the following errors: MMSYSERR_BADERRNUM, indicating the specified error number is out of range; MMSYSERR_NODRIVER, indicating there is no device driver present; or MMSYSERR_NOMEM, indicating that memory could not be allocated.

Example

Listing 3-7 reports both output and output errors. That's why its first parameter is IO_Direction, indicating input or output. The functions called in this procedure are input- or output-specific.

function WaveOutOpen   *mmsystem.pas*

Syntax

```
function WaveOutOpen(
  lphWaveOut: PHWaveOut;
  uDeviceID: UINT;
  lpFormatEx: PWaveFormatEx;
  dwCallback, dwInstance, dwFlags: DWORD
  ): MMRESULT; stdcall;
```

Description

This function opens the given waveform audio output device for playing with the number uDeviceID. If successful, the parameter lphWaveOut contains a handle for the device that will be used by other WaveOut functions.

Parameters

lphWaveOut: A PHWaveOut value that is the handle identifying the open waveform audio output device. This handle should be saved in a variable visible to other waveform output functions so that they can use it when they are called. This parameter can be NULL if WAVE_FORMAT_QUERY is specified in dwFlags.

uDeviceID: An integer identifying the waveform audio output device to open. It can be a device identifier, the handle of an open waveform audio output device, or the WAVE_MAPPER constant. In the latter case, the function will select a waveform audio output device capable of playing in the specified format.

3

Chapter

lpFormatEx: The address of a WAVEFORMATEX structure identifying the desired format for playing waveform audio data. You can free this structure immediately after WaveOutOpen() returns.

dwCallback: The address of a fixed callback function, an event handle, or the handle of a window or thread called during waveform audio playing to process messages related to the progress of playing. If no callback function is required, this value can be set to zero. In the Listing 3-16, two alternate approaches are shown: a callback function and a callback window. (One is commented out.)

dwInstance: User-instance data passed to the callback mechanism. This parameter is not used with the window callback mechanism and should be set to 0 in that case.

dwFlags: Flags for opening the device. Those flags are as follows:

Table 3-13: Values for the dwFlags member of WaveOutOpen()

Value	Meaning
CALLBACK_EVENT	The dwCallback parameter is an event handle.
CALLBACK_FUNCTION	The dwCallback parameter is a callback procedure address.
CALLBACK_NULL	No callback mechanism. This is the default setting.
CALLBACK_THREAD	The dwCallback parameter is a thread handle.
CALLBACK_WINDOW	The dwCallback parameter is a window handle.
WAVE_ALLOWSYNC	If this flag is specified, a synchronous waveform audio device can be opened. If this flag is not specified while opening a synchronous driver, the device will fail to open.
WAVE_FORMAT_QUERY	If this flag is specified, the WaveOutOpen() function will query the device to determine if it supports the given format, but the device will not be opened.
WAVE_MAPPED	If this flag is specified, the uDeviceID parameter specifies a waveform audio device to be mapped to by the wave mapper.

Return Value

Returns MMSYSERR_NOERROR if successful. Otherwise, it returns one of the following errors: MMSYSERR_ALLOCATED, indicating the specified resource is already allocated; MMSYSERR_BADDEVICEID, indicating the specified device identifier is out of range; MMSYSERR_NODRIVER, indicating that there is no device driver present; MMSYSERR_NOMEM, indicating that memory could not be allocated; WAVERR_BADFORMAT, indicating an attempt to open the device with an unsupported waveform audio format; or WAVERR_SYNC, indicating that the device is synchronous but WaveOutOpen() was called without using the WAVE_ALLOW-SYNC flag.

Example

The following segments of code show how to set up and manage a callback system for waveform output. In order to accomplish this, and to have these functions return as quickly as possible, we simply post a message—a message of our own creation. Those messages are defined as follows in the WavClass unit:

```
const
  WaveIn_Started = WM_User + 150;    // For WaveInOpen callbacks
  WaveIn_Recording = WM_User + 151;  // For WaveInOpen callbacks
  WaveIn_Stop = WM_User + 152;       // For WaveInOpen callbacks
  WaveOut_Started = WM_User + 153;   // For WaveOutOpen callbacks
  WaveOut_Stop = WM_User + 154;      // For WaveOutOpen callbacks
  WaveOut_Finished = WM_User + 155;  // For WaveOutOpen callbacks
```

In Listing 3-15, we respond to three of the standard waveform messages, WOM_OPEN, WOM_CLOSE, and WOM_DONE in our callback routine. These messages post further messages in the application's main window, this time using the PostMessage() function with our custom messages, WaveOut_Started, WaveOut_Stop, and WaveOut_Finished. The main application then responds to these custom messages in its DefaultHandler() method.

Listing 3-15: Callback routine for WaveOut

```
procedure waveOutProc(SomeWaveIn : HWaveIn; uMsg : UINT; dwInstance :
              DWORD; dwParam1, dwParam2 : DWORD); stdcall;
var
 ErrorMsg : string;
begin
 case uMsg of  // which message was sent?
  WOM_OPEN: PostMessage(HWND(MainFormHandle), WaveOut_Started, 0,
     dwParam1);
  WOM_CLOSE: PostMessage(HWND(MainFormHandle), WaveOut_Stop, 0, dwParam1);
  WOM_DONE:
   begin
    if Not WaveOut.ContinuePlaying(dwParam1, ErrorMsg) then exit;
```

3

Chapter

```
      PostMessage(HWND(MainFormHandle), WaveOut_Finished, 0, dwParam1);
    end;
  end;  // case
end;
```

Listing 3-16: Function for opening an audio output device

```
function TWaveOut.OpenSoundPlayDev(NumChannels : Channels;
      RequestedSamplingRate :SamplingRate; Bit16Use :
       boolean) : boolean;
 var
 FormatStruc : tWAVEFORMATEX;
 DevNum : integer;


function GetCaps(ChannelNum : Channels;
            SampRate : SamplingRate;
            var DeviceToUse : Integer;
            Use32Bits : boolean) : boolean;
var
 TotalsDevs : integer;
 j: Integer;
begin
 result := False;
 TotalsDevs := GetNumDevices;
 for j := 0 to (TotalsDevs-1) do           // Iterate
 begin
  CurrentMMRESULT := waveOutGetDevCaps(j, @WaveOutCaps, SizeOf(WaveOUt
      Caps){CapStructSize});
  if CurrentMMRESULT=MMSYSERR_NOERROR then
   DeviceToUse := j;
  if Bit16Use then
  case SampRate of                         // 16 bit only
   sr11_025 : if (((ChannelNum=chOne) and // 16 bit mono at slowest speed
    (WaveOutCaps.dwFormats and
    (1 shl WAVE_FORMAT_1M16)=(1 shl WAVE_FORMAT_1M16))
    or ((WaveOutCaps.dwFormats and         // 16 bit stereo slowest speed
    (1 shl WAVE_FORMAT_1S16))=(1 shl WAVE_FORMAT_1S16)))) then
     begin
      result := True;
      Break;
     end;
   sr22_05 : if (((ChannelNum=chOne) and // 16 bit mono at medium speed
    (WaveOutCaps.dwFormats and
    (1 shl WAVE_FORMAT_2M16)=(1 shl WAVE_FORMAT_2M16))
    or ((WaveOutCaps.dwFormats and       // 16 bit stereo at medium speed
    (1 shl WAVE_FORMAT_2S16))=(1 shl WAVE_FORMAT_2S16)))) then
     begin
```

```
      result := True;
       Break;
     end;
      sr44_1 : if (((ChannelNum=chOne) and // 16 bit mono fastest speed
    (WaveOutCaps.dwFormats and
    (1 shl WAVE_FORMAT_4M16)=(1 shl WAVE_FORMAT_4M16))
    or ((WaveOutCaps.dwFormats and  // 16 bit stereo at fastest speed
    (1 shl WAVE_FORMAT_4S16))=(1 shl WAVE_FORMAT_4S16)))) then
     begin
      result := True;
       Break;
      end;
   end                 // case
   else
   case SampRate of  // 8 bit only
    sr11_025 : if ((ChannelNum=chOne) // lowest rate *should* be supported
     or ((WaveOutCaps.dwFormats and    // 8 bit stereo at slowest speed
     (1 shl WAVE_FORMAT_1S08))=(1 shl WAVE_FORMAT_1S08))) then
     Break;
    sr22_05 : if (((ChannelNum=chOne) and // 8 bit mono at medium speed
     (WaveOutCaps.dwFormats and
     (1 shl WAVE_FORMAT_2M08)=(1 shl WAVE_FORMAT_2M08))
     or ((WaveOutCaps.dwFormats and      // 8 bit stereo at medium speed
     (1 shl WAVE_FORMAT_2S08))=(1 shl WAVE_FORMAT_2S08)))) then
      begin
       result := True;
       Break;
      end;
       sr44_1 : if (((ChannelNum=chOne) and // 8 bit mono at fastest speed
     (WaveOutCaps.dwFormats and
     (1 shl WAVE_FORMAT_4M08)=(1 shl WAVE_FORMAT_4M08))
     or ((WaveOutCaps.dwFormats and       // 8 bit stereo at fastest speed
     (1 shl WAVE_FORMAT_4S08))=(1 shl WAVE_FORMAT_4S08)))) then
      begin
       result := True;
       Break;
      end;
    end;
   end;        // for
  end;
begin
 DevNum := 0;
 if Not GetCaps(NumChannels, RequestedSamplingRate, DevNum, True) then
  begin
   FormatStruc.nChannels := WaveOutCaps.wChannels;
   FormatStruc.nSamplesPerSec := 22050;
```

```
     end
    else
     begin
      FormatStruc.nChannels := 2;
      FormatStruc.nSamplesPerSec := 44100;
     end;
    FormatStruc.wFormatTag := WAVE_FORMAT_PCM;
    FormatStruc.wBitsPerSample := 8;
    FormatStruc.nBlockAlign := Round((FormatStruc.nChannels *
               FormatStruc.wBitsPerSample) / 8);
    FormatStruc.nAvgBytesPerSec := FormatStruc.nSamplesPerSec *
               FormatStruc.nBlockAlign;
    FormatStruc.cbSize := 0;
    // An alternate callback:
    // CurrentMMRESULT := waveOutOpen(@AHandle, DevNum, @FormatStruc,
    //   DWORD(MainFormHandle), DWord(0), Cardinal(callback_window));
    CurrentMMRESULT := waveOutOpen(@AHandle, DevNum, (@FormatStruc),
       DWORD(@WaveOutProc), DWORD(MainFormHandle), DWORD(callback_function));
    result := (CurrentMMRESULT=MMSYSERR_NOERROR);
    PlayDevAvailable := result;
   end;
```

function WaveOutClose   mmsystem.pas

Syntax

```
function WaveOutClose(
hWaveOut: HWaveOut
): MMRESULT; stdcall;
MMRESULT; stdcall;
```

Description

This function closes the given waveform audio output device.

Parameter

hWaveOut: The handle of the waveform audio output device. If the function succeeds, the handle is no longer valid.

Return Value

Returns MMSYSERR_NOERROR if successful. Otherwise, it returns one of the following errors: MMSYSERR_INVALHANDLE, indicating that the specified device handle is invalid; MMSYSERR_NODRIVER, indicating that no device driver is present; MMSYSERR_NOMEM, indicating that

memory could not be allocated; or WAVERR_STILLPLAYING, indicating that one or more block buffers are still in the queue.

Example

Listing 3-17 shows how to properly shut down a playing device. First, you need to be certain that all block buffers have been returned by calling WaveOutReset(). WaveOutStop() is probably not required but doesn't do any harm. Then you need to call WaveOutUnprepareHeader() to clean up the buffers. The buffers can then be either disposed (their memory freed) or used again (prepared again). Finally, having done all of this you can call WaveOutClose().

Listing 3-17: A procedure to properly shut down a waveform output device

```
procedure TWaveOut.CloseDownPlayback;
var
 j: Integer;
begin
 WaveOutReset(AHandle);
 for j := 0 to (MaxBuffers-1) do  // Iterate
  WaveOutUnprepareHeader(AHandle, WaveBuffer.FWaveHeaderArray[j],
       SizeOf(WAVEHdr));
 WaveOutClose(AHandle);
end;
```

function WaveOutPrepareHeader   *mmsystem.pas*

Syntax

function WaveOutPrepareHeader(
hWaveOut: HWaveOut;
lpWaveOutHdr: PWaveHdr;
uSize: UINT
): MMRESULT; stdcall;

Description

This function prepares a buffer for waveform audio output. This is a temporary block buffer used for audio output to be stored in memory or in a file. Before calling this function it is essential that you initialize several of the WAVEHDR structure's members, particularly lpData, dwBufferLength, and dwFlags. The lpData member should point to a valid PChar for which memory has been set, and dwFlags must be set to zero.

Parameters

hWaveOut: The handle of the waveform audio output device.

lpWaveOutHdr: The address of a WAVEHDR structure that identifies the buffer to be prepared.

uSize: An integer indicating the size of the WAVEHDR structure. You can simply use the SizeOf(WAVEHDR) function for this parameter.

Return Value

Returns MMSYSERR_NOERROR if successful. Otherwise, it returns one of the following errors: MMSYSERR_INVALHANDLE, indicating that the specified device handle is invalid; MMSYSERR_NODRIVER, indicating that no device driver is present; or MMSYSERR_NOMEM, indicating that memory could not be allocated.

Example

Listing 3-18 shows how to properly set up the members for the WAVEHDR structure. Listing 3-19 shows how to use the WaveOutPrepareHeader() function.

Listing 3-18: Loading additional blocks of playback data

```
procedure TWaveOut.LoadNextDataBlock(var PlaybackLength : DWORD; var
 TempHdr : PWAVEHdr);
var
 TempBuffer : Array[0..32767] of byte;
begin
 with WaveBuffer do
 begin
 if WaveBuffer.FPlaybackBufferPosition<WaveBuffer.MainSoundBufferSize then
with TempHdr^ do
  begin
   PlaybackLength := MainSoundBufferSize - WaveBuffer
        .FPlaybackBufferPosition;
   if PlaybackLength>SecondaryBufferSize then
    PlaybackLength := SecondaryBufferSize;
   WaveBuffer.MainSoundBuffer.Read(TempBuffer, PlaybackLength);
   Move(TempBuffer, lpData^, PlaybackLength);
   WaveBuffer.FPlaybackBufferPosition :=
WaveBuffer.MainSoundBuffer.Position;
  end    // TempHdr^ do with
 else
  begin
```

```
    WaveOutStatus := wosDonePlaying;
   end;
   end;
end;
```

Listing 3-19: Starting the sound playing process

```
function TWaveOut.PlaySounds(var ResultMsg : string)    : boolean;
var
 j: Integer;
 CurrentLength : Cardinal;
begin { PlaySounds }
 result := False;
 CurrentLength := 0;
 WaveBuffer.MainSoundBuffer.Position := 0;
 WaveBuffer.FPlaybackBufferPosition := 0;
 (* if MM_Time=Nil then
 GetMem(MM_Time, SizeOf(MM_Time));
MM_Time^.wType := TIME_BYTES;
waveOutGetPosition(FOutputHandle, MM_Time, SizeOf(MMTime)); *)
 if (WaveOutStatus=wosDonePlaying) then
 begin { Make sure we are at the start and not already playing }
 WaveOutStatus := wosPlaying;
 waveOutPause(AHandle); //load first two buffers before starting play
 for j := 0 to (MaxBuffers-1) do  // Iterate
 begin
  LoadNextDataBlock(CurrentLength, WaveBuffer.FWaveHeaderArray[j]);
  WaveBuffer.FWaveHeaderArray[j].dwBufferLength := CurrentLength;
  CurrentMMRESULT := WaveOutPrepareHeader(AHandle,
   WaveBuffer.FWaveHeaderArray[j], SizeOf(WAVEHdr));
  if CurrentMMRESULT<>MMSYSERR_NOERROR then
   begin
    ResultMsg := 'Could not prepare header'; //HEADER_PREPARE_ERR_MSG;
    Exit;
   end;
  CurrentMMRESULT := WaveOutWrite(AHandle, WaveBuffer.FWaveHeaderArray[j],
   SizeOf(WaveHdr));
  if CurrentMMRESULT<>MMSYSERR_NOERROR then
   begin
    WaveOutStatus := wosError;
    WaveOutGetErrorText(CurrentMMRESULT, PChar(ResultMsg), MsgLength);
    Exit;
   end;
  end;
  WaveOutRestart(AHandle);
  result := True;
```

3

Chapter

```
end; { WaveOutStatus=wosDonePlaying }
end;
```

function WaveOutUnprepareHeader   *mmsystem.pas*

Syntax

function WaveOutUnprepareHeader(
hWaveOut: HWaveOut;
lpWaveOutHdr: PWaveHdr;
uSize: UINT
): MMRESULT; stdcall;

Description

This function cleans up the preparation performed by the WaveOut-PrepareHeader() function. After passing a buffer to the device driver with the WaveOutAddBuffer() function, you must wait until the driver is finished with the buffer before calling WaveOutUnprepareHeader(). Unpreparing a buffer that has not been prepared has no effect, and the function returns zero. You must call this function before freeing the buffer.

Parameters

hWaveOut: The handle of the waveform audio output device.

lpWaveOutHdr: The address of a WAVEHDR structure that identifies the buffer to be unprepared.

uSize: An integer indicating the size of the WAVEHDR structure. You can simply use the SizeOf(WAVEHDR) function for this parameter.

Return Value

Returns MMSYSERR_NOERROR if successful. Otherwise, it returns one of the following errors: MMSYSERR_INVALHANDLE, indicating that the specified device handle is invalid; MMSYSERR_NODRIVER, indicating that no device driver is present; MMSYSERR_NOMEM, indicating that memory could not be allocated; or WAVERR_STILLPLAYING, indicating that one or more block buffers are still in the queue.

Example

Listing 3-17 shows how to properly shut down a playing device including the use of the WaveOutUnprepareHeader() function.

function WaveOutWrite   *mmsystem.pas*

Syntax

```
function WaveOutWrite(
  hWaveOut: HWaveOut
  ): MMRESULT; stdcall;
```

Description

This is the function that actually starts the output process (playing) on the given waveform audio output device, hWaveOut. If you call this function when output has already started, it has no effect and the function returns with a value of zero. Buffers are returned to the application when they are full or when the WaveOutReset() function is called. The dwBytesRecorded member of the header will contain the length of data played. If there are no buffers in the queue, the data will be discarded without notifying the application and output continues.

Parameter

hWaveOut: The handle of the waveform audio output device.

Return Value

Returns MMSYSERR_NOERROR if successful. Otherwise, it returns one of the following errors: MMSYSERR_INVALHANDLE, indicating that the specified device handle is invalid; MMSYSERR_NODRIVER, indicating that no device driver is present; or MMSYSERR_NOMEM, indicating that memory could not be allocated.

Example

Listing 3-20 shows how WaveOutWrite() is used to continue to play sounds.

Listing 3-20: The process of continuing playback once it has begun

```
function TWaveOut.ContinuePlaying(WaveHdrPtr : Integer;
      var ResultMsg : string) : boolean;
var
 j: Integer;
 TempWavHdr : PWaveHdr;
 CurrentLength : Cardinal;

begin
```

3

Chapter

```
 result := False;
 CurrentLength := 0;
 TempWavHdr := PWaveHdr(WaveHdrPtr);
 MM_Time.wType := TIME_BYTES;
 waveOutGetPosition(AHandle, @MM_Time, SizeOf(MM_Time));
 CurrentTime := MM_Time.cb;
 if WaveOutStatus = wosPlaying then
 begin
  LoadNextDataBlock(CurrentLength, PWAVEHDR(TempWavHdr));
    TempWavHdr.dwBufferLength := CurrentLength;
  CurrentMMRESULT := WaveOutPrepareHeader(AHandle,
    TempWavHdr, SizeOf(WAVEHdr));
   if CurrentMMRESULT<>MMSYSERR_NOERROR then
    begin
     ResultMsg := 'Could not prepare header'; //HEADER_PREPARE_ERR_MSG;
     WaveOutStatus := wosError;
     Exit;
    end;
   CurrentMMRESULT := WaveOutWrite(AHandle, TempWavHdr,
   SizeOf(WaveHdr));
  if CurrentMMRESULT<>MMSYSERR_NOERROR then
   begin
    WaveOutStatus := wosError;
    WaveOutGetErrorText(CurrentMMRESULT, PChar(ResultMsg), MsgLength);

    Exit;
   end
  else
    result := True;
 end
 else
 begin
  for j := 0 to (MaxBuffers-1) do  // Iterate
   if ((WaveBuffer.FWaveHeaderArray[j].dwFlags and (1 shl WHdr_InQueue))=
    (1 shl WHdr_InQueue) ) then
   begin
    result := True;
    Exit;
   end;
  MM_Time.wType := TIME_BYTES;
  waveOutGetPosition(AHandle, @MM_Time, SizeOf(MM_Time));
  CurrentTime := MM_Time.cb;
  CloseDownPlayback;
 end;
end;
```

function WaveOutPause   *mmsystem.pas*

Syntax

function WaveOutPause(
  hWaveOut: HWAVEOUT
  ): MMRESULT; stdcall;

Description

This function pauses playback on the given waveform audio output device. The current position is saved. Use the WaveOutRestart() function to resume playback from the current position. If you call this function when the output is already paused, the function has no effect and returns with a value of zero.

Parameter

hWaveOut: The handle of the waveform audio input device.

Return Value

Returns MMSYSERR_NOERROR if successful. Otherwise, it returns one of the following errors: MMSYSERR_INVALHANDLE, indicating that the specified device handle is invalid; MMSYSERR_NODRIVER, indicating that no device driver is present; MMSYSERR_NOMEM, indicating that memory could not be allocated; or MMSYSERR_NOTSUPPORTED, indicating that the specified device is synchronous and does not support pausing.

Example

See Listing 3-19.

3

Chapter

function WaveOutRestart   *mmsystem.pas*

Syntax

```
function WaveOutRestart(
hWaveOut: HWAVEOUT
): MMRESULT; stdcall;
```

Description

This function resumes playback on a waveform audio output device that
has been paused. If you call this function when the output is not paused,
the function has no effect and returns with a value of zero.

Parameter

hWaveOut: The handle of the waveform audio output device.

Return Value

Returns MMSYSERR_NOERROR if successful. Otherwise, it returns one
of the following errors: MMSYSERR_INVALHANDLE, indicating that the
specified device handle is invalid; MMSYSERR_NODRIVER, indicating
that no device driver is present; MMSYSERR_NOMEM, indicating that
memory could not be allocated; or MMSYSERR_NOTSUPPORTED, indicating that the specified device is synchronous and does not support
pausing.

Example

See Listing 3-19.

function WaveOutReset   *mmsystem.pas*

Syntax

```
function WaveOutReset(
hWaveOut: HWaveOut
): MMRESULT; stdcall;
```

Description

This function stops output on the given waveform audio output device
and resets the current position to zero. Any pending buffers will be
marked as done and returned to the application.

Parameter

hWaveOut: The handle of the waveform audio output device.

Return Value

Returns MMSYSERR_NOERROR if successful. Otherwise, it returns one of the following errors: MMSYSERR_INVALHANDLE, indicating that the specified device handle is invalid; MMSYSERR_NODRIVER, indicating that no device driver is present; MMSYSERR_NOMEM, indicating that memory could not be allocated; or MMSYSERR_NOTSUPPORTED, indicating that the specified device is synchronous and does not support pausing.

Example

See Listing 3-17.

function WaveOutBreakLoop   *mmsystem.pas*

Syntax

```
function WaveOutBreakLoop(
  hWaveOut: HWAVEOUT
  ): MMRESULT; stdcall;
```

Description

This function breaks a loop begun earlier on the given waveform audio output device, hWaveOut. It allows playback to continue with the next block in the driver list. The blocks making up the loop are played to the end before the loop is terminated. If you call this function when nothing is playing or looping, the function has no effect and returns with a value of zero.

Parameter

hWaveOut: The handle of the waveform audio output device.

Return Value

Returns MMSYSERR_NOERROR if successful. Otherwise, it returns one of the following errors: MMSYSERR_INVALHANDLE, indicating that the specified device handle is invalid; MMSYSERR_NODRIVER, indicating that no device driver is present; or MMSYSERR_NOMEM, indicating that memory could not be allocated.

3

Chapter

Example

For an example of working with loops (but not terminating them), see
Listing 3-2. The following simple code shows how to terminate a loop
that is in progress:

```
procedure TWaveOut.BreakLoop;
begin
 waveOutBreakLoop(AHandle);
end;
```

function WaveOutGetPosition   *mmsystem.pas*

Syntax

```
function WaveOutGetPosition(
hWaveOut: HWaveOut;
lpInfo: PMMTime;
uSize: UINT
): MMRESULT; stdcall;
```

Description

Retrieves the current output position of the given waveform audio output device. The position is set to zero whenever the device is opened or
reset. Before calling this function, be sure to set the wType member of
the MMTIME structure to indicate the time format you want. After calling this function, check wType to determine whether the desired time
format is supported. If the format is not supported, the member will
specify an alternative format.

Parameters

hWaveOut: The handle of the waveform audio output device.

lpInfo: The address of an MMTIME structure.

uSize: An integer indicating the size of the MMTIME structure.

Return Value

Returns MMSYSERR_NOERROR if successful. Otherwise, it returns one
of the following errors: MMSYSERR_INVALHANDLE, indicating that the
specified device handle is invalid; MMSYSERR_NODRIVER, indicating
that no device driver is present; or MMSYSERR_NOMEM, indicating that
memory could not be allocated.

Example

See Listing 3-19.

function WaveOutGetPitch   *mmsystem.pas*

Syntax

```
function WaveOutGetPitch(
hWaveOut: HWAVEOUT;
lpdwPitch: PDWORD
):  MMRESULT;  stdcall;
```

Description

This function retrieves the current pitch setting for the specified wave-form audio output device. Changing the pitch does not change the playback rate, sample rate, or playback time. Not all devices support pitch changes. To determine whether the device supports pitch control, use the WAVECAPS_PITCH flag to test the dwSupport member of the WAVEOUTCAPS structure (filled by the WaveOutGetDevCaps() function).

Parameters

hWaveOut: The handle of the waveform audio output device.

lpdwPitch: A PDWORD value holding the address of a variable to be filled with the current pitch multiplier setting. The pitch multiplier indicates the current change in pitch from the original authored setting. The pitch multiplier must be a positive value and is specified as a fixed-point value. The high-order word of the variable contains the signed integer part of the number, and the low-order word contains the fractional part. A value of $8000 in the low-order word represents one half, and $4000 represents one quarter. For example, the value $00010000 specifies a multiplier of 1.0 (no pitch change), and a value of $000F8000 specifies a multiplier of 15.5.

Return Value

Returns MMSYSERR_NOERROR if successful. Otherwise, it returns one of the following errors: MMSYSERR_INVALHANDLE, indicating that the specified device handle is invalid; MMSYSERR_NODRIVER, indicating that no device driver is present; MMSYSERR_NOMEM, indicating that

memory could not be allocated; or MMSYSERR_NOTSUPPORTED indicating that the function is not supported.

Example

In the WavClass unit, the following type is defined for different pitch levels:

```
PitchPlaybackValue = (ppvQuarter, ppvHalf, ppvOriginal, ppvDouble,
ppvQuad);
```

Note how this is used in Listing 3-21. Also note how we check to make sure that the system supports this feature and how we exit gracefully if it does not.

Listing 3-21: Adjusting pitch on those systems that support it

```
procedure TWaveOut.AdjustPitch(AdjustPitchBy : PitchPlaybackValue;
         ChannelsNum : Channels;
         SamplingRateRequested :SamplingRate;
         UseBit16 : boolean);
var
 ADeviceID : UINT;
 APitch : DWORD;
 WOutCaps : TWaveOutCaps;
 ResultMsg : string;
begin
 if Not OpenSoundPlayDev(ChannelsNum, SamplingRateRequested,
            UseBit16) then
  begin
   ShowMessage('Could not open Sound Playing Device');
   Exit;
  end;
 WaveOutGetID(AHandle, @ADeviceID);
 WaveOutGetDevCaps(ADeviceID, @WOutCaps, SizeOf(WOutCaps));
 if (WOutCaps.dwSupport and (1 shl WaveCaps_Pitch)=
   (1 shl WaveCaps_Pitch)) then
  begin
   WaveOutGetPitch(AHandle, @APitch);
   case AdjustPitchBy of  //
    ppvQuarter: APitch := MakeLong(0, 8000);
    ppvHalf: APitch := MakeLong(0, 4000);
    ppvOriginal: APitch := MakeLong(0, 10000);
    ppvDouble: APitch := MakeLong(0, 20000);
    ppvQuad: APitch := MakeLong(0, 40000);
   end;  // case
   WaveOutSetPitch(AHandle, APitch);
```

```
if Not PlaySounds(ResultMsg) then
 begin
  ShowMessage(ResultMsg);
  exit;
 end;
end
else
 begin
  ShowMessage('This system does not support Pitch Manipulation');
  CloseDownPlayback;
 end;
end;
```

function WaveOutSetPitch   *mmsystem.pas*

Syntax

```
function WaveOutSetPitch(
 hWaveOut: HWAVEOUT;
 dwPitch: DWORD
 ): MMRESULT; stdcall;
```

Description

This function sets the pitch for the specified waveform audio output
device. Changing the pitch does not change the playback rate or the sample rate, nor does it change the playback time. Not all devices support
pitch changes. To determine whether the device supports pitch control,
use the WAVECAPS_PITCH flag to test the dwSupport member of the
WAVEOUTCAPS structure (filled by the WaveOutGetDevCaps()
function).

Parameters

hWaveOut: The handle of the waveform audio output device.

dwPitch: New pitch multiplier setting. This setting indicates the current
     change in pitch from the original authored setting. The pitch multi-
     plier must be a positive value and is specified as a fixed-point value.
     The high-order word contains the signed integer part of the number,
     and the low-order word contains the fractional part. A value of
     $8000 in the low-order word represents one half, and $4000 repre-
     sents one quarter. For example, the value $00010000 specifies a
     multiplier of 1.0 (no pitch change), and a value of $000F8000 spec-
     ifies a multiplier of 15.5.

Return Value

Returns MMSYSERR_NOERROR if successful. Otherwise, it returns one of the following errors: MMSYSERR_INVALHANDLE, indicating that the specified device handle is invalid; MMSYSERR_NODRIVER, indicating that no device driver is present; MMSYSERR_NOMEM, indicating that memory could not be allocated; or MMSYSERR_NOTSUPPORTED, indicating that the function is not supported.

Example

See Listing 3-21.

function WaveOutGetPlaybackRate   *mmsystem.pas*

Syntax

```
function WaveOutGetPlaybackRate(
  hWaveOut: HWAVEOUT;
  lpdwRate: PDWORD
  ): MMRESULT; stdcall;
```

Description

This function retrieves the current playback rate for the specified waveform audio output device. Changing the playback rate does not change the sample rate but does change the playback time. Not all devices support playback rate changes. To determine whether a device supports playback rate changes, use the WAVECAPS_PLAYBACKRATE flag to test the dwSupport member of the WAVEOUTCAPS structure (filled by the WaveOutGetDevCaps() function).

Parameters

hWaveOut: The handle of the waveform audio output device.

lpdwRate: A PDWORD containing the address of a variable to be filled with the current playback rate. The playback rate setting is a multiplier indicating the current change in playback rate from the original authored setting. The playback rate multiplier must be a positive value and is specified as a fixed-point value. The high-order word of the variable contains the signed integer part of the number, and the low-order word contains the fractional part. A value of $8000 in the low-order word represents one half, and $4000 represents one quarter. For example, the value $00010000 specifies a multiplier of 1.0 (no playback rate change), and a value of $000F8000 specifies a multiplier of 15.5.

Return Value

Returns MMSYSERR_NOERROR if successful. Otherwise, it returns one of the following errors: MMSYSERR_INVALHANDLE, indicating that the specified device handle is invalid; MMSYSERR_NODRIVER, indicating that no device driver is present; MMSYSERR_NOMEM, indicating that memory could not be allocated; or MMSYSERR_NOTSUPPORTED, indicating that the function is not supported.

Example

See Listing 3-22.

function WaveOutSetPlaybackRate   mmsystem.pas

Syntax

```
function WaveOutSetPlaybackRate(
  hWaveOut: HWAVEOUT;
  dwRate: DWORD
  ): MMRESULT; stdcall;
```

Description

This function sets the playback rate for the specified waveform audio output device. Changing the playback rate does not change the sample rate but does change the playback time. Not all devices support playback rate changes. To determine whether a device supports playback rate changes, use the WAVECAPS_PLAYBACKRATE flag to test the dwSupport member of the WAVEOUTCAPS structure (filled by the WaveOutGetDevCaps() function).

Parameters

hWaveOut: The handle of the waveform audio output device.

dwRate: A DWORD value indicating the new playback rate setting. This setting is a multiplier indicating the current change in playback rate from the original authored setting. The playback rate multiplier must be a positive value and is specified as a fixed-point value. The high-order word contains the signed integer part of the number, and

3

Chapter

the low-order word contains the fractional part. A value of $8000 in the low-order word represents one half, and $4000 represents one quarter. For example, the value $00010000 specifies a multiplier of 1.0 (no playback rate change), and a value of $000F8000 specifies a multiplier of 15.5.

Return Value

Returns MMSYSERR_NOERROR if successful. Otherwise, it returns one of the following errors: MMSYSERR_INVALHANDLE, indicating that the specified device handle is invalid; MMSYSERR_NODRIVER, indicating that no device driver is present; MMSYSERR_NOMEM, indicating that memory could not be allocated; or MMSYSERR_NOTSUPPORTED, indicating that the function is not supported.

Example

In the WavClass unit, the following type is defined for different playback rates:

```
RatePlaybackValue = (rpvQuarter, rpvHalf, rpvOriginal, rpvDouble,
        rpvQuad);
```

Note how this is used in Listing 3-22. Also note how we check to make sure that the system supports this feature and how we exit gracefully if it does not.

Listing 3-22: Adjusting the playback rate on those systems that support it

```
procedure TWaveOut.AdjustPlaybackRate(AdjustRateBy : RatePlaybackValue;
        ChannelsNum : Channels;
        SamplingRateRequested :SamplingRate;
        UseBit16 : boolean);
var
 ADeviceID : UINT;
 ASpeed : DWORD;
 WOutCaps : TWaveOutCaps;
 ResultMsg : string;
begin
 if Not OpenSoundPlayDev(ChannelsNum, SamplingRateRequested, UseBit16)
  then
  begin
   ShowMessage('Could not open Sound Playing Device');
   Exit;
  end;
 WaveOutGetID(AHandle, @ADeviceID);
```

```
WaveOutGetDevCaps(ADeviceID, @WOutCaps, SizeOf(WOutCaps));
if ((WOutCaps.dwSupport and (1 shl WaveCaps_PlayBackRate))
 = (1 shl WaveCaps_PlayBackRate)) then
 begin
  WaveOutGetPlayBackRate(AHandle, @ASpeed);
  case AdjustRateBy of  //
   rpvQuarter: ASpeed := MakeLong(0, 8000);
   rpvHalf: ASpeed := MakeLong(0, 4000);
   rpvOriginal: ASpeed := MakeLong(0, 10000);
   rpvDouble: ASpeed := MakeLong(0, 20000);
   rpvQuad: ASpeed := MakeLong(0, 40000);
  end;  // case
  WaveOutSetPlayBackRate(AHandle, ASpeed);
 if Not PlaySounds(ResultMsg) then
  begin
   ShowMessage(ResultMsg);
   exit;
  end;
 end
 else
  begin
   ShowMessage('This system does not support Playback Rates');
   CloseDownPlayback;
  end;
end;
```

3

Chapter

function WaveOutGetID   *mmsystem.pas*

Syntax

```
function WaveOutGetID(
 hWaveOut: HWaveOut;
 lpuDeviceID: PUINT
 ): MMRESULT;  stdcall;
```

Description

This function retrieves the device identifier for the given waveform audio output device. It is here mainly to support backward compatibility. New applications can cast a handle of the device rather than retrieving the device identifier.

Parameters

hWaveOut: The handle of the waveform audio output device.

lpuDeviceID: A pointer to a UINT (integer) that will receive the output device identifier. It is in the range from 0 to one less than the number of output devices.

Return Value

Returns MMSYSERR_NOERROR if successful. Otherwise, it returns one of the following errors: MMSYSERR_INVALHANDLE, indicating that the specified device handle is invalid; MMSYSERR_NODRIVER, indicating that no device driver is present; MMSYSERR_NOMEM, indicating that memory could not be allocated; or WAVERR_STILLPLAYING, indicating that one or more block buffers are still in the queue.

Example

See Listing 3-22.

function WaveOutMessage   *mmsystem.pas*

Syntax

```
function WaveOutMessage(
  hWaveOut: HWaveOut;
  uMessage: UINT;
  dw1, dw2: DWORD
  ): MMRESULT; stdcall;
```

Description

This function sends messages to the waveform audio output device drivers.

Parameters

hWaveOut: The handle of the waveform audio output device.

uMessage: An integer indicating the message to send.

dw1, dw2: Two DWORD parameters for message parameters.

Return Value

Returns a DWORD indicating the return value of the message.

Example

These messages are driver-specific, so we cannot show an example here that will definitely work on your system. To use this function you need to know the specific messages that your sound card and its driver(s) will accept. Here is a general example of how you might call this function:

```
procedure TWaveOut.SendMessage(ADriverMessage: UINT; MsgParam1,
    MsgParam2: DWORD);
begin
 waveOutMessage(AHandle, ADriverMessage, MsgParam1, MsgParam2);
end;
```

Putting It All Together—A Sample Application

With this seldom-used function, we have neared the end of a lengthy chapter. However, we have yet to show how a Delphi form can respond to the various messages we've been discussing. In order to accomplish this task we need to write a DefaultHandler() procedure as shown in Listing 3-23.

Listing 3-23: Default handler for waveform messages

```
procedure TForm1.DefaultHandler(var Msg);
begin
 ErrorMsg := '';
 inherited DefaultHandler(Msg);
 case TMessage(Msg).Msg of  //
  WaveIn_Started:
   begin
    Label1.Caption := DuringRecordingMsg;
    btnStartPlayback.Enabled := False;
    btnHigher.Enabled := False;
    btnFaster.Enabled := False;
   end;
  WaveIn_Recording:
   case WaveIn.CurrentSoundRecordTo of  //
   srtMemory: if WaveIn.WaveInStatus = wisRecording then exit
   { WaveIn.ContinueRecording(TMessage(Msg).lParam,
   ErrorMsg) }
    else
     begin
      Label1.Caption := AfterRecordingMsg;
      btnStartPlayback.Enabled := True;
      btnHigher.Enabled := True;
```

```
      btnFaster.Enabled := True;
      WaveIn.CloseDownRecording;
     end;
   srtFile: ; // Will be addressed in Chapter 5 on Multimedia File I/O
  end;  // case;
 WaveIn_Stop:
  begin
   Label1.Caption := AfterRecordingMsg;
   btnStartPlayback.Enabled := True;
   btnHigher.Enabled := True;
   btnFaster.Enabled := True;
  end;
 WaveOut_Started: Label1.Caption := DuringPlaybackMsg;
 WaveOut_Finished: ;
 WaveOut_Stop: Label1.Caption := AfterPlaybackMsg;
 end;  // case
end;
```

You can see the results in the sample application by studying Figures 3-5 through 3-9. Note how the large label changes in response to user actions and multimedia events. Since we're recording to and playing back from memory, nothing can occur until the user has recorded something. So the first screen shot provides directions on how to begin recording.

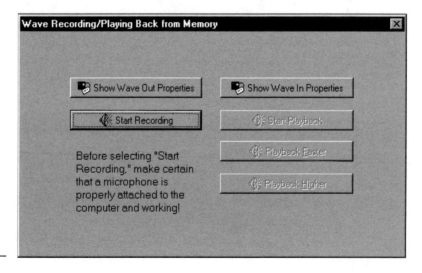

Figure 3-5

Note that prior to recording, all of the playback buttons are inactive. Once the user has hit the Start Recording button, a second message is displayed indicating that the individual should start talking into the microphone.

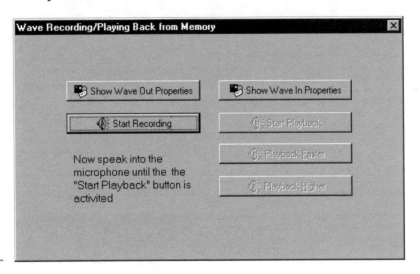

Figure 3-6

If the user has already recorded and played something, the playback buttons need to be deactivated again. All of this is accomplished in the following lines of code:

```
WaveIn_Started:
 begin
   Label1.Caption := DuringRecordingMsg;
   btnStartPlayback.Enabled := False;
   btnHigher.Enabled := False;
   btnFaster.Enabled := False;
 end;
```

Once recording is finished, the user is prompted to begin playback.

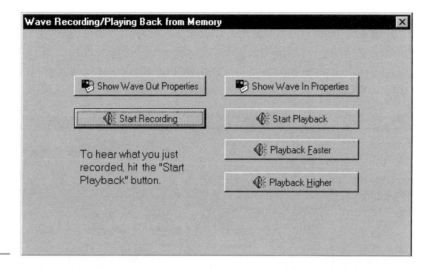

Figure 3-7

Once playback has begun, another message is played.

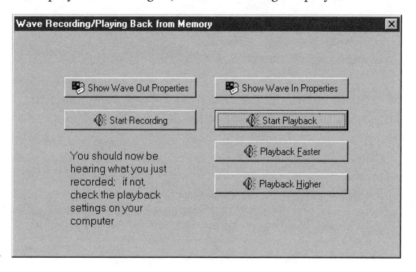

Figure 3-8

When playback is finished, the user is notified that he or she can record another message if desired.

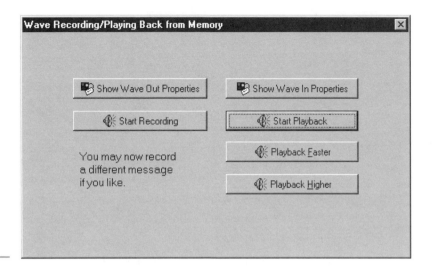

Figure 3-9

Some of the messages in the default handler are used simply to provide status messages; others are more important, calling sound recording or sound playing functions in the WavClass unit. Go ahead and compile and run the sample application to get a good idea of some of the issues involved. Experiment with using a status bar in place of the label to inform the user (we do that in the chapter on timers where we modify this code to provide an indication of bytes recorded and played).

Although we have covered all of the waveform audio functions in some detail, there are other details about which only an entire book on this subject could do justice. However, there are other important APIs in the Windows multimedia system that we are about to explore. As I think you will discover, the next API which supports MIDI, is equally useful and powerful as the one we presented in this chapter.

3

Chapter

Chapter Four

The MIDI API

In the last chapter, we explored the Wave API. Without a doubt this is one of the most important APIs in the entire multimedia system since it enables us to access the lowest level functionality of a computer's sound card. But there is another dimension to modern sound cards. That dimension, of course, is the built-in synthesizer that includes a large number of predefined sounds—sounds that are related to real-world musical instruments, called patches. This aspect of the sound system is controlled by MIDI, the Musical Instrument Digital Interface, which we'll be exploring in this chapter.

The World of MIDI

With waveform audio we were able to work with sound at the lowest level. Because of the level of detail present in waveform audio data, *.wav files can quickly become rather large. On the other hand, since MIDI is essentially accessing predefined data in a table, it can often get its job done with significantly fewer bytes of data. The disadvantage of MIDI is that it limits you in the amount of control you can exercise over the sounds you produce. However, if you're interested in playing music, MIDI is usually your best choice.

MIDI is a relatively new phenomena, but it is older than the PC and the Microsoft Windows platform. I remember working with electronic music in the late 1960s, in the pre-MIDI days, when a "patch" really was a patch—a patch cord, that is. In those days, you had to do a great deal of work manually. I can still remember some of the complex setups I created using the Moog synthesizer and a few other devices, with several dozen patch cords going here and there. At times it looked like the snake pit in one of those *Indiana Jones* movies.

4

Chapter

During the 1970s many other synthesizers and electronic devices became available. Naturally, musicians wanted to work with more than one synthesizer at a time. But there was a problem: There was no common interface through which different brands could communicate with each other. Thus, MIDI was born. When PCs started to include sound cards, it was only natural that MIDI should be included. Look on the back of your computer where the sound card plugs are located. Besides the speaker and microphone plugs you should see one or more others: very likely MIDI-IN, MIDI-OUT, and possibly MIDI-THRU. These enable you to connect your computer to a wide variety of MIDI-compliant devices including external synthesizers, sequencers, keyboards, and so on.

What exactly does MIDI define? General MIDI consists of 16 channels. Each channel can play one of 128 predefined musical instruments, including a few sound effects. These "instruments" are numbered 0 through 127. Since these names are standard, we have included them as an array of constants as follows in the MidClass.pas unit:

```
PatchArray : array [0..127] of string30 = ('Acoustic Grand Piano',
  'Bright Acoustic Piano','Electric Grand Piano','Honky-tonk Piano',
  'Rhodes Piano','Chorus Piano','Harpsichord','Clavinet','Celesta',
  'Glockenspiel','Music Box','Vibraphone','Marimba','Xylophone',
  'Tubular Bells','Dulcimer','Hammond Organ','Percuss. Organ',
  'Rock Organ','Church Organ','Reed Organ','Accordion','Harmonica',
  'Tango Accordion','Acoustic Guitar (nylon)','Acoustic Guitar
  (steel)','Electric Guitar (jazz)','Electric Guitar (clean)',
  'Electric Guitar (muted)','Overdriven Guitar','Distortion Guitar',
  'Guitar Harmonics','Acoustic Bass','Electric Bass (finger)',
  'Electric Bass (pick)','Fretless Bass','Slap Bass 1','Slap Bass 2',
  'Synth Bass 1','Synth Bass 2','Violin','Viola','Cello','Contra Bass',
  'Tremolo Strings','Pizzicato Strings','Orchestral Harp','Timpani',
  'String Ensemble 1','String Ensemble 2','Synth Strings 1',
  'Synth Strings 2','Choir Aahs','Voice Oohs','Synth Voice',
  'Orchestra Hit','Trumpet','Trombone','Tuba','Muted Trumpet',
  'French Horn','Brass Section','Synth Brass 1','Synth Brass 2',
  'Soprano Sax','Alto Sax','Tenor Sax','Baritone Sax','Oboe',
  'English Horn','Bassoon','Clarinet','Piccolo','Flute','Recorder',
  'Pan Flute','Bottle Blow','Shaku','Whistle','Ocarina','Lead 1 (square)',
  'Lead 2 (saw tooth)','Lead 3 (calliope lead)','Lead 4 (chiff lead)',
  'Lead 5 (charang)','Lead 6 (voice)','Lead 7 (fifths)','Lead 8 (bass +
  lead)','Pad 1 (new age)','Pad 2 (warm)','Pad 3 (poly synth)',
  'Pad 4 (choir)','Pad 5 (bowed)','Pad 6 (metallic)','Pad 7 (halo)',
  'Pad 8 (sweep)','FX 1 (rain)','FX 2 (sound track)','FX 3 (crystal)',
  'FX 4 (atmosphere)','FX 5 (bright)','FX 6 (goblins)','FX 7 (echoes)',
  'FX 8(sci-fi)','Sitar','Banjo','Shamisen','Koto','Kalimba','Bagpipe',
```

```
'Fiddle','Shanai','Tinkle Bell','Agogo','Steel Drums','Wood block',
'Taiko Drum','Melodic Tom','Synth Drum','Reverse Cymbal',
'Guitar Fret Noise','Breath Noise','Seashore','Bird Tweet',
'Telephone Ring','Helicopter','Applause','Gunshot');
```

References to MIDI channel numbers use the logical channel numbers 1 through 16. These logical channel numbers are mapped to physical channels, numbered 0 through 15. MIDI data takes the form of MIDI messages. These messages include, among other things, channel information. In MIDI, a musical composition is often referred to as a "song." We'll use that terminology here. To play a song, you simply send a series of MIDI messages to particular MIDI channels. Windows generally uses a MIDI mapper so it knows how to interpret and where to direct MIDI messages. The MIDI mapper, with its various settings, is used to help ensure that music played on different machines will sound similar. It includes three kinds of maps: channel maps, patch maps, and key maps. Let's examine each map a bit.

The channel map controls MIDI channel messages. These include messages for note-on, note-off, polyphonic key aftertouch, control change, program change, channel aftertouch, and pitch-bend change. The MIDI mapper uses just one channel map, but that channel map has an entry for each MIDI channel. Those entries hold the following information about the MIDI message: its destination channel, its output device's destination, and an optional patch map for other factors.

Each channel map entry may have an associated patch map. These maps are used specifically with MIDI program change and volume controller messages. Program change messages send a command to the synthesizer requesting it to switch from one instrumental sound to another on the specified channel. Naturally, volume controller messages manipulate the volume on a channel. Patch maps include a translation table with an entry for each of the 128 program change values.

That translation table contains specific performance information for each instrument. Performance information includes a destination program change value, a volume scalar, and an optional key map. When program change messages are received by the MIDI mapper, the destination program change value is mapped to the message's value. Each entry in a particular patch map translation table may be associated with a specific key map. Key maps are used with the following types of messages:

note-on, note-off, and polyphonic key aftertouch. They include a translation table with entries for each of the 128 MIDI key values.

We've discussed program change messages, but there's an important area we have not yet covered—volume or loudness. When you work with MIDI you have the opportunity to work with a lot of instruments, each of which has a different sound quality. Keeping all of those sounds in balance can be a challenge. The task is similar to that of a musical arranger who must consider the balance between the various instruments in a particular musical rendition. MIDI provides an answer: the volume scalar.

The volume scalar allows you to make adjustments between the relative output levels of various patches on a synthesizer. For example, if the trumpet patch on a synthesizer is too loud compared with the trombone patch, you can change the setup map to scale the trumpet volume down or the trombone volume up. The volume scalar specifies a percentage value for changing all MIDI main volume controller messages that follow an associated program change message. Now that we have a general idea of what MIDI is and how it works, let's examine Windows support for MIDI.

Windows Support for MIDI

Windows provides considerable support for MIDI. Many of the main capabilities are demonstrated in the sample application accompanying this chapter as shown in Figure 4-1 (the main screen) and Figure 4-2 (MIDI message dialog box).

You'll recall that we discussed Windows support for waveform audio in Chapter 3. Several of the constants we discussed there, those that support waveform audio, are also used with MIDI, especially MMRESULT. As with the waveform functions, this constant is commonly used as the return value for many of the various MIDI functions. See Table 3-1 for a description of this and other commonly used constants.

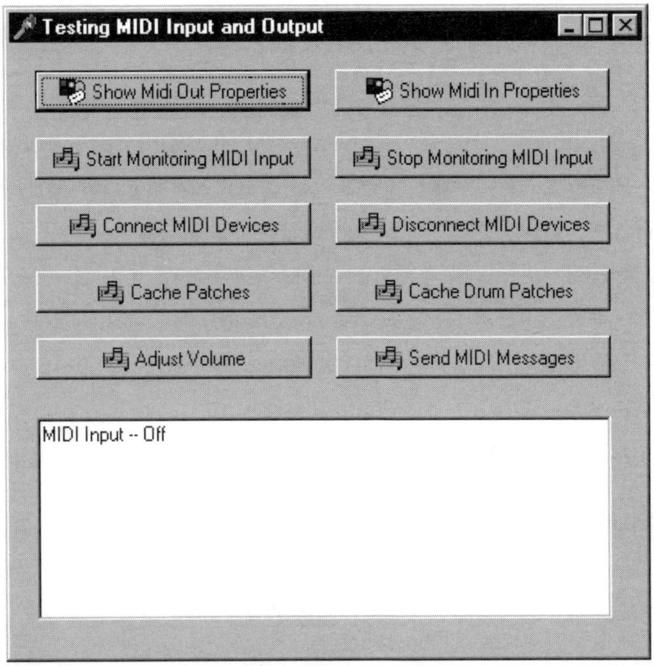

Figure 4-1

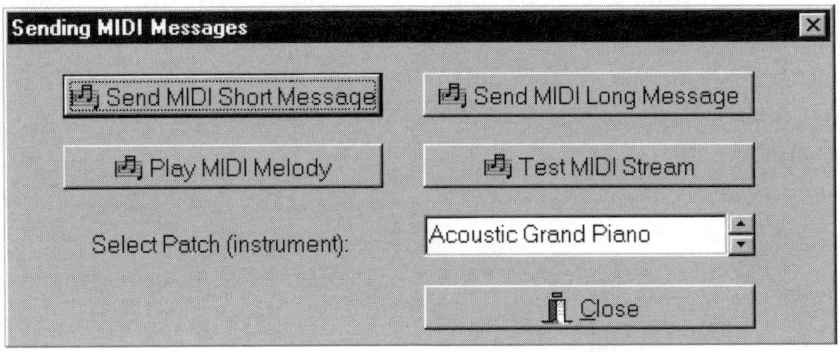

Figure 4-2

A particularly important new constant, MIDI_MAPPER, is used to provide standard patch services that enable device-independent playback of MIDI files. If you use MIDI files in your applications, you should use the MIDI mapper to ensure that the audio played will sound similar on different machines. The MIDI_MAPPER constant is defined in mmsystem.pas as follows:

```
MM_MIDI_MAPPER        = 1;
```

There are also error constants specific to MIDI. These constants and their meanings are given in Table 4-1.

Table 4-1: MIDI error messages and their meanings

Error Message	Meaning
MIDIERR_BASE	Base value for all MIDI error messages
MIDIERR_UNPREPARED	MIDI header has not been properly prepared
MIDIERR_STILLPLAYING	Something is still playing
MIDIERR_NOMAP	There is no current map
MIDIERR_NOTREADY	System not ready; hardware is currently busy
MIDIERR_NODEVICE	A MIDI port is no longer properly connected
MIDIERR_INVALIDSETUP	Setup is invalid
MIDIERR_BADOPENMODE	The requested operation is not supported in open mode
MIDIERR_DONT_CONTINUE	MIDI-thru device is not properly sending a message through the system
MIDIERR_LASTERROR	Last MIDI error in range

Now we'll take a look at some of the basic MIDI data types. The most basic one, HMidi, refers to any MIDI device. It does not appear to be used with any of the MIDI functions. Note that those types beginning with the letter "P" are generally pointers as in the following example from mmsystem.pas:

```
type
  PHMidi = ^HMIDI;
  HMidi = Integer;
  PHMidiIn = ^HMIDIIN;
  HMidiIn = Integer;
  PHMidiOut = ^HMIDIOUT;
  HMidiOut = Integer;
  PHMidiStrm = ^HMIDISTRM;
  HMidiStrm = Integer;
```

The PHMidiIn type is used for the first parameter in the MIDIInOpen() function. Likewise, the PHMidiOut type is used for the first parameter in the MIDIOutOpen() function. The PHMidiIn type is used for the first parameter in the MIDIInOpen() functions. Here, the value SomeMidiIn of type HMidiIn is used as the first parameter of the following callback routine.

We'll discuss this and other callback routines later in this chapter. We'll see that various callback functions can be used with MIDI operations.

However, there is just one standard callback type defined in mmsystem.pas (one I have not used or seen used, by the way):

```
type
  TFNMidiCallBack = TFNDrvCallBack;
```

There are several types common to both MIDI input and output; these are declared in our TMIDI class, as follows:

```
TMidi = class
  private
  { private values }
  public
  { public values }
  CurrentMMResult : MMRESULT; // used in all functions
  DeviceID : UINT;       // Midi input or output device
  BytesRecorded : Cardinal;
  CapStructSize: UINT; // used with MidiInCaps and MidiOutCaps
  NumDevices : UINT;
  function GetNumDevices : UINT; virtual; abstract;
  constructor Create(BufferSize, BlockSize : Cardinal);
  destructor Destroy(CloseBuffers : boolean); reintroduce;
  published
  { published values }
end;
```

You'll recall that before we opened a waveform device we needed to do certain things, including setting up memory buffers for waveform data; here we'll perform a similar task for MIDI messages as shown in Listing 4-1. As before, we take care of all of the buffer management in a single class, TMIDISupport. This class takes care of other tasks as well, such as handling MIDI timers and MIDI streams. The declaration for that class in the MidClass.pas unit is as follows:

```
TMidiSupport = class
public
// Timer Support
  FTimeCaps : TimeCaps;
  FTimerID : UINT;
  FTimeRes : UINT;
// Buffer Support
  MainMIDIBuffer : TMemoryStream; // Recording/Playback Buffer
                     // Calling app is responsible for getting and
                     // freeing memory; see example program
  SecondaryBufferSize,
  MainMIDIBufferSize : Cardinal;
```

```
    FPlaybackBufferPosition : cardinal;
    FBlockBuffers : PChar;
    MidiMelodyArray : TMelodyArray;
    MidiStreamArray : TMidiEventArray;
    FMidiStream : HMidiStrm;
    FNumberOfMessages : Cardinal;
    Dev : PUINT;               // Used with Midi Streams
// Header and Handles (not used in this implementation)
    FMidiHeader : PMidiHdr;    //MidiHeader;
    FbufHandle,
    FhdrHandle : THandle;
// Midi Property Elements
    MidiPropertyTempo :        MIDIPROPTEMPO;
    MidiPropertyTimeDivision : MIDIPROPTIMEDIV;
// Status Flags
    PlayDevAvailable: boolean;
    RecordDevAvailable: boolean;
    CurrentMMResult : MMRESULT; // used in all functions
    function SetupHighResTimer : boolean;
    procedure KillHighResTimer;
    function AllocateBuffers(var MainBlockSize, BufBlockSize : Cardinal):
        boolean;
    function DeAllocateBuffers: boolean;
    function ConnectMIDI: boolean;
    function DisConnectMIDI: boolean;
    constructor Create(ABlockSize, ABufferSize : Cardinal);
    destructor Destroy; override;
end;
```

We'll examine some of these methods presently. Before we do that, we need to understand MIDIHDR, a structure common to MIDI input, output, and streams. In fact, if MIDIHDR is not properly set up beforehand, many MIDI input, output, and stream functions will fail. Both MIDI input and output functions include a MIDIHdr parameter. Here is the declaration from mmsystem.pas:

```
type
  PMidiHdr = ^TMidiHdr;
  midihdr_tag = record
    lpData: PChar;              { pointer to locked data block }
    dwBufferLength: DWORD;      { length of data in data block }
    dwBytesRecorded: DWORD;     { used for input only }
    dwUser: DWORD;              { for client's use }
    dwFlags: DWORD;             { assorted flags (see defines) }
    lpNext: PMidiHdr;           { reserved for driver }
    reserved: DWORD;            { reserved for driver }
```

```
   dwOffset: DWORD;              { Callback offset into buffer }
   dwReserved: array[0..7] of DWORD; { Reserved for MMSYSTEM }
 end;
 TMidiHdr = midihdr_tag;
 MIDIHDR = midihdr_tag;
```

The fields of MIDIHDR are explained in Table 4-2.

Table 4-2: MIDIHDR fields

Field	Description and Use
lpData	A PChar that points to the data buffer used to store MIDI data.
dwBufferLength	This DWORD field indicates the length of the data buffer to which the lpData field points.
dwBytesRecorded	When the header is used in input, this DWORD field indicates the bytes recorded and ready to be passed to the operating system. This value is not necessarily the same as dwBufferLength. It should be set to 0 initially. See the RecordSounds() and ContinueRecording() methods of the TMIDIIn class for examples of using this parameter.
dwUser	Like Delphi's Tag field, you can use this DWORD field in any way you like. For example, you could initialize it to a particular value to keep track of the specific buffer being processed in a multi-buffering scheme.
dwFlags	Flags within a DWORD field that store information about the buffer and its use (see description of specific flags in Table 4-3). This field should be set initially to 0.
lpNext	This PMidiHdr field points to the next MIDIHDR structure in the application's queue.
reserved	Reserved; do not use.
dwOffset	Offset into the buffer when a callback is performed. You can use this field to determine which event caused the callback.
dwReserved	Reserved; do not use..

The dwFlags field is important in sending MIDI header information back to the application. These flags are described in Table 4-3.

4

Chapter

Table 4-3: Values of dwFlags flags field of the MIDIHDR structure

Value	Meaning
MHDR_DONE	Device driver communicating that it is finished with the buffer and is returning it to the application
MHDR_INQUEUE	Set by Windows to indicate that the buffer is queued for playback
MHDR_ISSTRM	Buffer is a MIDI stream buffer
MHDR_PREPARED	Buffer has been prepared with one of these functions: MIDIInPrepareHeader() or MIDIOutPrepareHeader()

The code shown in Listing 4-1 sets up memory for the MIDIHDR structure, initializes its fields, and sets up memory for the main buffer if needed.

Listing 4-I: Setting up the MIDIHDR structure and memory buffers

```
function TMidiSupport.AllocateBuffers(var MainBlockSize,
        BufBlockSize : Cardinal): boolean;
begin
  result := True;
  if BufBlockSize=0 then
    SecondaryBufferSize := MidiMsgBlockLength
  else
    SecondaryBufferSize := BufBlockSize;
  if MainBlockSize=0 then
    MainMIDIBufferSize := MidiMsgLength
  else
    MainMIDIBufferSize := MainBlockSize;
  try   // make sure we are able to allocate memory
    FBlockBuffers := Nil;
    FMidiHeader := NIl;
    FBlockBuffers := AllocMem(SecondaryBufferSize);
    FMidiHeader := AllocMem(SizeOf(MidiHdr));
  with FMidiHeader^ do
  begin
    lpData := PChar(FBlockBuffers);
    dwBufferLength := SecondaryBufferSize;
    dwBytesRecorded := 0;
    dwUser := 0;
    dwFlags := 0;
    Reserved := 0;
  end;    // for
  MainMIDIBuffer := TMemoryStream.Create;
  except
```

```
      if MainMIDIBuffer<>Nil then
        MainMIDIBuffer.Free;
      result := False;
    end;
end;
```

Of course, we also need to clean things up when we are finished. In this case, that means freeing all of the memory we allocated in Listing 4-1. Listing 4-2 shows how we do that in the TMidiSupport class.

Listing 4-2: Freeing all of the buffers created in Listing 4-1

```
function TMidiSupport.DeAllocateBuffers: boolean;
begin
  result := True;
  try
    FreeMem(FMidiHeader);
    FMidiHeader := Nil;
    FreeMem(FBlockBuffers);
    FBlockBuffers := Nil;
  except
    result := False;
  end;
  MainMIDIBuffer.Free;
end;
```

MIDI Messages: The Short and the Long of It

We've been discussing Windows messages and their use in callback routines since the previous chapter. But MIDI has its own messages— messages that are vital to how it functions. Various functions like MIDIOutShortMsg() and MIDIOutLongMsg() include these messages as a parameter and enable you to send data to a MIDI output device. We'll examine the details of how these messages are constructed in some actual examples. First, however, we need to understand the difference between short and long messages.

A MIDI short message conveys a MIDI command. These commands include status bytes that define the action to be performed such as note-on, note-off, system-exclusive (SysEx), end-of-system-exclusive (EOX), and patch change. Depending on the status byte, a number of different byte parameters follow. The note-on status byte tells the MIDI device to begin playing a note. Two additional bytes are required: a pitch byte, which tells the MIDI device which note to play, and a velocity byte ranging from 1 (softest) to 128 (loudest), which tells the device how loud to play the note. The command to stop playing a note is a separate note-off command and requires two additional bytes, the same bytes used for note-on.

The system-exclusive status byte indicates the beginning of a system-exclusive message. Such messages can accomplish powerful and useful functions such as exchanging banks of patches (instruments/sounds) between MIDI devices and controlling various aspects of a MIDI device. In addition to the status byte, a system-exclusive command requires at least three additional bytes. The first byte is a manufacturer's identification number or timing byte, the second byte is a data format or function byte, and the third is generally an end of transmission (EOX) byte. The following constants, borrowed from an impressive MIDI program written by David Churcher and included in the MidClass unit, define some of the common message bytes:

```
const
  MIDI_ALLNOTESOFF     = $7B;
  MIDI_NOTEON          = $90;
  MIDI_NOTEOFF         = $80;
  MIDI_KEYAFTERTOUCH   = $A0;
  MIDI_CONTROLCHANGE   = $B0;
  MIDI_PROGRAMCHANGE   = $C0;
  MIDI_CHANAFTERTOUCH  = $D0;
  MIDI_PITCHBEND       = $E0;
  MIDI_SYSTEMMESSAGE   = $F0;
  MIDI_BEGINSYSEX      = $F0;
  MIDI_MTCQUARTERFRAME = $F1;
  MIDI_SONGPOSPTR      = $F2;
  MIDI_SONGSELECT      = $F3;
  MIDI_ENDSYSEX        = $F7;
  MIDI_TIMINGCLOCK     = $F8;
  MIDI_START           = $FA;
  MIDI_CONTINUE        = $FB;
  MIDI_STOP            = $FC;
  MIDI_ACTIVESENSING   = $FE;
  MIDI_SYSTEMRESET     = $FF;
```

MIDI short messages are packed into a single DWORD value. A stream of MIDI messages can contain a running status byte. This means that once a MIDI command (status) has been issued (by the first message in a series), all of the MIDI short messages that follow may omit the command (status byte) from messages of the same command type. For example, if you're playing a 15-note tune consisting of 15 note-on commands, you can include the note-on status command byte in just the first MIDI short message. It will be understood or implied in subsequent messages. MIDI short messages do have some limitations. For example, unlike MIDI streams, which we'll discuss at the end of this chapter, they do not contain any timing information to control playback or recording. However, you can use the multimedia high-resolution timers to effect the correct flow of MIDI short messages to the MIDI output device. We show how to do this in the example program, which plays the first phrase of "Ode to Joy" from Beethoven's *Ninth Symphony*. While the tune is playing, the various bytes in the message are displayed as shown in Figure 4-3 (first in a series of notes played) and Figure 4-4 (end of a series of notes).

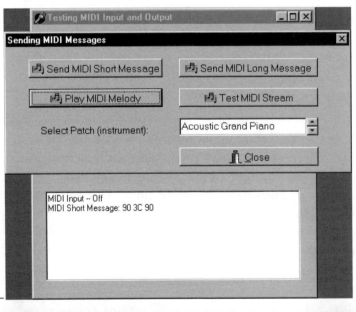

Figure 4-3

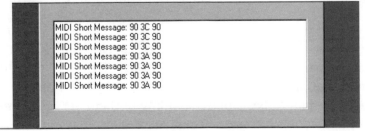

Figure 4-4

When used in MIDI functions, MIDI messages are packed into a DWORD (Double Word) parameter with the first byte of the message in the low-order byte. The message is packed like this:

High word	High-order byte	Not used.
	Low-order byte	Contains a second byte of MIDI data (when needed).
Low word	High-order byte	Contains the first byte of MIDI data (when needed).
	Low-order byte	Contains the MIDI status.

The two MIDI data bytes are optional, depending on the MIDI status byte. When a series of messages have the same status byte, the status byte can be omitted from messages after the first one in the series, creating a running status. A message for running status is packed like this:

High word	High-order byte	Not used.
	Low-order byte	Not used.
Low word	High-order byte	Contains a second byte of MIDI data (when needed)
	Low-order byte	Contains the first byte of MIDI data.

System-exclusive commands can sometimes be sent in short messages. But MIDI long messages are known specifically as system-exclusive messages. Here is an example of one such message that demonstrates the use of two of these status bytes. This test data, which includes a manufacturer ID of $7D, is reserved in the MIDI specification for non-commercial uses such as research and education. It is generally used to determine if an application is properly sending MIDI long (system exclusive) messages to the system. Note that it uses some of the constants defined above:

```
TestLongMsgData : array [0..6] of byte = (MIDI_BEGINSYSEX, $7D, $50,
                                          $61, $75, $6C, MIDI_ENDSYSEX);
```

In the sample application for this chapter on the companion CD, we display this message as shown in Figure 4-5. We'll explore MIDI short and long messages more when we take a look at the functions that use them. Now that we have a basic understanding of them, let's examine the various MIDI Windows messages. These are very similar to the Waveform messages we discussed in Chapter 3 and are listed in Table 4-4.

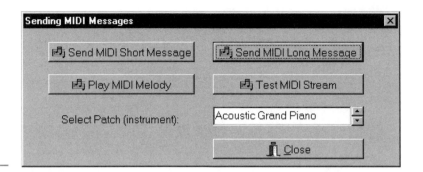

Figure 4-5

Table 4-4: MIDI messages sent to MidiIn, MidiOut, and MidiStream callback functions

Value	Meaning
MIM_OPEN	Message sent by the driver indicating that a MIDI input device was successfully opened.
MIM_CLOSE	Message sent by the driver when MIDI input device is closed.
MIM_DATA	Message sent when a complete MIDI message is received by a MIDI input device.
MIM_LONGDATA	Message sent when a buffer has been filled with data or when a complete MIDI system-exclusive message has been received.
MIM_ERROR	The MM_MIM_LONGDATA message is sent to a window when either a complete MIDI system-exclusive message is received or when a buffer has been filled with system-exclusive data.
MIM_LONGERROR	Message sent when an invalid MIDI system-exclusive message is received.
MOM_OPEN	Message sent when a MIDI output device is opened.
MOM_CLOSE	Message sent to a window when a MIDI output device is closed. The device handle is no longer valid once this message is sent.
MOM_DONE	Message sent when the specified system-exclusive buffer has been played and is being returned to the application.
MOM_POSITION	Message sent when a MEVT_F_CALLBACK event is reached in a MIDI output stream. Note that playback of the stream buffer continues even while the callback function is executing. Events in the buffer after the MEVT_F_CALLBACK event will be scheduled and sent on time regardless of how much time is spent in the callback function.

4

Chapter

Unlike the process we used with the Waveform callback procedures, here we place both callback routines in a DLL so that they will be readily available. Listing 4-3 shows the MIDIInProc() and MIDIOutProc() callback routines, defined in MidCBakU. The output of those two procedures is shown in Figures 4-6 and 4-7.

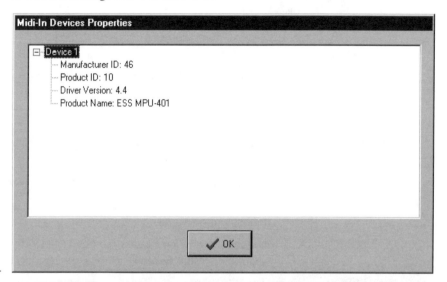

Figure 4-6

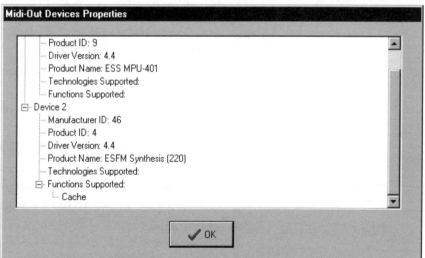

Figure 4-7

Listing 4-3: MIDIInProc() and MIDIOutProc() callback routines

```
procedure MidiInProc(hMidiInHandle : HMIDIIN; uMsg : UINT;
    dwInstance, dwParam1, dwParam2 : DWord); export; stdcall;
var
```

```
        lpMidiShort    : Pointer;
     hCallingWindow : THandle;
     bReturnValue   : Boolean;
begin
     hCallingWindow := THandle(dwInstance);
     case uMsg of
       MIM_Open : PostMessage (hCallingWindow, UINT(mm_MIM_Open), 0, 0);
       MIM_Error: PostMessage (hCallingWindow, UINT(mm_MIM_Error), 0, 0);
       MIM_Data :
         begin
           if hGMem <> 0 then
             begin
               lpMidiShort := GlobalLock(hGMem);
               with MidiShortMessage(lpMidiShort^) do
                 begin
                   MidiTime := dwParam2;
                   RawMidiData := dwParam1;
                 end; { with }
               bReturnValue := GlobalUnlock(hGMem);
               PostMessage(hCallingWindow, WM_USER, 0, hGMem);
             end; { if }
         end; { MIM_Data }
       MIM_Close: PostMessage (hCallingWindow, mm_MIM_Close, 0, 0);
       end; { case wMsg }
     end; { procedure MidiInCallback }

procedure MidiOutProc(hMidiInHandle : HMIDIIN; uMsg : UINT;
     dwInstance, dwParam1, dwParam2 : DWord); export; stdcall;
var
  hCallingWindow : THandle;
begin
     hCallingWindow := THandle(dwInstance);
     case uMsg of
       MOM_Open : PostMessage (hCallingWindow, UINT(mm_MIM_Open), 0, 0);
       MOM_PositionCB: PostMessage (hCallingWindow, UINT(mm_MOM_PositionCB
           ), 0, 0);
       MOM_Done : PostMessage(hCallingWindow, UINT(mm_MOM_Done), 0,
           dwParam1);
       MOM_Close: PostMessage (hCallingWindow, UINT(mm_MOM_Close), 0, 0);
     end;
end;
```

You'll recall that we discussed MIDI patches above. These sounds, which imitate so many familiar and exotic instruments, are at the heart of the MIDI system. Windows provides the following direct support for these patches. One constant defined in mmsystem.pas indicates the number of elements in an array of MIDI patches (which is the same number we used in our array of patch names above—no surprise!):

```
  MIDIPATCHSIZE   = 128;
The patch array itself is defined as the following type:
  PPatchArray = ^TPatchArray;
  TPatchArray = array[0..MIDIPATCHSIZE-1] of Word;
It is accompanied by the following array of MIDI keys.
  PKeyArray = ^TKeyArray;
  TKeyArray = array[0..MIDIPATCHSIZE-1] of Word;
```

As its name implies, the TPatchArray type defines an array of MIDI patches. Each element in the array corresponds to a particular MIDI patch; each of the 16 bits represents one of the 16 MIDI channels. Bits are set for each of the channels that use that particular patch. Similarly, the KeyArray type defines an array of keys. This time, each element in the array corresponds to a key-based percussion patch, each of the 16 bits representing one of the 16 MIDI channels. Bits are set for each of the channels that use that particular patch.

Remember the WAVEMAPPER from Chapter 3? We also have a MIDIMAPPER. The MIDI mapper constants are defined in mmsystem.pas as follows:

```
MIDIMAPPER      = UINT(-1);
MIDI_MAPPER     = UINT(-1);
```

The MIDIMAPPER is used to control patches, not to find a device with certain capabilities (as with waveform audio). There are other important differences between Waveform and MIDI functions. Unlike with the Waveform API, there are a couple of general MIDI functions for connecting and disconnecting a MIDI device. They are defined as follows:

function MIDIConnect   mmsystem.pas

Syntax

```
function MIDIConnect(
  hmi: HMIDI;
  hmo: HMIDIOUT;
  pReserved: Pointer
  ): MMRESULT; stdcall;
```

Description

This function connects a MIDI input device to a MIDI thru or output device, or connects a MIDI thru device to a MIDI output device. After this function has been called, the MIDI input device will receive event data in an MIM_DATA message whenever a message with the same event data is sent to the output device driver. A MIDI thru driver is a special form of MIDI output driver. The system will allow just one MIDI output device to be connected to a MIDI input device. However, multiple MIDI output devices may be connected to a MIDI thru device. Whenever the given MIDI input device receives event data in an MIM_DATA message, a message with the same event data is sent to the given output device driver (or through the thru driver to the output drivers).

Parameters

hmi: An HMIDI value that is the handle of a MIDI input device or a MIDI thru device. In the case of a MIDI thru device, this handle must have been returned by a call to the MIDIOutOpen() function.

hmo: An HMIDIOUT value that is the handle of the MIDI output or MIDI thru device.

pReserved: Reserved; must be set to NULL.

Return Value

Returns MMSYSERR_NOERROR if successful. Otherwise, it returns one of the following errors: MIDIERR_NOTREADY, indicating that the specified input device is already connected to an output device; or MMSYSERR_INVALHANDLE indicating that the specified device handle is invalid.

Example

The example given in Listing 4-4 shows how to connect a MIDI input device to a MIDI output device. It first checks to make certain that there are MIDI devices to connect, and then attempts to connect them. With additional code you could use this as a basis for recording MIDI input and echoing that to the computer's speakers.

Listing 4-4: Connecting a MIDI input and a MIDI output device

```
function TMidiSupport.ConnectMIDI: boolean;
var
  AMsg : string;
```

```
begin
  result := False;
 if MidiIn.AHandle=0 then
   begin
     MidiIn.CloseDownMidiIn;
     if NOT MidiIn.OpenRecordMidiDev(srtMemory, AMsg) then
       if ReportError(iodInput, 0, AMsg) then exit;
   end;
  CurrentMMResult := MidiConnect(MidiIn.AHandle, MidiOut.AHandle, Nil);
  if CurrentMMResult<> 0 then
    if ReportError(iodNone, CurrentMMResult, '') then exit;
  result := True; // if we get here, everything is fine
end;
```

function MIDIDisconnect   *mmsystem.pas*

Syntax

function MIDIDisconnect(
  hmi: HMIDI;
  hmo: HMIDIOUT;
  pReserved: Pointer
  ): MMRESULT; stdcall;

Description

This function disconnects a MIDI input device from a MIDI thru or output device, or disconnects a MIDI thru device from a MIDI output device. A MIDI input, output, or thru device can be connected by using the MIDIConnect() function. After that function has been called, the MIDI input device will receive event data in an MIM_DATA message whenever a message with the same event data is sent to the output device driver.

Parameters

hmi: An HMIDI value that is the handle of a MIDI input device or a MIDI thru device. In the case of a MIDI thru device, this handle must have been returned by a call to the MIDIOutOpen() function.

hmo: An HMIDIOUT value that is the handle of the MIDI output or MIDI thru device.

pReserved: Reserved; must be set to NULL.

Return Value

Returns MMSYSERR_NOERROR if successful. Otherwise, it returns MMSYSERR_INVALHANDLE, indicating that the specified device handle is invalid.

Example

The example in Listing 4-5 disconnects MIDI input and MIDI output devices that have been connected previously.

Listing 4-5: Disconnecting a MIDI input and a MIDI output device

```
function TMidiSupport.DisConnectMIDI: boolean;
begin
  result := False;
  CurrentMMResult := MidiDisconnect(MidiIn.AHandle, MidiOut.AHandle, Nil);
  if CurrentMMResult<> 0 then
    if ReportError(iodNone, CurrentMMResult, '') then exit;
  MidiIn.CloseDownMidiIn;
  MidiOut.ResetAndCloseDevice;
  result := True; // if we get here, everything is fine
end;
```

Recording Sounds with MIDI

We've examined all of the general MIDI issues. Now it's time to take a detailed look at MIDI input. Recording sounds with MIDI is similar to recording sound with waveform audio, but simpler. Here, you don't need to be concerned with driver capabilities such as monaural vs. stereo, 8 bit vs. 16 bit, or sampling speeds. However, like the Waveform API, the MIDI API does provide the MIDIINCAPS structure and the MIDIInGet-DevCaps() function to determine a MIDI device's capabilities.

The Windows multimedia system also provides the MIDIInGetNumDevs() function to return the number of input devices on a particular computer. Once you've found a suitable device you can open it with the MIDIInOpen() function. This function returns a handle in its first parameter. That handle is used by all of the other functions. The function also sets up the callback mechanism that will take care of MidiIn messages (see discussion above). We'll discuss more of these details when we discuss the MIDIInOpen() function. If at any point after this we want to get the device number (not the handle) of the input device, we can use the MIDIInGetID() function.

4

Chapter

Once you've chosen a MIDI input device, the process of recording is quite similar to that of recording waveform audio. If you haven't already done so, you need to get memory for your data buffers as we discussed above. Then you need to prepare the buffer block headers with the MIDIIn-PrepareHeader() function and add those buffers to the system queue with the MIDIInAddBuffer() function. While we used a double buffering system with waveform audio, that technique is not needed here. For long MIDI melodies, however, some type of circular queue would be helpful. One of the sample programs on the CD-ROM demonstrates such an approach.

The MIDIInStart() function begins the recording process. It continues to return data blocks to the system until it is finished. As with waveform audio, once the process of recording has been completed you need to close things down in a very specific manner. First, you must call MIDIInStop() and MIDIInReset() to make certain that recording is finished. It is good form to also call MIDIInUnprepareHeader() to clean up the block buffer headers. You must do this in any case before you free the memory associated with those headers and their associated block buffers. Finally, you need to call MIDIInClose(). After this the handle for the device is no longer valid.

As with the waveform audio functions, most of the MIDI functions report the result of their operations in MMRESULT, a constant integer. Once you have an MMRESULT value, you can use it to get a string that provides a description of the problem using the MIDIInGetErrorText() function. Now that we have taken a general look at the process of recording, let's take a detailed look at all of the functions and structures.

function MIDIInGetNumDevs   *mmsystem.pas*

Syntax

```
function MIDIInGetNumDevs
  : UINT; stdcall;
```

Description

This function takes no parameters and simply returns the number of input devices found on a machine. Once you determine the number of devices, you can then query each device to determine its capabilities.

Return Value

Returns the number of input devices.

Example

The following method in the TMIDIIn class encapsulates the MIDIInGetNumDevs function:

```
function TMIDIIn.GetNumDevices : UINT;
begin
  result :=MIDIInGetNumDevs;
end;
```

function MIDIInGetDevCaps   *mmsystem.pas*

Syntax

function MIDIInGetDevCaps(
  DeviceID: UINT;
  lpCaps: PMIDIInCaps;
  uSize: UINT
  ): MMRESULT; stdcall;

Description

This function queries the MIDI input device, DeviceID, determines its capabilities, and places them in the LPCAPS structure. The result is returned in MMRESULT. The MMRESULT type is used in most of the functions we'll be discussing in this chapter.

Parameters

DeviceID: An integer (UINT) identifying a MIDI input device. The MIDI_ MAPPER constant can also be used as the device identifier. To determine the number of MIDI device IDs, call MIDIInGetNumDevs().

lpCaps: The address of a MIDIINCAPS structure to be filled with information about the capabilities of the device specified by DeviceID. The declaration of the MIDIINCAPS structure in mmsystem.pas is given below. The various members of this structure are described in Table 4-5.

uSize: An integer (UINT) indicating the size of the MIDIINCAPS structure. Use SizeOf(MIDIINCAPS) to get this value.

4

Chapter

Return Value

Returns MMSYSERR_NOERROR if successful. Otherwise, it returns one
of the following errors: MMSYSERR_BADDEVICEID, indicating the
device identifier specified is out of range; MMSYSERR_NODRIVER, indicating that no device driver is present; or MMSYSERR_NOMEM,
indicating that memory could not be allocated.

The MIDIINCAPS structure, which holds information about a MIDI input
device's capabilities is defined as follows in mmsystem.pas:

```
type
  PMidiInCapsA = ^TMidiInCapsA;
  PMidiInCapsW = ^TMidiInCapsW;
  PMidiInCaps = PMidiInCapsA;
  tagMIDIINCAPSA = record
    wMid: Word;                    { manufacturer ID }
    wPid: Word;                    { product ID }
    vDriverVersion: MMVERSION;     { version of the driver }
    szPname: array[0..MAXPNAMELEN-1] of AnsiChar;  { product name (NULL
                                                     terminated string) }
    dwSupport: DWORD;              { functionality supported by driver }
  end;
  tagMIDIINCAPSW = record
    wMid: Word;                    { manufacturer ID }
    wPid: Word;                    { product ID }
    vDriverVersion: MMVERSION;     { version of the driver }
    szPname: array[0..MAXPNAMELEN-1] of WideChar;  { product name (NULL
                                                     terminated string) }
    dwSupport: DWORD;              { functionality supported by driver }
  end;
  tagMIDIINCAPS = tagMIDIINCAPSA;
  TMidiInCapsA = tagMIDIINCAPSA;
  TMidiInCapsW = tagMIDIINCAPSW;
  TMidiInCaps = TMidiInCapsA;
  MIDIINCAPSA = tagMIDIINCAPSA;
  MIDIINCAPSW = tagMIDIINCAPSW;
  MIDIINCAPS = MIDIINCAPSA;
```

Table 4-5: Values for the main fields of MIDIINCAPS

Field	Meaning
wMid	A word value indicating the manufacturer identifier for the device driver for the MIDI input device.
wPid	A word value indicating the product identifier for the MIDI input device.

Field	Meaning
vDriverVersion	An MMVERSION value indicating the version number of the device driver for the MIDI input device. The high-order byte is the major version number, and the low-order byte is the minor version number.
szPname	A null-terminated string holding the product name.
dwSupport	Reserved; must be set to zero.

Listing 4-6: Finding and displaying properties for all MidiIn devices on a computer

```
procedure TfrmMidiInDevicesProperties.FormCreate(Sender: TObject);
var
  FNumInputDevices : Cardinal;
  FMidiInCaps : TMidiInCaps;
  j: Integer;
  Node: TTreeNode;
begin
  if MidiIn=Nil then
    MidiIn := TMidiIn.Create(0, 0);
  FNumInputDevices := MidiIn.GetNumDevices;
  TreeView1.Items.Clear;
  for j := (FNumInputDevices-1) downto 0 do    // Iterate
  begin
    MidiInGetDevCaps(j, @FMidiInCaps, SizeOf(TMidiInCaps));
    Node := TreeView1.Items.AddChildFirst(nil, 'Device '+IntToStr(J+1));
    TreeView1.Items.AddChild(Node, 'Manufacturer ID: ' +
      IntToStr(FMidiInCaps.wMid));
    TreeView1.Items.AddChild(Node, 'Product ID: ' +
      IntToStr(FMidiInCaps.wPid));
    TreeView1.Items.AddChild(Node, 'Driver Version: ' +
      IntToStr(hi(FMidiInCaps.vDriverVersion)) +
      '.' + IntToStr(lo(FMidiInCaps.vDriverVersion)));
    TreeView1.Items.AddChild(Node, 'Product Name: ' +
      FMidiInCaps.szPname);
  end;    // for Input Devices
end;
```

function MIDIInGetErrorText   *mmsystem.pas*

Syntax

```
function MIDIInGetErrorText(
  mmrError: MMRESULT;
  lpText: PChar;
```

4

Chapter

uSize: UINT
): MMRESULT; stdcall;

Description

This function returns a textual description of the error identified by the given error number, mmrError. The error string is placed in the lpText parameter. See Listing 4-7 for an example of how to set up a general utility routine to return these strings for both input and output return values.

Parameters

mmrError: An MMRESULT error constant returned by one of the MidiIn functions.

lpText: The string explaining the error.

uSize: An integer (UINT) indicating the size of the PChar buffer that holds the description of the error. In the MidClass unit, the contant MsgLength is set to 128, sufficient for any of the message strings.

Return Value

Returns MMSYSERR_NOERROR if successful. Otherwise, it returns one of the following errors: MMSYSERR_BADERRNUM, indicating the specified error number is out of range; MMSYSERR_NODRIVER, indicating there is no device driver present; or MMSYSERR_NOMEM, indicating that memory could not be allocated.

Example

Listing 4-7 reports both input and output errors. That's why its first parameter is IO_Direction, indicating input or output. It is similar to the reporting function we used in the WavClass unit. The functions called in this procedure are input- or output-specific.

Listing 4-7: A routine for reporting MIDI input and MIDI output errors

```
function ReportError(
          IO_Direction : TIO_Direction; // (iodInput, iodOutput, iodNone)
          AMMResult : MMResult;         // applies to iodInput and iodOutput
          ErrMessage : string)          // if no MMresult send a string,
              : boolean;                // Otherwise set to ''
  var
    TempBuffer : Pchar;
    begin
```

```
     if ErrMessage='' then
     begin
       TempBuffer := Nil;
       StrNew(TempBuffer);
       if IO_Direction=iodInput then
          MidiInGetErrorText(AMMResult, PChar(TempBuffer), MsgLength)
       else if IO_Direction=iodOutput then
         MidiOutGetErrorText(AMMResult, PChar(TempBuffer), MsgLength)
       else exit;  // already have string; IO_Direction = iodNone
       ErrMessage := StrPas(TempBuffer);
       StrDispose(TempBuffer);
     end;
     case IO_Direction of    //
       iodInput: MidiIn.MidiInStatus := misError;
       iodOutput: MidiOut.MidiOutStatus := mosError;
     end;              // case
     ShowMessage('Error encountered; close application and try again');
     result := True;  // Always true; always exit on return
   end;
```

function MIDIInOpen   mmsystem.pas

Syntax

```
function MIDIInOpen(
    lphMIDIIn: PHMIDIIN;
    uDeviceID: UINT;
    dwCallback,
    dwInstance,
    dwFlags: DWORD
    ): MMRESULT; stdcall;
```

4

Chapter

Description

This function opens a specified MIDI input device. Use the MIDIInGetNumDevs() function to determine the number of MIDI input devices present in the system. The number for the device identifier specified by uDeviceID will be zero to one less than the number of MIDI devices present. If you choose a window or thread to receive callback information, the following messages will be sent to the window procedure or thread to indicate the progress of MIDI input: MM_MIM_OPEN, MM_MIM_CLOSE, MM_MIM_DATA, MM_MIM_LONGDATA, MM_MIM_ERROR, MM_MIM_LONGERROR, and MM_MIM_MOREDATA.

If you choose a function to receive callback information, these messages will be sent to the function to indicate the progress of MIDI input.

Parameters

lphMIDIIn: The address (PHMidiIn) of a handle (HMidiIn) identifying the opened MIDI input device. This handle will be used to identify the device in calls to other MIDI input functions

uDeviceID: An integer (UINT) that identifies the MIDI input device to be opened.

dwCallback: The address (DWORD) of a callback function, a thread identifier, or the handle of a window to receive information about incoming MIDI messages.

dwInstance: A DWORD value containing user instance data passed to the callback function; not used with window callback functions or threads.

dwFlags: A DWORD value containing the callback flag for opening the device and, optionally, a status flag that helps regulate rapid data transfers. (See Table 4-6 for possible flags and their meanings.) Most applications that use a callback mechanism will use CALLBACK_FUNCTION in this parameter.

Return Value

Returns MMSYSERR_NOERROR if successful. Otherwise, it returns one of the following errors: MMSYSERR_ALLOCATED, indicating the specified resource is already allocated; MMSYSERR_BADDEVICEID, indicating the specified device identifier is out of range; MMSYSERR_INVALFLAG, indicating the flags specified by dwFlags are invalid; MMSYSERR_IN-VALPARAM, indicating the specified pointer or structure is invalid; or MMSYSERR_NOMEM, indicating that memory could not be allocated.

Table 4-6: Flags for the dwFlags field of MIDIInOpen()

Flag	Meaning
CALLBACK_FUNCTION	The dwCallback parameter is the address of a callback procedure.
CALLBACK_NULL	There is no callback mechanism (this is the default setting).
CALLBACK_THREAD	The dwCallback parameter is a thread identifier.
CALLBACK_WINDOW	The dwCallback parameter is a window handle.

Flag	Meaning
MIDI_IO_STATUS	If you specify CALLBACK_FUNCTION or CALLBACK_WINDOW in dwFlags and this flag is set, MIM_MOREDATA messages are sent to the callback function or window as well as MIM_DATA messages. (This flag does not affect event or thread callbacks.) The special MIM_MOREDATA message is sent to a MIDI input callback function when a MIDI message is received by a MIDI input device but the application is processing MIM_DATA messages too slowly to keep up with the input device driver.

Example

The example code in Listing 4-8 from the MidClass unit gives you the choice of three different ways to open a MIDI in device using one of the following opening formats:

```
MidiOpenFormat = (mofCallbackFunc, mofCallbackWind, mofNoCallback);
```

Listing 4-8: Opening a MidiIn device

```
function TMidiIn.Open(AMidiOpenFormat : MidiOpenFormat): boolean;
begin
  case AMidiOpenFormat of  // (mofCallbackFunc, mofCallbackWind,
                               mofNoCallback)
    mofCallbackFunc: CurrentMMResult := MidiInOpen(@AHandle, 0,
      DWORD(@MidiInProc), Dword(MainFormHandle), callback_function);
    mofCallbackWind: CurrentMMResult := MidiInOpen(@AHandle, 0,
      DWord(MainFormHandle), Dword(0), callback_Window);
    mofNoCallback: CurrentMMResult := midiInOpen(@AHandle, $FFFF,
        0, 0, 0);
  end;   // case
  result := CurrentMMResult=MMSYSERR_NOERROR;
  MidiSupport.PlayDevAvailable := True;
end;
```

function MIDIInClose   mmsystem.pas

Syntax

```
function MIDIInClose(
  hMIDIIn: HMIDIIN
  ): MMRESULT; stdcall;
```

4

Chapter

Description

This function closes the given MIDI input device. Before calling this function it is important to return all pending buffers through the callback function. To make sure this has happened, use the MIDIInReset() function.

Parameter

hMIDIIn: The handle of the MIDI audio input device. If the function succeeds, the handle is no longer valid.

Return Value

Returns MMSYSERR_NOERROR if successful. Otherwise, it returns one of the following errors: MMSYSERR_INVALHANDLE, indicating that the specified device handle is invalid; MMSYSERR_NOMEM, indicating that memory could not be allocated; or MIDIRR_STILLPLAYING, indicating that one or more block buffers are still in the queue.

Example

Listing 4-9 shows how to properly shut down a MIDI input device. First, you need to be certain that all block buffers have been returned by calling MIDIInReset(). MIDIInStop() is probably not required but doesn't do any harm. Then you need to call MIDIInUnprepareHeader() to clean up the buffers. The buffers can then be either disposed (their memory freed) or used again (prepared again). Finally, having done all of this you can call MIDIInClose().

Listing 4-9: How to properly close a MIDI input device

```
procedure TMidiIn.CloseDownMidiIn;
begin
  CurrentMMResult :=  MidiInStop(AHandle);
  CurrentMMResult :=  MidiInReset(AHandle);
  CurrentMMResult :=  MidiInUnprepareHeader(AHandle, MidiSupport
        .FMidiHeader, SizeOf(MidiHdr));
  CurrentMMResult :=  MidiInClose(AHandle);
  MidiInStatus := misDoneRecording;
  MidiSupport.RecordDevAvailable := False;
end;
```

function MIDIInPrepareHeader   *mmsystem.pas*

Syntax

```
function MIDIInPrepareHeader(
 hMIDIIn: HMIDIIN;
 lpMIDIInHdr: PMIDIHdr;
 uSize: UINT
 ): MMRESULT; stdcall;
```

Description

This function prepares a buffer for MIDI input. This is a temporary block buffer used to input MIDI data to be stored in memory or in a file. Before calling this function, it is essential that you set the values of several of the MIDIHDR structure's fields, particularly lpData, dwBufferLength, and dwFlags. The lpData field should point to a valid PChar for which memory has been set and dwFlags must be set to zero.

Parameters

hMIDIIn: The handle of the MIDI audio input device.

lpMIDIInHdr: The address of a MIDIHDR structure that identifies the buffer to be prepared.

uSize: An integer indicating the size of the MIDIHDR structure. You can simply use the SizeOf(MIDIHDR) function for this parameter.

Return Value

Returns MMSYSERR_NOERROR if successful. Otherwise, it returns one of the following errors: MMSYSERR_INVALHANDLE, indicating that the specified device handle is invalid; MMSYSERR_NODRIVER, indicating that no device driver is present; or MMSYSERR_NOMEM, indicating that memory could not be allocated.

Example

Listing 4-10 shows how to use the MIDIInPrepareHeader() function.

Listing 4-10: Opening a recording device using MIDIInPrepareHeader() function

```
function TMidiIn.OpenRecordMidiDev(SaveTo : SoundRecordTo;
           var ReturnErrMsg : string) : boolean;
  var
    DevNum : integer;
```

4

Chapter

```
        k : integer;
     function GetCaps : boolean;
     var
       TotalsDevs : integer;
       j: Integer;
     begin
       result := False;
       TotalsDevs := GetNumDevices;
       for j := 0 to (TotalsDevs-1) do      // Iterate
       begin
         CurrentMMResult := MidiInGetDevCaps(j, @MidiInCaps, CapStructSize);
         if CurrentMMResult=MMSYSERR_NOERROR then
           begin
            DevNum := j;
            result := True;
            break;
           end;
       end;    // for
     end;
begin
  DevNum := 0;
  AHandle := 0;
  k := 0;
  result := False;
  if Not GetCaps then exit;
  CurrentMMResult := MidiInOpen(@AHandle, DevNum,
  DWORD(@MidiInProc), DWORD(MainFormHandle), DWORD(callback_function));
  if Not (CurrentMMResult = MMSYSERR_NOERROR) then
    if ReportError(iodInput, CurrentMMResult, '') then exit;
  CurrentMMResult := MidiInReset(AHandle);
  if Not (CurrentMMResult = MMSYSERR_NOERROR) then
    if ReportError(iodInput, CurrentMMResult, '') then exit;
  CurrentMMResult := MidiInPrepareHeader(AHandle, MidiSupport.FMidiHeader,
                   SizeOf(MidiHdr));
  if Not (CurrentMMResult = MMSYSERR_NOERROR) then
    if ReportError(iodInput, CurrentMMResult, '') then exit;
  CurrentMMResult := MidiInAddBuffer(AHandle, MidiSupport.FMidiHeader,
                   SizeOf(MidiHdr));
  if Not (CurrentMMResult = MMSYSERR_NOERROR) then
    if ReportError(iodInput, CurrentMMResult, '') then exit;
  CurrentMMResult := MidiInStart(AHandle);
  if Not (CurrentMMResult = MMSYSERR_NOERROR) then
    if ReportError(iodInput, CurrentMMResult, '') then exit;
  MidiSupport.RecordDevAvailable := True;
  result := True;
end;
```

function MIDIInUnprepareHeader   *mmsystem.pas*

Syntax

```
function MIDIInUnprepareHeader(
  hMIDIIn: HMIDIIN;
  lpMIDIInHdr: PMIDIHdr;
  uSize: UINT
  ): MMRESULT; stdcall;
```

Description

This function cleans up the preparation performed by the MIDIIn-
PrepareHeader() function. After passing a buffer to the device driver
with the MIDIInAddBuffer() function, you must wait until the driver is
finished with the buffer before calling MIDIInUnprepareHeader().
Unpreparing a buffer that has not been prepared has no effect, and the
function returns zero. You must call this function before freeing the
buffer.

Parameters

hMIDIIn: The handle of the MIDI audio input device.

lpMIDIInHdr: The address of a MIDIHDR structure that identifies the
buffer to be unprepared.

uSize: An integer indicating the size of the MIDIHDR structure. You can
simply use the SizeOf(MIDIHDR) function for this parameter.

Return Value

Returns MMSYSERR_NOERROR if successful. Otherwise, it returns one
of the following errors: MMSYSERR_INVALHANDLE, indicating that the
specified device handle is invalid; MMSYSERR_INVALPARAM, indicating
that the specified pointer or structure is invalid; or MIDIERR_STILL-
PLAYING, indicating that one or more block buffers are still in the queue.

Example

Listing 4-9 shows how to properly shut down a recording device including the use of the MIDIInUnprepareHeader() function.

4

Chapter

function MIDIInAddBuffer   *mmsystem.pas*

Syntax

```
function MIDIInAddBuffer(
hMIDIIn: HMIDIIN;
lpMIDIInHdr: PMIDIHdr;
uSize: UINT
): MMRESULT; stdcall;
```

Description

This function sends an input buffer to the given MIDI audio input device identified by hMidiIn. You need to prepare the buffer with the MIDIInPrepareHeader() function before you pass it to this function. When the buffer is filled, the application is notified. (See discussion of callbacks.) When the buffer is filled, the MHDR_DONE bit is set in the dwFlags member of the MIDIHDR structure.

Parameters

hMIDIIn: The handle of the MIDI input device.

lpMIDIInHdr: The address of a MIDIHDR structure that identifies the buffer to be unprepared.

uSize: An integer indicating the size of the MIDIHDR structure. You can simply use the SizeOf(MIDIHDR) function for this parameter.

Return Value

Returns MMSYSERR_NOERROR if successful. Otherwise, it returns one of the following errors: MMSYSERR_INVALHANDLE, indicating that the specified device handle is invalid; MMSYSERR_INVALPARAM, indicating that the specified pointer or structure is invalid; or MIDIERR_STILL-PLAYING, indicating that one or more block buffers are still in the queue.

Example

See Listing 4-10 on opening a MIDI input device.

function MIDIInStart   *mmsystem.pas*

Syntax

```
function MIDIInStart(
 hMIDIIn: HMIDIIN
 ): MMRESULT; stdcall;
```

Description

This is the function that actually starts the MIDI input process. It resets the time stamp to zero; time stamp values for subsequently received messages will be relative to the time that this function was called. Except for system-exclusive messages, all messages are sent directly to the client when they are received. System-exclusive messages are placed in the buffers supplied by the MIDIInAddBuffer() function. If there are no buffers in the queue, system-exclusive data will be thrown away without notifying the client and input continues. Buffers are returned to the client when they are full, when a complete system-exclusive message has been received, or when the MIDIInReset() function is used. The dwBytesRecorded member of the MIDIHDR structure will contain the actual length of data received. If you call this function when input has already started, it has no effect and returns with a value of zero.

Parameter

hMIDIIn: The handle of the MIDI audio input device.

Return Value

Returns MMSYSERR_NOERROR if successful. Otherwise, it returns MMSYSERR_INVALHANDLE, indicating that the specified device handle is invalid.

Example

See Listing 4-10 on opening a MIDI input device.

function MIDIInStop   *mmsystem.pas*

Syntax

```
function MIDIInStop(
 hMIDIIn: HMIDIIN
 ): MMRESULT; stdcall;
```

4

Chapter

Description

This function stops MIDI input, or recording. If there are any system-exclusive messages or stream buffers in the queue, the current buffer will be marked as done and the dwBytesRecorded member of the MIDIHDR structure will contain the actual length of data. Any empty buffers in the queue will remain there and will not be marked as done. If you call this function when input has already started, it will have no effect and will return with a value of zero.

Parameter

hMIDIIn: The handle of the MIDI audio input device. If the function succeeds, the handle is no longer valid.

Return Value

Returns MMSYSERR_NOERROR if successful. Otherwise, it returns one of the following errors: MMSYSERR_INVALHANDLE, indicating that the specified device handle is invalid; MMSYSERR_NODRIVER, indicating that no device driver is present; MMSYSERR_NOMEM, indicating that memory could not be allocated; or MIDIRR_STILLPLAYING, indicating that one or more block buffers are still in the queue.

Example

See Listing 4-9 on how to properly close a MIDI input device.

function MIDIInReset   *mmsystem.pas*

Syntax

```
function MIDIInReset(
  hMIDIIn: HMIDIIN
  ): MMRESULT; stdcall;
```

Description

This function stops MIDI input. Any pending buffers will be marked as done and returned to the callback function. It also sets the MHDR_DONE flag in the dwFlags member of the MIDIHDR structure.

Parameter

hMIDIIn: The handle of the MIDI audio input device. If the function succeeds, the handle is no longer valid.

Return Value

Returns MMSYSERR_NOERROR if successful. Otherwise, it returns MMSYSERR_INVALHANDLE, indicating that the specified device handle is invalid.

Example

See Listing 4-10 on opening a MIDI input device.

function MIDIInGetID   *mmsystem.pas*

Syntax

```
function MIDIInGetID(
  hMIDIIn: HMIDIIN;
  lpuDeviceID: PUINT
  ): MMRESULT; stdcall;
```

Description

This function gets the device identifier for the given MIDI input device. It is here mainly as a support for backward compatibility. New applications can cast a handle of the device rather than retrieving the device identifier.

Parameters

hMIDIIn: The handle of the MIDI audio input device.

lpuDeviceID: A PUINT (pointer to an integer) that will hold the device ID returned if the function succeeds.

Return Value

Returns MMSYSERR_NOERROR if successful. Otherwise, it returns one of the following errors: MMSYSERR_INVALHANDLE, indicating that the specified device handle is invalid; MMSYSERR_NODRIVER, indicating that no device driver is present; or MMSYSERR_NOMEM, indicating that memory could not be allocated.

Example

Listing 4-11 is a simple example of how to use this function.

4

Chapter

Listing 4-11: Using the MIDIInGetID() function

```
function TMidiIn.GetMidiInID: boolean;
begin
  CurrentMMResult := MidiInGetID(AHandle, @DeviceID);
  Result := CurrentMMResult=MMSYSERR_NOERROR;
end;
```

function MIDIInMessage   *mmsystem.pas*

Syntax

```
function MIDIInMessage(
  hMIDIIn: HMIDIIN;
  uMessage: UINT;
  dw1, dw2: DWORD
  ): MMRESULT; stdcall;
```

Description

This function sends messages to the MIDI device driver.

Parameters

hMIDIIn: The handle of the MIDI device.

uMessage: An integer indicating message to send.

dw1, dw2: Two DWORD parameters for message parameters.

Return Value

Returns a DWORD indicating the value returned by the driver.

Example

These messages are driver-specific, so we cannot show an example here that will definitely work on your system. To use this function you need to know the specific messages your sound card and its driver(s) will accept. Here is a general example of how you might call this function:

```
procedure TMIDIIn.SendMessage(ADriverMessage: UINT; MsgParam1,
    MsgParam2: DWORD);
begin
  MIDIInMessage(AHandle, ADriverMessage, MsgParam1, MsgParam2);
end;
```

Playing Sounds with MIDI

As with waveform audio, the process of playing MIDI data is similar to that of recording MIDI data. By now, some of the function names and their uses should be familiar. You can use the MIDIOutGetNumDevs() function to return the number of output devices on a particular computer and the MIDIOutGetDevCaps() function to ascertain the capabilities of a given MIDI device.

Once you have chosen a device, you can open it with the MIDIOutOpen() function. This function returns in its first parameter a handle that will be used by all of the other MidiOut functions. As with similar functions we have seen, it also sets up the callback mechanism that will take care of MidiOut messages (see the discussion on callbacks). We'll discuss more of these details when we discuss the MIDIOutOpen() function. If at any point after this you want to get the device number (not the handle) of the output device, you can use the MIDIOutGetID() function.

If you haven't already done so, you need to get memory for your data buffers as we discussed above. Then you need to prepare the buffer block headers with the MIDIOutPrepareHeader() function.

Once the output device is open and the header has been prepared, you can use the MIDIOutShortMsg() function to start and stop individual tones. As we discussed above, you can also use MIDI messages to perform many other functions like changing the patch, panning left to right, and so on. You can also play a MIDI melody using MIDI streams, which we discuss in the final section of this chapter. Shutting down a MIDI output device is similar to the processes we have seen before and should seem familiar. First, you need to call MIDIOutStop() and MIDIOutReset() to make certain that playing is finished. Again, you should call MIDIOut-UnprepareHeader() to clean up the block buffer headers. You must do this in any case before you free the memory associated with those headers and their associated block buffers. Finally, you must call MIDIOutClose(). After this the handle for the device is no longer valid.

As with MidiIn functions, most MidiOut functions also report their result in MMRESULT. Once you have an MMRESULT value, you can use it to get a string that provides a description of the problem using the MIDIOutGetErrorText() function. Now that we have taken a general look at the process of playing sounds, let's take a detailed look at all of the functions and structures.

function MIDIOutGetNumDevs   *mmsystem.pas*

Syntax

```
function MIDIOutGetNumDevs
  : UINT; stdcall;
```

Description

This function takes no parameters and simply returns the number of MIDI output devices found on a machine. Once you determine the number of devices, you can then query each device to determine its capabilities. Listing 4-12 shows how to do this using this function, the MIDIOutGetDevCaps() function, and the MIDIOUTCAPS structure.

Example

The code in Listing 4-12 from the MidClass.pas unit wraps this function in a method of the MidiOut class.

Listing 4-12: Getting the number of MidiOut devices and their capabilities on a system

```
function TMIDIOut.GetNumDevices : UINT;
begin
  result := MIDIOutGetNumDevs;
end;
function TMidiOut.GetMidiOutCaps(const ADeviceID: integer;
                          var AMMResult : MMRESULT;
                          var AMsg : string) : boolean;
begin
  AMMResult := MidiOutGetDevCaps(ADeviceID, @MidiOutCaps, CapStructSize);
  result := AMMResult=MMSYSERR_NOERROR;
  if NOT result then AMsg := GetMidiErrorString(AMMResult);
end;
```

function MIDIOutGetDevCaps   *mmsystem.pas*

Syntax

```
function MIDIOutGetDevCaps(
  uDeviceID: UINT;
  lpCaps: PMIDIOutCaps;
  uSize: UINT
  ): MMRESULT; stdcall;
```

Description

This function queries the MIDI output device identified by uDeviceID, determines its capabilities, and places that information in the LPCAPS structure. The result is returned in MMRESULT.

Parameters

uDeviceID: An integer (UINT) identifying a MIDI audio output device. It can be either a device identifier or the handle of an open MIDI audio output device. The MIDI_MAPPER constant can also be used as the device identifier. You can also use a properly cast device handle for this parameter.

lpCaps: The address of a MIDIOUTCAPS structure to be filled with information about the capabilities of the device specified by uDeviceID.

uSize: An integer (UINT) indicating the size of the MIDIOUTCAPS structure. Use SizeOf(MIDIOUTCAPS) to get this value.

Return Value

Returns MMSYSERR_NOERROR if successful. Otherwise, it returns one of the following errors: MMSYSERR_BADDEVICEID, indicating the device identifier specified is out of range; MMSYSERR_INVALPARAM, indicating the specified pointer or structure is invalid; MMSYSERR_NO-DRIVER, indicating that the driver has not been properly installed; or MMSYSERR_NOMEM, indicating that memory could not be allocated.

Example

See Listing 4-12.

The MIDIOUTCAPS structure holds information about a MIDI output device's capabilities. The members of that structure are described in Table 4-7; possible values for two of the members of this structure are shown in Tables 4-8 and 4-9. MIDIOUTCAPS and its related types are defined in mmsystem.pas as follows:

```
type
  PMidiOutCapsA = ^TMidiOutCapsA;
  PMidiOutCapsW = ^TMidiOutCapsW;
  PMidiOutCaps = PMidiOutCapsA;
  tagMIDIOUTCAPSA = record
    wMid: Word;                      { manufacturer ID }
    wPid: Word;                      { product ID }
```

4

Chapter

```
    vDriverVersion: MMVERSION;    { version of the driver }
    szPname: array[0..MAXPNAMELEN-1] of AnsiChar;  {product name (NULL
                                                terminated string) }
    wTechnology: Word;            { type of device }
    wVoices: Word;                { # of voices (internal synth only) }
    wNotes: Word;                 { max # of notes (internal synth only) }
    wChannelMask: Word;           { channels used (internal synth only) }
    dwSupport: DWORD;             { functionality supported by driver }
  end;
  tagMIDIOUTCAPSW = record
    wMid: Word;                   { manufacturer ID }
    wPid: Word;                   { product ID }
    vDriverVersion: MMVERSION;    { version of the driver }
    szPname: array[0..MAXPNAMELEN-1] of WideChar;  { product name (NULL
                                                terminated string) }
    wTechnology: Word;            { type of device }
    wVoices: Word;                { # of voices (internal synth only) }
    wNotes: Word;                 { max # of notes (internal synth only) }
    wChannelMask: Word;           { channels used (internal synth only) }
    dwSupport: DWORD;             { functionality supported by driver }
  end;
  tagMIDIOUTCAPS = tagMIDIOUTCAPSA;
  TMidiOutCapsA = tagMIDIOUTCAPSA;
  TMidiOutCapsW = tagMIDIOUTCAPSW;
  TMidiOutCaps = TMidiOutCapsA;
  MIDIOUTCAPSA = tagMIDIOUTCAPSA;
  MIDIOUTCAPSW = tagMIDIOUTCAPSW;
  MIDIOUTCAPS = MIDIOUTCAPSA;
```

Table 4-7: Members of the MIDIOUTCAPS structure

Field	Meaning
wMid	Manufacturer identifier of the device driver for the MIDI output device. For a list of identifiers, see the Microsoft Multimedia help file.
wPid	Product identifier of the MIDI output device. For a list of identifiers, see the Microsoft Multimedia help file.
vDriverVersion	Version number of the device driver for the MIDI output device. The high-order byte is the major version number, and the low-order byte is the minor version number.
szPname	Product name in a null-terminated string.
wTechnology	Flags describing the type of the MIDI output device. It can be one of the MOD_? flags described in Table 4-8.

Field	Meaning
wVoices	Number of voices supported by an internal synthesizer device. If the device is a port, this member is not meaningful and is set to 0.
wNotes	Maximum number of simultaneous notes that can be played by an internal synthesizer device. If the device is a port, this member is not meaningful and should be set to 0.
wChannelMask	Channels that an internal synthesizer device responds to, where the least significant bit refers to channel 0 and the most significant bit to channel 15. Port devices that transmit on all channels set this member to $FFFF.
dwSupport	Optional functionality supported by the device. It can be one or more of the MIDICAPS_? flags described in Table 4-9.

Table 4-8: Flags for the wTechnology field of MIDIOUTCAPS

Flag	Meaning
MOD_MIDIPORT	Output port
MOD_SYNTH	Generic internal synthesizer
MOD_SQSYNTH	Square MIDI internal synthesizer
MOD_FMSYNTH	Frequency modulating (FM) internal synthesizer
MOD_MAPPER	MIDI mapper

Table 4-9: Flags for the dwSupport field of MIDIOUTCAPS

Flag	Meaning
MIDICAPS_VOLUME	Supports volume control
MIDICAPS_LRVOLUME	Supports separate left-right control of volume
MIDICAPS_CACHE	Supports caching
MIDICAPS_STREAM	Driver includes direct support for MidiStreamOut

Listing 4-13: Getting and displaying MIDI output device capabilities

```
procedure TfrmMidiOutDevicesProperties.FormCreate(Sender: TObject);
var
  FNumOutputDevices : Cardinal;
  FMidiOutCaps : TMidiOutCaps;
  k: integer;
  j: Integer;
  Node,
  FormatNode: TTreeNode;
begin
```

4

Chapter

```
  FNumOutputDevices := MidiOut.GetNumDevices;
  TreeView1.Items.Clear;
  for j := (FNumOutputDevices-1) downto 0 do     // Iterate
  begin
    MidiOutGetDevCaps(j, @FMidiOutCaps, SizeOf(TMidiOutCaps));
    Node := TreeView1.Items.AddChildFirst(nil, 'Device '+IntToStr(J+1));
    TreeView1.Items.AddChild(Node, 'Manufacturer ID: ' +
      IntToStr(FMidiOutCaps.wMid));
    TreeView1.Items.AddChild(Node, 'Product ID: ' +
      IntToStr(FMidiOutCaps.wPid));
    TreeView1.Items.AddChild(Node, 'Driver Version: ' +
      IntToStr(hi(FMidiOutCaps.vDriverVersion)) +
      '.' + IntToStr(lo(FMidiOutCaps.vDriverVersion)));
    TreeView1.Items.AddChild(Node, 'Product Name: ' +
      FMidiOutCaps.szPname);
    FormatNode := TreeView1.Items.AddChild(Node, 'Technologies
        Supported: ');
      if (((FMidiOutCaps.wTechnology and (1 shl MOD_MIDIPORT))=
        (1 shl MOD_MIDIPORT)))then TreeView1.Items.AddChild(FormatNode,
        'Midi Hardware Port');
      if (((FMidiOutCaps.wTechnology and (1 shl MOD_SQSYNTH))=
        (1 shl MOD_SQSYNTH))) then TreeView1.Items.AddChild(FormatNode,
        'Squarewave Synthesizer');
      if (((FMidiOutCaps.wTechnology and (1 shl MOD_MIDIPORT))=
        (1 shl MOD_MIDIPORT))) then TreeView1.Items.AddChild(FormatNode,
        'Midi Hardware Port');
      if (((FMidiOutCaps.wTechnology and (1 shl MOD_FMSYNTH))=
        (1 shl MOD_FMSYNTH))) then TreeView1.Items.AddChild(FormatNode,
        'FM Synthesizer');
      if (((FMidiOutCaps.wTechnology and (1 shl MOD_MAPPER))=
        (1 shl MOD_MAPPER))) then TreeView1.Items.AddChild(FormatNode,
        'Midi Mapper');
    FormatNode := TreeView1.Items.AddChild(Node, 'Functions Supported: ');
      for k := 0 to MidiFunctionTotal-1 do
        if (FMidiOutCaps.dwSupport and (1 shl (k+1))=(1 shl (k+1))) then
          TreeView1.Items.AddChild(FormatNode, MidiFunctionArray[k]);
  end;     // for Output devices
end;
```

function MIDIOutGetVolume   *mmsystem.pas*

Syntax

```
function MIDIOutGetVolume(
  hmo: HMIDIOUT;
  lpdwVolume: PDWORD
  ): MMRESULT; stdcall;
```

Description

This function retrieves the current volume level of the specified MIDI output device. Volume settings are interpreted logarithmically—the perceived increase in volume is the same when increasing the volume level from $5000 to $6000 as it is from $4000 to $5000. Since not all devices support volume changes, it is important to determine whether a particular device supports volume control. To do this, use the MIDICAPS_VOLUME flag to test the dwSupport member of the MIDIOUTCAPS structure (filled by the MIDIOutGetDevCaps() function). To determine whether the device supports left- and right-channel volume control, use the MIDICAPS_LRVOLUME flag to test the dwSupport member of the MIDIOUTCAPS structure (filled by MIDIOutGetDevCaps()).

Parameters

hMIDIOut: The handle of an open MIDI output device; can also be a device identifier or the handle of a MIDI stream. In the latter case, cast that MIDI stream to HMidiOut.

lpdwVolume: The address of a variable to be filled with the current volume setting. The low-order word pointed to contains the left channel volume setting, and the high-order word contains the right channel setting. A value of $FFFF represents full volume, and a value of $0000 is silence. If a device does not support both left and right volume control, the low-order word of the specified location contains the mono volume level. Values set by using the MIDIOutSetVolume() function are returned, whether the MIDI device supports those values or not.

Return Value

Returns MMSYSERR_NOERROR if successful. Otherwise, it returns one of the following errors: MMSYSERR_INVALHANDLE, indicating that the specified device handle is invalid; MMSYSERR_INVALPARAM, indicating

4

Chapter

the specified pointer or structure is invalid; MMSYSERR_NOMEM, indicating that memory could not be allocated; or MMSYSERR_NOT-SUPPORTED, indicating that the function is not supported.

Example

In the WavClass unit, the following type is defined for different volume levels: VolumePlaybackValue = (vpvSilent, vpvSoft, vpvMedium, vpvLoud, rpvFull).

This type is used for both waveform and MIDI playback. Note how this is used in Listing 4-14. Also note how we check to make sure that the system supports this feature and how we exit gracefully if it does not.

Listing 4-14: Using the MIDIOutGetVolume() function

```
function TMidiOut.AdjustVolume(var Volume : PDWORD; SetVol : boolean):
boolean;
var
  TempMidiCaps : TMidiOutCaps;
  ADeviceID : UINT;
begin
  result := False;
  if NOT MidiSupport.PlayDevAvailable then  // Need to open device
    begin
      ADeviceID := 0; // Many computers have just one MIDI device
      if NOT (MidiOutOpen(@AHandle, ADeviceID, DWORD(@MidiOutProc),
          DWORD(MainFormHandle), DWORD(callback_function))=0) then
        if ReportError(iodOutput, 0, 'Could not open MIDI Output')
            then exit
        else
      else
        MidiSupport.PlayDevAvailable := True
    end
  else // Device already open; get its ID the old way
  if NOT (MidiOutGetID(AHandle, @ADeviceID)=0)  then
    if ReportError(iodOutput, 0, 'Could get MIDI ID') then exit;
  CurrentMMResult := MidiOutGetDevCaps(ADeviceID, @TempMidiCaps, SizeOf(
          MIDIOUTCAPS));
  if ((CurrentMMResult=0) and ((TempMidiCaps.dwSupport and
          (1 shl MIDICAPS_VOLUME)) = (1 shl MIDICAPS_VOLUME))) then
    begin
      CurrentMMResult := MidiOutGetVolume(AHandle, Volume);
      if NOT (CurrentMMResult=0)  then
        if ReportError(iodOutput, 0, 'Could not get Volume') then exit;
      if SetVol then
```

```
        CurrentMMResult := MidiOutGetVolume(AHandle, Volume);
     if NOT (CurrentMMResult=0)  then
         if ReportError(iodOutput, 0, 'Could not set Volume') then exit;
     result := True;
   end
 else
   ShowMessage('This sound card does not support MIDI Volume');
end;
```

function MIDIOutSetVolume   *mmsystem.pas*

Syntax

```
function MIDIOutSetVolume(
  hmo: HMIDIOUT;
  dwVolume: DWORD
  ): MMRESULT; stdcall;
```

Description

This function sets the volume level of the specified MIDI output device for the current instance. Changing the volume on a handle changes it for an instance of the device, rather than changing the default volume for the device (and thus affecting all instances of the device). Not all devices support volume changes. To determine whether the device supports volume control, use the MIDICAPS_VOLUME flag to test the dwSupport member of the MIDIOUTCAPS structure (filled by the MIDIOutGetDevCaps() function). To determine whether the device supports volume control on both the left and right channels, use the MIDICAPS_LRVOLUME flag. Note that most devices do not support the full 16 bits of volume level control and will not use the high-order bits of the requested volume setting. For example, if a given device supports 4 bits of volume control, requested volume level values of $4000, $4FFF, and $43BE will all produce the same physical volume setting: $4000. The MIDIOutGetVolume() function returns the full 16-bit setting set with MIDIOutSetVolume(). Volume settings are interpreted logarithmically—the perceived increase in volume is the same when increasing the volume level from $5000 to $6000 as it is from $4000 to $5000.

4

Chapter

Parameters

> *hmo*: The handle of an open MIDI output device; or a device identifier or the handle of a MIDI stream, cast to hMidiOut.

> *dwVolume*: A DWORD indicating the new volume setting. The low-order word contains the left channel volume setting, and the high-order word contains the right channel setting. A value of 0xFFFF represents full volume, and a value of 0x0000 is silence. If a device does not support both left and right volume control, the low-order word specifies the volume level, and the high-order word is ignored.

Return Value

> Returns MMSYSERR_NOERROR if successful. Otherwise, it returns one of the following errors: MMSYSERR_INVALHANDLE, indicating that the specified device handle is invalid; MMSYSERR_NOMEM, indicating that memory could not be allocated; or MMSYSERR_NOTSUPPORTED, indicating that the function is not supported.

Example

> See Listing 4-14.

function MIDIOutGetErrorText   *mmsystem.pas*

Syntax

```
function MIDIOutGetErrorText(
 mmrError: MMRESULT;
 pszText: PChar;
 uSize: UINT
 ): MMRESULT; stdcall;
```

Description

> This function returns a textual description of the error identified by the given error number, mmrError. The error string is placed in the pszText parameter. See Listing 4-7 for how to set up a general utility routine to return these strings for both output and output return values.

Parameters

> *mmrError*: An MMRESULT error constant returned by one of the MidiOut functions.

pszText: The string explaining the error, mmrError.

uSize: An integer (UINT) indicating the size of the PChar buffer that holds the description of the error. In the MidClass unit, the constant MsgLength is set to 128, sufficient for any of the message strings.

Return Value

Returns MMSYSERR_NOERROR if successful. Otherwise, it returns one of the following errors: MMSYSERR_BADERRNUM indicating the specified error number is out of range; or MMSYSERR_INVALPARAM, indicating that the specified pointer or structure is invalid.

Example

Listing 4-7 reports both output and output errors. That's why its first parameter is IO_Direction, indicating input or output. The functions called in this procedure are input- or output-specific.

function MIDIOutOpen   *mmsystem.pas*

Syntax

```
function MIDIOutOpen(
  lphMIDIOut: PHMIDIOut;
  uDeviceID: UINT;
  dwCallback, dwInstance, dwFlags: DWORD
  ): MMRESULT; stdcall;
```

Description

This function opens the given MIDI output device for playing with the number uDeviceID. If successful, the parameter lphMIDIOut contains a handle for the device that will be used by other MidiOut functions.

Parameters

lphMIDIOut: A PhMidiOut value that is the handle identifying the open MIDI output device. This handle should be saved in a variable visible to other MIDI output functions so that they can use it when they are called.

uDeviceID: An integer identifying the MIDI audio output device to open. It can be either a device identifier or the MIDI_MAPPER constant. In

4

Chapter

the latter case, the function will select a MIDI audio output device capable of playing in the specified format.

dwCallback: The address of a fixed callback function, an event handle, or a handle of a window or thread called during MIDI audio playing to process messages related to the progress of playing. If no callback function is required, this value can be NULL (0). In the example, two alternate approaches are shown: a callback function and a callback window.

dwInstance: User instance data passed to the callback mechanism. This parameter is not used with the window callback mechanism and should be set to zero in that case.

dwFlags: Flags for opening the device. Those flags are given in Table 4-10:

Table 4-10: Flags for the dwFlags field of MIDIOutOpen()

Flags	Meaning
CALLBACK_EVENT	The dwCallback parameter is an event handle.
CALLBACK_FUNCTION	The dwCallback parameter is a callback procedure address.
CALLBACK_NULL	No callback mechanism. This is the default setting.
CALLBACK_THREAD	The dwCallback parameter is a thread handle.
CALLBACK_WINDOW	The dwCallback parameter is a window handle.

Return Value

Returns MMSYSERR_NOERROR if successful. Otherwise, it returns one of the following errors: MMSYSERR_ALLOCATED, indicating the specified resource is already allocated; MMSYSERR_BADDEVICEID, indicating the specified device identifier is out of range; MIDIERR_NODEVICE, indicating that no MIDI port was found (this error can only occur when the mapper is opened); MMSYSERR_INVALPARAM, indicating that the specified pointer or structure is invalid; or MMSYSERR_NOMEM, indicating that memory could not be allocated.

Example

The following segments of code and code listings show several ways to set up and manage a callback system for MIDI output. As in MIDI input, the main MIDI output callback routine shown in Listing 4-15 is in a DLL.

Those messages are sent to the calling application that responds to them in its DefaultHandler() procedure as shown in Listing 4-16. The opening method itself is shown in listing 4-17. As with MIDI input, we provide three different means of opening the device—with a callback window, a callback procedure, or no callback at all. We also define custom messages that are used at various places in the MidClass.pas unit. Those messages are defined as follows in the MidClass.pas unit:

```
const
  MidiIn_Started = WM_User + 160;       // For MidiInOpen callbacks
  MidiIn_Recording = WM_User + 161;     // For MidiInOpen callbacks
  MidiIn_Stop = WM_User + 162;          // For MidiInOpen callbacks
  MidiOut_Started = WM_User + 163;      // For MidiOutOpen callbacks
  MidiOut_Stop = WM_User + 164;         // For MidiOutOpen callbacks
  MidiOut_Finished = WM_User + 165;     // For MidiOutOpen callbacks
  MidiOut_SendLongMsg = WM_User + 166;  // For MM_MOM_DONE messages
  MidiOut_ShortMsgSent = WM_User + 167; // Keep track of melody notes
  MidiStream_TempoProp = WM_User + 168; // Sends info back to calling app
  MidiStream_TimeDivProp = WM_User + 169;// Sends info back to calling app
```

In Listing 4-15 from the MidCBakU.pas unit, we respond to the standard MIDI output messages in our callback routine.

Listing 4-15: MidiOut callback routine in DLL

```
procedure MidiOutProc(hMidiInHandle : HMIDIIN; uMsg : UINT;
    dwInstance, dwParam1, dwParam2 : DWord); export; stdcall;
var
  j: Integer;
  hCallingWindow : THandle;
begin
    hCallingWindow := dwInstance;
    case uMsg of
      MOM_Open : PostMessage (hCallingWindow, mm_MIM_Open, 0, 0);
      MOM_PositionCB: PostMessage (hCallingWindow, mm_MOM_PositionCB,
              0, 0);
      MOM_Done : PostMessage(hCallingWindow, mm_MOM_Done, 0, dwParam1);
      MOM_Close: PostMessage (hCallingWindow, mm_MOM_Close, 0, 0);
    end;
end;
```

Note how we use these standard messages and some of our custom messages in the calling application's DefaultHandler() procedure in Listing 4-16 (see screen output in Figure 4-8). These messages are particularly useful in sending either data or status information to the calling application to be displayed as text.

Listing 4-16: Responding to MIDI input and output messages in a main calling application

```
procedure TForm1.DefaultHandler(var Msg);
var
  TempStr : string;
  j: Integer; // for iterations
begin
  ErrorMsg := '';
  inherited DefaultHandler(Msg);
  case TMessage(Msg).Msg of
  MidiOut_SendLongMsg:
    begin
      memo1.Lines.Add('System Exclusive (MIDI Long) Message: ');
      memo1.Lines.Add(IntToStr(Integer(PMidiHdr
              (TMessage(Msg).lParam).lpdata^)));
    end;
    MidiOut_ShortMsgSent:
      begin
        memo1.Lines.Add('MIDI Short Message: ' + Format
                ('%x %x %x ', [LoByte(
                    LoWord(TMessage(Msg).lParam)), HiByte(LoWord(
                    TMessage(Msg).lParam)), LoByte(
                    LoWord(TMessage(Msg).lParam))]));
      end;
  MM_MOM_DONE:
    begin
      if (((PMidiHdr(TMessage(Msg).lParam).dwFlags and (1 shl MHDR_
                DONE)) <> 0)
        and (PMidiHdr(TMessage(Msg).lParam).dwBytesRecorded > 0)) then
      begin
        // First make sure it's a long message, not a MIDI Stream by
                checking first byte
        if PMidiHdr(TMessage(Msg).lParam).lpData[0]=Chr($F0) then
          begin
            TempStr := 'System Exclusive (MIDI Long) Message: ';
            MidiSupport.MainMIDIBuffer.Position := 0;
            for j := 0 to (PMidiHdr(TMessage(Msg).lParam)
                    .dwBytesRecorded-1) do
              begin
                if MidiSupport.MainMIDIBuffer.Position>
                  (MidiSupport.MainMIDIBufferSize -4) then break;
                MidiSupport.MainMIDIBuffer.Read(PMidiHdr
```

```
                    (TMessage(Msg).lParam).lpdata[j], SizeOf(PMidiHdr
                    (TMessage(Msg).lParam).lpdata[j]));
               TempStr := Concat(TempStr, GetByteStr(TMessage(Msg)
                       .lParam, j));
          end;    // for
        MidiOut.MidiSysExStatus := sysexOff;
        MidiOut.ResetAndCloseDevice;
      end
    else
    begin
      TempStr := 'Done Playing MIDI Stream';
      MidiOut.CloseMidiStream;
    end;
    memo1.Lines.Add(TempStr);
   end;
  end;
 MM_MOM_OPEN: memo1.Lines.Add('MIDI Output device opened');
 MM_MOM_CLOSE: memo1.Lines.Add('MIDI Output device closed');
 MM_MIM_DATA: Memo1.Lines.Add(Format
   ('Short MIDI Message: %x, %x, %x', [LoByte(LoWord(TMessage
             (Msg).lParam)),
     HiByte(LoWord(TMessage(Msg).lParam)),
     LoByte(HiWord(TMessage(Msg).lParam))]));
 MM_MIM_LONGDATA: MidiIn.ProcessLongData(PMidiHdr(TMessage
             (Msg).lParam));
 MidiStream_TempoProp: Memo1.Lines.Add(Format
   ('MIDI Tempo: %d', [TMessage(Msg).lParam]));
 MidiStream_TimeDivProp: Memo1.Lines.Add(Format
   ('MIDI Time Division: %d', [TMessage(Msg).lParam]));
 end;    // case
end;
```

Listing 4-17: Function for opening a MIDI output device with one of the following: a callback function, a callback window, or no callback

```
function TMidiOut.Open(AMidiOpenFormat : MidiOpenFormat): boolean;
begin
 case AMidiOpenFormat of  // (mofCallbackFunc, mofCallbackWind,
                             mofNoCallback)
  mofCallbackFunc: CurrentMMResult := MidiOutOpen(@AHandle, 0,
    DWORD(@MidiOutProc), Dword(MainFormHandle), callback_function);
  mofCallbackWind: CurrentMMResult := MidiOutOpen(@AHandle, 0,
    DWord(MainFormHandle), Dword(0), callback_Window);
  mofNoCallback: CurrentMMResult := midiOutOpen(@AHandle, $FFFF,
             0, 0, 0);
 end;    // case
 result := CurrentMMResult=MMSYSERR_NOERROR;
```

```
  MidiSupport.PlayDevAvailable := True;
end;
```

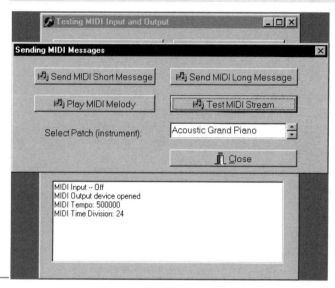

Figure 4-8

function MIDIOutClose   *mmsystem.pas*

Syntax

function MIDIOutClose(
  hMIDIOut: HMIDIOut
  ): MMRESULT; stdcall;

Description

This function closes the given MIDI output device. If the device is still playing, this function will fail.

Parameter

hMIDIOut: The handle of the MIDI audio output device. If the function succeeds, the handle is no longer valid.

Return Value

Returns MMSYSERR_NOERROR if successful. Otherwise, it returns one of the following errors: MMSYSERR_INVALHANDLE, indicating that the specified device handle is invalid; MMSYSERR_NODRIVER, indicating that no device driver is present; MMSYSERR_NOMEM, indicating that

memory could not be allocated; or MIDIRR_STILLPLAYING, indicating that one or more block buffers are still in the queue.

Example

Listing 4-18 shows how to properly shut down a playing device. For convenience, the process is divided into two routines, one that resets the MIDI output device and one that closes it. First, you need to be certain that all block buffers have been returned by calling MIDIOutReset(). MIDIOutStop() is probably not required but doesn't do any harm. Then you need to call MIDIOutUnprepareHeader() to clean up the buffers. The buffers can then be either disposed (their memory freed) or used again (prepared again). Finally, having done all of this you can call MIDIOutClose().

Listing 4-18: Three routines to properly shut down a MIDI output device

```
procedure TMidiOut.ResetAndCloseDevice;
begin
  Reset;
  Close;
  MidiSupport.PlayDevAvailable := False;
end;

function TMidiOut.Reset : boolean;
begin
  CurrentMMResult := midiOutPrepareHeader(AHandle,
    MidiSupport.FMidiHeader, SizeOf(MidiHdr));
  if CurrentMMResult=MMSYSERR_NOERROR then
    CurrentMMResult := MidiOutReset(AHandle);
  result := CurrentMMResult=MMSYSERR_NOERROR;
end;
function TMidiOut.Close: boolean;
begin
  CurrentMMResult := midiOutUnPrepareHeader(AHandle,
    MidiSupport.FMidiHeader, SizeOf(MidiHdr));
  if CurrentMMResult=MMSYSERR_NOERROR then
  CurrentMMResult := MidiOutClose(AHandle);
  result := CurrentMMResult=MMSYSERR_NOERROR;
end;
```

function MIDIOutPrepareHeader   *mmsystem.pas*

Syntax

```
function MIDIOutPrepareHeader(
hMIDIOut: HMIDIOUT;
lpMIDIOutHdr: PMIDIHdr;
uSize: UINT
): MMRESULT; stdcall;
```

Description

This function prepares a buffer for MIDI system-exclusive or stream buffer for output. As in waveform output, this is a temporary block. Before calling this function it is essential that you set the values of several of the MIDIHDR structure's fields, particularly lpData, dwBufferLength, and dwFlags. The lpData field should point to a valid PChar for which memory has been set and dwFlags must be set to zero.

Parameters

hMIDIOut: The handle of the MIDI output device or the handle of a MIDI stream cast to hMidiOut.

lpMIDIOutHdr: An address of a MIDIHDR structure that identifies the buffer to be prepared.

uSize: An integer indicating the size of the MIDIHDR structure. You can simply use the SizeOf(MIDIHDR) function for this parameter.

Return Value

Returns MMSYSERR_NOERROR if successful. Otherwise, it returns one of the following errors: MMSYSERR_INVALHANDLE, indicating that the specified device handle is invalid; or MMSYSERR_NOMEM, indicating that memory could not be allocated.

Example

Listing 4-19 shows how to use the MIDIOutPrepareHeader() function prior to sending a MIDI long message.

Listing 4-19 Sending a MIDI long message

```
function TMidiOut.SendLongMessage(MidiLongMessage : Array of byte;
                              ArraySize : Integer) : boolean;
var
```

```
  MsgLength : Integer;
  j: Integer;
begin
  result := False;
  MsgLength := ArraySize;
  Move(MidiLongMessage, MidiSupport.FMidiHeader.lpData^, MsgLength);
  MidiSupport.FMidiHeader.dwBytesRecorded := ArraySize;
  // Move(TempBuffer, MidiSupport.FBlockBuffers^, MsgLength);
  if MidiSupport.PlayDevAvailable then MidiOutClose(AHandle);
  CurrentMMResult := MidiOutOpen(@AHandle, 0, DWORD(@MidiOutProc),
    Dword(MainFormHandle), callback_function);
  MidiSupport.FMidiHeader.dwBufferLength := MsgLength;
  CurrentMMResult := MidiOutPrepareHeader(AHandle,
    MidiSupport.FMidiHeader, SizeOf(MidiHdr));
  CurrentMMResult := MidiOutLongMsg(AHandle,
    MidiSupport.FMidiHeader, SizeOf(MidiHdr));
  if CurrentMMResult<>MMSYSERR_NOERROR then
    if ReportError(iodOutput, CurrentMMResult, '') then exit;
  result := True;
  MidiSupport.PlayDevAvailable := True;
end;
```

function MIDIOutUnprepareHeader   *mmsystem.pas*

Syntax

```
function MIDIOutUnprepareHeader(
  hMIDIOut: HMIDIOUT;
  lpMIDIOutHdr: PMidiHdr;
  uSize: UINT
  ): MMRESULT; stdcall;
```

Description

This function cleans up the preparation performed by the MIDIOut-PrepareHeader() function. After passing a buffer to the device driver with the MIDIOutLongMsg() function, you must wait until the device driver is finished with the buffer before calling MIDIOutUnprepare-Header(). Unpreparing a buffer that has not been prepared has no effect, and the function returns zero. You must call this function before freeing the buffer.

Parameters

> *hMIDIOut*: The handle of the MIDI output device or the handle of a MIDI stream cast to hMidiOut.

> *lpMIDIOutHdr*: The address of a MIDIHDR structure that identifies the buffer to be unprepared.

> *uSize*: An integer indicating the size of the MIDIHDR structure. You can simply use the SizeOf(MIDIHDR) function for this parameter.

Return Value

Returns MMSYSERR_NOERROR if successful. Otherwise, it returns one of the following errors: MIDIERR_STILLPLAYING, indicating that the buffer pointed to by lpMIDIOutHdr is still in the queue; MMSYSERR_INVALHANDLE, indicating that the specified device handle is invalid; or MMSYSERR_INVALPARAM, indicating that the specified pointer or structure is invalid.

Example

Listing 4-18 shows how to properly shut down a MIDI output device using the MIDIOutUnprepareHeader() function.

function MIDIOutShortMsg   *mmsystem.pas*

Syntax

```
function MIDIOutShortMsg(
  hMIDIOut: HMIDIOUT;
  dwMsg: DWORD
  ): MMRESULT; stdcall;
```

Description

This function sends a short MIDI message to the specified MIDI output device. It can be used to send any MIDI message with the exception of system-exclusive and stream messages. The function might not return until the message has been sent to the output device. You can send short messages while streams are playing on the same device (although you will not be able to use a running status in this case).

Parameters

> *hMIDIOut*: The handle of the MIDI output device.

dwMsg: A MIDI message. The message is packed into a Double Word value with the first byte of the message in the low-order byte.

Return Value

Returns MMSYSERR_NOERROR if successful. Otherwise, it returns one of the following errors: MIDIERR_BADOPENMODE, indicating that the application sent a message without a status byte to a stream handle; MIDIERR_NOTREADY, indicating that the computer is busy with other data; or MMSYSERR_INVALHANDLE, indicating that the specified device handle is invalid.

Example

Listing 4-20 shows the general context for preparing to play a MIDI melody. Among other tasks, this method sets up the speed timer that will determine when to play the tones. The actual MIDIOutShortMsg() function is called in the high-level timer procedure in Listing 4-21. This example demonstrates how to send MIDI short messages at precise timing intervals.

Tip: The timer procedure, by nature, runs in its own thread. If you need to trace into it, you will find that it will be very slow going.

Listing 4-20: Sending a MIDI melody to a high-level timer procedure

```
procedure TMidiOut.PlayAMelody(AMelodyArray : TMelodyArray;
                               MidiMsgNum : Cardinal);
var
  j: Integer;
begin
  NotesInMelody := MidiMsgNum;
  if (MidiOutStatus=mosPlaying) or (MidiOutStatus=mosError) then
    if ReportError(iodOutput, 0,
      'Cannot play melody at this time; busy or error') then exit;
  SetLength(MidiSupport.MidiMelodyArray, MidiMsgNum);
  for j := 0 to MidiMsgNum-1 do    // Iterate
  begin
    MidiSupport.MidiMelodyArray[j].AMidiMessage :=
      AMelodyArray[j].AMidiMessage;
    MidiSupport.MidiMelodyArray[j].AMidiTimeInMs :=
      AMelodyArray[j].AMidiTimeInMs;
```

4

Chapter

```
end;    // for
NextShortMsg := 0;
CurrentPlaceInMs := 0;
CurrentMMResult := midiOutOpen(@AHandle, 1, 0, 0, 0);
if NOT CurrentMMResult=MMSYSERR_NOERROR then
  begin
    ReportError(iodOutput, 0, 'Could not Open MIDI Output Device');
    MidiOutStatus := mosError;
    exit;
  end;
MidiSupport.PlayDevAvailable := true;
// First send a message to set the proper patch
SendANote(BuildMidiMessage(CurrentPatch[CurrentMidiChannel],
  $CO + CurrentMidiChannel, 0));
if NOT MidiSupport.SetupHighResTimer then
  begin
    MidiOutStatus := mosError;
    if ReportError(iodOutput, 0, 'Could not Create Timer')  then
      exit;
  end;
  MidiOutStatus := mosPlaying;
end;
```

Listing 4-21: A high-resolution MIDI timer that sends MIDI messages at precise intervals

```
procedure MidiTimerProc(hMidiTimerHandle : UINT; uMsg : UINT;
    dwUser, dwParam1, dwParam2 : DWord);  stdcall;
var
  j: Integer;
begin
  for j := NextShortMsg to MidiOut.NotesInMelody-1 do
  // Iterate (Notes on/off)
    begin
    if MidiSupport.MidiMelodyArray[j].AMidiTimeInMs =
      CurrentPlaceInMs then
      begin
        MidiOut.CurrentMMResult := MidiOutShortMsg(MidiOut.AHandle,
          MidiSupport.MidiMelodyArray[j].AMidiMessage);
        NextShortMsg := j + 1;        // no need to check older messages
        PostMessage(dwUser, MidiOut_ShortMsgSent, 0,
          MidiSupport.MidiMelodyArray[j].AMidiMessage);
      end;
    end;
  inc(CurrentPlaceInMs);
  if NextShortMsg >= MidiOut.NotesInMelody then  // processed all of them
    begin
```

```
      MidiSupport.KillHighResTimer;
      MidiOut.ResetAndCloseDevice;
      MidiOut.MidiOutStatus := mosDonePlaying
    end;
end;
```

function MIDIOutLongMsg   *mmsystem.pas*

Syntax

```
function MIDIOutLongMsg(
  hMIDIOut: HMIDIOUT;
  lpMIDIOutHdr: PMidiHdr;
  uSize: UINT
  ): MMRESULT; stdcall;
```

Description

This function sends a system-exclusive MIDI message to the specified MIDI output device. Before the buffer is passed to MIDIOutLongMsg(), it must be prepared by using the MIDIOutPrepareHeader() function. The MIDI output device driver determines whether the data will be sent synchronously or asynchronously.

Parameters

hMIDIOut: The handle of the MIDI output device.

lpMIDIOutHdr: The address of a MIDIHDR structure that identifies the buffer to be unprepared.

uSize: An integer indicating the size of the MIDIHDR structure. You can simply use the SizeOf(MIDIHDR) function for this parameter.

Return Value

Returns MMSYSERR_NOERROR if successful. Otherwise, it returns one of the following errors: MIDIERR_NOTREADY, indicating that the computer is busy with other data; MIDIERR_UNPREPARED, indicating that the buffer pointed to by lpMidiOutHdr has not been prepared; MMSYSERR_INVALHANDLE, indicating that the specified device handle is invalid; or MMSYSERR_INVALPARAM, indicating that the specified pointer or structure is invalid.

4

Chapter

Example

See Listing 4-18.

function MIDIOutReset   *mmsystem.pas*

Syntax

```
function MIDIOutReset(
hMIDIOut: HMIDIOut
): MMRESULT; stdcall;
```

Description

This function turns off all notes on all MIDI channels for the specified MIDI output device. Pending system-exclusive or stream output buffers are returned to the callback function. The MHDR_DONE flag is set in the dwFlags member of the MIDIHDR structure. This function does not send an EOX (end-of-exclusive) byte when it terminates a system-exclusive message; applications are responsible for doing this. If the application terminates a system-exclusive message without first sending an EOX byte, this can cause problems for the receiving device. To turn off all notes, you must send a note-off message for each note in each channel. You must also turn off the sustain controller for each channel.

Parameter

hMIDIOut: The handle of the MIDI output device or the handle of a MIDI stream cast to hMidiOut. If the function succeeds, the handle is no longer valid.

Return Value

Returns MMSYSERR_NOERROR if successful. Otherwise, it returns the error MMSYSERR_INVALHANDLE, indicating that the specified device handle is invalid.

Example

See Listing 4-18.

function MIDIOutCachePatches   *mmsystem.pas*

Syntax

```
function MIDIOutCachePatches(
hMIDIOut: HMIDIOUT;
uBank: UINT;
lpwPatchArray: PWord;
uFlags: UINT
): MMRESULT; stdcall;
```

Description

This function requests that an internal MIDI synthesizer device preload and cache a particular set of patches. Not every synthesizer is capable of keeping all of the patches loaded simultaneously; some must load patch data from disk when they receive MIDI program change messages. To see if a device supports patch caching, use the MIDICAPS_CACHE flag to test the dwSupport member of the MIDIOUTCAPS structure filled by the MIDIOutGetDevCaps() function. Caching patches can improve performance by ensuring that the specified patches are immediately available. Each element in the PatchArray represents one of the 128 patches and has bits set for each of the 16 MIDI channels that use the particular patch. The least significant bit represents physical channel 0, and the most significant bit represents physical channel 15 ($0F).

Parameters

hMIDIOut: The handle of the MIDI audio input device. It must be an internal MIDI synthesizer or the handle of a MIDI stream, cast to hMidiOut.

uBank: The bank of patches to be used. Set this parameter to zero to cache the default patch bank.

lpwPatchArray: The address of the PatchArray pointing to the array of patches to be cached or uncached.

uFlags: Flags indicating options to be used in the caching operation. These are given in Table 4-11.

4

Chapter

Table 4-II: Flags for the uFlags field of MIDIOutCachePatches()

Flag	Meaning
MIDI_CACHE_ALL	Cache all of the specified patches. If all patches cannot be cached, then do the following: cache none, clear PatchArray, and return MMSYSERR_NOMEM.
MIDI_CACHE_BESTFIT	Try to cache all of the specified patches. If all patches cannot be cached, then cache as many patches as possible, change PatchArray to reflect which patches were cached, and return MMSYSERR_NOMEM.
MIDI_CACHE_QUERY	Change PatchArray to indicate which patches are currently cached.
MIDI_UNCACHE	Uncache the specified patches and clear PatchArray.

Return Value

Returns MMSYSERR_NOERROR if successful. Otherwise, it returns one of the following errors: MMSYSERR_INVALFLAG, indicating that the flag specified by wFlags is invalid; MMSYSERR_INVALHANDLE, indicating that the specified device handle is invalid; MMSYSERR_INVALPARAM, indicating that the array pointed to by lpwPatchArray is invalid; MMSYSERR_NOMEM, indicating that memory could not be allocated; or MMSYSERR_NOTSUPPORTED, indicating that the specified device is synchronous and does not support pausing.

Example

Listing 4-22 shows how to cache patches—normal MIDI patches or drum patches. Note that the parameter to this function allows you to choose either or both types of patches.

Listing 4-22: Caching MIDI patches

```
function TMidiOut.CachePatches(CachePatches : PatchesToCache) : boolean;
var
  TempMidiCaps : TMidiOutCaps;
  ADeviceID : UINT;
begin
  result := False;
  if NOT MidiSupport.PlayDevAvailable then  // Need to open device
    begin
      ADeviceID := 0; // Many computers have just one MIDI device
      if NOT (MidiOutOpen(@AHandle, ADeviceID, DWORD(@MidiOutProc),
          DWORD(MainFormHandle), DWORD(callback_function))=0) then
```

```
            if ReportError(iodOutput, 0, 'Could not open MIDI Output')
                      then exit
         else
       else
         MidiSupport.PlayDevAvailable := True
    end
  else // Device already open; get its ID the old way
  if NOT (MidiOutGetID(AHandle, @ADeviceID)=0)  then
    if ReportError(iodOutput, 0, 'Could get MIDI ID') then exit;
  CurrentMMResult := MidiOutGetDevCaps(ADeviceID, @TempMidiCaps, SizeOf(
                                  MIDIOUTCAPS));
  if ((CurrentMMResult=0) and ((TempMidiCaps.dwSupport and (1 shl
                    MIDICAPS_CACHE)) = (1 shl MIDICAPS_CACHE))) then
    if CachePatches=CacheBoth then
      begin
        MidiOutCacheDrumPatches(AHandle, ADeviceID, @DrumPatchArray,
                          MIDI_CACHE_QUERY);
        MidiOutCachePatches(AHandle, ADeviceID, @InstPatchArray,
                          MIDI_CACHE_QUERY);
      end
    else if CachePatches=CacheDrum then
        MidiOutCacheDrumPatches(AHandle, ADeviceID, @DrumPatchArray,
                          MIDI_CACHE_QUERY)
    else MidiOutCachePatches(AHandle, ADeviceID, @InstPatchArray,
                          MIDI_CACHE_QUERY);
  result := True;
end;
```

function MIDIOutCacheDrumPatches   *mmsystem.pas*

Syntax

```
function MIDIOutCacheDrumPatches(
  hMIDIOut: HMIDIOUT;
  uPatch: UINT;
  lpwKeyArray: PWord;
  uFlags: UINT
  ): MMRESULT; stdcall;
```

Description

This function requests that an internal MIDI synthesizer device preload
and cache a specified set of key-based percussion patches. Not every synthesizer is capable of keeping all of the percussion patches loaded
simultaneously; some must load patch data from disk when they receive

MIDI program change messages. To see if a device supports patch caching, use the MIDICAPS_CACHE flag to test the dwSupport member of the MIDIOUTCAPS structure filled by the MIDIOutGetDevCaps() function. Caching patches can improve performance by ensuring that the specified patches are immediately available. Each element in the KeyArray represents one of the 128 key-based percussion patches and has bits set for each of the 16 MIDI channels that use the particular patch. The least significant bit represents physical channel 0, and the most significant bit represents physical channel 15 ($0F).

Parameters

hMIDIOut: The handle of the MIDI input device. It must be an internal MIDI synthesizer or the handle of a MIDI stream, cast to hMidiOut.

uPatch: The drum patch number to be used. Set this parameter to zero to cache the default drum patch.

lpwKeyArray: The address of the KeyArray pointing to the key numbers of the specified percussion patches to be cached or uncached.

uFlags: Flags indicating options to be used in the caching operation. These are given in Table 4-12.

Table 4-12: Flags for the uFlag field of MIDIOutCacheDrumPatches()

Flag	Meaning
MIDI_CACHE_ALL	Cache all of the specified patches. If all patches cannot be cached, then do the following: cache none, clear KeyArray, and return MMSYSERR_NOMEM.
MIDI_CACHE_BESTFIT	Try to cache all of the specified patches. If all patches cannot be cached, than cache as many patches as possible, change KeyArray to reflect which patches were cached, and return MMSYSERR_NOMEM.
MIDI_CACHE_QUERY	Change KeyArray to indicate which patches are currently cached.
MIDI_UNCACHE	Uncache the specified patches and clear KeyArray.

Return Value

Returns MMSYSERR_NOERROR if successful. Otherwise, it returns one of the following errors: MMSYSERR_INVALFLAG, indicating that the flag specified by uFlags is invalid; MMSYSERR_INVALHANDLE, indicating that the specified device handle is invalid; MMSYSERR_INVALPARAM, indicating that the array pointed to by lpwPatchArray is invalid; MMSYSERR_NOMEM, indicating that memory could not be allocated; or MMSYSERR_NOTSUPPORTED, indicating that the specified device is synchronous and does not support pausing.

Example

See Listing 4-22.

function MIDIOutGetID   mmsystem.pas

Syntax

```
function MIDIOutGetID(
  hMIDIOut: HMIDIOut;
  lpuDeviceID: PUINT
  ): MMRESULT; stdcall;
```

Description

This function gets the device identifier for the given MIDI output device. It is here mainly as a support for backward compatibility. New applications can cast a handle of the device rather than retrieving the device identifier.

Parameters

hMIDIOut: The handle of the MIDI audio output device. If the function succeeds, the handle is no longer valid.

lpuDeviceID: A PUINT value that will receive the device identifier.

Return Value

Returns MMSYSERR_NOERROR if successful. Otherwise, it returns one of the following errors: MMSYSERR_INVALHANDLE, indicating that the specified device handle is invalid; MMSYSERR_NODRIVER, indicating that no device driver is present; MMSYSERR_NOMEM, indicating that memory could not be allocated; or MIDIRR_STILLPLAYING, indicating that one or more block buffers are still in the queue.

Example

Listing 4-22 shows how to get the MidiOut ID in the context of caching patches.

4

Chapter

function MIDIOutMessage   *mmsystem.pas*

Syntax

```
function MIDIOutMessage(
hMIDIOut: HMIDIOut;
uMessage: UINT;
dw1, dw2: DWORD
): MMRESULT; stdcall;
```

Description

This function sends messages to the MIDI device drivers. It is used only for driver-specific messages that are not supported by the MIDI API.

Parameters

hMIDIOut: The handle of the MIDI audio output device or the handle of a MIDI stream cast to hMidiOut.

uMessage: An integer indicating message to send.

dw1, dw2: Two DWORD parameters for message parameters.

Return Value

Returns a DWORD indicating the return value of the message.

Example

These messages are driver-specific, so we cannot show an example here that will definitely work on your system. To use this function you need to know the specific messages that your sound card and its driver(s) will accept. Here is a general example of how you might call this function:

```
procedure TMIDIOut.SendMessage(ADriverMessage: UINT; MsgParam1,
        MsgParam2: DWORD);
begin
  MIDIOutMessage(AHandle, ADriverMessage, MsgParam1, MsgParam2);
end;
```

MIDI Streams

When we worked with waveform audio in the last chapter we created our own memory stream for input and output. With MIDI we have some built-in stream support. There are a several structures that support MIDI

streams. The first one, MIDIHDR, we've seen already. When used with a
MIDI stream, the lpData member of the MIDIHDR structure points to a
stream buffer, and the dwBufferLength member specifies the actual size
of this buffer. The dwBytesRecorded member of MIDIHDR specifies the
number of bytes in the buffer that are actually used by the MIDI events.
Naturally, this value must be less than or equal to the value specified by
dwBufferLength.

Each MIDI event in the stream buffer is specified by a MIDIEVENT structure (see Table 4-13). This structure contains the time for the event, a
stream identifier, an event code, and (where appropriate) the parameters
for the event. Every MIDIEVENT structure must begin on a Double Word
boundary, e.g., some values may need to be padded to 4 bytes. I should
point out before going any further that I encountered a serious problem
using the MIDIEVENT structure in the sample program to send a series of
tones to the MIDI stream, which I will discuss presently. The MIDIEVENT
structure is defined as follows in mmsystem.pas:

```
PMidiEvent = ^TMidiEvent;
  midievent_tag = record
    dwDeltaTime: DWORD;              { Ticks since last event }
    dwStreamID: DWORD;              { Reserved; must be zero }
    dwEvent: DWORD;                 { Event type and parameters }
    dwParms: array[0..0] of DWORD;  { Parameters if this is a long event }
  end;
TMidiEvent = midievent_tag;
MIDIEVENT = midievent_tag;
```

Table 4-13: MIDIEVENT fields and their meanings

Field	Meaning
dwDeltaTime	Time, in MIDI ticks, between the previous event and the current event. The length of a tick is defined by the time format and could be affected by the tempo associated with the stream. This definition is identical to the specification for a tick in a standard MIDI file.
dwStreamID	Reserved; must be zero. This field will be set by the Windows operating system after the stream is properly opened.
dwEvent	Event code and event parameters or length. When sending notes, the pitch information will be included in the event code. You can parse this information by using the MEVT_EVENTTYPE and MEVT_EVENTPARM macros.

4

Chapter

Field	Meaning
dwEvent (cont.)	The high byte of this member contains one or more of the following constants and an event code. Either MEVT_F_LONG or MEVT_F_SHORT must be specified, but MEVT_F_CALLBACK is optional. Table 4-14 lists these and other possible constants that might be included in this member. One of the last seven constants will be part of the remainder of the high byte of this member.

Table 4-14: Constants that can be included in the dwEvent member of MIDIEVENT

Constant	Meaning
MEVT_F_CALLBACK	The system will generate a callback when the event is about to be executed.
MEVT_F_LONG	The event to be sent is a long event. The low 24 bits of the dwEvent field will contain the length of the event parameters.
MEVT_F_SHORT	The event to be sent is a short event. The event parameters are contained in the low 24 bits of the dwEvent field.
MEVT_COMMENT	Indicates a long event. This event is intended to store commentary information about a stream. This information might be useful in authoring programs or sequencers if the stream data were to be stored in a file in stream format. In a buffer containing this data, the zero byte identifies the comment class and subsequent bytes contain the comment data itself.
MEVT_LONGMSG	Indicates a long event. The event data will be transmitted verbatim. The event data is assumed to be system-exclusive data; a running status will be cleared when the event is executed and a running status from any previous events will not be applied to any channel events in the event data. You should not use this event to send a group of channel messages at the same time; instead, you should use a set of MEVT_SHORTMSG events with zero delta times.
MEVT_NOP	Indicates a short event that will act as a placeholder; it does nothing. The low 24 bits are ignored. Even though it serves no particular function, this event will still generate a callback if MEVT_F_CALLBACK is set in the dwEvent field.
MEVT_SHORTMSG	Indicates a short event. The data in the low 24 bits of the dwEvent field is a MIDI short message.

Constant	Meaning
MEVT_TEMPO	Indicates a short event. The data in the low 24 bits of the dwEvent field contain the new tempo for following events. The tempo is specified in the same format as it is for the tempo change meta-event in a MIDI file, that is, in microseconds per quarter note. (This event will have no effect if the time format specified for the stream is SMPTE time.)
MEVT_VERSION	Indicates a long event. The event data must contain a MIDISTRMBUFFVER structure.

When I sent simple note-playing data in this structure, the MIDIStream-Out() function failed. Fortunately, I discovered that another Delphi developer, Manuel Jander, had worked with MIDI streams and had come up with a modified structure that worked. Based on his code, I defined the following record, which omitted the last field—a field that is not used with MIDI short messages in a stream:

```
type
ShortMidiEvent = record
  dwDeltaTime : DWord;
  dwStreamID : DWord;
  dwEvent : DWord;
end;
```

The code shown in Listing 4-23 shows how to initialize each of the main fields you are responsible for, the dwDeltaTime field and the dwEvent field. First we fill an array of DWords with the intervals between time events and then we fill an array of ShortMidiEvents with note data and control data. The control data consists of three byte values: MEVT_F_CALLBACK, MEVT_F_SHORT, and MEVT_SHORTMSG, all of which are OR-ed together and then OR-ed with the pitch byte. All of this is preparatory to playing the opening phrase of Beethoven's "Ode to Joy" from the *Ninth Symphony*, the same example we used in sending MIDI short messages.

Listing 4-23: Preparing data for a MIDI stream

```
procedure TMIDIMsgDlg.btnTestMidiStreamClick(Sender: Tobject);
var
  j: Integer;
  DeltaTimeArray,
  EventArray : array of DWord;
```

```
   MidiEventFlags : DWORD;
   TestMidiEvent : array of ShortMidiEvent;
begin
  MidiEventFlags := MEVT_F_CALLBACK or MEVT_F_SHORT or MEVT_SHORTMSG;
  // will be "ORed" with event
  SetLength(TestMIDIEvent, 30);
  SetLength(EventArray, 30);
  SetLength(DeltaTimeArray, 30);
  DeltaTimeArray[0] := MakeLong(0, 0);
  j := 1;
  while j < 25 do
  begin       // notes of equal length, each successive one starting
              // when previous ends
     DeltaTimeArray[j] := 46;
     DeltaTimeArray[j+1] := 0;
     inc(j, 2);
  end;       // while
  DeltaTimeArray[25] := 69;
  DeltaTimeArray[26] := 0;
  DeltaTimeArray[27] := 23;
  DeltaTimeArray[28] := 0;
  DeltaTimeArray[29] := 200;
  for j := 0 to 29 do
  case j of    //
    0, 2, 12, 22, 24 : EventArray[j] := C_Start;
    1, 3, 13, 23, 25 : EventArray[j] := C_Stop;
    4, 10            : EventArray[j] := D_Flat_Start;
    5, 11            : EventArray[j] := D_Flat_Stop;
    6, 8             : EventArray[j] := E_Flat_Start;
    7, 9             : EventArray[j] := E_Flat_Stop;
    14, 20, 26, 28   : EventArray[j] := B_Flat_Start;
    15, 21, 27, 29   : EventArray[j] := B_Flat_Stop;
    16, 18           : EventArray[j] := A_Flat_Start;
    17, 19           : EventArray[j] := A_Flat_Stop;
  end;    // case

  for j := 0 to 29 do                      // Iterate
  with TestMIDIEvent[j] do
   begin
     dwDeltaTime := DeltaTimeArray[j];  //DWord(0); {}
     dwStreamID := MakeLong(0, 0); {   }
     dwEvent :=  EventArray[j] or MidiEventFlags;
   end;    // with
   // Now play beginning of "Ode to Joy" from Beethoven's Ninth Symphony
      MidiOut.PlayMidiStream({TestMidi}TestMIDIEvent {EventArray}, 30);
end;
```

As we've seen, the MIDIEVENT structure describes a MIDI event in a stream buffer. The other new structure, MIDISTRMBUFFVER, contains version information for a long MIDI event of the MEVT_VERSION type. MIDISTRMBUFFVER is defined in mmsystem.pas as follows:

```
PMidiStrmBuffVer = ^TMidiStrmBuffVer;
midistrmbuffver_tag = record
  dwVersion: DWORD;               { Stream buffer format version }
  dwMid: DWORD;                   { Manufacturer ID as defined in MMREG.H }
  dwOEMVersion: DWORD;            { Manufacturer version for custom ext }
end;
TMidiStrmBuffVer = midistrmbuffver_tag;
MIDISTRMBUFFVER = midistrmbuffver_tag;
```

There are also various MIDI stream functions that are quite similar in structure to ones we've seen already. However, their behavior is a bit different, so read the descriptions carefully.

function MIDIStreamOpen *mmsystem.pas*

Syntax

```
function MIDIStreamOpen(
  phms: PHMIDISTRM;
  puDeviceID: PUINT;
  cMIDI, dwCallback, dwInstance, fdwOpen: DWORD
  ): MMRESULT; stdcall
```

Description

This function opens a MIDI stream for output. By default, the device is opened in paused mode. The stream handle retrieved by this function must be used in all subsequent references to the stream.

Parameters

phms: A stream handle variable containing the address returned by the function. This handle should be saved in a variable visible to other MIDI output functions so that they can use it when they are called.

puDeviceID: An integer pointing to the address of the MIDI device identifier. The device is opened on behalf of the stream and closed again when the stream is closed.

cMIDI: Reserved; must be set to 1.

4

Chapter

dwCallback: A DWORD containing the address of a callback function, an event handle, a thread identifier, or a handle of a window or thread called during MIDI playback to process messages related to the progress of the playback. If no callback mechanism is desired, specify NULL for this parameter.

dwInstance: Instance data that is returned to the application with every callback function. Data is application-specific.

fdwOpen: Callback flag for opening the device; it must be one of the values given in Table 4-15.

Table 4-15: Callback flags for the fdwOpen field of MIDIStreamOpen

Flag	Meaning
CALLBACK_EVENT	The dwCallback parameter is an event handle.
CALLBACK_FUNCTION	The dwCallback parameter is a callback procedure address.
CALLBACK_NULL	No callback mechanism. This is the default setting.
CALLBACK_THREAD	The dwCallback parameter is a thread handle.
CALLBACK_WINDOW	The dwCallback parameter is a window handle.

Return Value

Returns MMSYSERR_NOERROR if successful. Otherwise, it returns one of the following errors: MMSYSERR_BADDEVICEID, indicating the specified device identifier is out of range; MMSYSERR_INVALPARAM, indicating that the specified pointer or structure is invalid; or MMSYSERR_NOMEM, indicating that memory could not be allocated.

Example

Listing 4-24 shows how to open a MIDI stream for playing.

Listing 4-24: Opening a MIDI stream and playing a MIDI melody from stream data

```
procedure TMidiOut.PlayMidiStream(AMidiStream : array of ShortMidiEvent;
              MidiMsgNum : Cardinal);
var
  TempPChar: Array [0..1024] of Char absolute AMidiStream;
  j: Integer;
  TempBuffer : array of Byte;
  BufferSize : Cardinal;
begin
// First set up the data buffer
```

```
   BufferSize := MidiMsgNum * SizeOf(ShortMidiEvent);
   SetLength(TempBuffer, MidiMsgNum*16);
   MidiSupport.FMidiHeader.dwBytesRecorded := SizeOf(ShortMidiEvent)
               * MidiMsgNum;
   MidiSupport.FMidiHeader.dwFlags := 0;
   Move(AMidiStream {TempBuffer}, MidiSupport.FMidiHeader.lpData^,
     MidiSupport.FMidiHeader.dwBytesRecorded);
// Next Open the Stream
   MidiSupport.Dev^ := 1;
   CurrentMMResult := midiStreamOpen(@MidiSupport.FMidiStream, MidiSupport
               .Dev, 1,
     MainFormHandle, 0, CallBack_Window);
   if CurrentMMResult<>MMSYSERR_NOERROR then
     if ReportError(iodOutput, CurrentMMResult, '') then exit;
   midiStreamPause(MidiSupport.FMidiStream);
   // Get default midi stream properties and send back to calling app for
   // Possible printing
   MidiSupport.MidiPropertyTempo.cbStruct :=  SizeOf(MIDIPROPTEMPO);
   MidiSupport.MidiPropertyTimeDivision.cbStruct := SizeOf
               (MIDIPROPTIMEDIV);
   MidiStreamProperty(MidiSupport.FMidiStream, @MidiSupport
               .MidiPropertyTempo,
     MIDIPROP_GET or MIDIPROP_TEMPO);
   MidiStreamProperty(MidiSupport.FMidiStream,
     @MidiSupport.MidiPropertyTimeDivision, MIDIPROP_GET or
               MIDIPROP_TIMEDIV);
   // Now send the info  back to the calling app
   PostMessage(MainFormHandle, MidiStream_TempoProp, 0,
     DWord(MidiSupport.MidiPropertyTempo.dwTempo));
   PostMessage(MainFormHandle, MidiStream_TimeDivProp, 0,
     DWord(MidiSupport.MidiPropertyTimeDivision.dwTimeDiv));
   // Send Midi Stream to output device, checking each step for errors
   // The HMidiOut type casting in the next call is a good idea
   CurrentMMResult :=
midiOutPrepareHeader(HMidiOut(MidiSupport.FMidiStream),
     MidiSupport.FMidiHeader, SizeOf(MidiHdr));
   if CurrentMMResult = MMSYSERR_NOERROR then
     CurrentMMResult := midiStreamRestart(MidiSupport.FMidiStream)
     else
       if ReportError(iodOutput, CurrentMMResult, '') then exit;
   if CurrentMMResult = MMSYSERR_NOERROR then
     CurrentMMResult := midiStreamOut(MidiSupport.FMidiStream,
     MidiSupport.FMidiHeader, SizeOf(MidiHdr));
   if NOT CurrentMMResult = MMSYSERR_NOERROR then if
     ReportError(iodOutput, CurrentMMResult, '') then exit;
end;
```

4

Chapter

function MIDIStreamClose   *mmsystem.pas*

Syntax

```
function MIDIStreamClose(
hms: HMIDISTRM
): MMRESULT; stdcall;
```

Description

This function closes an open MIDI stream.

Parameter

hms: The handle of the MIDI stream returned by the MIDIStreamOpen()
function.

Return Value

Returns MMSYSERR_NOERROR if successful. Otherwise, it returns
MMSYSERR_INVALHANDLE, indicating that the specified device handle
is invalid.

Example

Listing 4-25 shows how to properly close a MIDI stream.

Listing 4-25: Shutting down a MIDI stream

```
procedure TMidiOut.CloseMidiStream;
begin
  CurrentMMResult := midiOutUnPrepareHeader(HMidiOut
                 (MidiSupport.FMidiStream),
    MidiSupport.FMidiHeader, SizeOf(MidiHdr));
  if CurrentMMResult = MMSYSERR_NOERROR then
    CurrentMMResult := midiStreamStop(MidiSupport.FMidiStream);
  if CurrentMMResult = MMSYSERR_NOERROR then
    CurrentMMResult := midiStreamClose(MidiSupport.FMidiStream);
  if NOT CurrentMMResult = MMSYSERR_NOERROR then if
    ReportError(iodOutput, 0, 'Error Closing MIDI Stream') then exit;
  MidiOut.MM_Time.wType := TIME_MIDI;
  CurrentMMResult := midiStreamPosition(MidiSupport.FMidiStream,
    MidiOut.MM_Time, SizeOf(MMTime));
  if NOT CurrentMMResult = MMSYSERR_NOERROR then if
    ReportError(iodOutput, CurrentMMResult, '') then exit;
end;
```

function MIDIStreamProperty   *mmsystem.pas*

Syntax

```
function MIDIStreamProperty(
  hms: HMIDISTRM;
  lpPropData: PBYTE;
  dwProperty: DWORD
  ): MMRESULT; stdcall;
```

Description

This function sets or retrieves properties of a MIDI data stream associated with a MIDI output device. These properties are the default
properties defined by the system. Driver writers can implement and
document their own properties.

Parameters

hms: The handle of the MIDI device with which the property is
associated.

lpPropData: A byte holding the address of the property data.

dwProperty: A DWORD containing the flags that specify the action to
perform and that identify the appropriate property of the MIDI data
stream. Therefore, the MIDIStreamProperty() function requires setting two flags: one flag (either MIDIPROP_GET or MIDIPROP_SET)
specifies the action; the other flag identifies the specific property to
examine or edit. See Table 4-16.

Table 4-16: Flags for the dwProperty field of MIDIStreamProperty()

Flag	Meaning
MIDIPROP_GET	Retrieves the given property's current setting.
MIDIPROP_SET	Sets the given property's setting.
MIDIPROP_TEMPO	Retrieves the tempo property. The lpPropData parameter points to a MIDIPROPTEMPO structure. The current tempo value can be retrieved at any time. Output devices generally set the tempo by inserting MEVT_TEMPO events into the MIDI data.

4

Chapter

Flag	Meaning
MIDIPROP_TIMEDIV	Specifies the time division property. You can either retrieve or set this property. The lpPropData parameter points to a MIDIPROPTIMEDIV structure. This property can be set only when the device is stopped.

Return Value

Returns MMSYSERR_NOERROR if successful. Otherwise, it returns one of the following errors: MMSYSERR_INVALHANDLE, indicating that the specified handle is not a stream handle; or MMSYSERR_INVALPARAM, indicating that the given handle or flags parameter is invalid.

Two structures, MIDIPROPTIMEDIV and MIDIPROPTEMPO, defined in mmsystem.pas support MIDI properties:

```
type
  PMidiPropTimeDiv = ^TMidiPropTimeDiv;
  midiproptimediv_tag = record
    cbStruct: DWORD;
    dwTimeDiv: DWORD;
end;
TMidiPropTimeDiv = midiproptimediv_tag;
MIDIPROPTIMEDIV = midiproptimediv_tag;
PMidiPropTempo = ^TMidiPropTempo;
midiproptempo_tag = record
    cbStruct: DWORD;
    dwTempo: DWORD;
  end;
  TMidiPropTempo = midiproptempo_tag;
  MIDIPROPTEMPO = midiproptempo_tag;
```

Example

See Listing 4-24.

function MIDIStreamPosition   *mmsystem.pas*

Syntax

```
function MIDIStreamPosition(
 hms: HMIDISTRM;
 lpmmt: PMMTime;
 cbmmt: UINT
 ): MMRESULT; stdcall;
```

Description

This function retrieves the current position in a MIDI stream. The position is always set to zero when the device is opened or reset. Certain preparatory steps are required. Before calling MIDIStreamPosition(), be sure to set the wType member of the MMTIME structure to indicate the time format you desire. After calling this function, check the wType member to determine if the desired time format is supported. If the desired format is not supported, wType will specify an alternative format.

Parameters

hms: The handle of the MIDI stream returned by a call to the MIDIStreamOpen() function. This handle identifies the output device.

lpmmt: The address of an MMTIME structure.

cbmmt: A byte indicating the size of the MMTIME structure. You can simply use the SizeOf(MMTIME) function for this parameter.

Return Value

Returns MMSYSERR_NOERROR if successful. Otherwise, it returns one of the following errors: MMSYSERR_INVALHANDLE, indicating that the specified device handle is invalid; or MMSYSERR_INVALPARAM, indicating that the specified pointer or structure is invalid.

Example

See Listing 4-25.

function MIDIStreamOut   *mmsystem.pas*

Syntax

```
function MIDIStreamOut(
  hms: HMIDISTRM;
  pmh: PMIDIHDR;
  cbmh: UINT
  ): MMRESULT; stdcall;
```

Description

This function either plays or queues a stream (buffer) of MIDI data to a MIDI output device. The buffer pointed to by the MIDIHDR structure contains one or more MIDI events, each of which is defined by a MIDIEVENT structure. In the current version, that buffer must be smaller than 64K. Because the MIDIStreamOpen() function opens the output device in paused mode, you must call the MIDIStreamRestart() function before you can use MIDIStreamOut() to start the playback.

Parameters

hms: The handle of the MIDI stream returned by a call to the MIDIStreamOpen() function. This handle identifies the output device.

pmh: The address of a MIDIHDR structure that identifies the MIDI buffer.

cbmh: A UINT (integer) indicating the size of the MIDIHDR structure. You can simply use the SizeOf(MIDIHDR) function for this parameter.

Return Value

Returns MMSYSERR_NOERROR if successful. Otherwise, it returns one of the following errors: MIDIERR_STILLPLAYING, indicating that the output buffer pointed to by lpMIDIHdr is still playing or is queued from a previous call to MIDIStreamOut(); MIDIERR_UNPREPARED, indicating that the buffer pointed to by lpMIDIOutHdr has not been prepared; MMSYSERR_INVALHANDLE, indicating that the specified device handle is invalid; or MMSYSERR_INVALPARAM, indicating that the specified pointer or structure is invalid.

Example

See Listing 4-24.

function MIDIStreamPause   *mmsystem.pas*

Syntax

```
function MIDIStreamPause(
  hms: HMIDISTRM
  ): MMRESULT; stdcall;
```

Description

This function pauses playback of a specified MIDI stream. There is no danger of calling this function when the output is already paused; it simply returns with MMSYSERR_NOERROR. When playback is paused, the current playback position is saved. Call MIDIStreamRestart() to resume playback from the current position.

Parameter

hms: The handle of the MIDI stream returned by the MIDIStreamOpen() function.

Return Value

Returns MMSYSERR_NOERROR if successful. Otherwise, it returns MMSYSERR_INVALHANDLE, indicating that the specified device handle is invalid.

Example

See Listing 4-24.

function MIDIStreamRestart   *mmsystem.pas*

Syntax

```
function MIDIStreamRestart(
hms: HMIDISTRM
): MMRESULT; stdcall;
```

Description

This function restarts a MIDI stream that has been paused by calling MIDIStreamPause(). There is no danger of calling this function when the output is not paused; it simply returns with MMSYSERR_NOERROR.

Parameter

hms: The handle of the MIDI stream returned by the MIDIStreamOpen() function.

Return Value

Returns MMSYSERR_NOERROR if successful. Otherwise, it returns MMSYSERR_INVALHANDLE, indicating that the specified device handle is invalid.

Example

See Listing 4-24.

function MIDIStreamStop   *mmsystem.pas*

Syntax

```
function MIDIStreamStop(
  hms: HMIDISTRM
  ): MMRESULT; stdcall;
```

Description

This function turns off all notes on all MIDI channels for the specified MIDI output device. This function is similar to the MIDIOutReset() function. While the MIDIOutReset() function turns off all notes, MIDIStreamStop() turns off only those notes that have been turned on by a MIDI note-on message. By calling this function, all pending system-exclusive and stream output buffers are returned to the callback mechanism and the MHDR_DONE bit of MIDIHDR's dwFlags member is set.

Parameter

hms: The handle of the MIDI stream returned by the MIDIStreamOpen() function.

Return Value

Returns MMSYSERR_NOERROR if successful. Otherwise, it returns MMSYSERR_INVALHANDLE, indicating that the specified device handle is invalid.

Example

See Listing 4-25.

We've reached the end of another long chapter. This API gives us all of the tools we need to play music on a computer and to communicate with external MIDI devices. The next chapter will be a short one, for a change. Now we're going to explore the Auxiliary API, which gives us access to a variety of auxiliary audio devices.

Chapter Five

The Auxiliary API

Having worked with waveform audio and MIDI, we are now familiar with two of the most powerful ways of playing sounds in Windows. However, in terms of the possible sources of multimedia data we have only scratched the surface. In addition to a computer's sound card, there are a multitude of other devices adding to the richness of today's multimedia computing environment.

We can also get sound from other sources besides those we have been discussing so far. Auxiliary audio devices can be used alone or in combination with the MIDI and waveform audio output devices in a multimedia computer. Probably the best-known example of an auxiliary audio device is the CD audio output from a CD-ROM drive. Not every multimedia computer includes auxiliary audio support, but most do. You can use the AuxGetNumDevs() function to determine the number of available auxiliary devices present in a system. Then you can find out the capabilities of those devices by using the AuxGetDevCaps() function. Sound familiar? It should. We have already become acquainted with comparable functions in the chapters on waveform audio and MIDI. The multimedia APIs are conveniently consistent.

Remember the Wave mapper and the MIDI mapper? Guess what? We also have an auxiliary audio mapper which serves a similar function as the two previous mappers we encountered. It is defined as a constant in mmsystem.pas as follows:

```
AUX_MAPPER     = UINT(-1);
```

The general multimedia type we've been using consistently in the past two chapters, MMRESULT, is also used for error codes returned by many of the auxiliary audio functions. We'll see some of the same error codes we've seen before used here.

5

Chapter

The process of working with auxiliary devices is much simpler than with either waveform audio or MIDI devices. You don't have to worry about opening or closing devices, allocating memory buffers, preparing and unpreparing headers, and the myriad of other tasks we needed to complete with waveform and MIDI devices. While the functions themselves are similar, there are many fewer of them. In fact, the only support present is for controlling the volume of these devices or sending custom messages to them. Now that we have surveyed the general landscape, let's take a detailed look at all of the auxiliary functions and structures.

Using Auxiliary Devices

function AuxGetNumDevs   *mmsystem.pas*

Syntax

```
function AuxGetNumDevs
    : UINT; stdcall;
```

Description

This function takes no parameters and simply returns the number of auxiliary output devices found on a machine. Once you know the number of devices, you can then query each device to determine its capabilities. Listing 5-1 shows how to do this using this function, the AuxGetDevCaps() function, and the AUXCAPS structure.

Return Value

Returns a UINT giving the number of auxiliary output devices found on the computer.

Example

See Listing 5-1.

function AuxGetDevCaps   *mmsystem.pas*

Syntax

```
function auxGetDevCaps(
  uDeviceID: UINT;
  lpCaps: PAuxCaps;
  uSize: UINT
  ): MMRESULT; stdcall;
```

Description

This function queries the auxiliary output device, uDeviceID, determines its capabilities, and places them in the LPCAPS structure. The result is returned in MMRESULT. See below for possible return values.

Parameters

uDeviceID: An integer (UINT) identifying a waveform audio input device. It can be either a device identifier or the handle of an open waveform audio input device. The AUX_MAPPER constant can also be used as the device identifier. If the latter approach is used and there is no audio mapper installed, the function will return an error.

lpCaps: The address of an AUXCAPS structure to be filled with information about the capabilities of the device specified by uDeviceID.

uSize: An integer (UINT) indicating the size of the AUXCAPS structure. Use SizeOf(AUXCAPS) to get this value.

Return Value

Returns MMSYSERR_NOERROR if successful. Otherwise, it returns MMSYSERR_BADDEVICEID, indicating the device identifier specified is out of range.

Example

The following structure, defined in mmsystem.pas, holds information about an auxiliary device's capabilities. Table 5-1 describes the flags for the wTechnology field of the AUXCAPS structure shown below. Table 5-2 describes the flags for the dwSupport field of the AUXCAPS structure. Listing 5-1 shows how to determine and display the properties for an auxiliary device on a computer.

5

Chapter

```
type
  PAuxCapsA = ^TAuxCapsA;
  PAuxCapsW = ^TAuxCapsW;
  PAuxCaps = PAuxCapsA;
  tagAUXCAPSA = record
    wMid: Word;                          { manufacturer ID }
    wPid: Word;                          { product ID }
    vDriverVersion: MMVERSION;           { version of the driver }
    szPname: array[0..MAXPNAMELEN-1] of AnsiChar;  { product name (NULL
                                                     terminated string) }
    wTechnology: Word;                   { type of device }
    dwSupport: DWORD;                    { functionality supported by driver }
  end;
  tagAUXCAPSW = record
    wMid: Word;                          { manufacturer ID }
    wPid: Word;                          { product ID }
    vDriverVersion: MMVERSION;           { version of the driver }
    szPname: array[0..MAXPNAMELEN-1] of WideChar;  { product name (NULL
                                                     terminated string) }
    wTechnology: Word;                   { type of device }
    dwSupport: DWORD;                    { functionality supported by driver }
  end;
  tagAUXCAPS = tagAUXCAPSA;
  TAuxCapsA = tagAUXCAPSA;
  TAuxCapsW = tagAUXCAPSW;
  TAuxCaps = TAuxCapsA;
  AUXCAPSA = tagAUXCAPSA;
  AUXCAPSW = tagAUXCAPSW;
  AUXCAPS = AUXCAPSA;
```

Table 5-1: Flags for the wTechnology field in AUXCAPS structure

Flag	Meaning
AUXCAPS_CDAUDIO	Auxiliary audio from an internal CD-ROM drive
AUXCAPS_AUXIN	Auxiliary audio from one or more input jacks

Table 5-2: Flags for the dwSupport field in the AUXCAPS structure

Flag	Meaning
AUXCAPS_VOLUME	Supports volume control
AUXCAPS_LRVOLUME	Supports separate left-right volume control

Listing 5-1: Determining and displaying properties for an auxiliary device on a computer

```
procedure TForm1.GetAuxCapabilities;
var
  j: Integer;
begin
  SupportsCDAudio := False;
  SupportsLRVolume := False;
  for j := 0 to (Devices-1) do     // Iterate
    begin
      LocalMMResult := auxGetDevCaps(J, @TheAuxCaps, SizeOf(AuxCaps));
      if (LocalMMResult=MMSYSERR_NOERROR) then
        begin
          if (((TheAuxCaps.wTechnology and (1 shl AUXCAPS_CDAUDIO))
               and AUXCAPS_CDAUDIO)=0) then SupportsCDAudio := True;
          if (((TheAuxCaps.dwSupport and (1 shl AUXCAPS_LRVOLUME))
               and AUXCAPS_LRVOLUME)=0) then SupportsLRVolume := True;
        end;
    end;
end;
procedure TForm1.FormCreate(Sender: TObject);
begin
  Devices := auxGetNumDevs;
  Label1.Caption := Label1.Caption + IntToStr(Devices);
  GetAuxCapabilities;
  Label2.Caption := Label2.Caption + BoolToStr(SupportsCDAudio);
  Label3.Caption := Label3.Caption + BoolToStr(SupportsLRVolume);
end;
```

function AuxGetVolume   *mmsystem.pas*

Syntax

```
function auxGetVolume(
  uDeviceID: UINT;
  lpdwVolume: PDWORD
  ): MMRESULT; stdcall;
```

Description

This function retrieves the current volume level of the specified auxiliary output device. Volume settings are interpreted logarithmically—the perceived increase in volume is the same when increasing the volume level from $5000 to $6000 as it is from $4000 to $5000. Since not all devices support volume changes, it is important to determine whether a particular device supports volume control. To do this, use the AUXCAPS_VOLUME flag to test the dwSupport member of the AUXCAPS structure (filled by the AuxGetDevCaps() function). To determine whether the device supports left and right channel volume control, use the AUXCAPS_LRVOLUME flag to test the dwSupport member of the AUXCAPS structure (filled by AuxGetDevCaps()).

Parameters

uDeviceID: The handle of the auxiliary audio output device.

lpdwVolume: The address of a variable to be filled with the current volume setting. The low-order word of this location contains the left channel volume setting, and the high-order word contains the right channel setting. A value of $FFFF represents full volume, and a value of $0000 is silence. If a device does not support both left and right volume control, the low-order word of the specified location contains the mono volume level. The full 16-bit setting(s) set with the AuxSetVolume() function is returned, regardless of whether the device supports the full 16 bits of volume level control.

Return Value

Returns MMSYSERR_NOERROR if successful. Otherwise, it returns MMSYSERR_BADDEVICEID, indicating that the specified device identifier is out of range.

Example

In the AuxClass unit, the following type is defined for different volume levels: VolumePlaybackValue = (vpvSilent, vpvSoft, vpvMedium, vpvLoud, rpvFull); note how this is used in Listing 3-14. Also note how we check to make sure that the system supports this feature and how we exit gracefully if it does not. This example shows how to use the AuxGetVolume() function and other auxiliary audio functions. First, it determines if a CD device supports adjusting the volume. If a device is found that does, the volume is set to half the maximum ($7777).

Listing 5-2: Using the AuxGetVolume() function

```
procedure TForm1.btnSetVolumeToHalfClick(Sender: TObject);
var
  J : integer;
  LeftVal, RightVal : Word;
```

```
  VolumeVal : DWord;
begin
  for j := 0 to (Devices-1) do     // Iterate
    begin
      LocalMMResult := auxGetDevCaps(J, @TheAuxCaps, SizeOf(AuxCaps));
      if ((LocalMMResult=MMSYSERR_NOERROR) and (
           ((TheAuxCaps.wTechnology and (1 shl AUXCAPS_CDAUDIO))
            and AUXCAPS_CDAUDIO)=0) and (
           ((TheAuxCaps.dwSupport and (1 shl AUXCAPS_LRVOLUME))
            and AUXCAPS_LRVOLUME)=0)) then
             begin
               if auxGetVolume(j, @VolumeVal) <> MMSYSERR_NOERROR then
                 break;
               LeftVal := LoWord(VolumeVal);
               RightVal := HiWord(VolumeVal);
               if LeftVal > $7777 then
                 LeftVal := $7777;
               if ((RightVal > $7777) and
                    (((TheAuxCaps.dwSupport and (1 shl AUXCAPS_LRVOLUME))
                     and AUXCAPS_LRVOLUME) = 0)) then
                   RightVal := $7777;
               LocalMMResult := auxSetVolume(J, MakeLong(LeftVal,
                           RightVal));
             end;
    end;    // for
```

function AuxSetVolume   *mmsystem.pas*

Syntax

```
function auxSetVolume(
  uDeviceID: UINT;
  dwVolume: DWORD
  ): MMRESULT; stdcall;
```

Description

This function sets the volume level of the specified auxiliary output
device. Not all devices support volume changes. To determine whether
the device supports volume control, use the AUXCAPS_VOLUME flag to
test the dwSupport member of the AUXCAPS structure (filled by the
AuxGetDevCaps() function). To determine whether the device supports
volume control on both the left and right channels, use the
AUXCAPS_LRVOLUME flag.

5

Chapter

Most devices do not support the full 16 bits of volume level control and will not use the high-order bits of the requested volume setting. For example, if a given device supports 4 bits of volume control, requested volume level values of $4000, $4FFF, and $43BE will all produce the same physical volume setting: $4000. The WaveOutGetVolume() function returns the full 16-bit setting set with WaveOutSetVolume(). Volume settings are interpreted logarithmically—the perceived increase in volume is the same when increasing the volume level from $5000 to $6000 as it is from $4000 to $5000.

Parameters

uDeviceID: An integer (UINT) identifying an auxiliary output device.

dwVolume: A DWORD indicating the new volume setting. The low-order word contains the left channel volume setting, and the high-order word contains the right channel setting. A value of $FFFF represents full volume, and a value of $0000 is silence. If a device does not support both left and right volume control, the low-order word of dwVolume specifies the volume level, and the high-order word is ignored.

Return Value

Returns MMSYSERR_NOERROR if successful. Otherwise, it returns MMSYSERR_BADDEVICEID, indicating that the specified device identifier is out of range.

Example

See Listing 5-2.

function AuxOutMessage   *mmsystem.pas*

Syntax

```
function auxOutMessage(
  uDeviceID, uMessage: UINT;
  dw1, dw2: DWORD
  ): MMRESULT; stdcall;
```

Description

This function sends messages to the waveform audio input device drivers.

Parameters

uDeviceID: An integer (UINT) identifying an auxiliary output device.

uMessage: Message to send.

dw1, dw2: Two DWORD parameters for message parameters.

Return Value

Returns a DWORD indicating the return value of the message.

Example

These messages are driver-specific, so we cannot show an example here that will definitely work on your system. To use this function you need to know the specific messages, which your sound card and its driver(s) will accept. Here is a general example of how you might call this function:

```
procedure TAux.SendMessage(ADriverMessage: UINT; MsgParam1,
            MsgParam2: DWORD);
begin
 AuxOutMessage(AHandle, ADriverMessage, MsgParam1, MsgParam2);
end;
```

In this short chapter, we have explored the Auxiliary API. But how can we combine various audio sources? The answer to that question will be found in the next chapter on audio mixers.

Chapter Six

Multimedia Mixers

With waveform audio, MIDI, and a host of auxiliary devices, we have no shortage of multimedia sources. But how do we manage to get all of these sources to work together? How do we control the overall audio volume and other sound qualities on a computer? The answer to both of these questions is mixers. Mixers have probably been around as long as any device, except the recording and playing devices themselves.

Mixers—An Introduction

Windows audio mixer services have two general uses: They allow you to route audio lines to a destination device (either input or output) and they allow you to control volume and other aspects of sound recording or reproduction. Many of the techniques involved in using these services are similar to those we have discussed in earlier chapters. Let's examine some of the basic principles.

The central element within the mixer architecture is the audio line. The audio line is the conduit through which an audio signal is sent from one location to another. It can contain one or more channels of data. The data transmitted can originate from a particular device or from a system resource. More than one sound can be sent through a single line. Though a stereo audio line has two channels, it is still considered a single audio line since it comes from a single source.

The mixer architecture, defined by the API functions and structures we'll present in this chapter, provides routing services to manage a computer's audio lines. To use these services you must have adequate hardware devices and software drivers to control those devices. The level of support can vary considerably from one computer to another. In the sample application for this chapter on the companion CD, we use slider controls for volume, treble, and bass. While all of these were functional on the author's desktop computer (see Figure 6-1), only the volume control was functional on his laptop computer (see Figure 6-2). Note that in the latter case, the treble and bass sliders are deactivated, since they are non-functional.

Figure 6-1

Figure 6-2

As in traditional audio mixers, the Windows mixer architecture allows you to map several audio source lines to a single destination audio line. Furthermore, each audio line can have one or more mixer controls associated with it. A mixer control can perform any number of functions; the most common function is controlling the volume. The functions available will depend on the characteristics of the associated audio line.

As in the previous multimedia APIs, the Mixer API includes several general types, constants, and error messages defined in mmsystem.pas. The main mixer objects are defined as follows:

```
type
  PHMIXEROBJ = ^HMIXEROBJ;
  HMIXEROBJ = Integer;

  PHMIXER = ^HMIXER;
  HMIXER = Integer;
```

For each of the various mixer controls, Microsoft Windows provides a
short name and a long name. The following constants, defined in
mmsystem.pas, provide the maximum lengths of these names:

```
MIXER_SHORT_NAME_CHARS   = 16;
MIXER_LONG_NAME_CHARS    = 64;
```

While the various mixer functions use many of the return values we have
seen before, the following MMRESULT error return values, which are
described under the functions that return them, are specific to the Mixer
API:

```
MIXERR_INVALLINE
MIXERR_INVALCONTROL
MIXERR_INVALVALUE
MIXERR_LASTERROR
```

There are hosts of other constants that define specific mixer types and
line devices. There are three structures central to this API:
MIXERCONTROL, which describes the state and metrics of a single
control of an audio line; MIXERLINECONTROLS, which contains
information about the controls of an audio line; and MIXERCONTROL-
DETAILS, which refers to various control detail structures and is used to
retrieve or set state information for an audio mixer control. These three
structures (the first two of which are very complex) and their related
structures are defined in mmsystem.pas as follows:

```
type
  PMixerControlA = ^TMixerControlA;
  PMixerControlW = ^TMixerControlW;
  PMixerControl = PMixerControlA;
  tagMIXERCONTROLA = packed record
    cbStruct: DWORD;              { size in bytes of MIXERCONTROL }
    dwControlID: DWORD;           { unique control id for mixer device }
    dwControlType: DWORD;         { MIXERCONTROL_CONTROLTYPE_xxx }
    fdwControl: DWORD;            { MIXERCONTROL_CONTROLF_xxx }
    cMultipleItems: DWORD;        { if MIXERCONTROL_CONTROLF_MULTIPLE set }
    szShortName: array[0..MIXER_SHORT_NAME_CHARS - 1] of AnsiChar;
```

```
    szName: array[0..MIXER_LONG_NAME_CHARS - 1] of AnsiChar;
    Bounds: record
      case Integer of
        0: (lMinimum, lMaximum: Longint);
        1: (dwMinimum, dwMaximum: DWORD);
        2: (dwReserved: array[0..5] of DWORD);
    end;
    Metrics: record
      case Integer of
        0: (cSteps: DWORD);          { # of steps between min & max }
        1: (cbCustomData: DWORD);  { size in bytes of custom data }
        2: (dwReserved: array[0..5] of DWORD);
    end;
  end;
  tagMIXERCONTROLW = packed record
    cbStruct: DWORD;           { size in bytes of MIXERCONTROL }
    dwControlID: DWORD;        { unique control id for mixer device }
    dwControlType: DWORD;      { MIXERCONTROL_CONTROLTYPE_xxx }
    fdwControl: DWORD;         { MIXERCONTROL_CONTROLF_xxx }
    cMultipleItems: DWORD;     { if MIXERCONTROL_CONTROLF_MULTIPLE set }
    szShortName: array[0..MIXER_SHORT_NAME_CHARS - 1] of WideChar;
    szName: array[0..MIXER_LONG_NAME_CHARS - 1] of WideChar;
    Bounds: record
      case Integer of
        0: (lMinimum, lMaximum: Longint);
        1: (dwMinimum, dwMaximum: DWORD);
        2: (dwReserved: array[0..5] of DWORD);
    end;
    Metrics: record
      case Integer of
        0: (cSteps: DWORD);          { # of steps between min & max }
        1: (cbCustomData: DWORD);  { size in bytes of custom data }
        2: (dwReserved: array[0..5] of DWORD);
    end;
  end;
  tagMIXERCONTROL = tagMIXERCONTROLA;
  TMixerControlA = tagMIXERCONTROLA;
  TMixerControlW = tagMIXERCONTROLW;
  TMixerControl = TMixerControlA;
  MIXERCONTROLA = tagMIXERCONTROLA;
  MIXERCONTROLW = tagMIXERCONTROLW;
  MIXERCONTROL = MIXERCONTROLA;


type
  PMixerLineControlsA = ^TMixerLineControlsA;
```

```
PMixerLineControlsW = ^TMixerLineControlsW;
PMixerLineControls = PMixerLineControlsA;
tagMIXERLINECONTROLSA = record
  cbStruct: DWORD;                   { size in bytes of MIXERLINECONTROLS }
  dwLineID: DWORD;                   { line id (from MIXERLINE.dwLineID) }
  case Integer of
    0: (dwControlID: DWORD);         { MIXER_GETLINECONTROLSF_ONEBYID }
    1: (dwControlType: DWORD;        { MIXER_GETLINECONTROLSF_ONEBYTYPE }
        cControls: DWORD;            { count of controls pmxctrl points to }
        cbmxctrl: DWORD;             { size in bytes of _one_ MIXERCONTROL }
        pamxctrl: PMixerControlA);   { pointer to first MIXERCONTROL
                                        array }
end;
tagMIXERLINECONTROLSW = record
  cbStruct: DWORD;                   { size in bytes of MIXERLINECONTROLS }
  dwLineID: DWORD;                   { line id (from MIXERLINE.dwLineID) }
  case Integer of
    0: (dwControlID: DWORD);         { MIXER_GETLINECONTROLSF_ONEBYID }
    1: (dwControlType: DWORD;        { MIXER_GETLINECONTROLSF_ONEBYTYPE }
        cControls: DWORD;            { count of controls pmxctrl points to }
        cbmxctrl: DWORD;             { size in bytes of _one_ MIXERCONTROL }
        pamxctrl: PMixerControlW);   { pointer to first MIXERCONTROL
                                        array }
end;
tagMIXERLINECONTROLS = tagMIXERLINECONTROLSA;
TMixerLineControlsA = tagMIXERLINECONTROLSA;
TMixerLineControlsW = tagMIXERLINECONTROLSW;
TMixerLineControls = TMixerLineControlsA;
MIXERLINECONTROLSA = tagMIXERLINECONTROLSA;
MIXERLINECONTROLSW = tagMIXERLINECONTROLSW;
MIXERLINECONTROLS = MIXERLINECONTROLSA;

type
  PMixerControlDetails = ^TMixerControlDetails;
  tMIXERCONTROLDETAILS = record
    cbStruct: DWORD;       { size in bytes of MIXERCONTROLDETAILS }
    dwControlID: DWORD;    { control id to get/set details on }
    cChannels: DWORD;      { number of channels in paDetails array }
    case Integer of
      0: (hwndOwner: HWND);        { for MIXER_SETCONTROLDETAILSF_CUSTOM }
      1: (cMultipleItems: DWORD;   { if _MULTIPLE, the number of items per
                                      channel }
          cbDetails: DWORD;        { size of _one_ details_XX struct }
          paDetails: Pointer);     { pointer to array of details_XX
                                      structs }
  end;
```

Types of Mixer Controls and Structures

Having examined the basic structures, we need to look further into the kind of mixers available under Windows. We could define a mixer as a collection of controls that perform various functions, usually associated with input or output. The Windows mixer architecture includes eight types of controls: custom controls, faders, list controls, meters, number controls, sliders, switches, and timing controls. Custom controls are vendor specific. They are the most generic of all the mixer controls, allowing a mixer driver to define the control's characteristics and, by implication, its visual design.

Fader Controls

Fader controls are usually vertical in orientation, can be adjusted up or down, and have a linear scale. These controls come in five flavors, as shown in Table 6-1. Use the MIXERCONTROLDETAILS_UNSIGNED structure to retrieve and set control details. That structure is defined in mmsystem.pas as follows:

```
type
PMixerControlDetailsUnsigned = ^TMixerControlDetailsUnsigned;
  tMIXERCONTROLDETAILS_UNSIGNED = record
    dwValue: DWORD;
  end;
  TMixerControlDetailsUnsigned = tMIXERCONTROLDETAILS_UNSIGNED;
  MIXERCONTROLDETAILS_UNSIGNED = tMIXERCONTROLDETAILS_UNSIGNED;
```

Table 6-1: Five types of fader controls

Control	Description
Fader	General fade control. Acceptable values range from 0 through 65,535.
Volume	General volume fade control. Acceptable values range from 0 through 65,535.
Bass	Bass volume fade control. Acceptable values range from 0 through 65,535. The limits of the bass frequency band vary and are hardware specific.
Treble	Treble volume fade control. Acceptable values range from 0 through 65,535. The limits of the treble frequency band vary and are hardware specific.

Control	Description
Equalizer	Graphic equalizer control. Acceptable values for a single equalizer band range from 0 through 65,535. The number of equalizer bands and their limits are hardware specific. You can use the MIXERCONTROLDETAILS_LISTTEXT structure to retrieve text labels for the equalizer.

List Controls

List controls provide single-select or multiple-select states for complex audio lines. Like the fader controls, the list controls also come in a variety of flavors. Table 6-2 describes the various types of list controls. These controls use the MIXERCONTROLDETAILS_BOOLEAN structure to retrieve and set their properties. In addition, the MIXERCONTROL-DETAILS_LISTTEXT structure is used to retrieve all text descriptions of a multiple-item control. These two structures and their related structures are defined in mmsystem.pas as follows:

```
type
 PMixerControlDetailsBoolean = ^TMixerControlDetailsBoolean;
  tMIXERCONTROLDETAILS_BOOLEAN = record
    fValue: Longint;
  end;
  TMixerControlDetailsBoolean = tMIXERCONTROLDETAILS_BOOLEAN;
   MIXERCONTROLDETAILS_BOOLEAN = tMIXERCONTROLDETAILS_BOOLEAN;

  PMixerControlDetailsListTextA = ^TMixerControlDetailsListTextA;
  PMixerControlDetailsListTextW = ^TMixerControlDetailsListTextW;
  PMixerControlDetailsListText = PMixerControlDetailsListTextA;
  tagMIXERCONTROLDETAILS_LISTTEXTA = record
    dwParam1: DWORD;
    dwParam2: DWORD;
    szName: array[0..MIXER_LONG_NAME_CHARS - 1] of AnsiChar;
  end;
  tagMIXERCONTROLDETAILS_LISTTEXTW = record
    dwParam1: DWORD;
    dwParam2: DWORD;
    szName: array[0..MIXER_LONG_NAME_CHARS - 1] of WideChar;
  end;
  tagMIXERCONTROLDETAILS_LISTTEXT = tagMIXERCONTROLDETAILS_LISTTEXTA;
  TMixerControlDetailsListTextA = tagMIXERCONTROLDETAILS_LISTTEXTA;
  TMixerControlDetailsListTextW = tagMIXERCONTROLDETAILS_LISTTEXTW;
  TMixerControlDetailsListText = TMixerControlDetailsListTextA;
  MIXERCONTROLDETAILS_LISTTEXTA = tagMIXERCONTROLDETAILS_LISTTEXTA;
```

```
MIXERCONTROLDETAILS_LISTTEXTW = tagMIXERCONTROLDETAILS_LISTTEXTW;
MIXERCONTROLDETAILS_LISTTEXT = MIXERCONTROLDETAILS_LISTTEXTA;
```

Table 6-2: Four types of list controls

Control	Description
Single-select	A list control that restricts the selection to just one item. Unlike the multiplexer control, this control can be used to control more than just audio source lines. For example, you could use this control to select a low-pass filter from a list of filters supported by a mixer device.
Multiplexer (MUX)	A list control that restricts the selection to just one item. This can only be used with one source line at a time.
Multiple-select	A list control that allows simultaneous selection of multiple items and control of more than one audio source line.
Mixer	A list control that allows simultaneous selection of source lines.

Meter Controls

The meter controls measure data passing through an audio line. Table 6-3 describes the different types of meter controls. These controls use the MIXERCONTROLDETAILS_BOOLEAN, MIXERCONTROLDETAILS_SIGNED, and MIXERCONTROLDETAILS_UNSIGNED structures to retrieve and set control properties. The MIXERCONTROLDETAILS_SIGNED structure is defined in mmsystem.pas as follows:

```
type
  PMixerControlDetailsSigned = ^TMixerControlDetailsSigned;
  tMIXERCONTROLDETAILS_SIGNED = record
    lValue: Longint;
  end;
  TMixerControlDetailsSigned = tMIXERCONTROLDETAILS_SIGNED;
  MIXERCONTROLDETAILS_SIGNED = tMIXERCONTROLDETAILS_SIGNED;
```

Table 6-3: Four types of meter controls

Control	Description
Boolean	Control that measures whether an integer value is FALSE/OFF (zero) or TRUE/ON (nonzero).
Peak	Control that measures the deflection from 0 in both the positive and negative directions. The range of integer values for the peak meter is –32,768 through 32,767.

Control	Description
Signed	Control that measures integer values in the range of –2,147,483,648 through 2,147,483,647. The mixer driver defines the limits of this meter.
Unsigned	Control that measures integer values in the range of 0 through 4,294,967,295. The mixer driver defines the limits of this meter.

Number Controls

With number controls, a user can enter numerical data associated with an audio line. The numerical data can be expressed as signed integers, unsigned integers, or integer decibel values. These controls use the MIXERCONTROLDETAILS_SIGNED and MIXERCONTROL-DETAILS_UNSIGNED structures to retrieve and set the control properties. Table 6-4 describes the types of number controls.

Table 6-4: Four types of number controls

Control	Description
Signed	A control that allows integer values entered in the range of –2,147,483,648 through 2,147,483,647.
Unsigned	Allows integer values entered in the range of 0 through 4,294,967,295.
Decibel	Allows integer decibel values to be entered in tenths of decibels. The range of values for this control is –32,768 through 32,767.
Percent	Allows values to be entered as percentages.

Slider Controls

Slider controls are typically horizontal in orientation and can be adjusted to the left or right. These controls use the MIXERCONTROLDETAILS_ SIGNED structure to retrieve and set their properties. Table 6-5 describes the types of sliders.

Table 6-5: Three types of slider controls

Control	Description
Slider	Control with a range of –32,768 through 32,767. The mixer driver defines the limits of this control.
Pan	Control with a range of –32,768 through 32,767. The mixer driver defines the limits of this control, with 0 as the midrange value.
QSound Pan	Control that provides expanded sound control through QSound. This control has a range of –15 through 15.

Switch Controls

Switch controls are simply two-state switches. These controls use the MIXERCONTROLDETAILS_BOOLEAN structure to retrieve and set control properties. Table 6-6 describes the various types of switches.

Table 6-6: Seven types of switch controls

Control	Description
Boolean	A generic switch control. It can be set to TRUE or FALSE.
Button	Set to TRUE for all buttons that the driver should handle as though they had been pressed. If the value is FALSE, no action is taken.
On/Off	An alternative switch that is represented by a graphic other than the one used for the Boolean switch. It can be set to ON or OFF.
Mute	A control that mutes an audio line (suppressing the data flow of the line) or allows the audio data to play. This switch is frequently used to help control the lines feeding into the mixer.
Mono	A toggle control that switches between mono and stereo output for a stereo audio line. Set to OFF to play stereo data as separate channels. Set to ON to combine data from both channels into a mono audio line.
Loudness	Boosts low-volume bass for an audio line. Set to ON to boost low-volume bass. Set to OFF to set volume levels to normal. The amount of boost is hardware specific. For more information, see the documentation for your mixer device.
Stereo Enhanced	Increases stereo separation. Set to ON to increase stereo separation. Set to OFF for no enhancement.

The sample application for this chapter on the companion CD uses three of these controls: loudness, stereo enhanced, and mute. Only the mute control was supported on all of the various test computers, however.

Time Controls

With time controls you can allow the user to enter timing-related data, such as an echo delay or reverberation time. The time data is expressed as positive integers. The two types of time controls are described in Table 6-7.

Table 6-7: Two types of time controls

Control	Description
Microsecond	Time control that supports timing data expressed in microseconds. The range of acceptable values is 0 through 4,294,967,295.
Millisecond	Time control that supports timing data expressed in milliseconds. The range of acceptable values is 0 through 4,294,967,295.

Mixer Functions

In addition to the structures and types described above, the Mixer API includes ten functions for working with mixers. Again, you'll notice considerable similarity between these and the functions we've seen in previous chapters. As before, we have functions for opening and closing mixers, querying their capabilities, and so forth. We also have functions for connecting mixers to the devices they control and for retrieving or setting their properties. Let's take a detailed look at all of the functions.

We'll begin by discussing functions related to the mixer capabilities of a particular system. As in previous APIs, we have two functions—MixerGetNumDevs() to retrieve the number of devices and MixerGetDevCaps() to retrieve the capabilities of those devices.

function MixerGetNumDevs   *mmsystem.pas*

Syntax

```
function MixerGetNumDevs
  : UINT; stdcall;
```

Description

This function takes no parameters and simply returns the number of mixer devices found on the machine. There is usually just one mixer device.

Example

Listing 6-1 shows how to use this function. To determine the number of mixers on a machine, a calling application can call the GetNumDevices() method defined in the MixClass.pas unit, which wraps the MixerGet-NumDevs() function.

Listing 6-1: Using the MixerGetNumDevs() function

```
function TMixer.GetNumDevices : UINT;
begin
  result := MixerGetNumDevs;
end;
```

function MixerGetDevCaps   *mmsystem.pas*

Syntax

```
function MixerGetDevCaps(
uMxId: UINT;
pmxcaps: PMixerCaps;
cbmxcaps: UINT
): MMRESULT; stdcall;
```

Description

This function queries the specified mixer device, uMxId, determines its capabilities, and places them in the pmxcaps structure. This function can also accept a mixer device handle returned by the MixerOpen() function as the uMxId parameter. In that case, be sure to cast the HMIXER handle to a UINT. The function's result is returned in MMRESULT.

Parameters

uMxId: An integer (UINT) identifying a mixer device. It can be either a device identifier or the handle of an open mixer device.

pmxcaps: The address of a MIXERCAPS structure to be filled with information about the capabilities of the device specified by uMxId.

cbmxcaps: An integer (UINT) indicating the size of the MIXERCAPS structure. Use SizeOf(MIXERCAPS) to get this value.

Return Value

Returns MMSYSERR_NOERROR if successful. Otherwise, it returns one of the following errors: MMSYSERR_BADDEVICEID, indicating the device identifier specified is out of range; MMSYSERR_INVALHANDLE, indicating that the mixer device handle is invalid; or MMSYSERR_IN-VALPARAM, indicating that one or more parameters are invalid.

Example

The MIXERCAPS structure holds information about a mixer device's capabilities. Its main members are described in Table 6-8. MIXERCAPS and its related structures are defined as follows in mmsystem.pas:

```
type
  PMixerCapsA = ^TMixerCapsA;
  PMixerCapsW = ^TMixerCapsW;
  PMixerCaps = PMixerCapsA;
  tagMIXERCAPSA = record
    wMid: WORD;                            { manufacturer id }
    wPid: WORD;                            { product id }
    vDriverVersion: MMVERSION;             { version of the driver }
    szPname: array [0..MAXPNAMELEN - 1] of AnsiChar;   { product name }
    fdwSupport: DWORD;                     { misc. support bits }
    cDestinations: DWORD;                  { count of destinations }
  end;
  tagMIXERCAPSW = record
    wMid: WORD;                            { manufacturer id }
    wPid: WORD;                            { product id }
    vDriverVersion: MMVERSION;             { version of the driver }
    szPname: array [0..MAXPNAMELEN - 1] of WideChar;   { product name }
    fdwSupport: DWORD;                     { misc. support bits }
    cDestinations: DWORD;                  { count of destinations }
  end;
  tagMIXERCAPS = tagMIXERCAPSA;
  TMixerCapsA = tagMIXERCAPSA;
  TMixerCapsW = tagMIXERCAPSW;
  TMixerCaps = TMixerCapsA;
  MIXERCAPSA = tagMIXERCAPSA;
  MIXERCAPSW = tagMIXERCAPSW;
  MIXERCAPS = MIXERCAPSA;
```

Table 6-8: Values for the main members of the MIXERCAPS structure

Member	Meaning
wMid	A Word value indicating the manufacturer identifier for the device driver for the waveform audio input device.
wPid	A Word value indicating the product identifier for the mixer device.

Member	Meaning
vDriverVersion	An MMVERSION value indicating the version number of the device driver for the mixer device. The high-order byte is the major version number, and the low-order byte is the minor version number.
szPname	A null-terminated string holding the product name.
fdwSupport	A DWORD value holding various types of support information for the mixer device driver. No extended support bits are currently defined.
cDestinations	A DWORD value specifying the number of audio line destinations available through the mixer device. All mixer devices must support at least one destination line, so this member cannot be zero. Destination indexes used in the dwDestination member of the MIXERLINE structure (see below) range from zero to the value specified in the cDestinations member minus one.

The MIXERLINE and its related structures are defined in mmsystem.pas as follows:

```
type
  PMixerLineA = ^TMixerLineA;
  PMixerLineW = ^TMixerLineW;
  PMixerLine = PMixerLineA;
  tagMIXERLINEA = record
    cbStruct: DWORD;                { size of MIXERLINE structure }
    dwDestination: DWORD;           { zero based destination index }
    dwSource: DWORD;                { zero based source index (if source) }
    dwLineID: DWORD;                { unique line id for mixer device }
    fdwLine: DWORD;                 { state/information about line }
    dwUser: DWORD;                  { driver specific information }
    dwComponentType: DWORD;         { component type line connects to }
    cChannels: DWORD;               { number of channels line supports }
    cConnections: DWORD;            { number of connections [possible] }
    cControls: DWORD;               { number of controls at this line }
    szShortName: array[0..MIXER_SHORT_NAME_CHARS - 1] of AnsiChar;
    szName: array[0..MIXER_LONG_NAME_CHARS - 1] of AnsiChar;
    Target: record
      dwType: DWORD;                { MIXERLINE_TARGETTYPE_xxxx }
      dwDeviceID: DWORD;            { target device ID of device type }
      wMid: WORD;                             { of target device }
      wPid: WORD;                             {      "  }
      vDriverVersion: MMVERSION;              {      "  }
      szPname: array[0..MAXPNAMELEN - 1] of AnsiChar;  {      "  }
```

```
      end;
  end;
  tagMIXERLINEW = record
    cbStruct: DWORD;              { size of MIXERLINE structure }
    dwDestination: DWORD;         { zero based destination index }
    dwSource: DWORD;              { zero based source index (if source) }
    dwLineID: DWORD;              { unique line id for mixer device }
    fdwLine: DWORD;               { state/information about line }
    dwUser: DWORD;                { driver specific information }
    dwComponentType: DWORD;       { component type line connects to }
    cChannels: DWORD;             { number of channels line supports }
    cConnections: DWORD;          { number of connections [possible] }
    cControls: DWORD;             { number of controls at this line }
    szShortName: array[0..MIXER_SHORT_NAME_CHARS - 1] of WideChar;
    szName: array[0..MIXER_LONG_NAME_CHARS - 1] of WideChar;
    Target: record
      dwType: DWORD;              { MIXERLINE_TARGETTYPE_xxxx }
      dwDeviceID: DWORD;          { target device ID of device type }
      wMid: WORD;                                { of target device }
      wPid: WORD;                                {      " }
      vDriverVersion: MMVERSION;                 {      " }
      szPname: array[0..MAXPNAMELEN - 1] of WideChar; {      " }
      end;
  end;
  tagMIXERLINE = tagMIXERLINEA;
  TMixerLineA = tagMIXERLINEA;
  TMixerLineW = tagMIXERLINEW;
  TMixerLine = TMixerLineA;
  MIXERLINEA = tagMIXERLINEA;
  MIXERLINEW = tagMIXERLINEW;
  MIXERLINE = MIXERLINEA;
```

The members of the MIXERLINE structure are defined in Table 6-9.

Table 6-9: Members of the MIXERLINE structure

Member	Meaning
cbStruct	Size, in bytes, of the MIXERLINE structure. This field must be initialized before calling the MixerGetLineInfo() function. The size specified in this field must be large enough to contain the MIXERLINE structure. When MixerGetLineInfo() returns, this field contains the actual size of the information returned. The returned information will not exceed the requested size.

Member	Meaning
dwDestination	Destination line index. This field ranges from zero to one less than the value specified in the cDestinations field of the MIXERCAPS structure retrieved by the MixerGetDevCaps() function. When the MixerGetLineInfo() function is called with the MIXER_GETLINEINFOF_DESTINATION flag, properties for the destination line are returned. (The dwSource field must be set to zero in this case.) When called with the MIXER_GETLINE-INFOF_SOURCE flag, the properties for the source given by the dwSource field that is associated with the dwDestination field are returned.
dwSource	Index for the audio source line associated with the dwDestination field. That is, this field specifies the nth audio source line associated with the specified audio destination line. This field is not used for destination lines and must be set to zero when MIXER_GETLINEINFOF_DESTINATION is specified in the MixerGetLineInfo() function. When the MIXER_GETLINE-INFOF_SOURCE flag is specified, this field ranges from zero to one less than the value specified in the cConnections field for the audio destination line given in the dwDestination field.
dwLineID	An identifier defined by the mixer device that uniquely refers to the audio line described by the MIXERLINE structure. This identifier is unique for each mixer device and can be in any format. An application should use this identifier only as an abstract handle.
fdwLine	Status and support flags for the audio line. This field is always returned to the application and requires no initialization. The following three values are defined:

MIXERLINE_LINEF_ACTIVE   Audio line is active. An active line indicates that a signal is probably passing through the line.

MIXERLINE_LINEF_DISCONNECTED   Audio line is disconnected. A disconnected line's associated controls can still be modified, but the changes have no effect until the line is connected.

MIXERLINE_LINEF_SOURCE   Audio line is an audio source line associated with a single audio destination line. If this flag is not set, it indicates that this line is an audio destination line associated with one or more audio source lines. |

Member	Meaning
dwUser	Instance data defined by the audio device for the line. This field is intended for custom mixer applications designed specifically for the mixer device returning this information. Other applications should ignore this data.
dwComponentType	Component type for this audio line. An application can use this information to display tailored graphics or to search for a particular component. If an application does not use component types, this field should be ignored. This field can be one of the values shown in Table 6-10.
cChannels	Maximum number of separate channels that can be manipulated independently for the audio line. The minimum value for this field is 1 because a line must have at least one channel. Most modern computer sound cards are stereo devices; for them, the value of this field is 2. Channel 1 is assumed to be the left channel; channel 2 is assumed to be the right channel. A multichannel line might have one or more uniform controls (controls that affect all channels of a line uniformly) associated with it.
cConnections	Number of connections that are associated with the audio line. This field is used only for audio destination lines and specifies the number of audio source lines that are associated with it. This field is always zero for source lines and for destination lines that do not have any audio source lines associated with them.
cControls	Number of controls associated with the audio line. This value can be zero. If no controls are associated with the line, the line is likely to be a source that might be selected in a MIXERCONTROL_CONTROLTYPE_MUX or MIXERCONTROL_CONTROLTYPE_MIXER but allows no manipulation of the signal.
szShortName	Short string that describes the audio mixer line specified in the dwLineID field. This description should be appropriate as a concise label for the line.
szName	String that describes the audio mixer line specified in the dwLineID field. This description should be appropriate as a complete description for the line.
Target	Target media information.
dwType	Target media device type associated with the audio line described in the MIXERLINE structure. An application must ignore target information for media device types it does not use. The values shown in Table 6-11 are defined for this member.

Member	Meaning
dwDeviceID	Current device identifier of the target media device when the dwType field is a target type other than MIXERLINE_TARGET-TYPE_UNDEFINED. This identifier is identical to the current media device index of the associated media device. When calling the MixerGetLineInfo() function with the MIXER_GETLINE-INFOF_TARGETTYPE flag, this field is ignored on input and will be returned to the caller by the audio mixer manager.
wMid	Manufacturer identifier of the target media device when the dwType field is a target type other than MIXERLINE_TARGET-TYPE_UNDEFINED. This identifier is identical to the wMid field of the device capabilities structure for the associated media. Manufacturer identifiers are defined in the manufacturer and product identifiers established by Microsoft Corporation.
wPid	Product identifier of the target media device when the dwType field is a target type other than MIXERLINE_TARGETTYPE_UNDEFINED. This identifier is identical to the wPid field of the device capabilities structure for the associated media. Product identifiers are defined in the manufacturer and product identifiers established by Microsoft.
vDriverVersion	Driver version of the target media device when the dwType field is a target type other than MIXERLINE_TARGETTYPE_UNDEFINED. This version is identical to the vDriverVersion field of the device capabilities structure for the associated media.
szPname	Product name of the target media device when the dwType field is a target type other than MIXERLINE_TARGETTYPE_UNDEFINED. This name is identical to the szPname field of the device capabilities structure for the associated media.

Table 6-10: Destination and source values that can be used for the dwComponentType member of the MIXERLINE structure

Value	Meaning
MIXERLINE_COMPONENTTYPE_DST_DIGITAL	This value indicates that the audio line is a digital destination (for example, digital input to a DAT or CD audio device).
MIXERLINE_COMPONENTTYPE_DST_HEADPHONES	This value indicates that the audio line is an adjustable (gain and/or attenuation) destination intended to drive headphones. Most sound cards use the same audio destination line for both speakers and headphones, in which case, the

Value	Meaning
MIXERLINE_COMPONENTTYPE_ DST_HEADPHONES (cont.)	mixer device simply uses the MIXERLINE_ COMPONENTTYPE_DST_SPEAKERS type.
MIXERLINE_COMPONENTTYPE_ DST_LINE	This value indicates that the audio line is a line level destination (for example, line level input from a CD audio device) that will be the final recording source for the analog-to-digital converter (ADC). Because most computer sound cards provide some sort of gain for the recording audio source line, the mixer device will use the MIXERLINE_COMPONENTTYPE_ DST_WAVEIN type.
MIXERLINE_COMPONENTTYPE_ DST_MONITOR	This value indicates that the audio line is a destination used for a monitor.
MIXERLINE_COMPONENTTYPE_ DST_SPEAKERS	This value indicates that the audio line is an adjustable (gain and/or attenuation) destination intended to drive speakers. This is the typical component type for the audio output of computer sound cards.
MIXERLINE_COMPONENTTYPE_ DST_TELEPHONE	This value indicates that the audio line is a destination that will be routed to a telephone line. This can be used in TAPI applications.
MIXERLINE_COMPONENTTYPE_ DST_UNDEFINED	This value indicates that the audio line is a destination that cannot be defined by one of the standard component types. A mixer device is required to use this component type for line component types that have not been defined by Microsoft.
MIXERLINE_COMPONENTTYPE_ DST_VOICEIN	This value indicates that the audio line is a destination that will be the final recording source for voice input. This component type is exactly like MIXERLINE_COMPONENTTYPE_ DST_WAVEIN but is intended specifically for settings used during voice recording/recognition. Support for this line is optional for a mixer device. Many mixer devices provide only MIXERLINE_COMPONENTTYPE_DST_ WAVEIN.

Value	Meaning
MIXERLINE_COMPONENTTYPE_ DST_WAVEIN	This value indicates that the audio line is a destination that will be the final recording source for the waveform audio input (ADC). This line typically provides some sort of gain or attenuation. This is the typical component type for the recording line of most computer sound cards.
MIXERLINE_COMPONENTTYPE_ SRC_ANALOG	This value indicates that the audio line is an analog source (for example, analog output from a video cassette).
MIXERLINE_COMPONENTTYPE_ SRC_AUXILIARY	This value indicates that the audio line is a source originating from the auxiliary audio line. This line type is intended as a source with gain or attenuation that can be routed to the MIXERLINE_COMPONENTTYPE_DST_SPEAK ERS destination and/or recorded from the MIXERLINE_COMPONENTTYPE_DST_ WAVEIN destination.
MIXERLINE_COMPONENTTYPE_ SRC_COMPACTDISC	This value indicates that the audio line is a source originating from the output of an internal audio CD. This component type is provided for sound cards that provide an audio source line intended to be connected to an audio CD (or CD-ROM playing an audio CD).
MIXERLINE_COMPONENTTYPE_ SRC_DIGITAL	This value indicates that the audio line is a digital source (for example, digital output from a DAT or audio CD).
MIXERLINE_COMPONENTTYPE_ SRC_LINE	This value indicates that the audio line is a line-level source (for example, line-level input from an external stereo) that can be used as an optional recording source. Because most computer sound cards provide some sort of gain for the recording source line, the mixer device will use the MIXERLINE_COMPONENTTYPE_ SRC_AUXILIARY type.

Value	Meaning
MIXERLINE_COMPONENTTYPE_SRC_MICROPHONE	This value indicates that the audio line is a microphone recording source. Most computer sound cards provide at least two types of recording sources: an auxiliary audio line and microphone input. A microphone audio line typically provides some sort of gain. Sound cards that use a single input for use with a microphone or auxiliary audio line should use the MIXERLINE_COMPONENTTYPE_SRC_MICROPHONE component type.
MIXERLINE_COMPONENTTYPE_SRC_PCSPEAKER	This value indicates that the audio line is a source originating from a personal computer speaker. Several computer sound cards provide the ability to mix what would typically be played on the internal speaker with the output of a sound card. Some sound cards support the ability to use this output as a recording source.
MIXERLINE_COMPONENTTYPE_SRC_SYNTHESIZER	This value indicates that the audio line is a source originating from the output of an internal synthesizer. Most computer sound cards provide some sort of MIDI synthesizer (for example, an Adlib®-compatible or OPL/3 FM synthesizer).
MIXERLINE_COMPONENTTYPE_SRC_TELEPHONE	This value indicates that the audio line is a source originating from an incoming telephone line. Can be used in TAPI applications.
MIXERLINE_COMPONENTTYPE_SRC_UNDEFINED	This value indicates that the audio line is a source that cannot be defined by one of the standard component types. A mixer device is required to use this component type for line component types that have not been defined by Microsoft.
MIXERLINE_COMPONENTTYPE_SRC_WAVEOUT	This value indicates that the audio line is a source originating from the waveform audio output digital-to-analog converter (DAC). Most computer sound cards provide this component type as a source to the MIXERLINE_COMPONENTTYPE_DST_SPEAKERS destination. Some cards also allow this source to be routed to the MIXERLINE_COMPONENTTYPE_DST_WAVEIN destination.

Table 6-11: Values that can be used for the dwType Member of the MIXERLINE structure

Value	Meaning
MIXERLINE_TARGETTYPE_AUX	This value indicates that the audio line described by the MIXERLINE structure is strictly bound to the auxiliary device detailed in the remaining fields of the Target structure field of the MIXERLINE structure.
MIXERLINE_TARGETTYPE_MIDIIN	This value indicates that the audio line described by the MIXERLINE structure is strictly bound to the MIDI input device detailed in the remaining fields of the Target structure field of the MIXERLINE structure.
MIXERLINE_TARGETTYPE_MIDIOUT	This value indicates that the audio line described by the MIXERLINE structure is strictly bound to the MIDI output device detailed in the remaining fields of the Target structure field of the MIXERLINE structure.
MIXERLINE_TARGETTYPE_UNDEFINED	This value indicates that the audio line described by the MIXERLINE structure is not strictly bound to a defined media type. All remaining Target structure fields of the MIXERLINE structure should be ignored. An application cannot use the MIXER-LINE_TARGETTYPE_UNDEFINED target type when calling the MixerGetLineInfo() function with the MIXER_GETLINEINFOF_TARGETTYPE flag.
MIXERLINE_TARGETTYPE_WAVEIN	This value indicates that the audio line described by the MIXERLINE structure is strictly bound to the waveform audio input device detailed in the remaining fields of the Target structure field of the MIXERLINE structure.
MIXERLINE_TARGETTYPE_WAVEOUT	This value indicates that the audio line described by the MIXERLINE structure is strictly bound to the waveform audio output device detailed in the remaining fields of the Target structure field of the MIXERLINE structure.

When you work with this complex structure and the devices it controls, you need to be mindful of certain conditions, particularly the type of device that is being connected to the mixer. If an application is not using a waveform audio output device, the audio line associated with that device would not be active (that is, the MIXERLINE_LINEF_ACTIVE flag would not be set). If the waveform audio output device is opened, then the audio line is considered active and the MIXERLINE_LINEF_ACTIVE flag will be set. A paused or starved waveform audio output device is still considered active. That is, whenever a waveform audio output device is opened by an application, the associated audio line is considered active whether data is being played or not. If a line cannot be strictly defined as active, the mixer device will always set the MIXERLINE_LINEF_ACTIVE flag.

You also need to be mindful about how you set some of the members of the structure. For example, consider these two methods defined in the MixClass.pas unit used with the example program that accompanies this chapter. In the SetFaderControlValues() method, because the TMIXERCONTROLDETAILS structure's paDetails member points to a MIXERCONTROLDETAILS_UNSIGNED structure (declared as an array [0..1024] of integer), we use the following code to determine the size of the cChannels member we must initialize:

```
CurrentChannels := LocalMixerLine.cChannels;
if ((LocalMixerControl.fdwControl AND (1 SHL MIXERCONTROL_CONTROLF_
          UNIFORM)) =
   1 SHL MIXERCONTROL_CONTROLF_UNIFORM)
  then CurrentChannels := 1;
...
LocalMixerControlDetails.cChannels      := CurrentChannels;
```

Later, in the SetBooleanControlValues(), where the paDetails member points instead to a MIXERCONTROLDETAILS_BOOLEAN structure, and where the control in question (mute) applies to all controls, we must use a value of 1. Using the above code in this situation (which the author tried) results in an error. Instead, you simply need to use this line of code in place of the above snippet:

```
LocalMixerControlDetails.cChannels      := 1; // Required for Boolean
                                                 control
```

Opening and Closing Mixer Devices

Now we'll turn our attention to opening and closing mixer devices. There's one important difference between mixer devices and waveform devices: You don't need to open a mixer device to use it! You can simply begin using it or you can explicitly open the device before using it. Explicitly opening a mixer device does offer two important benefits:

■ It guarantees that the mixer device will continue to exist and be available.

■ It provides a means for you to receive notification of changes to the audio line or control.

The changes to the audio line or control can come from applications other than the ones you write. For example, if you create your own master volume control (as in the sample application for this chapter on the companion CD), changes to the Windows volume control will affect your volume control and vice versa. So how do you explicitly open a mixer device?

The MixerOpen() function, which we'll examine shortly, provides the means to do this. As we'll see, it takes as its main parameters a device identifier and a pointer to a memory location. The memory location is filled with a device handle. You can use this device handle to identify the open mixer device when calling other audio mixer functions.

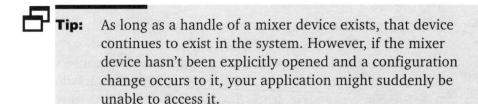

Tip: As long as a handle of a mixer device exists, that device continues to exist in the system. However, if the mixer device hasn't been explicitly opened and a configuration change occurs to it, your application might suddenly be unable to access it.

In working with mixers, you need to be aware of the difference between device identifiers and device handles. As we'll see presently, you retrieve a device handle when you open a device driver by calling the MixerOpen() function. However, since device identifiers are determined by the number of devices present in a system, you retrieve the set of valid numbers by calling the MixerGetNumDevs() function we discussed earlier. Once you have opened and finished using a mixer device, you can close it by calling the MixerClose() function. You should always close a device after you have finished using it.

function MixerOpen   *mmsystem.pas*

Syntax

```
function MixerOpen(
  phMx: PHMIXER;
  uMxId: UINT;
  dwCallback, dwInstance, fdwOpen: DWORD
  ): MMRESULT; stdcall;
```

Description

This function opens the mixer device with the number, uMxId, and ensures that the device will not be removed until the application closes the handle. If successful, the parameter phmx contains a handle for the device that will be used by other mixer functions. If a window is chosen to receive callback information, the MM_MIXM_LINE_CHANGE and MM_MIXM_CONTROL_CHANGE messages are sent to the window procedure function to indicate when an audio line or control state changes. For both messages, the wParam parameter is the handle of the mixer device. The lParam parameter is the line identifier for MM_MIXM_ LINE_CHANGE or the control identifier for MM_MIXM_CONTROL_ CHANGE that changed state. To query for audio mixer support or a media device, use the MixerGetID() function discussed later in this chapter.

Parameters

phMx: A PHMixer value that is the handle identifying the open mixer device. This handle should be saved in a variable visible to other mixer functions so that they can use it when they are called. This parameter cannot be NULL.

uMxID: An integer identifying the mixer device to open. It can be either a device identifier or any HMIXEROBJ (see the MixerGetID() function for a description of mixer object handles) value. Since there is currently no mapper for audio mixer devices, an identifier of –1 is not valid.

dwCallback: The handle of the window called when the state of an audio line and/or a control associated with the device being opened is changed. If no callback function is required, this value can be zero.

dwInstance: User instance data passed to the callback mechanism. This parameter is not used with the window callback mechanism and should be set to 0 in that case.

fdwOpen: Flags for opening the device. Those flags are shown in Table 6-12.

Return Value

Returns MMSYSERR_NOERROR if successful. Otherwise, it returns one of the following errors: MMSYSERR_ALLOCATED, indicating the specified resource is already allocated; MMSYSERR_BADDEVICEID, indicating the specified device identifier is out of range; MMSYSERR_INVALFLAG, indicating that one or more flags are invalid; MMSYSERR_INVAL-HANDLE, indicating that the uMxId parameter specifies an invalid handle; MMSYSERR_INVALPARAM, indicating that one or more parameters are invalid; MMSYSERR_NODRIVER, indicating that no mixer device is available for the object specified by uMxId (note that the location referenced by uMxId will also contain the value –1); MMSYSERR_NO-DRIVER, indicating that there is no device driver present; or MMSYSERR_NOMEM, indicating that memory could not be allocated.

Example

A special type and two methods in Listing 6-2 show how to explicitly open a mixer with some level of flexibility.

Listing 6-2: A type and two methods for opening a mixer

```
TMixerObject = (moNone, moHandle, moMixer, moHMixer, moWaveOut,
                moHWaveOut,
   moWaveIn, moHWaveIn, moMidiOut, moHMidiOut, moMidiIn, moHMidiIn,
                moAux,
   moUnspecified);
function TMixer.GetMixerObject(AMixerObject : TMixerObject) : DWord;
begin
  result := 0;
  case AMixerObject of
    moNone   : result :=  0;
    moHandle : result :=  MIXER_OBJECTF_HANDLE;
    moMixer  : result :=  MIXER_OBJECTF_MIXER;
```

```
    moHMixer   : result :=  MIXER_OBJECTF_HMIXER;
    moWaveOut  : result :=  MIXER_OBJECTF_WAVEOUT;
    moHWaveOut : result :=  MIXER_OBJECTF_HWAVEOUT;
    moWaveIn   : result :=  MIXER_OBJECTF_WAVEIN;
    moHWaveIn  : result :=  MIXER_OBJECTF_HWAVEIN;
    moMidiOut  : result :=  MIXER_OBJECTF_MIDIOUT;
    moHMidiOut : result :=  MIXER_OBJECTF_HMIDIOUT;
    moMidiIn   : result :=  MIXER_OBJECTF_MIDIIN;
    moHMidiIn  : result :=  MIXER_OBJECTF_HMIDIIN;
    moAux      : result :=  MIXER_OBJECTF_AUX;
  end;
end;

function TMixer.OpenMixerDev(RequestedMixerObject : TMixerObject) :
boolean;
var
  TempFlags : DWord;
begin
  result := False;
  DevNum := 0;  // Most systems have just one mixer device
  if mixerGetNumDevs=0 then if
    ReportMixerError('No mixer device available')
      then exit;
  if RequestedMixerObject = moNone then
    CurrentMMResult := MixerOpen(@AHandle, DevNum, DWORD(MainFormHandle),
                  DWord(0), Cardinal(callback_window))
  else
    begin
      TempFlags := GetMixerObject(RequestedMixerObject);
      CurrentMMResult := MixerOpen(@AHandle, DevNum, DWORD
                  (MainFormHandle), DWord(0), Cardinal
                  (TempFlags or callback_window));
    end;
  result := (CurrentMMResult=MMSYSERR_NOERROR);
  if result then
    begin
      AObjectHandle := 0; // Placeholder
      mixerGetID(AHandle, AMixerID, MIXER_OBJECTF_HMIXER);
    end;

  if NOT result then
    ReportMixerError('Could not open mixer device');
end;
```

Table 6-12: Flags for the fdwOpen field of MixerOpen()

Flag	Meaning
CALLBACK_WINDOW	The dwCallback parameter is a window handle.
MIXER_OBJECTF_AUX	The uMxId parameter is an auxiliary device identifier in the range of zero to one less than the number of devices returned by the AuxGetNumDevs() function.
MIXER_OBJECTF_HMIDIIN	The uMxId parameter is the handle of a MIDI input device. This handle must have been returned by the MIDIInOpen() function.
MIXER_OBJECTF_HMIDIOUT	The uMxId parameter is the handle of a MIDI output device. This handle must have been returned by the MIDIOutOpen() function.
MIXER_OBJECTF_HMIXER	The uMxId parameter is a mixer device handle returned by the MixerOpen() function. This flag is optional.
MIXER_OBJECTF_HWAVEIN	The uMxId parameter is a waveform audio input handle returned by the WaveInOpen() function.
MIXER_OBJECTF_HWAVEOUT	The uMxId parameter is a waveform audio output handle returned by the WaveOutOpen() function.
MIXER_OBJECTF_MIDIIN	The uMxId parameter is the identifier of a MIDI input device. This identifier must be in the range of zero to one less than the number of devices returned by the MIDIInGetNumDevs() function.
MIXER_OBJECTF_MIDIOUT	The uMxId parameter is the identifier of a MIDI output device. This identifier must be in the range of zero to one less than the number of devices returned by the MIDIOutGetNumDevs() function.
MIXER_OBJECTF_MIXER	The uMxId parameter is a mixer device identifier in the range of zero to one less than the number of devices returned by the MixerGetNumDevs() function. This flag is optional.
MIXER_OBJECTF_WAVEIN	The uMxId parameter is the identifier of a waveform audio input device in the range of zero to one less than the number of devices returned by the WaveInGetNumDevs() function.
MIXER_OBJECTF_WAVEOUT	The uMxId parameter is the identifier of a waveform audio output device in the range of zero to one less than the number of devices returned by the WaveOutGetNumDevs() function.

function MixerClose   *mmsystem.pas*

Syntax

```
function MixerClose(
  hMx: HMIXER
  ): MMRESULT; stdcall;
```

Description

This function closes the given mixer device.

Parameter

hMx: The handle of the mixer device. If the function succeeds, the handle is no longer valid.

Return Value

Returns MMSYSERR_NOERROR if successful. Otherwise, it returns MMSYSERR_INVALHANDLE, indicating that the specified device handle is invalid.

Example

The following very simple method shows how to call the MixerClose() function in a class's method, thus nullifying its AHandle variable.

```
procedure TMixer.CloseMixerDev;
begin
  MixerClose(AHandle);
end;
```

function MixerGetControlDetails   *mmsystem.pas*

Syntax

```
function MixerGetControlDetails(
  hmxobj: HMIXEROBJ;
  pMxCd: PMixerControlDetails;
  fdwDetails: DWORD
  ): MMRESULT; stdcall;
```

Description

This function retrieves details about a single control associated with an audio line. All members of the MIXERCONTROLDETAILS structure must be initialized before calling this function.

Parameters

hmxobj: The handle of the mixer device object being queried.

pMxCd: The address of a MIXERCONTROLDETAILS structure, which is filled with state information about the control.

fdwDetails: Flags for retrieving control details. The values defined for this parameter can include any of those in Table 6-13.

Return Value

Returns MMSYSERR_NOERROR if successful. Otherwise, it returns one of the following errors: MIXERR_INVALCONTROL, indicating that the control reference is invalid; MMSYSERR_BADDEVICEID, indicating that the hmxobj parameter specifies an invalid device identifier; MMSYSERR_INVALFLAG, indicating that one or more flags are invalid; MMSYSERR_INVALHANDLE, indicating that the specified device handle is invalid; MMSYSERR_INVALPARAM, indicating that one or more parameters are invalid; or MMSYSERR_NODRIVER, indicating that no device driver is present.

Example

Listings 6-3 and 6-4 show two ways to use the MixerGetControlDetails() function, the first with a slider control and the second with a Boolean switch control.

Listing 6-3: Using the MixerGetControlDetails() function with a slider control

```
function TMixer.ChangeControl(NewPosition : Integer; ALongParam :
                             DWORD) : boolean;
var
  LocalMixerControlDetails : TMIXERCONTROLDETAILS;
  LocalControlData : array [0..15] of Integer;
  Channels : integer;
  TheMixerLineControls : MixerLineControls;
  Max : Integer;
  procedure InitMixerLineControls(AControlID : Cardinal);
  begin
    TheMixerLineControls.cbStruct := SizeOf(TheMixerLineControls);
```

```
      TheMixerLineControls.dwLineID :=  AMixerLine.dwLineID;
      TheMixerLineControls.dwControlID := AControlID{0};
     // TheMixerLineControls.dwControlType := GetControlType(ControlType);
      TheMixerLineControls.cControls := AMixerLine.cControls;
      TheMixerLineControls.cbmxctrl := SizeOf(MixerControl);
      TheMixerLineControls.pamxctrl := @AMixerControl;
   end;
begin
  FillChar(LocalControlData, SizeOf(LocalControlData), 0);
  Channels := AMixerLine.cChannels;
  if ((AMixerControl.fdwControl and MIXERCONTROL_CONTROLF_UNIFORM)=0) then
     Channels := 1;
  LocalMixerControlDetails.hwndOwner := MainFormHandle;
  LocalMixerControlDetails.cbStruct :=
sizeof(LocalControlData{LocalMixerControlDetails}{TMIXERCONTROLDETAILS});
  LocalMixerControlDetails.dwControlID := ALongParam;
  LocalMixerControlDetails.cChannels  := Channels;
  LocalMixerControlDetails.cMultipleItems := AMixerControl.cMultipleItems;
  LocalMixerControlDetails.cbDetails :=
sizeof({integer}MIXERCONTROLDETAILS_UNSIGNED);
  LocalMixerControlDetails.paDetails :=
@LocalControlData{MixerControlDetails};
  CurrentMMResult :=  mixerGetControlDetails(AHandle,
                        @LocalMixerControlDetails, 0
                        {MIXER_GETCONTROLDETAILSF_VALUE});
  result := (CurrentMMResult=MMSYSERR_NOERROR);
  Max := Round((High(FaderControlRange)) / 10);
  LocalControlData[0] :=  MulDiv((Max - NewPosition),
    $FFFF, Max);
  LocalControlData[1] :=  MulDiv((Max - NewPosition),
    $FFFF, Max);
  CurrentMMResult :=  mixerSetControlDetails(AHandle,
                        @LocalMixerControlDetails, 0
                        {MIXER_GETCONTROLDETAILSF_VALUE});
  result := (CurrentMMResult=MMSYSERR_NOERROR);
end;
```

Listing 6-4: Using the MixerGetControlDetails() function with a Boolean switch control

```
procedure TMixer.ChangeBoolControl(CurrentCBState : boolean;
                                   ALongParam : DWORD);
var
  LocalMixerControlDetails : TMIXERCONTROLDETAILS;
  LocalControlData : array [0..15] of Integer;
  TheMixerLineControls : MixerLineControls;
```

```
  procedure InitMixerLineControls(AControlID : Cardinal);
  begin
    TheMixerLineControls.cbStruct := SizeOf(TheMixerLineControls);
    TheMixerLineControls.dwLineID := AMixerLine.dwLineID;
    TheMixerLineControls.dwControlID := AControlID{0};
    TheMixerLineControls.cControls := AMixerLine.cControls;
    TheMixerLineControls.cbmxctrl := SizeOf(MixerControl);
    TheMixerLineControls.pamxctrl := @AMixerControl;
  end;
begin
  FillChar(LocalControlData, SizeOf(LocalControlData), 0);
  LocalMixerControlDetails.hwndOwner := MainFormHandle;
  LocalMixerControlDetails.cbStruct :=
sizeof(LocalControlData{LocalMixerControlDetails}{TMIXERCONTROLDETAILS});
  LocalMixerControlDetails.dwControlID := ALongParam;
  LocalMixerControlDetails.cChannels  := 1; //Channels;
  LocalMixerControlDetails.cMultipleItems := AMixerControl.cMultipleItems;
  LocalMixerControlDetails.cbDetails :=
sizeof({integer}MIXERCONTROLDETAILS_UNSIGNED);
  LocalMixerControlDetails.paDetails :=
@{LocalControlData}MixerControlDetails;
  CurrentMMResult :=  mixerGetControlDetails(AHandle,
                       @LocalMixerControlDetails, 0
                       {MIXER_GETCONTROLDETAILSF_VALUE});
  if NOT CurrentCBState then
    MixerControlDetails.dwValue := 0
  else
    MixerControlDetails.dwValue := 1;
  CurrentMMResult :=  mixerSetControlDetails(AHandle,
                       @LocalMixerControlDetails,  0
                       {MIXER_GETCONTROLDETAILSF_VALUE});
end;
```

Table 6-13: Flag constants that can be used with the fdwDetails parameter of MixerGetControlDetails()

Flag	Meaning
MIXER_GETCONTROLDETAILSF_LISTTEXT	The paDetails member of the MIXERCONTROLDETAILS structure points to one or more MIXERCONTROL-DETAILS_LISTTEXT structures to receive text labels for multiple-item controls. An application must get all list text items for a multiple-item control at once. This

6

Chapter

Flag	Meaning
	flag cannot be used with MIXERCONTROL_CONTROLTYPE_ CUSTOM controls.
MIXER_GETCONTROLDETAILSF_ VALUE	Current values for a control are retrieved. The paDetails member of the MIXERCONTROLDETAILS structure points to one or more detail structures appropriate for the control class.
MIXER_OBJECTF_AUX	The hmxobj parameter is an auxiliary device identifier in the range of zero to one less than the number of devices returned by the AuxGetNumDevs() function.
MIXER_OBJECTF_HMIDIIN	The hmxobj parameter is the handle of a MIDI (Musical Instrument Digital Interface) input device. This handle must have been returned by the MIDIInOpen() function.
MIXER_OBJECTF_HMIDIOUT	The hmxobj parameter is the handle of a MIDI output device. This handle must have been returned by the MIDIOutOpen() function.
MIXER_OBJECTF_HMIXER	The hmxobj parameter is a mixer device handle returned by the MixerOpen() function. This flag is optional.
MIXER_OBJECTF_HWAVEIN	The hmxobj parameter is a waveform audio input handle returned by the WaveInOpen() function.
MIXER_OBJECTF_HWAVEOUT	The hmxobj parameter is a waveform audio output handle returned by the WaveOutOpen() function.
MIXER_OBJECTF_MIDIIN	The hmxobj parameter is the identifier of a MIDI input device. This identifier must be in the range of zero to one less than the number of devices returned by the MIDIInGetNumDevs() function.
MIXER_OBJECTF_MIDIOUT	The hmxobj parameter is the identifier of a MIDI output device. This identifier must be in the range of zero to one less than the number of devices returned by the MIDIOutGetNumDevs() function.

Flag	Meaning
MIXER_OBJECTF_MIXER	The hmxobj parameter is the identifier of a mixer device in the range of zero to one less than the number of devices returned by the MixerGetNumDevs() function. This flag is optional.
MIXER_OBJECTF_WAVEIN	The hmxobj parameter is the identifier of a waveform audio input device in the range of zero to one less than the number of devices returned by the WaveInGetNum-Devs() function.
MIXER_OBJECTF_WAVEOUT	The hmxobj parameter is the identifier of a waveform audio output device in the range of zero to one less than the number of devices returned by the WaveOutGetNum-Devs() function.

function MixerGetLineControls   mmsystem.pas

Syntax

```
function MixerGetLineControls(
  hmxobj: HMIXEROBJ;
  pmxlc: PMixerLineControls;
  fdwControls: DWORD
  ): MMRESULT; stdcall;
```

Description

This function retrieves one or more controls associated with an audio line.

Parameters

hmxobj: The handle of the mixer device object that is being queried.

pmxlc: The address of a MIXERLINECONTROLS structure. This structure is used to reference one or more MIXERCONTROL structures to be filled with information about the controls associated with an audio line. The cbStruct member of the MIXERLINECONTROLS structure must always be initialized to be the size, in bytes, of the MIXERLINECONTROLS structure.

6

fdwControls: Flags for retrieving information about one or more controls associated with an audio line. Values defined are shown in Table 6-14.

Return Value

Returns MMSYSERR_NOERROR if successful. Otherwise, it returns one of the following errors: MIXERR_INVALCONTROL, indicating that the control reference is invalid; MIXERR_INVALLINE, indicating that the audio line reference is invalid; MMSYSERR_BADDEVICEID, indicating that the hmxobj parameter specifies an invalid device identifier; MMSYSERR_INVALFLAG, indicating that one or more flags are invalid; MMSYSERR_INVALHANDLE, indicating that the specified device handle is invalid; MMSYSERR_INVALPARAM, indicating that one or more parameters are invalid; or MMSYSERR_NODRIVER, indicating that no device driver is present.

Example

Listing 6-5 show how to locate a specific control on a line using the MixerGetLineControls() function.

Listing 6-5: Using MixerGetLineControls() to locate a specific control

```
function TMixer.LocateControl(MixerLineInfoOf : TMixerLineInfoOf;
        ControlType : TMixerControlType;
        var ALine: TMixerLine;
        var TheMixerControl : TMixerControl;
        CurrentControlNum : Cardinal;
        MixerLineObject : TMixerLineObject;
        RequestedSource : TSource;
        RequestedDestination : TDestination): boolean;
var
    TheMixerLineControls : MixerLineControls;
    AMixerType : DWord;
    j: Integer;
    MixerControlArray :  Array of TMixerControl;
  procedure InitMixerLineControls(AControlID : Cardinal);
    begin  { InitMixerLineControls }
    TheMixerLineControls.cbStruct := SizeOf(TheMixerLineControls);
    TheMixerLineControls.dwLineID :=  ALine.dwLineID;
    TheMixerLineControls.dwControlID := AControlID;
    TheMixerLineControls.dwControlType := GetControlType(ControlType);
    TheMixerLineControls.cControls := AMixerLine.cControls;
    TheMixerLineControls.cbmxctrl := SizeOf(MixerControl);
    TheMixerLineControls.pamxctrl := @TheMixerControl;
```

```
    end;    { InitMixerLineControls }
    procedure GetFlags;
    begin { GetFlags }
      case MixerLineInfoOf of     //
        mliComponentType: FMixerGetLineFlags := FMixerGetLineFlags or
          MIXER_GETLINEINFOF_COMPONENTTYPE;
        mliDestination: FMixerGetLineFlags := FMixerGetLineFlags or
          MIXER_GETLINEINFOF_DESTINATION;
        mliLineID: FMixerGetLineFlags := FMixerGetLineFlags or
          MIXER_GETLINEINFOF_LINEID;
        mliSource: FMixerGetLineFlags := FMixerGetLineFlags or
          MIXER_GETLINEINFOF_SOURCE;
        mliTarget  : FMixerGetLineFlags := FMixerGetLineFlags or
          MIXER_GETLINEINFOF_TARGETTYPE;
      end;    // case
    end; { GetFlags }
begin { LocateControl }
  SetLength(MixerControlArray, ControlsToImplement);
  result := False;
  FMixerGetLineFlags := 0;
  AMixerLine.cbStruct := SizeOf(AMixerLine{MixerLineControls});
  AMixerLine.dwDestination := GetDestination(RequestedDestination);
  CurrentMMResult := mixerGetLineInfo(AHandle, @AMixerLine,
    MIXER_GETLINEINFOF_LINEID);
  if NOT CurrentMMResult = MMSYSERR_NOERROR then exit;
  if AMixerLine.cControls=0 then if
    ReportMixerError('No controls associated with this line') then exit;
  for j := 0 to AMixerLine.cControls-1 do    // Iterate thorough controls
  begin
    InitMixerLineControls(j);
    CurrentMMResult := mixerGetLineControls(AHandle,
                  @TheMixerLineControls,
      MIXER_GETLINECONTROLSF_ONEBYTYPE);
    if (CurrentMMResult = MMSYSERR_NOERROR) then break
    else
      if j=AMixerLine.cControls-1 then // tried them all - none available
        exit;
  end;    // for
    AMixerType := GetControlType(ControlType);
    if NOT((TheMixerControl.fdwControl and MIXERCONTROL_CONTROLF_
            DISABLED)=0)  then
      begin
        ShowMessage('Requested Control is not active and cannot be
                    modified');
        exit;
      end;
```

```
for j := 0 to TheMixerLineControls.cControls-1 do  // Iterate through
                                                         controls
begin
  if TheMixerLineControls.dwControlType=AMixerType then
  begin
    // Check to make sure we have the right control type
    if NOT ((MixerControlArray[j].dwControlType and AMixerType)
          = 0) then
      begin
        ShowMessage('Incorrect Control Type');
        exit;
      end;
  end;
end;    // for
result := True;  // If we get this far, everything worked OK
end;  { LocateControl }
```

Table 6-14: Values defined for the fdwControls parameter of MixerGetLineControls()

Value	Meaning
MIXER_GETLINECONTROLSF_ALL	The pmxlc parameter references a list of MIXERCONTROL structures that will receive information on all controls associated with the audio line identified by the dwLineID member of the MIXERLINECONTROLS structure. The cControls member must be initialized to the number of controls associated with the line. This number is retrieved from the cControls member of the MIXERLINE structure returned by the MixerGetLineInfo function. The cbmxctrl member must be initialized to the size, in bytes, of a single MIXERCONTROL structure. The pamxctrl member must point to the first MIXERCONTROL structure to be filled. The dwControlID and dwControlType members are ignored for this query.
MIXER_GETLINECONTROLSF_ONEBYID	The pmxlc parameter references a single MIXERCONTROL structure that will receive information on the control identified by the dwControlID member of the MIXERLINECONTROLS structure. The cControls member must be initialized to 1. The cbmxctrl member must be initialized to the size, in bytes, of a single MIXERCONTROL structure. The

Value	Meaning
	pamxctrl member must point to a MIXERCONTROL structure to be filled. The dwLineID and dwControlType members are ignored for this query. This query is usually used to refresh a control after receiving a MM_MIXM_CONTROL_CHANGE control change notification message by the user-defined callback (see MixerOpen()).
MIXER_GETLINECONTROLSF_ ONEBYTYPE	The MixerGetLineControls() function retrieves information about the first control of a specific class for the audio line that is being queried. The pmxlc parameter references a single MIXERCONTROL structure that will receive information about the specific control. The audio line is identified by the dwLineID member. The control class is specified in the dwControlType member of the MIXERLINECONTROLS structure.
	The dwControlID member is ignored for this query. This query can be used by an application to get information on a single control associated with a line. For example, you might want your application to use a peak meter only from a waveform audio output line.
MIXER_OBJECTF_AUX	The hmxobj parameter is an auxiliary device identifier in the range of zero to one less than the number of devices returned by the AuxGetNumDevs() function.
MIXER_OBJECTF_HMIDIIN	The hmxobj parameter is the handle of a MIDI input device. This handle must have been returned by the MIDIInOpen() function.
MIXER_OBJECTF_HMIDIOUT	The hmxobj parameter is the handle of a MIDI output device. This handle must have been returned by the MIDIOutOpen() function.
MIXER_OBJECTF_HMIXER	The hmxobj parameter is a mixer device handle returned by the MixerOpen() function. This flag is optional.
MIXER_OBJECTF_HWAVEIN	The hmxobj parameter is a waveform audio input handle returned by the WaveInOpen() function.

Value	Meaning
MIXER_OBJECTF_HWAVEOUT	The hmxobj parameter is a waveform audio output handle returned by the WaveOutOpen() function.
MIXER_OBJECTF_MIDIIN	The hmxobj parameter is the identifier of a MIDI input device. This identifier must be in the range of zero to one less than the number of devices returned by the MIDIInGetNumDevs() function.
MIXER_OBJECTF_MIDIOUT	The hmxobj parameter is the identifier of a MIDI output device. This identifier must be in the range of zero to one less than the number of devices returned by the MIDIOutGetNumDevs() function.
MIXER_OBJECTF_MIXER	The hmxobj parameter is the identifier of a mixer device in the range of zero to one less than the number of devices returned by the MixerGetNumDevs() function. This flag is optional.
MIXER_OBJECTF_WAVEIN	The hmxobj parameter is the identifier of a waveform audio input device in the range of zero to one less than the number of devices returned by the WaveInGetNumDevs() function.
MIXER_OBJECTF_WAVEOUT	The hmxobj parameter is the identifier of a waveform audio output device in the range of zero to one less than the number of devices returned by the WaveOutGetNumDevs() function.

function MixerGetLineInfo   mmsystem.pas

Syntax

```
function MixerGetLineInfo(
  hmxobj: HMIXEROBJ;
  pmxl: PMixerLine;
  fdwInfo: DWORD
  ): MMRESULT; stdcall;
```

Description

This function retrieves information about a specific line of a mixer device.

Parameters

hmxobj: The handle of the mixer device object that controls the specific audio line.

pmxl: The address of a MIXERLINE structure. This structure is filled with information about the audio line for the mixer device. The cbStruct member must always be initialized to be the size, in bytes, of the MIXERLINE structure.

fdwInfo: Flags for retrieving information about an audio line. These flags, which are explained in Table 6-15, give you a great deal of flexibility when querying audio line. For that reason, we include the same flexibility in the MixClass.pas unit, as shown in the nested GetFlags() procedure in Listing 6-5.

Return Value

Returns MMSYSERR_NOERROR if successful. Otherwise, it returns one of the following errors: MIXERR_INVALLINE, indicating that the audio line reference is invalid; MMSYSERR_BADDEVICEID, indicating that the hmxobj parameter specifies an invalid device identifier; MMSYSERR_ INVALFLAG, indicating that one or more flags are invalid; MMSYSERR_INVALHANDLE, indicating that the specified device handle is invalid; MMSYSERR_INVALPARAM, indicating that one or more parameters are invalid; or MMSYSERR_NODRIVER, indicating that no device driver is present.

Example

Listing 6-6 shows how to use the MixerGetLineInfo() function to retrieve information on an audio line. The ChangeLine method defined in MixClass.pas is called in the second sample application for this chapter, one that monitors multimedia activity on a computer and responds whenever a line changes. It returns a MIXERLINE structure to the calling application. The UpdateLineInfo() method in the calling application responds to MM_MIXM_LINE_CHANGE messages. The GetComponent-Type() method in MixClass.pas is used to return a string value based on MIXERLINE's dwComponentType member.

Listing 6-6: Using the MixerGetLineInfo() function to return information on an audio line

```
function TMixer.ChangeLine(ALongParam : DWORD;
        var LocalMixerLine : MIXERLINE) : boolean;
var
  LocalLineID : DWORD;
begin
  LocalLineID := ALongParam;
```

```pascal
   LocalMixerLine.cbStruct := SizeOf(MIXERLINE);
   LocalMixerLine.dwLineID := LocalLineID;
   CurrentMMResult := mixerGetLineInfo(AHandle, @LocalMixerLine,
                     MIXER_GETLINEINFOF_LINEID);
   result := CurrentMMResult=MMSYSERR_NOERROR;
end;

procedure TForm1.UpdateLineInfo(AWordMessage : Word;
       ALongMessage : DWord);
var
  CurrentMixerLine : MIXERLINE;
  AListItem: TListItem;
begin
 if Mixer.ChangeLine(ALongMessage, CurrentMixerLine) then
   begin
     AListItem := lvMMLineInfo.Items.Add;
     AListItem.Caption := CurrentMixerLine.szName;
     AListItem.SubItems.Add(IntToStr(ALongMessage));
     AListItem.SubItems.Add(Mixer.GetComponentType
       (CurrentMixerLine.dwComponentType));
     AListItem.SubItems.Add(IntToStr(CurrentMixerLine.cConnections));
     AListItem.SubItems.Add(IntToStr(CurrentMixerLine.cControls));
   end;
end;

function TMixer.GetComponentType(dwComponentTypeIn : DWord):
               string;
begin
  result := 'Unknown';
  case dwComponentTypeIn of     //
    MIXERLINE_COMPONENTTYPE_DST_UNDEFINED: Result :=
      'DST_UNDEFINED';
    MIXERLINE_COMPONENTTYPE_DST_DIGITAL: Result :=
      'DST_DIGITAL';
    MIXERLINE_COMPONENTTYPE_DST_LINE: Result :=
      'DST_LINE';
    MIXERLINE_COMPONENTTYPE_DST_MONITOR: Result :=
      'DST_MONITOR';
    MIXERLINE_COMPONENTTYPE_DST_SPEAKERS: Result :=
      'DST_SPEAKERS';
    MIXERLINE_COMPONENTTYPE_DST_HEADPHONES: Result :=
      'DST_HEADPHONES';
    MIXERLINE_COMPONENTTYPE_DST_TELEPHONE: Result :=
      'DST_TELEPHONE';
    MIXERLINE_COMPONENTTYPE_DST_WAVEIN: Result :=
      'DST_WAVEIN';
```

```
      MIXERLINE_COMPONENTTYPE_DST_VOICEIN: Result :=
        'DST_VOICEIN';
      MIXERLINE_COMPONENTTYPE_SRC_FIRST: Result :=
        'SRC_FIRST';
      MIXERLINE_COMPONENTTYPE_SRC_DIGITAL: Result :=
        'SRC_DIGITAL';
      MIXERLINE_COMPONENTTYPE_SRC_LINE: Result :=
        'SRC_LINE';
      MIXERLINE_COMPONENTTYPE_SRC_MICROPHONE: Result :=
        'SRC_MICROPHONE';
      MIXERLINE_COMPONENTTYPE_SRC_SYNTHESIZER: Result :=
        'SRC_SYNTHESIZER';
      MIXERLINE_COMPONENTTYPE_SRC_COMPACTDISC: Result :=
        'SRC_COMPACTDISC';
      MIXERLINE_COMPONENTTYPE_SRC_TELEPHONE: Result :=
        'SRC_TELEPHONE';
      MIXERLINE_COMPONENTTYPE_SRC_PCSPEAKER: Result :=
        'SRC_PCSPEAKER';
      MIXERLINE_COMPONENTTYPE_SRC_WAVEOUT: Result :=
        'SRC_WAVEOUT';
      MIXERLINE_COMPONENTTYPE_SRC_AUXILIARY: Result :=
        'SRC_AUXILIARY';
      MIXERLINE_COMPONENTTYPE_SRC_ANALOG: Result :=
        'SRC_ANALOG';
  end;     // case
end;
```

Table 6-15: FdwInfo values that can be used in the MixerGetLineInfo() function

Value	Meaning
MIXER_GETLINEINFOF_COMPONENTTYPE	The pmxl parameter will receive information about the first audio line of the type specified in the dwComponentType member of the MIXERLINE structure. This flag is used to retrieve information about an audio line of a specific component type. Remaining structure members except cbStruct require no further initialization.
MIXER_GETLINEINFOF_DESTINATION	The pmxl parameter will receive information about the destination audio line specified by the dwDestination member of the MIXERLINE structure. This index ranges from zero to one less than the value in the cDestinations member of the MIXERCAPS structure. All remaining structure members except cbStruct require no further initialization.

Value	Meaning
MIXER_GETLINEINFOF_LINEID	The pmxl parameter will receive information about the audio line specified by the dwLineID member of the MIXERLINE structure. This is usually used to retrieve updated information about the state of an audio line. All remaining structure members except cbStruct require no further initialization.
MIXER_GETLINEINFOF_SOURCE	The pmxl parameter will receive information about the source audio line specified by the dwDestination and dwSource members of the MIXERLINE structure. The index specified by dwDestination ranges from zero to one less than the value in the cDestinations member of the MIXERCAPS structure. The index specified by dwSource ranges from zero to one less than the value in the cConnections member of the MIXERLINE structure returned for the audio line stored in the dwDestination member. All remaining structure members except cbStruct require no further initialization.
MIXER_GETLINEINFOF_TARGETTYPE	The pmxl parameter will receive information about the audio line that is for the dwType member of the Target structure, which is a member of the MIXERLINE structure. This flag is used to retrieve information about an audio line that handles the target type (for example, MIXERLINE_TARGETTYPE_WAVEOUT). An application must initialize the dwType, wMid, wPid, vDriverVersion, and szPname members of the MIXERLINE structure before calling MixerGetLineInfo(). All of these values can be retrieved from the device capabilities structures for all media devices. Remaining structure members except cbStruct require no further initialization.
MIXER_OBJECTF_AUX	The hmxobj parameter is an auxiliary device identifier in the range of zero to one less than the number of devices returned by the AuxGetNumDevs() function.
MIXER_OBJECTF_HMIDIIN	The hmxobj parameter is the handle of a MIDI input device. This handle must have been returned by the MIDIInOpen() function.
MIXER_OBJECTF_HMIDIOUT	The hmxobj parameter is the handle of a MIDI output device. This handle must have been returned by the MIDIOutOpen() function.

Value	Meaning
MIXER_OBJECTF_HMIXER	The hmxobj parameter is a mixer device handle returned by the MixerOpen() function. This flag is optional.
MIXER_OBJECTF_HWAVEIN	The hmxobj parameter is a waveform audio input handle returned by the WaveInOpen() function.
MIXER_OBJECTF_HWAVEOUT	The hmxobj parameter is a waveform audio output handle returned by the WaveOutOpen() function.
MIXER_OBJECTF_MIDIIN	The hmxobj parameter is the identifier of a MIDI input device. This identifier must be in the range of zero to one less than the number of devices returned by the MIDIInGetNumDevs() function.
MIXER_OBJECTF_MIDIOUT	The hmxobj parameter is the identifier of a MIDI output device. This identifier must be in the range of zero to one less than the number of devices returned by the MIDIOutGetNumDevs() function.
MIXER_OBJECTF_MIXER	The hmxobj parameter is a mixer device identifier in the range of zero to one less than the number of devices returned by the MixerGetNumDevs() function. This flag is optional.
MIXER_OBJECTF_WAVEIN	The hmxobj parameter is the identifier of a waveform audio input device in the range of zero to one less than the number of devices returned by the WaveInGetNumDevs() function.
MIXER_OBJECTF_WAVEOUT	The hmxobj parameter is the identifier of a waveform audio output device in the range of zero to one less than the number of devices returned by the WaveOutGetNumDevs() function.

function MixerMessage   *mmsystem.pas*

Syntax

```
function MixerMessage(
hMx: HMIXER;
uMsg: UINT;
dwParam1, dwParam2: DWORD
): DWORD; stdcall;
```

6

Chapter

Description

This function sends a custom mixer driver message directly to a mixer driver. User-defined messages must be sent only to a mixer driver that supports such messages. The application should verify that the mixer driver is a driver that supports the message by retrieving the mixer capabilities and checking the wMid, wPid, vDriverVersion, and szPname fields of the MIXERCAPS structure.

Parameters

hMx: The handle of the mixer device.

uMsg: An integer indicating the custom mixer driver message to be sent to the mixer driver. This message must be equal to or above the MXDM_USER constant.

dwParam1, *dwParam2*: Two DWORD parameters for message parameters.

Return Value

Returns a DWORD indicating the return value of the message.

Example

The following simple method from MixClass.pas wraps this function call.

```
procedure TMixer.SendMixerMessage(ADriverMessage: UINT; MsgParam1,
                      MsgParam2: DWORD);
begin
  MixerMessage(AHandle, ADriverMessage, MsgParam1, MsgParam2);
end;
```

function MixerGetID   *mmsystem.pas*

Syntax

```
function MixerGetID(
  hmxobj: HMIXEROBJ;
  var puMxId: UINT;
  fdwId: DWORD
  ): MMRESULT; stdcall;
```

Description

This function gets the device identifier for a mixer device associated with a specified device handle.

Parameters

hmxobj: The handle of the audio mixer object to map to a mixer device identifier.

puMxId: The address of a variable that receives the mixer device identifier. If no mixer device is available for the hmxobj object, the value −1 is placed in this location and the MMSYSERR_NODRIVER error value is returned.

fdwID: Flags for mapping the mixer object hmxobj. The following values are defined:

Table 6-16: Flags for the fdwID field of function MixerGetID()

Flag	Meaning
MIXER_OBJECTF_AUX	The hmxobj parameter is an auxiliary device identifier in the range of zero to one less than the number of devices returned by the AuxGetNumDevs() function.
MIXER_OBJECTF_HMIDIIN	The hmxobj parameter is the handle of a MIDI input device. This handle must have been returned by the MIDIInOpen() function.
MIXER_OBJECTF_HMIDIOUT	The hmxobj parameter is the handle of a MIDI output device. This handle must have been returned by the MIDIOutOpen() function.
MIXER_OBJECTF_HMIXER	The hmxobj parameter is a mixer device handle returned by the MixerOpen() function. This flag is optional.
MIXER_OBJECTF_HWAVEIN	The hmxobj parameter is a waveform audio input handle returned by the WaveInOpen() function.
MIXER_OBJECTF_HWAVEOUT	The hmxobj parameter is a waveform audio output handle returned by the WaveOutOpen() function.
MIXER_OBJECTF_MIDIIN	The hmxobj parameter is the identifier of a MIDI input device. This identifier must be in the range of zero to one less than the number of devices returned by the MIDIInGetNumDevs() function.

Flag	Meaning
MIXER_OBJECTF_MIDIOUT	The hmxobj parameter is the identifier of a MIDI output device. This identifier must be in the range of zero to one less than the number of devices returned by the MIDIOutGetNumDevs() function.
MIXER_OBJECTF_MIXER	The hmxobj parameter is the identifier of a mixer device in the range of zero to one less than the number of devices returned by the MixerGetNumDevs() function. This flag is optional.
MIXER_OBJECTF_WAVEIN	The hmxobj parameter is the identifier of a waveform audio input device in the range of zero to one less than the number of devices returned by the WaveInGetNumDevs() function.
MIXER_OBJECTF_WAVEOUT	The hmxobj parameter is the identifier of a waveform audio output device in the range of zero to one less than the number of devices returned by the WaveOutGetNumDevs() function.

Return Value

Returns MMSYSERR_NOERROR if successful. Otherwise, it returns one of the following errors: MMSYSERR_BADDEVICEID, indicating that the hmxobj parameter specifies an invalid device identifier; MMSYSERR_INVALFLAG, indicating that one or more flags are invalid; MMSYSERR_INVALHANDLE, indicating that the specified device handle is invalid; MMSYSERR_INVALPARAM, indicating that one or more parameters are invalid; or MMSYSERR_NODRIVER, indicating that no audio mixer device is available for the object specified by hmxobj (the location referenced by puMxId also contains the value –1).

Example

See the OpenMixerDev() method under Listing 6-2.

function MixerSetControlDetails   *mmsystem.pas*

Syntax

```
function MixerSetControlDetails(
  hmxobj: HMIXEROBJ;
  pmxcd: PMixerControlDetails;
  fdwDetails: DWORD
  ): MMRESULT; stdcall;
```

Description

This function sets properties of a single control associated with an audio line. All members of the MIXERCONTROLDETAILS structure must be initialized before calling MixerSetControlDetails(). If an application needs to retrieve only the current state of a custom mixer control and not display a dialog box, then MixerGetControlDetails() can be used with the MIXER_GETCONTROLDETAILSF_VALUE flag.

Parameters

hmxobj: The handle of the mixer device object for which properties are being set.

pmxcd: The address of a MIXERCONTROLDETAILS structure, which is used to reference control detail structures that contain the desired state for the control.

fdwDetails: Flags for setting control details. Possible values defined for this parameter are described in Table 6-17.

Return Value

Returns MMSYSERR_NOERROR if successful. Otherwise, it returns one of the following errors: MIXERR_INVALCONTROL, indicating that the control reference is invalid; MMSYSERR_BADDEVICEID, indicating that the hmxobj parameter specifies an invalid device identifier; MMSYSERR_INVALFLAG, indicating that one or more flags are invalid; MMSYSERR_INVALHANDLE, indicating that the specified device handle is invalid; MMSYSERR_INVALPARAM, indicating that one or more parameters are invalid; or MMSYSERR_NODRIVER, indicating that no device driver is present.

Example

See Table 6-17.

Table 6-17: Flags for the fdwDetails parameter of MixerSetControlDetails()

Flag	Meaning
MIXER_OBJECTF_AUX	The hmxobj parameter is an auxiliary device identifier in the range of zero to one less than the number of devices returned by the AuxGetNumDevs() function.

Flag	Meaning
MIXER_OBJECTF_HMIDIIN	The hmxobj parameter is the handle of a MIDI (Musical Instrument Digital Interface) input device. This handle must have been returned by the MIDIInOpen() function.
MIXER_OBJECTF_HMIDIOUT	The hmxobj parameter is the handle of a MIDI output device. This handle must have been returned by the MIDIOutOpen() function.
MIXER_OBJECTF_HMIXER	The hmxobj parameter is a mixer device handle returned by the MixerOpen() function. This flag is optional.
MIXER_OBJECTF_HWAVEIN	The hmxobj parameter is a waveform audio input handle returned by the WaveInOpen() function.
MIXER_OBJECTF_HWAVEOUT	The hmxobj parameter is a waveform audio output handle returned by the WaveOutOpen() function.
MIXER_OBJECTF_MIDIIN	The hmxobj parameter is the identifier of a MIDI input device. This identifier must be in the range of zero to one less than the number of devices returned by the MIDIInGetNumDevs() function.
MIXER_OBJECTF_MIDIOUT	The hmxobj parameter is the identifier of a MIDI output device. This identifier must be in the range of zero to one less than the number of devices returned by the MIDIOutGetNumDevs() function.
MIXER_OBJECTF_MIXER	The hmxobj parameter is the identifier of a mixer device in the range of zero to one less than the number of devices returned by the MixerGetNumDevs() function. This flag is optional.
MIXER_OBJECTF_WAVEIN	The hmxobj parameter is the identifier of a waveform audio input device in the range of zero to one less than the number of devices returned by the WaveInGetNumDevs() function.
MIXER_OBJECTF_WAVEOUT	The hmxobj parameter is the identifier of a waveform audio output device in the range of zero to one less than the number of devices returned by the WaveOutGetNumDevs() function.

Flag	Meaning
MIXER_SETCONTROL DETAILSF_CUSTOM	A custom dialog box for the specified custom mixer control is displayed. The mixer device gathers the required information from the user and returns the data in the specified buffer. The handle for the owning window is specified in the hwndOwner member of the MIXERCONTROLDETAILS structure. (This handle can be set to NULL.) The application can then save the data from the dialog box and use it later to reset the control to the same state by using the MIXER_SETCONTROL DETAILSF_VALUE flag.
MIXER_SETCONTROL DETAILSF_VALUE	The current value(s) for a control are set. The paDetails member of the MIXERCONTROLDETAILS structure points to one or more mixer control details structures of the appropriate class for the control.

We have reached the end of an important chapter demonstrating how to combine various audio devices with the multimedia Mixer API. In the next chapter, we will examine two secondary topics: timers and joysticks.

Chapter Seven

Timers and Joysticks

We have built a great deal of multimedia functionality up to this point. The Wave API, which we have been using since we worked with wave-form audio, is connected with Windows timers. In this chapter, we have expanded the application from Chapter 3 to respond to timer messages. See Figures 7-1 and 7-2, showing timing status for recording and playback.

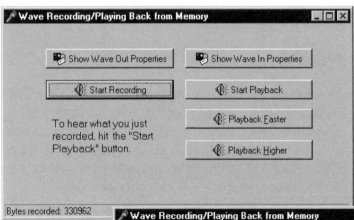

Figure 7-1

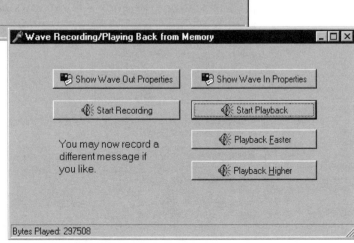

Figure 7-2

As we mentioned in the introduction, these low-level timers are the most powerful in the entire operating system. These timer services allow applications to schedule timer events with the greatest resolution (or accuracy) possible and are useful for applications that demand high-resolution timing. Take MIDI, for example. A MIDI sequencer requires a high-resolution timer because it must maintain the pace of MIDI events within a resolution of one millisecond.

On the other hand, applications that do not require high-resolution timing may use Delphi's built-in timer instead. This timer uses the Windows SetTimer() function, which posts WM_TIMER messages to a message queue—hardly the most accurate approach. The multimedia timer services, on the other hand, rely on a callback function. We'll explore these timer services in detail in this chapter.

One input device often associated with multimedia, especially with multimedia games, is the joystick. This device generally provides positional input on at least two axes and one or more buttons. We will explore both of these APIs in this chapter, beginning with timers.

Multimedia Timers

Before an application begins using the multimedia timer services, it needs a reference point against which to measure subsequent timing events. Generally, it uses the system time. Therefore, the first step is to retrieve the current system time. This is defined as the time, in milliseconds, since the Microsoft Windows operating system was started. A sample application (see Figure 7-3) shows how to do this.

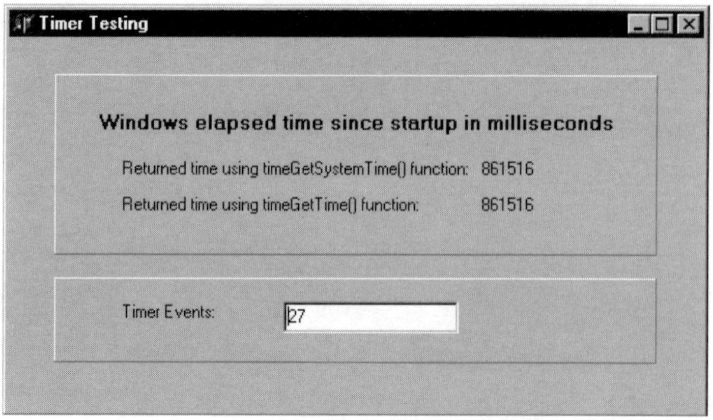

Figure 7-3

To get this time, you can use the TimeGetTime() or TimeGetSystem-Time() functions. While very similar, these two functions have subtle differences. TimeGetTime() simply returns the system time, while TimeGetSystemTime() fills an MMTIME structure with that time. That structure and its related structures are defined in mmsystem.pas as follows:

```
type
  PMMTime = ^TMMTime;
  mmtime_tag = record
    case wType: UINT of   { indicates the contents of the variant record }
    TIME_MS:      (ms: DWORD);
    TIME_SAMPLES: (sample: DWORD);
    TIME_BYTES:   (cb: DWORD);
    TIME_TICKS:   (ticks: DWORD);
    TIME_SMPTE: (
        hour: Byte;
        min: Byte;
        sec: Byte;
        frame: Byte;
        fps: Byte;
        dummy: Byte;
        pad: array[0..1] of Byte);
      TIME_MIDI : (songptrpos: DWORD);
  end;
  TMMTime = mmtime_tag;
  MMTIME = mmtime_tag;
```

The variant elements in this record in the wType field make it very flexible. That field can have any of the values included in mmsystem.pas:

```
{ types for wType field in MMTIME struct }
const
  TIME_MS       = $0001;  { time in milliseconds }
  TIME_SAMPLES  = $0002;  { number of wave samples }
  TIME_BYTES    = $0004;  { current byte offset }
  TIME_SMPTE    = $0008;  { SMPTE time }
  TIME_MIDI     = $0010;  { MIDI time }
  TIME_TICKS    = $0020;  { ticks within MIDI stream }
```

A wType field can be indicative of any of the following time formats, specific to a particular use:

■ TIME_BYTES   time based on the current byte offset from beginning of the file

■ TIME_MIDI   time in support of a MIDI event

- TIME_MS   time in milliseconds
- TIME_SAMPLES   number of samples with waveform audio
- TIME_SMPTE   SMPTE time (Society of Motion Picture and Television Engineers)
- TIME_TICKS   ticks within a MIDI stream

As with waveform devices, MIDI devices, and all of the other devices we have examined, timer devices can have different capabilities on different machines, particularly with respect to their accuracy (resolutions). These capabilities are stored in the TIMECAPS structure defined in mmsystem.pas as follows:

```
Type
  TTimeCaps = timecaps_tag;
  TIMECAPS = timecaps_tag;
```

MIDI support is based upon the following constants and a structure defined in mmsystem.pas:

```
Const                                { These are intentionally both non-zero
  MIDIPROP_TIMEDIV  = $00000001;  so the app cannot accidentally leave
  MIDIPROP_TEMPO    = $00000002;  the operation off and happen to appear
type                                 to work due to default action. }
  PMidiPropTimeDiv = ^TMidiPropTimeDiv;
  midiproptimediv_tag = record
    cbStruct: DWORD;
    dwTimeDiv: DWORD;
  end;
  TMidiPropTimeDiv = midiproptimediv_tag;
  MIDIPROPTIMEDIV = midiproptimediv_tag;
```

Returning to timers in general, in order to determine their capabilities (the minimum and maximum timer resolutions supported by the timer services), you should call the TimeGetDevCaps() function. This function fills the wPeriodMin and wPeriodMax members of the TIMECAPS structure with the minimum and maximum resolutions. This range can vary with both different computers and different Windows platforms. That rather simple structure is defined in mmsystem.pas as follows:

```
type
  PTimeCaps = ^TTimeCaps;
  timecaps_tag = record
    wPeriodMin: UINT;      { minimum period supported }
    wPeriodMax: UINT;      { maximum period supported }
  end;
```

After you've determine the minimum and maximum available timer resolutions, you need to establish the minimum resolution you want your application to use. To accomplish this task you must use the Time-BeginPeriod() and TimeEndPeriod() functions to set and clear the resolution. You need to be sure to match each call to TimeBeginPeriod() with a subsequent call to TimeEndPeriod(), specifying the same minimum resolution in both calls. You can make multiple calls to TimeBeginPeriod(), as long as each one is matched with a call to TimeEndPeriod(). As you'll see when we discuss them further, in both the TimeBeginPeriod() and TimeEndPeriod() functions, the uPeriod parameter indicates the minimum timer resolution, in milliseconds. You can specify any timer resolution value within the range supported by the timer.

Once you've set up a timer you can start using it to control timer events. To start a timer event, use the TimeSetEvent() function. This function returns a timer identifier that you can use to either stop or identify timer events. As we'll see when we discuss it further, one of this function's parameters is the address of a TimeProc() callback function that will be called when the timer event takes place. The following constants are defined in mmsystem.pas to enable you to work with the wFlags parameter of the TimeSetEvent() function:

```
const
  TIME_ONESHOT      = 0;      { program timer for single event }
  TIME_PERIODIC     = 1;      { program for continuous periodic event }
  TIME_CALLBACK_FUNCTION    = $0000; { callback is function }
  TIME_CALLBACK_EVENT_SET   = $0010; { callback is event - use SetEvent }
  TIME_CALLBACK_EVENT_PULSE = $0020; {callback is event - use PulseEvent}
```

What is the nature of a timer event? Actually, there are two types of timer events: single and periodic. A single timer event occurs only once, after a specified number of milliseconds; a periodic timer event occurs every time a specified number of milliseconds has elapsed. The interval between periodic events is called an event delay. Note that periodic timer events with an event delay of 10 milliseconds or less consume a significant portion of CPU resources.

The relationship between the resolution of a timer event and the length of the event delay is important in timer events. For example, if you specify a resolution of 5 and an event delay of 100, the timer services will notify the callback function after an interval ranging from 95 to 105 milliseconds. Finally, you can cancel an active timer event at any time by using the TimeKillEvent() function. You must be sure to cancel any outstanding timers before freeing the memory containing the callback function. One final note: A multimedia timer runs in its own thread. For this reason, tracing into a timer callback routine can slow things down.

As with other multimedia APIs, there are a few error messages specific to timers. These messages are explained in Table 7-1.

Table 7-1: Timer error messages

Message	Meaning
TIMERR_NOERROR	No error; has a value of 0
TIMERR_NOCANDO	The requested operation cannot be completed
TIMERR_STRUCT	Error getting a timer's device capabilities

The following is the prototype for a timer callback message as defined in mmsystem.pas:

```
type
  TFNTimeCallBack = procedure(uTimerID, uMessage: UINT;
    dwUser, dw1, dw2: DWORD) stdcall;
```

Now we'll examine the various timer functions.

Multimedia Timer Functions

function TimeGetSystemTime   *mmsystem.pas*

Syntax

```
function TimeGetSystemTime(
lpTime: PMMTime;
uSize: Word
): MMRESULT; stdcall;
```

Description

This function retrieves the system time, in milliseconds. The system time is the time elapsed since Windows was started. This function works very much like the TimeGetTime() function. See the entry for TimeGetTime() for details of its operation.

Parameters

lpTime: A PMMTime value identifying an MMTIME structure.

uSize: A word value indicating the size, in bytes, of the MMTIME structure. Use SizeOf(MMTIME) to get this value.

Return Value

Returns TIMERR_NOERROR. The system time is returned in the ms member of the MMTIME structure.

Example

Listing 7-1 shows how to set up a form to use the TimeGetSystemTime() function. Listing 7-2 shows how to create a TimerProc() callback routine to send timer messages to an application and set up the Default-Handler() procedure to respond to messages.

Listing 7-I: Setting up a timer in an application's FormCreate method

```
procedure TForm1.FormCreate(Sender: TObject);
begin
  AHandle := Handle;
  // First deal with the system time
  Events := 0;
  AMMTime.wType := TIME_MS;
  timeGetSystemTime(@AMMTime, SizeOf(MMTIME));
  TimeInMS := timeGetTime;
  lblGetSystemTime.Caption := IntToStr(AMMTime.ms);
  lblGetTime.Caption := IntToStr(TimeInMS);
  // Now do the timer test
  ATimerID := 0;
  TargetMs := 500;
  timeGetDevCaps(@TimerCaps, SizeOf(TIMECAPS));
  // First make sure we are within bounds
  if TargetMs < TimerCaps.wPeriodMin then
    TargetMs := TimerCaps.wPeriodMin else
  if TargetMs > TimerCaps.wPeriodMax then
    TargetMs := TimerCaps.wPeriodMax;
  timeBeginPeriod(TargetMs);
  ATimerID := timeSetEvent(TargetMs, TargetMs, TimerProc,
             DWord(AHandle), TIME_PERIODIC);
  if ATimerID=0 then
    begin
      timeEndPeriod(TargetMs);
      ShowMessage('Error initializing timer');
```

7

Chapter

```
      exit;
    end;
end;
```

Listing 7-2: Setting up a timer callback routine to send messages and a DefaultHandler() routine to respond to messages

```
const
  Time_Elapsed_Msg = Wm_User + 1;
procedure TimerProc(hTimerHandle : UINT; uMsg : UINT;
    dwUser, dwParam1, dwParam2 : DWord);  stdcall;
begin
  PostMessage(HWnd(dwUser), Time_Elapsed_Msg, 0, 0);
end;

procedure TForm1.DefaultHandler(var Msg);
begin
  inherited DefaultHandler(Msg);
  case TMessage(Msg).Msg of    //
  Time_Elapsed_Msg:
    begin
      inc(Events);
      Edit1.Text := IntToStr(Events);
      Exit;
    end;
  end;    // case
end;
```

function TimeGetTime   *mmsystem.pas*

Syntax

```
function TimeGetTime: DWORD;
  stdcall;
```

Description

This function, which does not take any parameters, retrieves the system time, in milliseconds. The system time is the time elapsed since Windows was started. The only difference between this function and the TimeGetSystemTime() function is that the latter function uses the MMTIME structure to return the system time. Therefore, the TimeGet-Time() function has less overhead than TimeGetSystemTime. Note that the value returned by the TimeGetTime() function is a DWORD value. The return value wraps around to 0 every 2^{32} milliseconds, which is about 49.71 days. This can cause problems in code that directly uses the TimeGetTime() return value in computations, particularly where the value is used to control code execution. It is recommended that you always use the difference between two TimeGetTime() return values in computations.

There are special considerations related to using this function under Windows NT. The default precision of the TimeGetTime() function can be 5 milliseconds or more, depending on the machine. You can use the TimeBeginPeriod() and TimeEndPeriod() functions to increase the precision of TimeGetTime(). If you do so, the minimum difference between successive values returned by TimeGetTime() can be as large as the minimum period value set using TimeBeginPeriod() and TimeEndPeriod(). Therefore, under Windows NT, use the QueryPerformanceCounter() and QueryPerformanceFrequency() functions to measure short time intervals at a high resolution. Under Windows 95, the default precision of the TimeGetTime() function is 1 millisecond. In other words, in that environment, the TimeGetTime() function can return successive values that differ by just 1 millisecond. This is true no matter what calls have been made to the TimeBeginPeriod() and TimeEndPeriod() functions.

Return Value

Returns the system time, in milliseconds.

Example

See Listing 7-1.

function TimeSetEvent   *mmsystem.pas*

Syntax

```
function TimeSetEvent(
  uDelay, uResolution: UINT;
  lpFunction: TFNTimeCallBack;
  dwUser: DWORD;
  uFlags: UINT
  ): MMRESULT; stdcall;
```

Description

This function starts a specified timer event. As mentioned above, a multimedia timer runs in its own thread. After the event is activated, it calls the specified callback function. Note that each call to TimeSetEvent() for periodic timer events must be matched with a call to the TimeKillEvent() function.

Parameters

uDelay: Event delay, in milliseconds. If this value is not in the range of the minimum and maximum event delays supported by the timer, the function returns an error.

uResolution: Resolution of the timer event, in milliseconds. The resolution increases with smaller values; a resolution of 0 indicates periodic events should occur with the greatest possible accuracy. To reduce system overhead, however, you should use the maximum value appropriate for your application.

lpFunction: The address of a callback function that can be called either once upon expiration of a single event or periodically upon expiration of periodic events.

dwUser: User-supplied callback data.

uFlags: Timer event type. The defined values are shown in Table 7-2.

Table 7-2: Values for the uFlags field of TimeSetEvent()

Value	Meaning
TIME_ONESHOT	Event occurs once, after uDelay milliseconds.
TIME_PERIODIC	Event occurs every uDelay milliseconds.

Return Value

Returns an identifier for the timer event, if successful, or an error otherwise. This function returns NULL if it fails and the timer event was not created. (This identifier is also passed to the callback function.)

Example

See Listing 7-1.

function TimeKillEvent   *mmsystem.pas*

Syntax

```
function TimeKillEvent(
uTimerID: UINT
): MMRESULT; stdcall;
```

Description

This function cancels a specified timer event.

Parameter

uTimerID: The identifier of the timer event to cancel. This identifier was returned by the TimeSetEvent() function when the timer event was set up.

Return Value

Returns TIMERR_NOERROR, if successful, or MMSYSERR_INVALPARAM if the specified timer event does not exist.

Example

Listing 7-3 shows how to clean things up when closing an application that has used timer functions.

Listing 7-3: Using TimeKillEvent() and TimeEndPeriod() when closing down an application

```
procedure TForm1.FormDestroy(Sender: TObject);
begin
  timeKillEvent(ATimerID);
  timeEndPeriod(TargetMs);
end;
```

function TimeGetDevCaps   *mmsystem.pas*

Syntax

```
function TimeGetDevCaps(
lpTimeCaps: PTimeCaps;
uSize: UINT
): MMRESULT; stdcall;
```

7

Chapter

Description

This function queries the timer device to determine its resolution.

Parameters

lpTimeCaps: The address of a TIMECAPS structure. This structure is filled with information about the resolution of the timer device.

uSize: The size, in bytes, of the TIMECAPS structure. Use SizeOf(TIMECAPS) to get this value.

Return Value

Returns TIMERR_NOERROR, if successful, or TIMERR_STRUCT if it fails to return the timer device capabilities.

Example

See Listing 7-1.

function TimeBeginPeriod   *mmsystem.pas*

Syntax

```
function TimeBeginPeriod(
uPeriod: UINT
): MMRESULT; stdcall;
```

Description

This function sets the minimum timer resolution for an application or device driver. Be sure to call this function immediately before using any of the timer services. Also, be sure to call the TimeEndPeriod() function immediately after you are finished using the timer services. You must match each call to TimeBeginPeriod() with a call to TimeEndPeriod(), specifying the same minimum resolution in both calls. An application can make multiple TimeBeginPeriod() calls as long as each call is matched with a call to TimeEndPeriod().

Parameter

uPeriod: Minimum timer resolution, in milliseconds, for the application or device driver.

Return Value

Returns TIMERR_NOERROR, if successful, or TIMERR_NOCANDO if the resolution specified in uPeriod is out of range.

Example

See Listing 7-1.

function TimeEndPeriod   *mmsystem.pas*

Syntax

```
function TimeEndPeriod(
  uPeriod: UINT
  ): MMRESULT; stdcall;
```

Description

This function clears a previously set minimum timer resolution. You must be sure to call this function immediately after you are finished using any of the timer services. You must match each call to TimeBeginPeriod() with a call to TimeEndPeriod(), specifying the same minimum resolution in both calls. An application can make multiple TimeBeginPeriod() calls as long as each call is matched with a call to TimeEndPeriod().

Parameter

uPeriod: Minimum timer resolution specified in the previous call to the TimeBeginPeriod() function.

Return Value

Returns TIMERR_NOERROR if successful, or TIMERR_NOCANDO if the resolution specified in uPeriod is out of range.

Example

See Listings 7-1 and 7-3.

7

Chapter

Joysticks

When you think of computer games, particularly fast-paced action games, you might also think of the joystick. This ancillary input device provides a powerful alternative to using the keyboard or the mouse. In fact, some games give you the choice of all three. The joystick provides positional information within a coordinate system that has absolute maximum and minimum values in each axis of movement. The sample application for this chapter on the companion CD allows you to get the properties of a joystick and its current status (Figure 7-4).

Figure 7-4

As with other input devices, drivers to control joystick services are loaded when the operating system is started. These joystick services can simultaneously monitor two joysticks, each with two- or three-axis movement. Modern joysticks can have as many as four buttons; these services provide the opportunity to monitor exactly that many. As with the other multimedia devices we have discussed, you can determine the capabilities of a joystick and its driver through the joystick functions we'll be discussing. Also, you can process a joystick's positional and button information by querying the joystick directly or by capturing the joystick and processing messages from it. The latter method is simpler because your application does not have to manually query the joystick or track the time to generate queries at regular intervals. The following constants defined in mmsystem.pas are used when working with joysticks:

```
const
  MM_JOY1MOVE       = $3A0;
  MM_JOY2MOVE       = $3A1;
  MM_JOY1ZMOVE      = $3A2;
  MM_JOY2ZMOVE      = $3A3;
  MM_JOY1BUTTONDOWN = $3B5;
  MM_JOY2BUTTONDOWN = $3B6;
  MM_JOY1BUTTONUP   = $3B7;
  MM_JOY2BUTTONUP   = $3B8;
```

What about the capabilities of a joystick? As mentioned already, joysticks can support two- or three-axis movement and may include up to four buttons. They also support different ranges of motion and various polling frequencies. Range of motion is defined as the distance a joystick handle can move from its resting (central) position to the position farthest from its resting position. Polling frequency is defined as the time interval between joystick queries. Figure 7-5 shows the properties of a joystick.

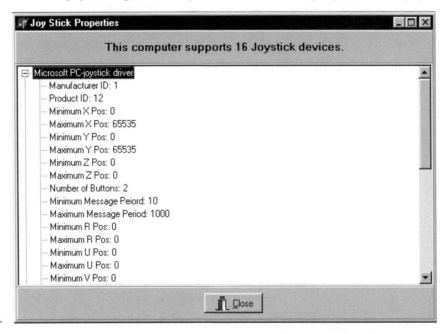

Figure 7-5

As stated above, joystick drivers may support either one or two joysticks. You can determine the number of joysticks supported by a particular joystick driver by using the JoyGetNumDevs() function, which returns an unsigned integer containing the number of supported joysticks. If there is no joystick support, this function returns a value of zero. The return value indicates the driver's capabilities and does not necessarily indicate the number of joysticks attached to a system. (The author is quite certain that he does not have 12 joysticks attached to his desktop computer!) To determine if a joystick is attached to the system, use the JoyGetPos() function. This function will return JOYERR_NOERROR if the specified device is attached. Otherwise, it returns JOYERR_UNPLUGGED.

We've seen that different joysticks can have different capabilities. To determine these capabilities, use the JoyGetDevCaps() function. This function fills a JOYCAPS structure with joystick capabilities such as the minimum and maximum values for its coordinate system, the number of buttons on a joystick, and the minimum and maximum polling frequencies.

One of the most important joystick issues we need to monitor is its position. The other is which buttons, if any, have been pressed. You can query a joystick for both the position and the button information by using the JoyGetPos() function. An application can query the joystick for baseline position values just as the Windows Control Panel property sheet does in the process of calibrating it. By the way, you should calibrate a joystick when you attach it to your system for the first time. You can also query a joystick or a related device that has extended capabilities by using the JoyGetPosEx() function.

As with other multimedia devices, joysticks send information back to the system and running applications through messages. If you need to capture direct joystick messages to be sent to a function, use the JoySetCapture() function. Figure 7-6 shows the display of such information in our sample application.

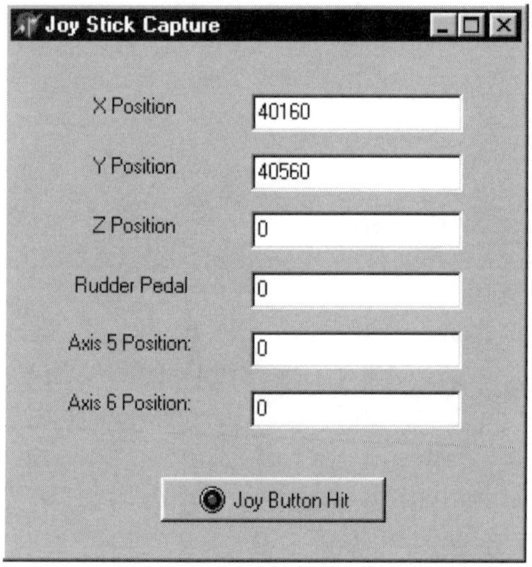

Figure 7-6

There's one important constraint: Only one application at a time can capture messages from a joystick. As we mentioned above, you can query the joystick from another application by using the JoyGetPos() and JoyGetPosEx() functions. But there's another issue: Joystick messages can fail to reach the application that captured the joystick if a second application uses either the JoyGetPos() or the JoyGetPosEx() functions to query the joystick at approximately the same time that the message was sent. In this case, the second application could intercept the message.

If you need to capture messages from two joysticks attached to the system, use JoySetCapture() twice, once for each joystick. Then, your window will receive separate and distinct messages for each device. You can release a captured joystick by using the JoyReleaseCapture() function. Conveniently, if an application does not release a joystick before ending, that joystick will be automatically released shortly after the capture window has been destroyed. Naturally, you cannot capture an unplugged joystick. If a joystick or related device is unplugged, the JoySetCapture() function will return JOYERR_UNPLUGGED.

As with other multimedia devices, timing can be critical when working with joysticks. For this reason, Windows automatically sets up a timer event with each call to the JoySetCapture() function. Additionally, you can have the operating system send joystick messages to an application at regular time intervals by setting the fChanged parameter of the JoySetCapture() to FALSE and by specifying the interval length between successive messages. To do this, assign the uPeriod parameter a value between the minimum and maximum polling frequencies for the joystick. You can determine this range by using the JoyGetDevCaps() function, which fills the wPeriodMin and wPeriodMax members in the JOYCAPS structure. If the uPeriod value is outside the range of valid polling frequencies for the joystick, the joystick driver will use the minimum or maximum polling frequency, whichever is closer to the uPeriod value.

In addition to timing, the position of the joystick is also crucial. You can notify Windows to send joystick messages to an application whenever the position of a joystick axis changes by a value greater than the movement threshold of the device. The movement threshold is the distance the joystick must be moved before a WM_JOYMOVE message is sent to a window that has captured the device. The threshold is initially zero. You can set the movement threshold by using the JoySetThreshold() function. You can retrieve the minimum polling frequency of the joystick by using the JoyGetDevCaps() function.

Joystick Messages

We've alluded to joystick messages already. Let's take a more detailed look at the nature and use of these messages. The purpose of a joystick message is to notify an application when the joystick has changed position or when one of its buttons has changed state. Messages beginning with MM_JOY1 are sent to the function if the application requests input from the joystick using the identifier JOYSTICKID1; MM_JOY2 messages are sent if the application requests input from the joystick using the identifier JOYSTICKID2. The messages in Table 7-3 identify the status of the joystick buttons.

Table 7-3: Messages identifying the status of joystick buttons

Message	*Description*
MM_JOY1BUTTONDOWN	A button on joystick JOYSTICKID1 has been pressed.
MM_JOY1BUTTONUP	A button on joystick JOYSTICKID1 has been released.
MM_JOY1MOVE	Joystick JOYSTICKID1 changed position in the x- or y-direction.
MM_JOY1ZMOVE	Joystick JOYSTICKID1 changed position in the z-direction.
MM_JOY2BUTTONDOWN	A button on joystick JOYSTICKID2 has been pressed.
MM_JOY2BUTTONUP	A button on joystick JOYSTICKID2 has been released.
MM_JOY2MOVE	Joystick JOYSTICKID2 changed position in the x- or y-direction.
MM_JOY2ZMOVE	Joystick JOYSTICKID2 changed position in the z-direction.

All of the above messages report non-existent buttons as released. Now we'll explore programming joysticks in more detail.

Programming Joysticks

There are three aspects involved in programming joysticks, each of which we'll examine in detail. These three aspects are concerned with the following tasks:

- Getting the joystick driver's capabilities
- Capturing the joystick input
- Processing the joystick messages

The Windows Multimedia SDK help file includes several examples (in C) taken from a simple joystick application that retrieves position and button state information from the joystick services, plays waveform audio resources, and paints bullet holes on the screen when a user presses the joystick buttons. Those examples, which demonstrate each of the above tasks, have been translated into Pascal below. When we discuss the various joystick functions, we'll see further code examples from the sample application that accompanies this chapter. We'll begin with the first task of determining the capabilities of the joystick driver.

The first example uses the JoyGetNumDevs() and the JoyGetPos() functions to determine whether the joystick services are available and if a joystick is attached to one of the ports.

Listing 7-4: Port of Microsoft (C) example using JoyGetNumDevs() to return number of devices

```
Function TestForJoystick : boolean;
Var
   AMMResult : MMRESULT;
   currentJoyinfo : JOYINFO;
   wNumDevs, wDeviceID : UINT;
   bDev1Attached, bDev2Attached : boolean;
begin
   Result := False // assume there is no joystick until we find one
   wNumDevs := joyGetNumDevs;
   if wNumDevs=0 then exit; // No joystick devices; might as well leave
   Result := True; // We know there is at least one device;
   AMMResult :=    joyGetPos(JOYSTICKID1,@joyinfo);
   bDev1Attached :=  AMMResult<> JOYERR_UNPLUGGED;
   AMMResult :=    joyGetPos(JOYSTICKID2,@joyinfo);
   bDev2Attached :=  ((wNumDevs = 2) AND (AMMResult<> JOYERR_UNPLUGGED));
   If (wNumDevs = 2) then
   wDeviceID = ChooseJoyStick // simple dialog to choose between
                           // JOYSTICKID1 or JOYSTICKID2
```

```
    wDeviceID =  JOYSTICKID1;
end;
```

Once you know that you have a functional joystick available you can
begin to work with it. Most of the code controlling the joystick will be in
your main unit. In the following code, the application tries to capture
input from the joystick, JOYSTICKID1, by calling JoySetCapture(). Note
that it shows an error message if it cannot capture the joystick.

Listing 7-5: Capturing a joystick

```
Procedure CaptureJoyStick;
begin
    if (joySetCapture(Self, JOYSTICKID1, 0, FALSE)) <> JOYERR_NOERROR
    Then ShowMessage('Couldn''t capture the joystick');
end;
```

The only task remaining is to deal with the messages that the joystick
sends to the application. The following code snippet shows how to
enable an application to respond to joystick movements and changes in
the button states. In this example, when the joystick changes position,
the application will move the cursor; additionally, if either joystick button is pressed, it will draw a bullet hole on the desktop. When a joystick
button is pressed, the application also plays a sound continuously until a
button is released. The messages to watch are MM_JOY1MOVE,
MM_JOY1BUTTONDOWN, and MM_JOY1BUTTONUP. Again, this is a
port of the Microsoft SDK example. Please note that the author has not
implemented either the DrawFire() procedure or the DrawSight()
procedure.

Listing 7-6: Processing joystick messages

```
case Message of
  MM_JOY1MOVE :                        // changed position
    Begin
      if((UINT) wParam AND (JOY_BUTTON1 OR  JOY_BUTTON2)) then
          DrawFire;                    // Procedure to draw bullet hole
        DrawSight(lParam);             // calculates new cursor position
    End;
  MM_JOY1BUTTONDOWN :                  // button is down
    Begin
      if((UINT) wParam AND JOY_BUTTON1) then
        Begin
          PlaySound(lpButton1, SND_LOOP or SND_ASYNC or SND_MEMORY);
          DrawFire;
```

```
        End
      else if((UINT) wParam and JOY_BUTTON2)
      then
        Begin
          PlaySound(lpButton2, SND_ASYNC or SND_MEMORY or  SND_LOOP);
          DrawFire;
        End;
      end;
  MM_JOY1BUTTONUP :                     // button is up
      sndPlaySound(NULL, 0);            // stops the sound
  end;
```

Other Constants and Structures Used to Monitor Joysticks

As with the Wave API, the MIDI API, and the Mixer API, the Joystick API includes a number of constants and structures used to hold and return information to an application. The following constants, defined in mmsystem.pas, provide error information for joystick functions:

```
const
  JOYERR_NOERROR        = 0;                  { no error }
  JOYERR_PARMS          = JOYERR_BASE+5;      { bad parameters }
  JOYERR_NOCANDO        = JOYERR_BASE+6;      { request not completed }
  JOYERR_UNPLUGGED      = JOYERR_BASE+7;      { joystick is unplugged }
```

The following constants defined in mmsystem.pas, are used with the JOYINFO and the JOYINFOEX structures outlined below. They are also used with the various MM_JOY? messages.

```
const
  JOY_BUTTON1         = $0001;
  JOY_BUTTON2         = $0002;
  JOY_BUTTON3         = $0004;
  JOY_BUTTON4         = $0008;
  JOY_BUTTON1CHG      = $0100;
  JOY_BUTTON2CHG      = $0200;
  JOY_BUTTON3CHG      = $0400;
  JOY_BUTTON4CHG      = $0800;
```

The following constants, defined in mmsystem.pas, are used with the JOYINFOEX structure outlined below.

```
  JOY_BUTTON5         = $00000010;
  JOY_BUTTON6         = $00000020;
  JOY_BUTTON7         = $00000040;
  JOY_BUTTON8         = $00000080;
```

```
JOY_BUTTON9     = $00000100;
JOY_BUTTON10    = $00000200;
JOY_BUTTON11    = $00000400;
JOY_BUTTON12    = $00000800;
JOY_BUTTON13    = $00001000;
JOY_BUTTON14    = $00002000;
JOY_BUTTON15    = $00004000;
JOY_BUTTON16    = $00008000;
JOY_BUTTON17    = $00010000;
JOY_BUTTON18    = $00020000;
JOY_BUTTON19    = $00040000;
JOY_BUTTON20    = $00080000;
JOY_BUTTON21    = $00100000;
JOY_BUTTON22    = $00200000;
JOY_BUTTON23    = $00400000;
JOY_BUTTON24    = $00800000;
JOY_BUTTON25    = $01000000;
JOY_BUTTON26    = $02000000;
JOY_BUTTON27    = $04000000;
JOY_BUTTON28    = $08000000;
JOY_BUTTON29    = $10000000;
JOY_BUTTON30    = $20000000;
JOY_BUTTON31    = $40000000;
JOY_BUTTON32    = $80000000;
```

The following constants, defined in mmsystem.pas, are used with the
JOYINFOEX structure outlined below:

```
JOY_POVCENTERED     = -1;
JOY_POVFORWARD      = 0;
JOY_POVRIGHT        = 9000;
JOY_POVBACKWARD     = 18000;
JOY_POVLEFT         = 27000;
JOY_RETURNX         = $00000001;
JOY_RETURNY         = $00000002;
JOY_RETURNZ         = $00000004;
JOY_RETURNR         = $00000008;
JOY_RETURNU         = $00000010; { axis 5 }
JOY_RETURNV         = $00000020; { axis 6 }
JOY_RETURNPOV       = $00000040;
JOY_RETURNBUTTONS   = $00000080;
JOY_RETURNRAWDATA   = $00000100;
JOY_RETURNPOVCTS    = $00000200;
JOY_RETURNCENTERED  = $00000400;
JOY_USEDEADZONE     = $00000800;
JOY_RETURNALL       = (JOY_RETURNX or JOY_RETURNY or JOY_RETURNZ or
```

```
    JOY_RETURNR or JOY_RETURNU or JOY_RETURNV or JOY_RETURNPOV
    or JOY_RETURNBUTTONS);
  JOY_CAL_READALWAYS   = $00010000;
  JOY_CAL_READXYONLY   = $00020000;
  JOY_CAL_READ3        = $00040000;
  JOY_CAL_READ4        = $00080000;
  JOY_CAL_READXONLY    = $00100000;
  JOY_CAL_READYONLY    = $00200000;
  JOY_CAL_READ5        = $00400000;
  JOY_CAL_READ6        = $00800000;
  JOY_CAL_READZONLY    = $01000000;
  JOY_CAL_READRONLY    = $02000000;
  JOY_CAL_READUONLY    = $04000000;
  JOY_CAL_READVONLY    = $08000000;
```

The following constants, defined in mmsystem.pas, are used for joystick
IDs for Joystick 1 and/or Joystick 2:

```
const
  JOYSTICKID1          = 0;
  JOYSTICKID2          = 1;
```

The following constants, defined in mmsystem.pas, are used for joystick
driver capabilities:

```
const
  JOYCAPS_HASZ         = $0001;
  JOYCAPS_HASR         = $0002;
  JOYCAPS_HASU         = $0004;
  JOYCAPS_HASV         = $0008;
  JOYCAPS_HASPOV       = $0010;
  JOYCAPS_POV4DIR      = $0020;
  JOYCAPS_POVCTS       = $0040;
```

The following structures, defined in mmsystem.pas, are also used to support working with joysticks. As in previous APIs, we have a complex data
structure that holds the joystick device capabilities. That structure,
JOYCAPS, and its related structures are defined as follows in
mmsystem.pas:

```
type
  PJoyCapsA = ^TJoyCapsA;
  PJoyCapsW = ^TJoyCapsW;
  PJoyCaps = PJoyCapsA;
  tagJOYCAPSA = record
    wMid: Word;                      { manufacturer ID }
```

```
  wPid: Word;                        { product ID }
  szPname: array[0..MAXPNAMELEN-1] of AnsiChar; { product name (NULL
                                                  terminated string) }
  wXmin: UINT;                       { minimum x position value }
  wXmax: UINT;                       { maximum x position value }
  wYmin: UINT;                       { minimum y position value }
  wYmax: UINT;                       { maximum y position value }
  wZmin: UINT;                       { minimum z position value }
  wZmax: UINT;                       { maximum z position value }
  wNumButtons: UINT;                 { number of buttons }
  wPeriodMin: UINT;                  { minimum message period when captured }
  wPeriodMax: UINT;                  { maximum message period when captured }
  wRmin: UINT;                       { minimum r position value }
  wRmax: UINT;                       { maximum r position value }
  wUmin: UINT;                       { minimum u (5th axis) position value }
  wUmax: UINT;                       { maximum u (5th axis) position value }
  wVmin: UINT;                       { minimum v (6th axis) position value }
  wVmax: UINT;                       { maximum v (6th axis) position value }
  wCaps: UINT;                       { joystick capabilites }
  wMaxAxes: UINT;                    { maximum number of axes supported }
  wNumAxes: UINT;                    { number of axes in use }
  wMaxButtons: UINT;                 { maximum number of buttons supported }
  szRegKey: array[0..MAXPNAMELEN - 1] of AnsiChar; { registry key }
  szOEMVxD: array[0..MAX_JOYSTICKOEMVXDNAME - 1] of AnsiChar;
                     { OEM VxD in use }
end;
tagJOYCAPSW = record
  wMid: Word;                        { manufacturer ID }
  wPid: Word;                        { product ID }
  szPname: array[0..MAXPNAMELEN-1] of WideChar; { product name (NULL
                                                  terminated string) }
  wXmin: UINT;                       { minimum x position value }
  wXmax: UINT;                       { maximum x position value }
  wYmin: UINT;                       { minimum y position value }
  wYmax: UINT;                       { maximum y position value }
  wZmin: UINT;                       { minimum z position value }
  wZmax: UINT;                       { maximum z position value }
  wNumButtons: UINT;                 { number of buttons }
  wPeriodMin: UINT;                  { minimum message period when captured }
  wPeriodMax: UINT;                  { maximum message period when captured }
  wRmin: UINT;                       { minimum r position value }
  wRmax: UINT;                       { maximum r position value }
  wUmin: UINT;                       { minimum u (5th axis) position value }
  wUmax: UINT;                       { maximum u (5th axis) position value }
  wVmin: UINT;                       { minimum v (6th axis) position value }
  wVmax: UINT;                       { maximum v (6th axis) position value }
```

```
    wCaps: UINT;                    { joystick capabilites }
    wMaxAxes: UINT;                 { maximum number of axes supported }
    wNumAxes: UINT;                 { number of axes in use }
    wMaxButtons: UINT;              { maximum number of buttons supported }
    szRegKey: array[0..MAXPNAMELEN - 1] of WideChar; { registry key }
    szOEMVxD: array[0..MAX_JOYSTICKOEMVXDNAME - 1] of WideChar;
                                    { OEM VxD in use }
  end;
  tagJOYCAPS = tagJOYCAPSA;
  TJoyCapsA = tagJOYCAPSA;
  TJoyCapsW = tagJOYCAPSW;
  TJoyCaps = TJoyCapsA;
  JOYCAPSA = tagJOYCAPSA;
  JOYCAPSW = tagJOYCAPSW;
  JOYCAPS = JOYCAPSA;
```

The next two structures, JOYINFO and JOYINFOEX, and their related
structures are defined as follows in mmsystem.pas:

```
type
  PJoyInfo = ^TJoyInfo;
  joyinfo_tag = record
    wXpos: UINT;                    { x position }
    wYpos: UINT;                    { y position }
    wZpos: UINT;                    { z position }
    wButtons: UINT;                 { button states }
  end;
  TJoyInfo = joyinfo_tag;
  JOYINFO = joyinfo_tag;

  PJoyInfoEx = ^TJoyInfoEx;
  joyinfoex_tag = record
    dwSize: DWORD;                  { size of structure }
    dwFlags: DWORD;                 { flags to indicate what to return }
    wXpos: UINT;                    { x position }
    wYpos: UINT;                    { y position }
    wZpos: UINT;                    { z position }
    dwRpos: DWORD;                  { rudder/4th axis position }
    dwUpos: DWORD;                  { 5th axis position }
    dwVpos: DWORD;                  { 6th axis position }
    wButtons: UINT;                 { button states }
    dwButtonNumber: DWORD;          { current button number pressed }
    dwPOV: DWORD;                   { point of view state }
    dwReserved1: DWORD;             { reserved for communication between winmm
                                      & driver }
    dwReserved2: DWORD;             { reserved for future expansion }
```

```
end;
TJoyInfoEx = joyinfoex_tag;
JOYINFOEX = joyinfoex_tag;
```

Now that we have a general idea of working with joysticks and have seen the constants and structures, we'll examine the various joystick functions in some detail.

Joystick Functions

function JoyGetNumDevs   mmsystem.pas

Syntax

function JoyGetNumDevs:
  UINT; stdcall;

Description

This function, which takes no parameters, queries the joystick driver for the number of joysticks it supports. Use the JoyGetPos() function to determine whether a given joystick is physically attached to the system. If the specified joystick is not connected, JoyGetPos() returns a JOYERR_UNPLUGGED error value.

Return Value

Returns the number of joysticks supported by the joystick driver or zero if no driver is present.

Example

See Listing 7-4.

function JoyGetDevCaps   mmsystem.pas

Syntax

function JoyGetDevCaps(
  uJoyID: UINT;
  lpCaps: PJoyCaps;
  uSize: UINT
  ): MMRESULT; stdcall;

Description

This function queries a joystick to determine its capabilities. Use the JoyGetNumDevs() function to determine the number of joystick devices supported by the driver.

Parameters

uJoyID: The identifier of the joystick (JOYSTICKID1 or JOYSTICKID2) to be queried.

lpCaps: The address of a JOYCAPS structure to contain the capabilities of the joystick.

uSize: The size, in bytes, of the JOYCAPS structure. Use sizeof(JOYCAPS) to get this amount.

Return Value

Returns JOYERR_NOERROR if successful. Otherwise, it returns one of the following errors: MMSYSERR_NODRIVER, indicating that the joystick driver is not present, or MMSYSERR_INVALPARAM, indicating that an invalid parameter was passed.

Example

Listing 7-7 shows how to query for the properties of a joystick using this function.

Listing 7-7: Using the JoyGetDevCaps() function to get joystick properties

```
procedure TfrmJoyStickProp.FormActivate(Sender: TObject);
var
  SetClose: boolean;
  ADeviceTreeNode, APropTreeNode: TTreeNode;
  j: Integer;
begin
  SetClose := False;
  iJStickDev := joyGetNumDevs;
  Joy_ID := 0; // First Joystick device
  pnNumDevices.Caption := 'This computer supports ' + IntToStr(iJStickDev)
        + ' Joystick devices.';
  CurrentMMResult := joyGetPos(Joy_ID, @JoyInformation);
  if CurrentMMResult<>0 then
    begin
      ShowMessage
        ('Error: ' + GetJoystickError(CurrentMMResult)+#10#13+
```

```
            'Make sure a joystick is connected');
      SetClose := True;
      ModalResult := mrCancel;
    end;
TreeView1.Items.Clear; { Start Fresh by removing any existing nodes }
if SetClose then
with TreeView1.Items do
  ADeviceTreeNode := Add(nil,
      'No joystick device attached; exit and correct the problem')
else
for j := 0 to (iJStickDev-1) do      // Iterate
  with TreeView1.Items do
  begin
    CurrentMMResult := JoyGetDevCaps(j, @JoyProperties,
              SizeOf(JoyCaps));
    ADeviceTreeNode := Add(nil, JoyProperties.szPname); { Add a root
                                                          node }
    //{ Add a child node to the node just added }
    AddChild(ADeviceTreeNode,'Manufacturer ID: '+ IntToStr(
      JoyProperties.wMid));
    AddChild(ADeviceTreeNode,'Product ID: '+ IntToStr(
      JoyProperties.wPid));
    AddChild(ADeviceTreeNode,'Minimum X Pos: '+ IntToStr(
      JoyProperties.wXmin));
    AddChild(ADeviceTreeNode,'Maximum X Pos: '+ IntToStr(
      JoyProperties.wXmax));
    AddChild(ADeviceTreeNode,'Minimum Y Pos: '+ IntToStr(
      JoyProperties.wYmin));
    AddChild(ADeviceTreeNode,'Maximum Y Pos: '+ IntToStr(
      JoyProperties.wYmax));
    AddChild(ADeviceTreeNode,'Minimum Z Pos: '+ IntToStr(
      JoyProperties.wZmin));
    AddChild(ADeviceTreeNode,'Maximum Z Pos: '+ IntToStr(
      JoyProperties.wZmax));
    AddChild(ADeviceTreeNode,'Number of Buttons: '+ IntToStr(
      JoyProperties.wNumButtons));
    AddChild(ADeviceTreeNode,'Minimum Message Peiord: '+ IntToStr(
      JoyProperties.wPeriodmin));
    AddChild(ADeviceTreeNode,'Maximum Message Period: '+ IntToStr(
      JoyProperties.wPeriodmax));
    AddChild(ADeviceTreeNode,'Minimum R Pos: '+ IntToStr(
      JoyProperties.wRmin));
    AddChild(ADeviceTreeNode,'Maximum R Pos: '+ IntToStr(
      JoyProperties.wRmax));
    AddChild(ADeviceTreeNode,'Minimum U Pos: '+ IntToStr(
      JoyProperties.wUmin));
```

```
      AddChild(ADeviceTreeNode,'Maximum U Pos: '+ IntToStr(
        JoyProperties.wUmax));
      AddChild(ADeviceTreeNode,'Minimum V Pos: '+ IntToStr(
        JoyProperties.wVmin));
      AddChild(ADeviceTreeNode,'Maximum V Pos: '+ IntToStr(
        JoyProperties.wVmax));
      AddChild(ADeviceTreeNode,'Maximum number of axes: '+ IntToStr(
        JoyProperties.wMaxAxes));
      AddChild(ADeviceTreeNode,'Axes in use: '+ IntToStr(
        JoyProperties.wNumAxes));
      AddChild(ADeviceTreeNode,'Maximum number of buttons: '+ IntToStr(
        JoyProperties.wMaxAxes));
    end;    // for
  if SetClose then Close;
end;
```

7

Chapter

function JoyGetPos   *mmsystem.pas*

Syntax

```
function JoyGetPos(
  uJoyID: UINT;
  lpInfo: PJoyInfo
  ): MMRESULT; stdcall;
```

Description

This function queries a joystick for its position and button status. For devices that have four to six axes of movement, a point-of-view control, or more than four buttons, use the JoyGetPosEx() function.

Parameters

uJoyID: The identifier of the joystick (JOYSTICKID1 or JOYSTICKID2) to be queried.

lpInfo: The address of a JOYINFO structure to contain the capabilities of the joystick.

Return Value

Returns JOYERR_NOERROR if successful. Otherwise, it returns one of the following errors: MMSYSERR_NODRIVER, indicating that the joystick driver is not present; MMSYSERR_INVALPARAM, indicating that an invalid parameter was passed; or JOYERR_UNPLUGGED, indicating that the specified joystick is not connected to the system.

Example

See Listing 7-7.

function JoyGetPosEx   *mmsystem.pas*

Syntax

```
function JoyGetPosEx(
  uJoyID: UINT;
  lpInfo: PJoyInfoEx
  ): MMRESULT; stdcall; stdcall;
```

Description

This function queries a joystick or related device for its position and button status. This function provides access to extended devices such as rudder pedals, point-of-view hats, devices with a large number of buttons, and coordinate systems using up to six axes. For joystick devices that use three axes or fewer and have fewer than four buttons, use the JoyGetPos function.

Parameters

uJoyID: The identifier of the joystick (JOYSTICKID1 or JOYSTICKID2) to be queried.

lpInfo: The address of a JOYINFOEX structure to contain the capabilities of the joystick.

Return Value

Returns JOYERR_NOERROR if successful. Otherwise, it returns one of the following errors: MMSYSERR_NODRIVER, indicating that the joystick driver is not present; MMSYSERR_INVALPARAM, indicating that an invalid parameter was passed; MMSYSERR_BADDEVICEID, indicating that the specified joystick identifier is invalid; or JOYERR_UNPLUGGED, indicating that the specified joystick is not connected to the system.

Example

Listing 7-8 shows how to get the current joystick position using the JoyGetPosEx() function.

Listing 7-8: Getting the current position of a joystick using the JoyGetPosEx() function

```
procedure TfrmJoyStickCapture.DefaultHandler(var Msg);
var
  LocalJOYINFO : JOYINFO;
  LocalJOYINFOEX : JOYINFOEX;
begin
  inherited DefaultHandler(Msg);
  case TMessage(Msg).Msg of
  // Messages related to Joystick activity
    MM_JOY1BUTTONDOWN:   btnJoyButtonHit.Glyph.LoadFromFile
              ('led2off.bmp');
    MM_JOY1BUTTONUP:     btnJoyButtonHit.Glyph.LoadFromFile('led2on.bmp');
    MM_JOY1MOVE:
      begin
        joyGetPos(JOYSTICKID1, @LocalJOYINFO);
        joyGetPosEx(JOYSTICKID1, @LocalJOYINFOEX);
        edXPos.Text := IntToStr(LocalJOYINFO.wXpos);
        edYPos.Text := IntToStr(LocalJOYINFO.wYpos);
        edZPos.Text := IntToStr(LocalJOYINFO.wZpos);
        if (((LocalJOYINFOEX.dwFlags AND (1 shl JOY_RETURNR)) =
          JOY_RETURNR)) then edRudderPed.Text :=
            IntToStr(LocalJOYINFOEX.dwRpos)
        else
          edRudderPed.Text := '0';
        if (((LocalJOYINFOEX.dwFlags AND (1 shl JOY_RETURNU)) =
          JOY_RETURNU)) then edAxis5.Text :=
            IntToStr(LocalJOYINFOEX.dwUpos)
        else
          edAxis5.Text := '0';
        if (((LocalJOYINFOEX.dwFlags AND (1 shl JOY_RETURNV)) =
          JOY_RETURNV)) then edAxis6.Text :=
            IntToStr(LocalJOYINFOEX.dwVpos)
        else
          edAxis6.Text := '0';
      end;
    end;    // case
end;
```

7

Chapter

function JoyGetThreshold   *mmsystem.pas*

Syntax

```
function JoyGetThreshold(
uJoyID: UINT;
lpuThreshold: PUINT
): MMRESULT; stdcall;
```

Description

This function queries a joystick for its current movement threshold. The movement threshold is the distance the joystick must be moved before a WM_JOYMOVE message is sent to a window that has captured the device. The threshold is initially zero.

Parameters

uJoyID: The identifier of the joystick (JOYSTICKID1 or JOYSTICKID2) to be queried.

lpuThreshold: The address of a variable that contains the movement threshold value.

Return Value

Returns JOYERR_NOERROR if successful. Otherwise, it returns one of the following errors: MMSYSERR_NODRIVER, indicating that the joystick driver is not present, or MMSYSERR_INVALPARAM, indicating that an invalid parameter was passed.

Example

Listing 7-9 shows how to use this function in a form's Activate method.

Listing 7-9: Capturing a joystick in a form's Activate method

```
procedure TfrmJoyStickCapture.FormActivate(Sender: TObject);
begin
  AMMResult := joySetCapture(Self.Handle, JOYSTICKID1, 0, False);
  if AMMResult<>0 then
    begin
      ShowMessage('Cannot capture the joystick; Make sure it''s
                   connected');
      Exit;
    end;
  joyGetThreshold(JOYSTICKID1, @JoyStickThreshold);
```

```
    if (JoyStickThreshold < 100)
      then
        begin
          JoyStickThreshold := 100;
          joySetThreshold(JOYSTICKID1, JoyStickThreshold);
        end;
end;
```

function JoyReleaseCapture　　　　*mmsystem.pas*

Syntax

```
function JoyReleaseCapture(
  uJoyID: UINT
): MMRESULT; stdcall;
```

Description

This function releases the specified captured joystick.

Parameters

uJoyID: The identifier of the joystick (JOYSTICKID1 or JOYSTICKID2) to be queried.

Return Value

Returns JOYERR_NOERROR if successful. Otherwise, it returns one of the following errors: MMSYSERR_NODRIVER, indicating that the joystick driver is not present, or JOYERR_PARMS, indicating that the specified joystick device identifier uJoyID is invalid.

Example

The following simple procedure shows how to release a joystick using the JoyReleaseCapture() function:

```
procedure TfrmJoyStickCapture.FormDeactivate(Sender: TObject);
begin
  joyReleaseCapture(JOYSTICKID1);
end;
```

function JoySetCapture   *mmsystem.pas*

Syntax

```
function JoySetCapture(
  Handle: HWND;
  uJoyID, uPeriod: UINT;
  bChanged: BOOL
  ): MMRESULT; stdcall;
```

Description

This function captures a joystick by causing its messages to be sent to the specified window. This function will fail if the specified joystick is currently captured. Call the JoyReleaseCapture() function to release the captured joystick, or destroy the window to release the joystick automatically.

Parameters

Handle: The handle of the window to receive the joystick messages.

uJoyID: The identifier of the joystick (JOYSTICKID1 or JOYSTICKID2) to be captured.

uPeriod: Polling frequency, in milliseconds.

bChanged: Change position flag. Specify TRUE for this parameter to send messages only when the position changes by a value greater than the joystick movement threshold. Otherwise, messages are sent at the polling frequency specified in uPeriod.

Return Value

Returns JOYERR_NOERROR if successful. Otherwise, it returns one of the following errors: MMSYSERR_NODRIVER, indicating that the joystick driver is not present; or JOYERR_UNPLUGGED, indicating that the specified joystick is not connected to the system.

Example

See Listing 7-9.

function JoySetThreshold   *mmsystem.pas*

Syntax

```
function JoySetThreshold(
  uJoyID, uThreshold: UINT
  ): MMRESULT; stdcall;
```

Description

This function sets the movement threshold of a joystick. The movement threshold is the distance the joystick must be moved before a WM_JOYMOVE message is sent to a window that has captured the device. The threshold is initially zero.

Parameters

uJoyID: The identifier of the joystick (JOYSTICKID1 or JOYSTICKID2) to be queried.

uThreshold: New movement threshold.

Return Value

Returns JOYERR_NOERROR if successful. Otherwise, it returns one of the following errors: MMSYSERR_NODRIVER, indicating that the joystick driver is not present, or JOYERR_PARMS, indicating that the specified joystick device identifier, uJoyID, is invalid.

Example

See Listing 7-9.

Joysticks and timers can add a great deal to our multimedia applications. One important topic we have not covered up to this point is multimedia input and output. That is the topic of Chapter 8.

7

Chapter

Chapter Eight

Multimedia Input and Output Support

In Windows, as in other operating environments, one of the most common operations is file input and output. This is a subject we have largely ignored until now. Most multimedia applications require file input and output (I/O) to create, read, and write disk files. Clearly, Delphi has an abundance of support for input and output. Why not just use those services? The answer is simple—those built-in services are limited. The multimedia file I/O services provide more functionality than the standard I/O services, functionality that is specific to the Windows multimedia system. These multimedia file I/O services provide buffered and unbuffered file I/O and support for Resource Interchange File Format (RIFF) files, or memory files. The services can even be extended using custom I/O procedures. They can also be shared among applications.

Which of these services will be most important to you in writing multimedia applications? Most of the time, you'll need only the basic file I/O services and the RIFF file I/O services. However, if your application has special file I/O needs, you can access some of the low-level functions to meet those needs. One example mentioned in the Microsoft help file is a situation in which an application must stream data from a compact disc in real time. In such a time critical case, you can optimize performance by using these low-level services to directly access the file I/O buffer. Another example mentioned concerns applications that need to access files in custom storage systems such as file archives or databases. In that case, you can provide your own I/O procedures to read and write elements to the storage system. This will become clearer when we look at some of the structures and functions involved.

Types of Multimedia Input/Output Services

The Multimedia I/O API provides most or all of the multimedia input/output services that you might require. Those services can be divided into the following four categories:

- Basic services
- Buffered services
- Resource Interchange File Format (RIFF) services
- Custom services

Let's examine each of these in turn.

Basic Multimedia I/O Services

The basic multimedia I/O services are similar to the basic file I/O services available in Delphi and cover the essential operations of opening, closing, reading, writing, and saving files. They also allow you to change the current read or write location within an open file.

Obviously, before you complete any other I/O operation, you must open the file with which you're going to work. In the multimedia file I/O system, you use the MmioOpen() function, which returns a file handle of the type HMMIO to accomplish this. After that, you can use this file handle to identify the open file when calling other file I/O functions. Be aware that this HMMIO file handle is not a standard file handle and cannot be used with other file operations outside of the multimedia I/O system.

When you use MmioOpen() to open a file, you need to use a flag to specify whether you are opening it for reading, writing, or both. You can also specify flags that enable you to create or delete a file. Always be sure to use the MmioClose() function to close a file when you are finished reading or writing to it.

After the file has been opened, you can read it and write to it by using the MmioRead() and MmioWrite() functions, respectively. These functions will then ensure that the next read or write operation will occur at the current file position or location pointer in a file. The current file position is advanced each time a segment of the file is read or written. To get this kind of functionality with standard input/output services, you would need to write a good deal of code yourself.

You can also change the current file position by using the MmioSeek() function. You should be sure that you specify a valid location in a file. If you specify an invalid location (such as past the end of the file), MmioSeek() may not return an error, but subsequent I/O operations could fail. As with previous APIs, it is always a good policy to check the values returned by multimedia functions, particularly when debugging an application that uses these services.

There are flags you can use with the MmioOpen() function for operations beyond basic file I/O. For example, by specifying an MMIOINFO structure, you can open memory files, specify a custom I/O procedure, or supply a buffer for buffered I/O. We'll examine this structure in some detail, when we describe the MmioOpen() function. Now, let's examine the buffered services available.

Buffered Services

Most of the overhead in file I/O occurs when accessing a media device such as a disk drive. If you're reading or writing many small blocks of information, the device can spend a lot of time moving to the physical location on the media for each read or write operation. In such a situation, you can achieve better performance by using the buffered file I/O services. With these services, the file I/O manager maintains an intermediate buffer larger than the blocks of information you are reading or writing. This allows it to access the device only when the buffer must be filled from disk or written to disk. This reduces the number of read or write operations.

Before you set up and use buffered file I/O, you have an important decision to make: You need to decide whether you want the file I/O manager or the application (your code) to allocate the buffer. Of course, it is simpler to let the file I/O manager do the work. However, if you want to directly access the buffer or open a memory file, you should allocate the buffer yourself in the application.

A buffer allocated by the file I/O manager is called an internal I/O buffer. The default size of this kind of buffer is 8K. If you need or want a larger buffer, you can use the MmioSetBuffer() function to change its size. The sample application for this chapter on the companion CD shows how to do this. If you want to open a file for buffered I/O using an internal buffer, you must specify the MMIO_ALLOCBUF flag when you open the file using the MmioOpen() function. This flag and all of the others are described under the MmioOpen() function. You can also use this function to enable buffering for a file opened for unbuffered I/O or to supply your own buffer to use as a memory file. These capabilities further demonstrate the power of the multimedia input/output system.

You can force the contents of the I/O buffer to be written to disk at any time by using the MmioFlush() function. However, when you close a file using the MmioClose() function, the flushing (writing) occurs automatically and you don't have to call MmioFlush() explicitly. Be aware that if you run out of disk space, a call to MmioFlush() could fail, even if the preceding calls to the MmioWrite() function were successful. Similarly, a call to MmioClose() could fail if it is unable to flush its I/O buffer.

Applications for which performance is an issue, such as those that stream data in real time from a CD-ROM, can optimize file I/O performance by directly accessing the I/O buffer. You should be careful if you decide to do this because you will be bypassing some of the safeguards and error checking provided by the file I/O manager. Let's see how this file manager works.

Multimedia File Manager

The multimedia file I/O manager uses the MMIOINFO structure to maintain state information about an open file. As demonstrated in the sample application for this chapter on the companion CD, you can use three members in this structure to read from and write to the I/O buffer: pchNext, pchEndRead, and pchEndWrite. The pchNext member points to the next location in the buffer that will be read or written. You must increment this member yourself as you read and write the buffer. The pchEndRead member identifies the last valid character you can read from the buffer. Likewise, this member identifies the last location in the buffer to which you can write. More precisely, both pchEndRead and pchEndWrite point to the memory location that follows the last valid data in the buffer. The MMIOINFO structure is defined in mmsystem.pas as follows:

```
type
  PMMIOInfo = ^TMMIOInfo;
  _MMIOINFO = record
    { general fields }
    dwFlags: DWORD;        { general status flags }
    fccIOProc: FOURCC;     { pointer to I/O procedure }
```

```
      pIOProc: TFNMMIOProc;    { pointer to I/O procedure }
      wErrorRet: UINT;         { place for error to be returned }
      hTask: HTASK;            { alternate local task }

      { fields maintained by MMIO functions during buffered I/O }
      cchBuffer: Longint;      { size of I/O buffer (or OL) }
      pchBuffer: PChar;        { start of I/O buffer (or NULL) }
      pchNext: PChar;          { pointer to next byte to read/write }
      pchEndRead: PChar;       { pointer to last valid byte to read }
      pchEndWrite: PChar;      { pointer to last byte to write }
      lBufOffset: Longint;     { disk offset of start of buffer }

      { fields maintained by I/O procedure }
      lDiskOffset: Longint;              { disk offset of next read or write }
      adwInfo: array[0..2] of DWORD;  { data specific to type of MMIOPROC }

      { other fields maintained by MMIO }
      dwReserved1: DWORD;      { reserved for MMIO use }
      dwReserved2: DWORD;      { reserved for MMIO use }
      hmmio: HMMIO;            { handle to open file }
    end;
  TMMIOInfo = _MMIOINFO;
  MMIOINFO = _MMIOINFO;
```

Before you can use the MMIOINFO structure (in this case,
CurrentMMIoInfo, which is declared as a pointer to the MMIOINFO
structure, or PMMIOINFO in the sample application), you need to set
aside memory for it with a statement like the following:

```
    GetMem(CurrentMMIoInfo, SizeOf(MMIOINFO));
```

Of course, you should free the memory as soon as you are finished using
the structure to avoid a memory leak. Then you must initialize the various fields as in Listing 8-1.

Listing 8-1: Initializing the fields in the MMIOINFO structure

```
  procedure InitMMIOInfo; // Initialize MMIOINFO structure
  begin
    CurrentMMIoInfo^.dwFlags     := 0;
    CurrentMMIoInfo^.fccIOProc   := mmioStringToFOURCC('WAV ', 0);
    CurrentMMIoInfo^.pIOProc     := TFNMMIOProc(PChar('waveInIOProc'));
    CurrentMMIoInfo^.wErrorRet   := 0;
    CurrentMMIoInfo^.htask       := 0;
    CurrentMMIoInfo^.cchBuffer   := 0;
    CurrentMMIoInfo^.pchBuffer   := nil;
```

```
    CurrentMMIoInfo^.pchNext     := nil;
    CurrentMMIoInfo^.pchEndRead  := nil;
    CurrentMMIoInfo^.pchEndWrite := nil;
    CurrentMMIoInfo^.lBufOffset  := 0;
    CurrentMMIoInfo^.lDiskOffset := 0;
    CurrentMMIoInfo^.adwInfo[0]   := 0;
    CurrentMMIoInfo^.adwInfo[1]   := 0;
    CurrentMMIoInfo^.adwInfo[2]   := 0;
    CurrentMMIoInfo^.dwReserved1 := 0;
    CurrentMMIoInfo^.dwReserved2 := 0;
    CurrentMMIoInfo^.hmmio        := 0;
  end; {InitMMIOInfo}
```

Not surprisingly, the multimedia input/output system contains a number of functions specifically designed to manage buffers. These include the functions MmioGetInfo() and MmioSetInfo(), which are used to retrieve and set state information about the file I/O buffer, respectively, as well as the MmioAdvance() function, which is used to move the process forward during a read or write operation. During a read operation, this latter function fills the buffer and sets the pchEndRead pointer to point to the end of the buffer. These functions rely heavily on pointers to navigate multimedia files. An application will always read from the I/O buffer at the location specified by the pchNext pointer and then advance that pointer. In a similar fashion, an application will write to the I/O buffer and then advance the pchNext pointer.

After the application fills the buffer, it calls MmioAdvance() to flush the buffer to disk. This function resets pchNext to point to the beginning of the buffer. To see how to use this function, see the example under the MmioAdvance() function description. When you reach the end of the I/O buffer, you must advance the buffer to fill it from the disk (if you are reading) or flush it to the disk (if you are writing). In the sample application, the following Boolean statement tests for this condition:

```
CurrentMMIoInfo^.pchNext = CurrentMMIoInfo^.pchEndWrite
```

As we've discussed, you use the MmioAdvance() function to advance an I/O buffer. The operation differs for input or output operations. When reading, you can fill an I/O buffer from disk by using the Mmio-Advance() function with the MMIO_READ flag. If the data remaining to be read from the file is insufficient to fill the buffer, the pchEndRead member of the MMIOINFO structure points to the location following the last valid byte in the buffer, not the actual end of the buffer. (Imagine having to write code to accomplish this!) When writing to a file, you can flush a buffer to disk by first setting the MMIO_DIRTY flag in the dwFlags member of the MMIOINFO structure and then calling MmioAdvance() with the MMIO_WRITE flag. These techniques are demonstrated in the sample application for this chapter on the companion CD.

RIFF File Services

The preferred format for multimedia files is Resource Interchange File Format, or RIFF. The RIFF file I/O functions work with the basic buffered and unbuffered file I/O services. Conveniently, you can open, read, or write RIFF files in the same way as other file types. RIFF files have a number of special characteristics, however. Let's take a look.

RIFF files use four-character codes to identify file elements, including the type of multimedia data the file contains. These codes are 32-bit values representing a sequence of one to four ASCII alphanumeric characters, padded on the right with space characters. Not surprisingly, the data type for four-character codes is called FOURCC. You can use the Mmio-FOURCC() function to convert any four characters into this special four-character code. While writing an article on TAPI (Telephony Application Programming Interface) for *Delphi Informant* magazine with Keith Elias, we found that this function had not been implemented in mmsystem.pas. Keith wrote the following straightforward function that got the job done:

```
function mmioFOURCC(A:Char; B:Char; C:Char; D:Char) : DWORD;
begin
Result := DWORD(A)          OR
          DWORD(B) shl 8    OR
          DWORD(C) shl 16   OR
          DWORD(D) shl 24;
end;
```

Another function is also used with the FOURCC structure, the Mmio-StringToFOURCC() function. This function, which is implemented in mmsystem.pas, converts a null-terminated string into a four-character code. This function and its related functions are defined in mmsystem.pas as follows:

8

Chapter

```
function mmioStringToFOURCCA(sz: PAnsiChar; uFlags: UINT): FOURCC;
        stdcall;
function mmioStringToFOURCCW(sz: PWideChar; uFlags: UINT): FOURCC;
        stdcall;
function mmioStringToFOURCC(sz: PChar; uFlags: UINT): FOURCC; stdcall;
```

Let's examine the general structure of RIFF files. The basic building block of a RIFF file is a chunk. A chunk is a logical unit of multimedia data, such as a single frame in a video clip. Each chunk contains the following fields:

- A four-character code specifying the chunk identifier
- A DWORD value specifying the size of the data member in the chunk
- A data field

Some chunks can contain other chunks, called subchunks. Specifically these container chunks have a chunk identifier of "RIFF" or "LIST" and are the only ones that are permitted to contain subchunks. These chunks (that contain other chunks) are called parent chunks. The first chunk in a RIFF file must be a "RIFF" chunk. All other chunks in the file are subchunks of the "RIFF" chunk. Figures 8-1 and 8-2 show the beginning of a WAV file with a "RIFF" chunk that contains two subchunks (fmt and data).

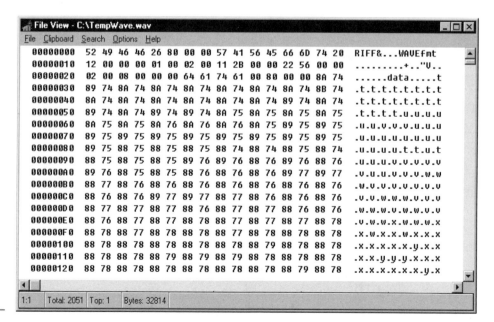

Figure 8-1

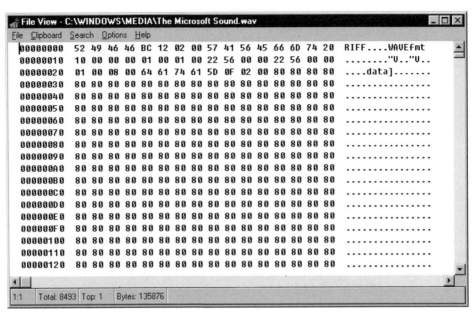

Figure 8-2

"RIFF" chunks include an additional field in the first four bytes of the data field. This additional field provides the form type of the field. The form type is a four-character code identifying the format of the data stored in the file. For example, Microsoft waveform audio files have a form type of WAVE. Similarly, "LIST" chunks also include an additional field in the first four bytes of the data field, a field indicating the list type of the field. The list type is a four-character code identifying the contents of the list. As explained in the Microsoft help file, a specific "LIST" chunk with a list type of INFO could contain "ICOP" and "ICRD" chunks. These chunks provide copyright and creation date information, respectively.

Multimedia file I/O services include two functions that you can use to navigate a RIFF file's chunks: MmioAscend() and MmioDescend(). You can use either of these two functions to perform high-level seek operations in RIFF files. As with many of the multimedia I/O functions, each is used in both input and output. When you descend into a chunk, the file position is set to the data field of the chunk (8 bytes from the beginning of the chunk). For "RIFF" and "LIST" chunks, the file position is set to the location following the form type or list type (12 bytes from the beginning of the chunk). When you ascend out of a chunk, the file position is set to the location following the end of the chunk.

When you write to a new WAVE file using the MMIO services, you need to create these chunks. To accomplish this you must use the

MmioCreateChunk() function to write a chunk header at the current position in the file. The three functions we have been discussing, MmioAscend(), MmioDescend(), and MmioCreateChunk(), all use the MMCKINFO structure to specify and retrieve information about "RIFF" chunks. This structure is defined in mmsystem.pas as follows:

```
type
  PMMCKInfo = ^TMMCKInfo;
  _MMCKINFO = record
    ckid: FOURCC;             { chunk ID }
    cksize: DWORD;            { chunk size }
    fccType: FOURCC;          { form type or list type }
    dwDataOffset: DWORD;      { offset of data portion of chunk }
    dwFlags: DWORD;           { flags used by MMIO functions }
  end;
  TMMCKInfo = _MMCKINFO;
  MMCKINFO = _MMCKINFO;
```

Custom Multimedia I/O Services

Multimedia file I/O services use I/O procedures to handle the physical input and output associated with reading and writing multimedia data to different types of storage systems, such as file archival systems and database-storage systems. Predefined I/O procedures exist for the standard file systems and for memory files, but you can supply a custom I/O procedure for accessing a unique storage system by using the Mmio-InstallIOProc() function. This process is demonstrated in the sample application accompanying this chapter.

When you use the MMIO functions, you must first call the MmioOpen() function to open the file. You have a number of options in opening a file with this function. You can include a plus sign (+) or the CFSEPCHAR constant in the filename to separate the name of the physical file from the name of a specific element of the file you want to open. For example, the following statement opens a file element named "MyElement" from a file named FILENAME.ARC. The handle for the file (which can be used only with MMIO functions) is returned in AMM_IO:

```
AMM_IO := mmioOpen(PChar('filename.arc+MyElement'), Nil, MMIO_READ);
```

When the multimedia file I/O manager encounters the plus sign character (+) in a filename, it uses the filename extension to determine with which I/O procedure to associate the file. In the previous example, the file I/O manager would attempt to use the I/O procedure associated with the .arc filename extension; this I/O procedure would first have to be installed by using MmioInstallIOProc(). If no I/O procedure is installed, MmioOpen() returns an error. I/O procedures must respond to one of the messages shown in Table 8-1:

Table 8-1: Messages responded to by MMIO procedures

Message	Purpose, Parameters, and Return Value
MMIOM_CLOSE	This message is sent to an I/O procedure by the MmioClose() function to request that a file be closed. It has two parameters: IParam1, which points to ICloseFlags, and IParam2, which is reserved. The ICloseFlags parameter contains the flags of the wFlags parameter of the MmioClose() function.
MMIOM_OPEN	This message is sent to an I/O procedure by the MmioOpen() function to request that a file be opened or deleted. It has two parameters: IParam1, which points to a null-terminated string containing the filename, and IParam2, which is reserved.
MMIOM_READ	This message is sent to an I/O procedure by the MmioRead() function to request that a specified number of bytes be read from an open file. It has two parameters: IParam1 (IBuffer), which points to the address of a buffer to be filled with data read from the file and IParam2 (cbRead), which contains the number of bytes to read from file. This message returns the number of bytes read from the file.
MMIOM_WRITE	This message is sent to an I/O procedure by the MmioWrite() function to request that data be written to an open MMIO file. It has two parameters: IParam1 (lpBuffer) and IParam2 (cbWrite). The lpBuffer parameter points to the address of the buffer that contains the data to be written to the file. The cbWrite parameter contains the number of bytes to write to the file. This message returns the number of bytes written to the file.

Message	Purpose, Parameters, and Return Value
MMIOM_SEEK	This message is sent to an I/O procedure by the MmioSeek() function to request that the current file position be moved. It has two parameters: lParam1 (lNewFilePos) and lParam2 (lChangeFlag). The first parameter indicates the new file position. The meaning of this value is dependent on the flag specified in the second parameter, lChangeFlag. This flag specifies how the file position will be changed. It can be any of the following values: SEEK_CUR, moving the file position lNewFilePos (positive or negative) bytes from the current position; SEEK_END, moving the file position lNewFilePos bytes from the end of the file; and SEEK_SET, moving the file position lNewFilePos bytes from the beginning of the file. This message returns the new file position.
MMIOM_RENAME	This message is sent to an I/O procedure by the MmioRename() function to request that the specified file be renamed. It has two parameters: lParam1 (lpszOldFilename) and lParam2 (lpszNewFilename). The first, lpszOldFilename, contains the address of a string indicating the current name of the file to be renamed. The second, lpszNewFilename, is the address of a string containing the new filename. This message returns zero if the file is renamed successfully. If the specified file cannot be found, the return value is MMIOERR_FILENOT-FOUND.
MMIOM_WRITEFLUSH	This message is sent to an I/O procedure by the MmioWrite() function to request that data be written to an open file and that any internal buffers used by the I/O procedure be flushed to disk. It has two parameters, lParam1 (lpBuffer) and lParam2 (cbWrite.) The first, lpBuffer, is the address of a buffer containing the data to write to the file. The second, cbWrite, is the number of bytes to write to file. This message returns the number of bytes written to the file. If there is an error, the return value will be −1. This message is equivalent to the MMIOM_WRITE message with one exception: It requests that the I/O procedure flush its internal buffers, if any. Therefore, unless an I/O procedure performs internal buffering, this message can be handled exactly like the MMIOM_WRITE message.

Sometimes you will need to do something unusual that is not supported by the above messages. In that case, you can create a custom message and send it to your I/O procedure by using the MmioSendMessage() function. If you define your own message, be sure to define it by giving it a value above that defined by the MMIOM_USER constant.

Multimedia I/O messages have an important housekeeping function to perform: They must maintain the lDiskOffset member of the MMIOINFO structure (pointed to by the lpmmioinfo parameter of the MmioOpen() function). That lDiskOffset member must always contain the file offset to the location that will be accessed by the next MMIOM_READ or MMIOM_WRITE message. This offset, specified in bytes, is relative to the beginning of the file. The I/O procedure can use the adwInfo member to maintain any required state information. However, the I/O procedure should not modify any other members in the MMIOINFO structure. Now let's take a detailed look at the various constants used in the MMIO system.

Constants Used in Multimedia Input/Output

As with waveform audio, MIDI, and other parts of the multimedia system, multimedia input/output has its own collection of error constants. These constants, defined in mmsystem.pas, are shown in Tables 8-2 through 8-6.

Table 8-2: Multimedia input/output error constants

Constant Name	Value	Meaning
MMIOERR_BASE	256	Base value from which the others are determined
MMIOERR_FILENOTFOUND	MMIOERR_BASE + 1	File not found
MMIOERR_OUTOFMEMORY	MMIOERR_BASE + 2	Out of memory
MMIOERR_CANNOTOPEN	MMIOERR_BASE + 3	Cannot open file
MMIOERR_CANNOTCLOSE	MMIOERR_BASE + 4	Cannot close file
MMIOERR_CANNOTREAD	MMIOERR_BASE + 5	Cannot read file
MMIOERR_CANNOTWRITE	MMIOERR_BASE + 6	Cannot write to file
MMIOERR_CANNOTSEEK	MMIOERR_BASE + 7	Cannot seek in file
MMIOERR_CANNOTEXPAND	MMIOERR_BASE + 8	Cannot expand file
MMIOERR_CHUNKNOTFOUND	MMIOERR_BASE + 9	Chunk not found

8

Chapter

Constant Name	Value	Meaning
MMIOERR_UNBUFFERED	MMIOERR_BASE + 10	Error because file is unbuffered
MMIOERR_PATHNOTFOUND	MMIOERR_BASE + 11	Specified path is incorrect
MMIOERR_ACCESSDENIED	MMIOERR_BASE + 12	File is protected
MMIOERR_SHARINGVIOLATION	MMIOERR_BASE + 13	File is in use
MMIOERR_NETWORKERROR	MMIOERR_BASE + 14	Network is not responding
MMIOERR_TOOMANYOPENFILES	MMIOERR_BASE + 15	No more file handles
MMIOERR_INVALIDFILE	MMIOERR_BASE + 16	Default MMIO error

Additionally, there are a number of constants used for bit field masks as described in Table 8-3. The first two constants are related to a file's mode, the next three are related to the manner in which a file will be opened in Read/Write mode, and the last five are concerned only with files opened in Share mode.

Table 8-3: Constants used for bit field masks

Constant Name	Value	Meaning
MMIO_RWMODE	$00000003	Open file for reading/writing/both
MMIO_SHAREMODE	$00000070	File sharing mode number
MMIO_READ	$00000000	Open file for reading only
MMIO_WRITE	$00000001	Open file for writing only
MMIO_READWRITE	$00000002	Open file for reading and writing
MMIO_COMPAT	$00000000	Compatibility mode
MMIO_EXCLUSIVE	$00000010	Exclusive-access mode
MMIO_DENYWRITE	$00000020	Deny writing to other processes
MMIO_DENYREAD	$00000030	Deny reading to other processes
MMIO_DENYNONE	$00000040	Deny nothing to other processes

In addition to bitmap constants, the MMIO API includes a number of flag constants that are used with the various functions we'll be discussing presently. For easy reference, all of those constants are in Table 8-4. The first six flags are associated with the dwFlags field of the MMIOINFO structure. The next three are associated specifically with the MmioSeek() function and indicate one of the three locations in a file from which you can seek. The next one, MMIO_DIRTY, is used with I/O buffers. The remaining 13 are associated with various other MMIO functions.

Table 8-4: Constants used for various flags associated with MMIO functions

Constant Name	Value	Meaning
MMIO_CREATE	$00001000	Create new file or truncate file
MMIO_PARSE	$00000100	Parse new file returning its path
MMIO_DELETE	$00000200	Delete file
MMIO_EXIST	$00004000	Check for the existence of file
MMIO_ALLOCBUF	$00010000	MmioOpen() should allocate a buffer
MMIO_GETTEMP	$00020000	MmioOpen() should retrieve temp name
SEEK_SET	0	Seek to an absolute position
SEEK_CUR	1	Seek relative to current position
SEEK_END	2	Seek relative to end of file
MMIO_DIRTY	$10000000	I/O buffer is dirty
MMIO_FHOPEN	$0010	MmioClose() should keep file handle open
MMIO_EMPTYBUF	$0010	MmioFlush() should empty the I/O buffer
MMIO_TOUPPER	$0010	MmioStringToFOURCC() should convert string to uppercase
MMIO_INSTALLPROC	$00010000	MmioInstallIOProc() should install an MMIOProc custom procedure
MMIO_GLOBALPROC	$10000000	MmioInstallIOProc() should install an MMIOProc custom procedure globally
MMIO_REMOVEPROC	$00020000	MmioInstallIOProc() should remove an MMIOProc custom procedure
MMIO_UNICODEPROC	$01000000	MmioInstallIOProc() should install a Unicode MMIOProc custom procedure
MMIO_FINDPROC	$00040000	MmioInstallIOProc() should find an MMIOProc custom procedure
MMIO_FINDCHUNK	$0010	MmioDescend() should find a chunk by its ID
MMIO_FINDRIFF	$0020	MmioDescend() should find a "RIFF" chunk
MMIO_FINDLIST	$0040	MmioDescend() should find a "LIST" chunk
MMIO_CREATERIFF	$0020	MmioCreateChunk() should create a "RIFF" chunk
MMIO_CREATELIST	$0040	MmioCreateChunk() should create a "LIST" chunk

As we mentioned above, MMIOPROC I/O procedures use various messages. The constants shown in Table 8-5 are used for those messages.

Table 8-5: MMIOPROC I/O message constants

Constant Name	Value	Meaning
MMIOM_READ	MMIO_READ	Read from an MMIO file
MMIOM_WRITE	MMIO_WRITE	Write to an MMIO file
MMIOM_SEEK	2	Seek to a new position in an MMIO file
MMIOM_OPEN	3	Open an MMIO file
MMIOM_CLOSE	4	Close an MMIO file
MMIOM_WRITEFLUSH	5	Write data to an MMIO file and flush its contents
MMIOM_RENAME	6	Rename specified MMIO file
MMIOM_USER	$8000	Beginning of user-defined messages

Two constants are associated with FOURCC codes and two with the standard built-in I/O procedures that use them. There are also two miscellaneous constants associated with the default buffer size and the plus character sometimes used with filenames. These constants are listed in Table 8-6.

Table 8-6: FOURCC and miscellaneous constants

Constant Name	Value	Meaning
FOURCC_RIFF	$46464952	'RIFF'
FOURCC_LIST	$5453494C	'LIST'
FOURCC_DOS	$20532F44	'DOS '
FOURCC_MEM	$204D454D	'MEM '
MMIO_DEFAULTBUFFER	8192	Default buffer size
CFSEPCHAR	'+'	Compound file name separator character

In addition to these constants, there are several variables and types defined in mmsystem.pas as follows:

```
FOURCC = DWORD;              {a four-character code used with a RIFF file}
PHMMIO = ^HMMIO;             {pointer to a file handle}
HMMIO = Integer;             {a handle to an open file}
TFNMMIOProc = function(lpmmioinfo: PChar; uMessage: UINT; lParam1,
           lParam2: LPARAM): Longint stdcall;
         { prototype of a custom multimedia I/O function }
```

Multimedia Input/Output Functions

function MmioInstallIOProc   *mmsystem.pas*

Syntax

```
function MmioInstallIOProc(
 fccIOProc: FOURCC;
 pIOProc: TFNMMIOProc;
 dwFlags: DWORD
 ): TFNMMIOProc; stdcall;
```

Description

This function installs or removes a custom I/O procedure. It can also locate an installed I/O procedure by using its corresponding four-character code.

Parameters

fccIOProc: A four-character code that identifies the I/O procedure to install, remove, or locate. All characters in this code should be uppercase.

pIOProc: The address of the I/O procedure to install. To remove or locate an I/O procedure, you should set this parameter to NULL.

dwFlags: A flag indicating whether the I/O procedure is being installed, removed, or located. The following values are defined: MMIO_FINDPROC, indicating that the function will search for the specified I/O procedure; MMIO_GLOBALPROC, a modifier to the MMIO_INSTALLPROC flag that indicates the I/O procedure should be installed for global use (ignored if MMIO_FINDPROC or MMIO_REMOVEPROC is specified); MMIO_INSTALLPROC, indicating the specified I/O procedure should be installed; and MMIO_REMOVEPROC, indicating the specified I/O procedure should be removed.

Return Value

Returns the address of the I/O procedure installed, removed, or located. Returns zero if there is an error.

8

Chapter

Example

Listing 8-2 shows how to install a custom procedure. Before you install it, you'll need to do some preliminary work. You will need to declare a constant that holds a version number for your procedure as we do in the sample application with:

```
WaveIn_CustomProcVersion = WM_USER+10001;
```

Then, you'll need to write a callback procedure (of type STADCALL; this is required) that can respond to all of the standard messages. Our callback procedure, WaveInFileProc(), responds to the three general WIM messages by sending three custom messages to the calling application, WaveIn_Started, WaveIn_Stop, and WaveIn_RecordingToFile. Each of these messages is responded to in the DefaultHandler() procedure of the calling application. Figures 8-3 and 8-4 show the calling application responding to two of these messages during a recording operation.

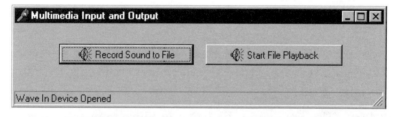

Figure 8-3

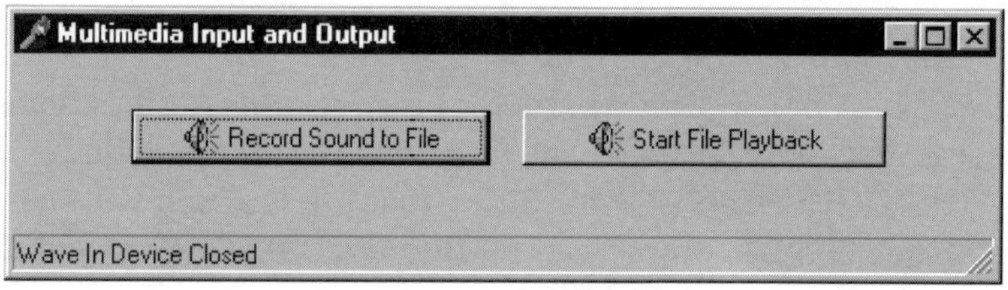

Figure 8-4

Likewise, Figures 8-5 and 8-6 show the calling application responding to two of these messages during a playback operation.

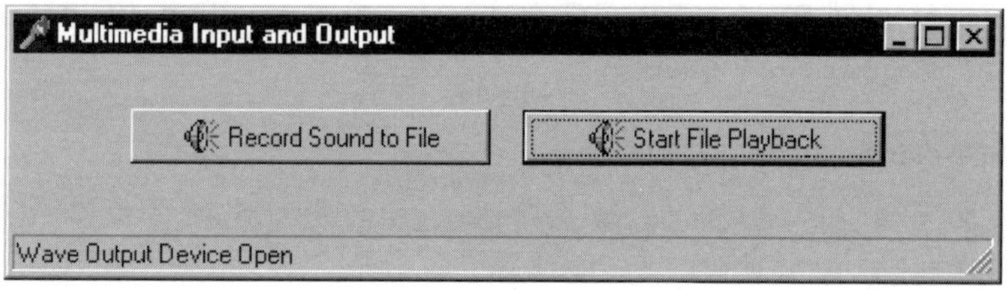

Figure 8-5

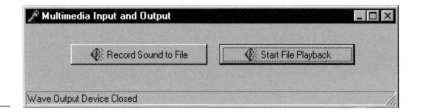

Figure 8-6

The last one, WaveIn_RecordingToFile, calls our procedure, WaveInIOProc(). In Listing 8-2, there is the following line of code:

```
CurrentMMIoInfo^.pIOProc    := TFNMMIOProc(PChar('waveInIOProc'));
```

which stores the name of our all-purpose procedure that consists of a large case statement that includes all of the MMIOPROC I/O message constants explained in Table 8-5.

Listing 8-2: Defining, installing, running, and uninstalling a custom multimedia I/O procedure

```
procedure waveInFileProc(SomeWaveIn : HWaveIn; uMsg : UINT; dwInstance :
                         DWORD; dwParam1, dwParam2 : DWORD); stdcall;
begin
  case uMsg of        // check possible messages
    WIM_OPEN: PostMessage(HWND(MainFormHandle), WaveIn_Started, 0,
            dwParam1);
    WIM_CLOSE: PostMessage(HWND(MainFormHandle), WaveIn_Stop, 0,
            dwParam1);
    WIM_DATA:        // next line modified 1/9/00
      PostMessage(HWND(MainFormHandle{dwInstance}), WaveIn_
            RecordingToFile,
          0, dwParam1);
  end;              // case

function TWaveIn.InstallACustomIOProc: boolean;
begin
  @AMMIOProc := Nil;
  AMMIOProc := mmioInstallIOProc(FOURCC(mmioStringToFOURCC('WAV', 0)),
            TFNMMIOProc(PChar('waveInIOProc')), MMIO_INSTALLPROC);
  result := (@AMMIOProc<>Nil);
end;
// Main MMIO Procedure that processes messages
function waveInIOProc(MM_IOInfo : MMIOInfo; AMsg : UINT; lParam1, lParam2
                     : LPARAM) : longint; stdcall;
var
  AFile : Integer;
  TheFlags : Integer;
```

```
  ShortStatus : Integer;
  LongStatus : LongInt;
begin
  case AMsg of    // responds to MMIOPROC I/O message constants explained
                     in Table 8-5.
    MMIOM_OPEN:    // Open File
      if ((MM_IOInfo.dwFlags AND MMIO_READ)=0) then
          TheFlags := OF_READ
      else if ((MM_IOInfo.dwFlags AND MMIO_WRITE)=0) then
          TheFlags := OF_WRITE
      else if ((MM_IOInfo.dwFlags AND MMIO_CREATE)=0) then
        begin
          AFile := _lcreat(LPSTR(lParam1), 0);
          if (AFile = -1) then
              result := MMIOERR_CANNOTOPEN
          else
            begin
              MM_IOInfo.lDiskOffset := 0;
              result := 0;
            end
        end
          else  // default
            begin
              TheFlags := OF_READWRITE;
              Afile := _lopen(LPSTR(lParam1), TheFlags);
              if (AFile = -1) then
                if ((MM_IOInfo.dwFlags AND MMIO_WRITE)=0) then
                  AFile := _lcreat(LPSTR(lParam1), 0);
              if (AFile = -1) then
                result := MMIOERR_CANNOTOPEN
              else
                begin
                  MM_IOInfo.lDiskOffset := 0;
                  result := 0;
                end;
          exit;
        end;
    MMIOM_CLOSE:  // Close File
      result := _lclose(AFile);
    MMIOM_READ:    // Read File
      begin
        ShortStatus := _lread(AFile, LPSTR(lParam1), Integer(lParam2));
        MM_IOInfo.lDiskOffset := MM_IOInfo.lDiskOffset + Integer
                  (lParam2);
        result := LongInt(ShortStatus);
      end;
```

```
      MMIOM_WRITE: ; // Write File not implemented
      MMIOM_WRITEFLUSH:
        begin
          ShortStatus := _lwrite(AFile, LPSTR(lParam1), Integer(lParam2));
          MM_IOInfo.lDiskOffset := MM_IOInfo.lDiskOffset + Integer
                    (lParam2);
          result := LongInt(ShortStatus);
        end;
      MMIOM_SEEK:    // Seek in File
        begin
          LongStatus := _llseek(AFile, LONGInt(lParam1), Integer
                    (lParam2));
          MM_IOInfo.lDiskOffset := LongStatus;
          result := LongStatus;
        end;
      WaveIn_CustomProcVersion:  // Version (custom message)
      result := MAKELONG(0, 1);  // version 1.00
      else
        result := 0;
    end;             // case
end;

procedure TForm1.DefaultHandler(var Msg);
begin
  inherited DefaultHandler(Msg);
  case TMessage(Msg).Msg of
  // Messages related to standard Input/Output
    MM_WOM_OPEN: StatusBar1.Panels[0].Text := 'Wave Output Device Open';
    MM_WOM_DONE:
      begin
        StatusBar1.Panels[0].Text := 'Done Playing Wave File';
        WaveOut.ClosePlayFromFile;
      end;
    MM_WOM_CLOSE: StatusBar1.Panels[0].Text := 'Wave Output Device
                  Closed';
    WaveIn_Started: StatusBar1.Panels[0].Text := 'Wave In Device Opened';
    WaveIn_Stop: StatusBar1.Panels[0].Text := 'Wave In Device Closed';
    WaveIn_Recording:
    begin
      StatusBar1.Panels[0].Text := 'Wave In Recording ...';
      case WaveIn.CurrentSoundRecordTo of    //
        srtMemory: if WaveIn.WaveInStatus = wisRecording then exit
        else
          begin
            WaveIn.CloseDownRecording;
          end;
```

```
        srtFile: WaveIn.CompleteFileRecording;
    end;   // internal case;
  end;
  // Message related to multimedia I/O
  WaveIn_RecordingToFile : WaveIn.CompleteFileRecording;
 end;    // case
end;

procedure TWaveIn.UnInstallACustomIOProc;
begin
  mmioInstallIOProc(FOURCC(mmioStringToFOURCC('WAV', 0)),
              TFNMMIOProc(PChar('waveInIOProc')), MMIO_REMOVEPROC);
end;
```

function MmioOpen　　*mmsystem.pas*

Syntax

```
function MmioOpen(
  szFilename: PChar;
  lpmmioinfo: PMMIOInfo;
  dwOpenFlags: DWORD
  ): HMMIO; stdcall;
```

Description

This is probably the most important multimedia input/output function. It opens a file for unbuffered or buffered input and/or output. The file can be a standard file, a memory file, or an element of a custom storage system. As we discussed in the introductory part of this chapter, the handle returned by MmioOpen() is not a standard file handle; you cannot use it with any of the standard file I/O functions other than multimedia file I/O functions described in this chapter. Also, since open files are not automatically closed when an application exits, you must always be sure to call MmioClose() to close a file that was opened using MmioOpen().

Parameters

szFilename: The address of a string containing the filename of the file to open. If no I/O procedure is specified to open the file, the filename determines how the file is opened, as follows:

- If the filename does not contain a plus sign (+), it is assumed to be the name of a standard file (that is, a file whose type is not HMMIO).

- If the filename is of the form EXAMPLE.EXT+ABC, the extension EXT is assumed to identify an installed I/O procedure, which is called to perform I/O on the file. For more information, see the entry for MmioInstallIOProc().

- If the filename is NULL and no I/O procedure is given, the adwInfo member of the MMIOINFO structure is assumed to be the standard (non-HMMIO) file handle of a currently open file. The filename should not be longer than 128 bytes, including the terminating NULL character. When opening a memory file, set szFilename to NULL.

lpmmioinfo: The address of an MMIOINFO structure containing extra parameters used by the MmioOpen() function. Unless you are opening a memory file, specifying the size of a buffer for buffered I/O, or specifying an uninstalled I/O procedure to open a file, this parameter should be nil. If this parameter is not nil, all unused members of the MMIOINFO structure it references must be set to zero, including the reserved members. See Table 8-8 for instructions on setting specific members to accomplish certain tasks.

dwOpenFlags: Flags for the open operation. The MMIO_READ, MMIO_WRITE, and MMIO_READWRITE flags are mutually exclusive—only one should be specified. The MMIO_COMPAT, MMIO_EXCLUSIVE, MMIO_DENYWRITE, MMIO_DENYREAD, and MMIO_DENYNONE flags are file sharing flags. Table 8-7 explains how the values are defined.

Return Value

Returns a handle of the opened file. If the file cannot be opened, the return value is zero. If lpmmioinfo is not nil, the wErrorRet member of the MMIOINFO structure will contain one of the following error values: MMIOERR_ACCESSDENIED indicating that the file is protected and cannot be opened; MMIOERR_INVALIDFILE, the default error value for an open file failure; MMIOERR_NETWORKERROR, indicating that the network is not responding to the request to open a remote file; MMIOERR_PATHNOTFOUND, indicating that the directory specification is incorrect; MMIOERR_SHARINGVIOLATION, indicating that the file is

being used by another application and is unavailable; and
MMIOERR_TOOMANYOPENFILES, indicating that the number of files
currently open is already at the maximum level and that the system has
run out of available file handles.

Table 8-7: Flags used in the dwOpenFlags parameter of the MmioOpen() function

Flag	Meaning
MMIO_ALLOCBUF	This flag opens a file for buffered I/O. To allocate a buffer larger or smaller than the default buffer size (8K, defined as MMIO_DEFAULTBUFFER), set the cchBuffer member of the MMIOINFO structure to the desired buffer size. If cchBuffer is zero, the default buffer size is used. If you are providing your own I/O buffer, this flag should not be used.
MMIO_COMPAT	This flag opens the file with compatibility mode, allowing any process on a given machine to open the file any number of times. Note that if the file has been opened with any of the other sharing modes, the call to MmioOpen() will fail.
MMIO_CREATE	This flag creates a new file. If the file already exists, it will be truncated to zero length. For memory files, this flag indicates the end of the file will be initially set to the start of the buffer.
MMIO_DELETE	This flag deletes a file. If this flag is specified, szFilename should not be NULL. The return value will be TRUE (cast to HMMIO) if the file was deleted successfully, or FALSE otherwise. You should not call the MmioClose() function for a file that has been deleted. If this flag is specified, all other flags that open files will be ignored.
MMIO_DENYNONE	This flag opens the file without denying other processes read or write access to the file. Note that if the file has been opened in compatibility mode by any other process, the call to MmioOpen() will fail.
MMIO_DENYREAD	This flag opens the file and denies other processes read access to it. Note that if the file has been opened in compatibility mode or for read access by any other process, the call to MmioOpen() will fail.
MMIO_DENYWRITE	This flag opens the file and denies other processes write access to the file. Note that if the file has been opened in compatibility mode or for write access by any other process, the call to MmioOpen() will fail.

Flag	Meaning
MMIO_EXCLUSIVE	This flag opens the file and denies other processes read and write access to the file. Note that if the file has been opened in any other mode for read or write access, even by the current process, the call to MmioOpen() will fail.
MMIO_EXIST	This flag determines whether the specified file exists and creates a fully qualified filename from the path specified in szFilename. The filename is placed in the szFilename parameter. The return value is TRUE (cast to HMMIO) if the qualification was successful and the file exists, or FALSE otherwise. This flag does not open the file nor does the function return a valid multimedia file I/O file handle; therefore, you should not attempt to close the file.
MMIO_GETTEMP	This flag creates a temporary filename, optionally using the parameters passed in szFilename. For example, you can specify "C:F" to create a temporary file residing on drive C, starting with letter F. The resulting filename will be placed in the buffer pointed to by szFilename. The return value is MMSYSERR_NOERROR (cast to HMMIO), if the temporary filename was created successfully, or MMIOERR_FILENOT-FOUND otherwise. The file will not be opened, and the function will not return a valid multimedia file I/O file handle; therefore, you should not attempt to close the file. This flag overrides all other flags.
MMIO_PARSE	This flag creates a fully qualified filename from the path specified in szFilename. The filename is placed back into szFilename. The return value will be TRUE (cast to HMMIO) if the qualification was successful, or FALSE otherwise. The file will not be opened, and the function will not return a valid multimedia file I/O file handle; therefore, you should not attempt to close the file. If this flag is specified, all flags that open files are ignored.
MMIO_READ	This flag opens the file for reading only. This is the default if MMIO_WRITE and MMIO_READWRITE are not specified.
MMIO_READWRITE	This flag opens the file for reading and writing.
MMIO_WRITE	This flag opens the file for writing only.

8

Chapter

Table 8-8: Using the lpmmioinfo parameter of MmioOpen() to accomplish certain tasks

MMIO Task	Means of Accomplishing Task
Open file with installed MMIO procedure	Set fcclOProc to the four-character code of the I/O procedure, and set pIOProc to 0.
Open file with uninstalled MMIO procedure	Set IOProc to point to the I/O procedure, and set fcclOProc to NULL.
Have MmioOpen() function determine the I/O procedure to use to open the file specified by szFilename	Set fcclOProc and pIOProc to NULL; default behavior when no MMIOINFO structure is specified.
Open a memory file using an internally allocated and managed buffer	Set pchBuffer to NULL, fcclOProc to FOURCC_MEM, cchBuffer to initial size of the buffer, and adwInfo to incremental expansion size of the buffer. A memory file will automatically be expanded in increments of the number of bytes specified in adwInfo when necessary. Specify the MMIO_CREATE flag for the dwOpenFlags parameter to initially set the end of the file to be the beginning of the buffer.
Open a memory file using an application-supplied buffer	Set pchBuffer to point to the memory buffer, fcclOProc to FOURCC_MEM, cchBuffer to the size of the buffer, and adwInfo to the incremental expansion size of the buffer. The expansion size in adwInfo should be non-zero only if pchBuffer is a pointer obtained by calling the GlobalAlloc() and GlobalLock() functions; in this case, the GlobalReAlloc() function will be called to expand the buffer. In other words, if pchBuffer points to a local or global array or a block of memory in the local heap, adwInfo must be zero. Specify the MMIO_CREATE flag for the dwOpenFlags parameter to initially set the end of the file to be the beginning of the buffer. Otherwise, the entire block of memory is considered readable.

MMIO Task	Means of Accomplishing Task
Use a currently open standard file handle (that is, a file handle that does not have the HMMIO type) with multimedia file I/O services	Set fccIOProc to FOURCC_DOS, pchBuffer to NULL, and adwInfo to the standard file handle. Offsets within the file will be relative to the beginning of the file and are not related to the position in the standard file at the time MmioOpen() is called; the initial multimedia file I/O offset will be the same as the offset in the standard file when MmioOpen() is called. To close the multimedia file I/O file handle without closing the standard file handle, pass the MMIO_FHOPEN flag to MmioClose().

Examples

Listing 8-3 shows how to use MmioOpen() to open a file for input. Listing 8-4 shows how to open a file for output.

Listing 8-3: Opening a file with MmioOpen() for input

```
procedure TWaveIn.MMFileRecord;
var
  ARiffChunk : MMCKINFO;  // main RIFF chunk information
  ASubChunk : MMCKINFO;   // subchunk information
  CurrentMMIoInfo : PMMIOINFO;

  function OpenMMFile: boolean;
  begin
    // First backup existing 'new.wav' file to 'new.bak'
    CurrentMMResult := mmioRename(PChar(WaveInFilename), PChar
                 ('C:\WaveFile.bak'),
      Nil, 0);
    AMM_IO := mmioOpen(PChar(WaveInFilename), Nil, (MMIO_CREATE OR
                 MMIO_WRITE OR MMIO_ALLOCBUF));
    result := NOT (AMM_IO=0); // indicates an error
    if NOT result then
        ShowMessage('Failed to open MMIO file because of error ' +
        IntToStr(CurrentMMIoInfo.wErrorRet));
    // Try to increase the size of the buffer to MainSoundBufferSize
    CurrentMMResult := mmioSetBuffer(AMM_IO, 0, WaveBuffer
                 .SecondaryBufferSize,{WaveBuffer.MainSoundBufferSize,} 0);
    // Retrieve custom I/O proc version number; can be used to display
      number
    ACustomIOVersion := mmioSendMessage(AMM_IO, WaveIn_CustomProcVersion,
                 0, 0);
  end;
```

```
begin   {MMFileRecord}
  // Next, open wave file using an internal I/O buffer
  GetMem(CurrentMMIoInfo, SizeOf(MMIOINFO));
  InitMMIOInfo;
  if NOT OpenMMFile then
    begin
      FreeMem(CurrentMMIoInfo);
      exit;
    end;
  CreateRiffChunks;
  MMIOWriteSpecial;
  CleanupMMIO;
  FreeMem(CurrentMMIoInfo);
end;  {MMFileRecord}
```

Listing 8-4: Opening a file with MmioOpen() for output

```
function TWaveOut.PlaySoundFromFile(FileName : string): boolean;
var
  FmtSize, DataSize: LongInt;
  ARiffChunk : MMCKINFO;  // main RIFF chunk information
  ASubChunk : MMCKINFO;   // subchunk information
  CurrentMMIoInfo : PMMIOINFO;
  FmtInfo, TempData : PChar;
  //ATempString : string;
begin
  if FileName='' then
    WaveOutFilename := 'C:\TempFile.wav'
    else
      WaveOutFilename := FileName;
  AMM_IO := mmioOpen(PChar(WaveOutFilename), Nil, (MMIO_READ OR MMIO_
            ALLOCBUF));
    result := AMM_IO<>0;  // indicates an error
    if NOT result then
      begin
        ShowMessage('Failed to open MMIO file because of error ' +
        IntToStr(CurrentMMIoInfo.wErrorRet));
        Exit;
      end;
    // after moving to file start, find the WAVE chunk within the main
      'RIFF' chunk
    CurrentMMResult := mmioSeek(AMM_IO, 0, SEEK_SET);
    ARiffChunk.fccType := mmioFOURCC('W', 'A', 'V', 'E');
    CurrentMMResult := mmioDescend(AMM_IO, @ARiffChunk , Nil,
            MMIO_FindRIFF);
```

```
    // Next the 'fmt ' chunk
    ASubChunk.ckid   :=  mmioFOURCC('f', 'm', 't', ' ');
    CurrentMMResult  :=  mmioDescend(AMM_IO, @ASubChunk , @ARiffChunk,
       MMIO_FindChunk);
    // Now setup the buffer
    FmtSize :=  ASubChunk.cksize;
    GetMem(FmtInfo, FmtSize);
    // Read the 'fmt ' cunck
    CurrentMMResult  := mmioRead(AMM_IO, FmtInfo, FmtSize);
    // ascend out of 'fmt' chunk back to the main 'RIFF' chunk
    CurrentMMResult  :=  mmioAscend(AMM_IO, @ASubChunk, 0);
    // next three lines create the 'data' chunk
    // if the cksize is incorrect, when we ascend out of the chunk,
    // the cksize will be updated to it's actual size
    ASubChunk.ckid   :=  mmioFOURCC('d', 'a', 't', 'a');
    CurrentMMResult  :=  mmioDescend(AMM_IO, @ASubChunk, @ARiffChunk,
       MMIO_FINDCHUNK);
    DataSize := ASubChunk.cksize;
    GetMem(TempData, DataSize);
    CurrentMMResult := mmioRead(AMM_IO, TempData, DataSize);
    CurrentMMResult := mmioClose(AMM_IO, 0);
    PlayWaveFile(FmtInfo, TempData, DataSize);
    FreeMem(TempData);
    FreeMem(FmtInfo);
 end;
```

8

Chapter

function MmioRename   *mmsystem.pas*

Syntax

```
function MmioRename(
  szFileName, szNewFilename: PChar;
  lpmmioinfo: PMMIOInfo;
  dwRenameFlags: DWORD
  ): MMRESULT; stdcall;
```

Description

This function renames the specified file.

Parameters

szFilename: The address of a string containing the filename of the file to
     be renamed.

szNewFilename: The address of a string containing the new filename.

lpmmioinfo: The address of an MMIOINFO structure containing extra parameters used by this function. If this parameter is not nil, all unused members of the MMIOINFO structure must be set to zero, including reserved members.

dwRenameFlags: Flags for the rename operation. This parameter should be set to zero.

Return Value

Returns zero if the file was renamed successfully. Otherwise, returns an error code returned from MmioRename() or from the I/O procedure.

Example

The following lines of code from Listing 8-3 shows how to rename a file as a backup:

```
CurrentMMResult := mmioRename(PChar(WaveInFilename), PChar
    ('C:\WaveFile.bak'), Nil, 0);
```

function MmioClose   *mmsystem.pas*

Syntax

```
function MmioClose(
  hmmio: HMMIO;
  uFlags: UINT
  ): MMRESULT; stdcall;
```

Description

This function closes a file that was opened by using the MmioOpen() function. You must always call this function when you open a file with MmioOpen().

Parameters

hmmio: An HMMIO value that contains the file handle of the file to be closed.

uFlags: A UINT value containing the flags for the close operation. The following value is defined: MMIO_FHOPEN. If the file were opened by passing a standard file handle (not HMMIO), using this flag tells the MmioClose() function to close the multimedia file handle but not the standard file handle.

Return Value

Returns zero if successful, or an error otherwise. The error value can originate from the MmioFlush() function or from the I/O procedure. Possible error values include MMIOERR_CANNOTWRITE, indicating that the contents of the buffer could not be written to disk.

Example

Listing 8-5 shows how to shut down a recording session, including using the MmioClose() function.

Listing 8-5: Closing down a file recording session with MmioClose()

```
procedure CleanupMMIO;
begin
  CurrentMMResult := mmioAscend(AMM_IO, @ASubChunk, 0);
  // ascend out of the main 'RIFF' chunk
  CurrentMMResult := mmioAscend(AMM_IO, @ARiffChunk, 0);
  // flush buffer and close file
  CurrentMMResult := mmioFlush(AMM_IO, 0);
  CurrentMMResult := mmioClose(AMM_IO, 0);
end;
```

8

Chapter

function MmioRead   *mmsystem.pas*

Syntax

```
function MmioRead(
  hmmio: HMMIO;
  pch: PChar;
  cch: Longint
  ): Longint; stdcall;
```

Description

This function reads a specified number of bytes from a file opened with the MmioOpen() function.

Parameters

hmmio: An HMMIO value that contains the file handle of the file to be read.

pch: A PChar pointing to the address of a buffer that will contain the data read from the file.

cch: A Longint indicating the number of bytes to read from the file.

Return Value

Returns the number of bytes read. If the end of the file has been reached and no more bytes can be read, the return value is 0. If there is an error reading from the file, the return value is –1.

Example

The following three lines of code (from Listing 8-4), set up and execute a Read operation:

```
DataSize := ASubChunk.cksize;
GetMem(TempData, DataSize);
CurrentMMResult := mmioRead(AMM_IO, TempData, DataSize);
```

function MmioWrite   *mmsystem.pas*

Syntax

```
function mmioWrite(
hmmio: HMMIO;
pch: PChar;
cch: Longint
): Longint; stdcall;
```

Description

This function writes a specified number of bytes to a file opened by using the MmioOpen() function. The current file position is incremented by the number of bytes written.

Parameters

hmmio: An HMMIO value that contains the file handle of the file to which to write.

pch: A PChar pointing to the address of a buffer that will contain the data to be written to the file.

cch: A Longint indicating the number of bytes to write to the file.

Return Value

Returns the number of bytes written. If there is an error writing to the file, the return value is –1.

Example

The following line of code is given in a comment in Listing 8-6, which shows how to write data the hard way, one byte at a time. This example demonstrates many of the MMIO functions. This line of code represents the easy way to accomplish this:

```
CurrentMMResult := mmioWrite(AMM_IO,
              PChar(WaveBuffer.FWaveHeaderArray[0].lpData),
              WaveBuffer.FWaveHeaderArray[0].dwBytesRecorded);
```

Listing 8-6: Routine for writing data to an MMIO file

```
procedure mmIOWriteSpecial;        // Write to custom file IO system, one
                                   //    byte at a time

  var
    i : LongInt;
    TempChar : Char;
    TempByte : Byte absolute TempChar;

  function IncrementNextPosition(var LocalBuffer : PChar; BufferPos :
                 integer) : Char;
  begin
    result := Char(LocalBuffer[BufferPos]);
  end;


  begin
    CurrentMMResult := mmioGetInfo(AMM_IO, CurrentMMIoInfo, 0);
{ If you call the next line, you can skip all of the lines after it ! }
(*  CurrentMMResult := mmioWrite(AMM_IO,
                 PChar(WaveBuffer.FWaveHeaderArray[0].lpData),
                 WaveBuffer.FWaveHeaderArray[0].dwBytesRecorded); *)
    for i := 0 to {(WaveBuffer.MainSoundBufferSize-1) do }
      (WaveBuffer.FWaveHeaderArray[0].dwBytesRecorded - 1) do
      begin
        if (CurrentMMIoInfo^.pchNext = CurrentMMIoInfo^.pchEndWrite) then
          begin
            CurrentMMIoInfo^.dwFlags := (CurrentMMIoInfo^.dwFlags or
                      MMIO_DIRTY);  // we have modified the buffer
            CurrentMMResult := mmioAdvance(AMM_IO, CurrentMMIoInfo,
                      MMIO_WRITE);
          end;
        // Move ahead one
          CurrentMMIoInfo^.pchNext^ := IncrementNextPosition(
            WaveBuffer.FWaveHeaderArray[0].lpData, i);
          Inc(CurrentMMIoInfo^.pchNext);
      end;
```

```
    // Change flags to indicate that the buffer has been modified
    CurrentMMIoInfo^.dwFlags := (CurrentMMIoInfo^.dwFlags OR MMIO_DIRTY);
    mmioSetInfo(AMM_IO, CurrentMMIoInfo, 0);
  end; {mmIOWriteSpecial}
```

function MmioSeek   *mmsystem.pas*

Syntax

```
function MmioSeek(
  hmmio: HMMIO;
  lOffset: Longint;
  iOrigin: Integer
  ): Longint; stdcall;
```

Description

This function changes the current file position in a file opened by using the MmioOpen() function. Seeking to an invalid location in the file (such as past the end of the file) might not cause MmioSeek() to return an error. However, it could cause subsequent I/O operations on the file to fail.

Parameters

hmmio: An HMMIO value that contains the file handle of the file in which to seek.

lOffset: A Longint value indicating the offset that will be used when changing the file position.

iOrigin: Flags indicating how the offset specified by lOffset will be interpreted. The following values are defined: SEEK_CUR, indicating seeks to lOffset bytes from the current file position; SEEK_END, indicating seeks to lOffset bytes from the end of the file; and SEEK_SET, indicating seeks to lOffset bytes from the beginning of the file. If you need to locate the end of a file, call MmioSeek() with lOffset set to zero and iOrigin set to SEEK_END.

Return Value

Returns the new file position, in bytes, relative to the beginning of the file. If there is an error, the return value is –1.

Example

Listing 8-7 shows how to create the various "RIFF" chunks using
MmioSeek() and other functions.

Listing 8-7: Creating a RIFF file header, including essential chunks

```
procedure CreateRiffChunks;
begin { CreateRiffChunks }
  // Now create the main 'RIFF' chunk
  mmioSeek(AMM_IO, 0, SEEK_SET); // reset position (seek) to start of
                                 file
  ARiffChunk.fccType   :=  mmioFOURCC('W', 'A', 'V', 'E');
  ARiffChunk.cksize    := 0;  // mmio will determine corect size
  CurrentMMResult := mmioCreateChunk(AMM_IO, @ARiffChunk,
                        MMIO_CREATERIFF);
  // Now create the 'fmt' chunk
  ASubChunk.ckid   := mmioStringToFOURCC('fmt ', 0);
  ASubChunk.cksize := sizeof(TWaveFormatEx);
  CurrentMMResult := mmioCreateChunk(AMM_IO, @ASubChunk, 0);
  // return value of next function is bytes written
  CurrentMMResult := mmioWrite(AMM_IO, @(AWaveFormatEx),
                        sizeof(TWAVEFORMATEX));
  // ascend out of 'fmt' chunk back to the main 'RIFF' chunk
  CurrentMMResult :=  mmioAscend(AMM_IO, @ASubChunk {@ARiffChunk}, 0);
  // next three lines create the 'data' chunk
  // if the cksize is incorrect, when we ascend out of the chunk,
  // the cksize will be updated to it's actual size
  ASubChunk.ckid   := mmioStringToFOURCC('data', 0);
  ASubChunk.cksize := CustomIOBufferSize;
  CurrentMMResult := mmioCreateChunk(AMM_IO, @ASubChunk, 0);
end; { CreateRiffChunks }
```

function MmioGetInfo   *mmsystem.pas*

Syntax

```
function MmioGetInfo(
  hmmio: HMMIO;
  lpmmioinfo: PMMIOInfo;
  uFlags: UINT
  ): MMRESULT; stdcall;
```

Description

This function retrieves information about a file opened with the
MmioOpen() function. This information allows the application to directly
access the I/O buffer if the file is opened for buffered I/O. See the following section on accessing I/O buffers for constraints and additional
information.

Parameters

hmmio: An HMMIO value that contains the file handle of the file about
which to get information.

lpmmioinfo: The address of an MMIOINFO structure that MmioGetInfo()
fills with information about the file.

uFlags: Reserved; must be zero.

Returns

Returns zero, if successful, or an error otherwise.

Example

See Listing 8-6 for an example of this function in use.

Directly Accessing I/O Buffers

As mentioned in its description, the MmioGetInfo() function allows you
to directly access the I/O buffer of a file opened for buffered I/O. To do
so, use the following members of the MMIOINFO structure filled by
MmioGetInfo() as described in Table 8-9.

Table 8-9: MMIOINFO members used in accessing an I/O buffer

Member	Purpose, Use, and Constraints
pchNext	This member points to the next byte in the buffer that can be read or written. Whenever you read or write to a file, you must increment pchNext by the number of bytes read or written. After you finish the operation and modify pchNext, do not call any multimedia file I/O functions except MmioAdvance() until you call the MmioSetInfo() function. Be sure to call MmioSetInfo() when you are finished directly accessing the

Member	Purpose, Use, and Constraints
	buffer. Do not decrement pchNext or modify any members in the MMIOINFO structure other than pchNext and dwFlags. Do not set any flags in dwFlags except MMIO_DIRTY.
pchEndRead	This member points to a location that is one byte past the last valid byte in the buffer that can be read. When you reach the end of the buffer specified by the pchEndRead, be sure to call MmioAdvance() to fill the buffer from the disk. The MmioAdvance() function updates the pchNext and pchEndRead members in the MMIOINFO structure for the file.
pchEndWrite	This member points to a location that is one byte past the last location in the buffer that can be written. When you reach the end of the buffer specified by the pchEndWrite member, be sure to call MmioAdvance() to write the buffer to the disk. The MmioAdvance() function updates the pchNext and pchEndWrite members in the MMIOINFO structure for the file.

Before you call MmioAdvance() or MmioSetInfo() to flush a buffer to disk, be sure to set the MMIO_DIRTY flag in the dwFlags member of the MMIOINFO structure for the file. Otherwise, the buffer will not be written to disk. All of the above principles are demonstrated in the sample application accompanying this chapter.

8

Chapter

function MmioSetInfo   mmsystem.pas

Syntax

```
function MmioSetInfo(
  hmmio: HMMIO;
  lpmmioinfo: PMMIOInfo;
  uFlags: UINT
  ): MMRESULT; stdcall;
```

Description

This function updates the information retrieved by the MmioGetInfo() function about a file opened with the MmioOpen() function. Use this function to terminate direct buffer access of a file opened for buffered I/O. (See the previous section.) As mentioned, if you have written to the file I/O buffer, be sure to set the MMIO_DIRTY flag in the dwFlags member of the MMIOINFO structure before calling MmioSetInfo() to terminate direct buffer access. Otherwise, the buffer will not get flushed to disk.

Parameters

hmmio: An HMMIO value that contains the file handle of the file about which to get information.

lpmmioinfo: The address of an MMIOINFO structure that MmioGetInfo() fills with information about the file.

uFlags: Reserved; must be zero.

Return Value

Returns zero if successful, or an error otherwise.

Example

See Listing 8-6.

function MmioSetBuffer   *mmsystem.pas*

Syntax

```
function MmioSetBuffer(
hmmio: HMMIO;
pchBuffer: PChar;
cchBuffer: Longint;
uFlags: Word
): MMRESULT; stdcall;
```

Description

This function enables or disables buffered I/O, or changes the buffer or buffer size for a file opened with the MmioOpen() function. To enable buffering using an internal buffer, set pchBuffer to NULL and cchBuffer to the desired buffer size. If you want to create your own buffer, set pchBuffer to point to the buffer, and set cchBuffer to the size of the buffer. To disable buffered I/O, set pchBuffer to NULL and cchBuffer to 0. If buffered I/O has already been enabled using an internal buffer, you can reallocate the buffer to a different size by setting pchBuffer to nil and cchBuffer to the new buffer size. The contents of the buffer can be changed after resizing.

Parameters

hmmio: An HMMIO value that contains the file handle of the file associated with the buffer.

pchBuffer: A PChar pointing to the address of an application-defined buffer to use for buffered I/O. If this parameter is nil, MmioSetBuffer() allocates an internal buffer for buffered I/O.

cchBuffer: A Longint indicating the size, in characters, of the application-defined buffer, or the size of the internal buffer for MmioSetBuffer() to allocate.

uFlags: Reserved; must be zero.

Return Value

Returns zero if successful, or an error otherwise. If an error occurs, the file handle remains valid. The following values are defined: MMIOERR_CANNOTWRITE, indicating that the contents of the old buffer could not be written to disk, causing the operation to be aborted; and MMIOERR_OUTOFMEMORY, indicating that the new buffer could not be allocated, most likely due to a lack of available memory.

Example

This function is called in the OpenMMFile() function included under Listing 8-3. The following line of code attempts to increase the size of the buffer to the value in WaveBuffer.SecondaryBufferSize:

```
CurrentMMResult := mmioSetBuffer(AMM_IO, 0, WaveBuffer.Secondary
          BufferSize, {WaveBuffer.MainSoundBufferSize,} 0);
```

function MmioFlush   *mmsystem.pas*

Syntax

```
function MmioFlush(
hmmio: HMMIO;
uFlags: UINT
): MMRESULT; stdcall;
```

Description

This function writes the I/O buffer of a file to disk if the buffer has been written to.

Parameters

hmmio: An HMMIO value that contains the file handle of the file to be flushed.

uFlags: A UINT value containing the flag that determines how the flush will be carried out. It can be zero or MMIO_EMPTYBUF, indicating that the buffer should be emptied after writing it to the disk. Closing a file with the MmioClose() function automatically flushes its buffer. If there is insufficient disk space to write the buffer, MmioFlush() fails, even if the preceding calls of the MmioWrite() function were successful.

Return Value

Returns zero if successful, or an error otherwise. The following value is defined: MMIOERR_CANNOTWRITE, indicating that the contents of the buffer could not be written to disk.

Example

See Listing 8-5 for an example of how to use this function in shutting down multimedia input/output.

function MmioAdvance   *mmsystem.pas*

Syntax

```
function MmioAdvance(
hmmio: HMMIO;
lpmmioinfo: PMMIOInfo;
uFlags: UINT
): MMRESULT; stdcall;
```

Description

Advances the I/O buffer of a file set up for direct I/O buffer access with the MmioGetInfo() function. As with most of these functions, this one is used for both input and output. If the file is opened for reading, the I/O buffer is filled from the disk. If the file is opened for writing and the MMIO_DIRTY flag is set in the dwFlags member of the MMIOINFO structure, the buffer is written to disk. The pchNext, pchEndRead, and pchEndWrite members of the MMIOINFO structure will be updated to reflect the new state of the I/O buffer. In the MMIO system, files can also be opened for both input and output. In this case, or if the specified file is opened for writing alone, the I/O buffer is flushed to disk before the next buffer is read. If the I/O buffer cannot be written to disk because the disk is full, MmioAdvance() returns MMIOERR_CANNOTWRITE.

If the specified file is open only for writing, the MMIO_WRITE flag must be specified. After you have written to the I/O buffer, you must set the MMIO_DIRTY flag in the dwFlags member of the MMIOINFO structure before calling MmioAdvance(). Otherwise, the buffer will not be written to disk. If the end of file is reached, MmioAdvance() still returns successfully even though no more data can be read. To check for the end of the file, check if the pchNext and pchEndRead members of the MMIOINFO structure are equal after calling MmioAdvance().

Parameters

hmmio: An HMMIO value that contains the file handle of the file opened by using the MmioOpen() function.

lpmmioinfo: The address of an MMIOINFO structure obtained by using the MmioGetInfo() function. This structure is used to set the current file information, and then it is updated after the buffer is advanced. This parameter is optional.

uFlags: Flag that controls the operation. It can be either of the following: MMIO_READ, indicating that the buffer will be filled from the file, or MMIO_WRITE, indicating that the buffer will be written to the file.

Return Value

Returns MMSYSERR_NOERROR if successful, or an error otherwise. Possible error values include the following: MMIOERR_CANNOTEXPAND, indicating that the specified memory file cannot be expanded, probably because the adwInfo member of the MMIOINFO structure was set to zero in the initial call to the MmioOpen() function; MMIOERR_CANNOT-READ, indicating that an error occurred while refilling the buffer; MMIOERR_CANNOTWRITE, indicating that the contents of the buffer could not be written to disk; MMIOERR_OUTOFMEMORY, indicating that there was not enough memory to expand a memory file for further writing; and MMIOERR_UNBUFFERED, indicating that the specified file was not opened for buffered I/O.

8

Chapter

Example

See Listing 8-6 for an example of using this function.

function MmioSendMessage   *mmsystem.pas*

Syntax

```
function MmioSendMessage(
hmmio: HMMIO;
uMessage: UINT;
lParam1, lParam2: DWORD
): Longint; stdcall;
```

Description

This function sends a message to the I/O procedure associated with the specified file. You should use this function to send custom user-defined messages only. Do not use it to send the built-in MMIOM_OPEN, MMIOM_CLOSE, MMIOM_READ, MMIOM_WRITE, MMIOM_WRITE-FLUSH, or MMIOM_SEEK messages. When you define custom messages, be sure that their value is equal to or greater than the MMIOM_USER constant.

Parameters

hmmio: An HMMIO value that contains the file handle of the file opened by using the MmioOpen() function.

uMessage: A UINT value holding the message to send to the I/O procedure.

lParam1, lParam2: Parameters for the message.

Return Value

Returns a value that corresponds to the message. If the I/O procedure does not recognize the message, the return value should be zero.

Example

See Listing 8-3 for an example of using this function.

Descending into a RIFF Chunk

In the introduction to this chapter, we discussed "RIFF" chunks. We pointed out that a "RIFF" chunk consists of several parts. There is a four-byte chunk identifier (type FOURCC), a four-byte (DWORD) value giving the chunk size, the data portion of the chunk, and a null pad byte if the size of the data portion is odd. When the chunk identifier is either "RIFF" or "LIST," the first four bytes of the data portion of the chunk are a *form* type or *list* type (type FOURCC).

When you use the MmioDescend() function to search for a chunk, make sure the file position is at the beginning of a chunk before calling the function. The searching process begins at the current position in the file and continues to the end of the file. If a parent chunk is specified, the file position should be somewhere within the parent chunk before calling MmioDescend(). In this case, the search begins at the current file position and continues to the end of the parent chunk.

If MmioDescend() is unsuccessful in searching for a chunk, the current file position will be undefined. On the other hand, if MmioDescend() is successful, the current file position will be changed. If the chunk is a "RIFF" or "LIST" chunk, the new file position will be just after the form type or list type (12 bytes from the beginning of the chunk). For other chunk types, the new file position will be the start of the data portion of the chunk (eight bytes from the beginning of the chunk). The Mmio-Descend() function fills the MMCKINFO structure pointed to by the lpck parameter with the information shown in Table 8-10.

8

Chapter

function MmioDescend   *mmsystem.pas*

Syntax

```
function MmioDescend(
  hmmio: HMMIO;
  lpck: PMMCKInfo;
  lpckParent: PMMCKInfo;
  uFlags: UINT
  ): MMRESULT; stdcall;
```

Description

This function descends into a chunk of a RIFF file that was opened by using the MmioOpen() function. It can also search for a given chunk.

Parameters

> *hmmio*: An HMMIO value that contains the file handle of an open RIFF file.

> *lpck*: The address of an application-defined MMCKINFO structure.

> *lpckParent*: The address of an optional application-defined MMCKINFO structure identifying the parent of the chunk being searched for. If this parameter is not nil, MmioDescend() assumes the MMCKINFO structure to which it refers was filled when MmioDescend() was called to descend into the parent chunk. In this case MmioDescend() searches for a chunk within the parent chunk. Set this parameter to nil if no parent chunk is being specified.

> *uFlags*: Search flags. If no flags are specified, MmioDescend() descends into the chunk beginning at the current file position. The following values are defined: MMIO_FINDCHUNK, indicating to search for a chunk with the specified chunk identifier; MMIO_FINDLIST, indicating to search for a chunk with the chunk identifier "LIST" and with the specified form type; or MMIO_FINDRIFF, indicating to search for a chunk with the chunk identifier "RIFF" and with the specified form type.

Return Value

Returns MMSYSERR_NOERROR if successful, or an error otherwise. Possible error values include the following: MMIOERR_CHUNKNOTFOUND, indicating that the end of the file (or the end of the parent chunk, if given) was reached before the desired chunk was found.

Example

See Listing 8-4 for an example of using this function.

Table 8-10: MMCKINFO members set by MmioDescend()

Member	How Member is Set
ckid	This member is the chunk. If the MMIO_FINDCHUNK, MMIO_FINDRIFF, or MMIO_FINDLIST flag is specified for wFlags, the MMCKINFO structure will also be used to pass parameters to MmioDescend(). In this case, the ckid member will specify the four-character code of the chunk identifier, the form type, or the list type for which to search.
cksize	This member is the size, in bytes, of the data portion of the chunk. The size includes the form type or the list type (if any). Note that it does not include the eight-byte chunk header nor the pad byte at the end of the data (if any).
fccType	The value of this member depends on the chunk type. If ckid is "RIFF," it is the form type; if ckid is "LIST," it is the list type. Otherwise, it is NULL.
dwDataOffset	If the chunk is a "RIFF" chunk or a "LIST" chunk, this member is the offset of the form type or list type. Otherwise, this member is the file offset of the beginning of the data portion of the chunk.
dwFlags	This member contains other information about the chunk. However, this information is not currently used and is set to zero.

function MmioAscend　　*mmsystem.pas*

Syntax

```
function MmioAscend(
  hmmio: HMMIO;
  lpck: PMMCKInfo;
  uFlags: UINT
  ): MMRESULT; stdcall;
```

Description

This function ascends out of a chunk in a RIFF file descended into with the MmioDescend() function or created with the MmioCreateChunk() function. If the chunk was descended into by using MmioDescend(), MmioAscend() seeks to the location following the end of the chunk (past the extra pad byte, if there is one). If the chunk had been created and descended into by using MmioCreateChunk(), or if the MMIO_DIRTY flag were set in the dwFlags member of the MMCKINFO structure referenced by lpck, the current file position is assumed to be the end of the data portion of the chunk. If the chunk size is not the same as the value stored in the cksize member of the MMCKINFO structure when MmioCreateChunk() was called, MmioAscend() corrects the chunk size in the file before ascending from the chunk. If the chunk size is odd, MmioAscend() writes a null pad byte at the end of the chunk. After ascending from the chunk, the current file position will be the location following the end of the chunk (past the extra pad byte, if any).

Parameters

hmmio: An HMMIO value that contains the file handle of an open RIFF file.

lpck: The address of an application-defined MMCKINFO structure previously filled by the MmioDescend() function or the MmioCreateChunk() function.

uFlags: Reserved; must be zero.

Return Value

Returns MMSYSERR_NOERROR if successful or an error otherwise. Possible error values include the following: MMIOERR_CANNOTSEEK, indicating that there was an error while seeking to the end of the chunk, or MMIOERR_CANNOTWRITE, indicating that the contents of the buffer could not be written to disk.

Example

See Listing 8-7 for an example of using this function.

function MmioCreateChunk   *mmsystem.pas*

Syntax

```
function MmioCreateChunk(
  hmmio: HMMIO;
  lpck: PMMCKInfo;
  uFlags: UINT
  ): MMRESULT; stdcall;
```

Description

This function creates a chunk in a RIFF file that was opened by using the MmioOpen() function. The new chunk is created at the current file position. After the new chunk is created, the current file position will be the beginning of the data portion of the new chunk. Note that this function cannot insert a chunk into the middle of a file. If an application attempts to create a chunk somewhere other than at the end of a file, MmioCreateChunk() overwrites existing information in the file.

Parameters

hmmio: An HMMIO value that contains the file handle of an open RIFF file.

lpck: The address of an application-defined MMCKINFO structure previously containing information about the chunk to be created. The structure should be set up as shown in Table 8-11.

uFlags: Flags identifying what type of chunk to create. The following values are defined: MMIO_CREATELIST, indicating a "LIST" chunk, or MMIO_CREATERIFF, indicating a "RIFF" chunk.

Return Value

Returns MMSYSERR_NOERROR if successful, or an error otherwise. Possible error values include the following: MMIOERR_CANNOTSEEK, indicating the function was unable to determine the offset of the data portion of the chunk; or MMIOERR_CANNOTWRITE, indicating the function was unable to write the chunk header.

Example

See Listing 8-7 for an example of using this function.

Table 8-11: Setting up the MMCKINFO structure pointed to by the lpck parameter

Member	Setting Up the Member
ckid	The member specifies the chunk identifier. If uFlags includes MMIO_CREATERIFF or MMIO_CREATELIST, this member will be filled by MmioCreateChunk().
cksize	The member specifies the size of the data portion of the chunk, including the form type or list type (if any). If this value is not correct when the MmioAscend() function is called to mark the end of the chunk, MmioAscend() corrects the chunk size.

8

Chapter

Member	Setting Up the Member
fccType	The member specifies the form type or list type if the chunk is a "RIFF" or "LIST" chunk. If the chunk is not a "RIFF" or "LIST" chunk, this member does not need to be filled in.
dwDataOffset	The member does not need to be filled in. The MmioCreateChunk() function fills this member with the file offset of the data portion of the chunk.
dwFlags	The member does not need to be filled in. The MmioCreateChunk() function sets the MMIO_DIRTY flag in dwFlags.

We have reached the end of another complex chapter with many useful functions and capabilities. One question that has probably come up for you if you have studied all of the chapters up to this point is this, "Isn't there an easier way to do this?" The answer is "Yes!" Of course, to achieve greater ease, you must give up some level of control. That is always the trade-off. In our final chapter, we'll explore the higher level Media Control Interface (MCI), which provides a great deal of the functionality of the previous chapters with a simplified set of functions.

Chapter Nine

The Media Control Interface API

In earlier chapters, we examined several low-level multimedia APIs. We also examined some of the support services for timing, mixing, and working with various audio devices. But what if you don't need the level of control found in the low-level APIs and would prefer to work at a more general level? The good news is, you can! The Media Control Interface (MCI) API makes this possible. To conclude our exploration of the Windows multimedia APIs, we'll explore the MCI API in this chapter.

The Media Control Interface (MCI) provides a standard set of commands for playing multimedia devices and recording multimedia resource files. These commands provide a general, device-independent interface to nearly every kind of multimedia device. Applications can use the MCI to control any supported multimedia device. These devices include waveform audio devices, MIDI sequencers, CD audio devices, digital video (video playback) devices, and others.

As we discussed in Chapter 1 and in the Introduction, there are two ways you can work with the MCI: command strings and command messages. You can use either approach or both in your applications. We'll be examining each approach in some detail, but here is an overview of the main characteristics of each:

- The command message interface consists of constants and structures. It uses the MciSendCommand() function to send a message to an MCI device.

- The command string interface provides a textual version of the command messages. It uses the MciSendString() function to send a string to an MCI device. Command strings duplicate the functionality of the command messages. The Microsoft Windows operating system converts the command strings to command messages before sending them to the MCI driver for processing.

∎ As we pointed out in the Introduction, command strings are ideal for prototyping an application since they are easy to use. On the other hand, command messages are better suited for production software, as they have no need to be interpreted and thus this run faster. In some cases, command messages might be easier to use than the command strings. However, command strings are easy to remember and implement. (And there are quite a few commands and command parameters, as we'll see.) Some MCI applications use command strings when the return value will not be used (other than to verify success) and command messages when retrieving information from the device.

The command messages that retrieve information do so using records, which are easy to interpret in a Delphi application. These records can contain information on many different aspects of a device. On the other hand, the command strings that retrieve information do so in the form of strings, and can only retrieve one string at a time. Therefore, an application must parse or test each string to interpret it.

In discussing specific commands, we'll follow the convention used in the Microsoft Multimedia help file that ships with Delphi and use the string form of the command followed by the message form in parentheses.

Command Strings

To send a string command you need to use the MciSendString() function. This function, which we'll discuss in detail later, includes parameters for the string command and a buffer for any information returned. In addition to the MciSendString() function, Windows provides the MciGetErrorString() function to return the error string that corresponds to a particular error number. Like many other multimedia functions, the MciSendString() function returns zero when successful. However, if the function fails, the low-order word of the return value contains an error code. You can pass this error code to MciGetErrorString() to get a text description of it.

MCI command strings use a consistent syntax of verb-object-modifier. Each command string includes a command (verb), a device identifier (object), and command arguments. For some commands, arguments are optional; for others, they are required. All command strings have the following form:

```
command device_id [arguments]
```

The three components contain the following types of information. The command specifies one of the MCI commands, such as open(), close(), or play(). The device_id identifies an MCI driver. This identifier is created when the device is opened. The arguments specify various flags and variables used by the command. Flags are keywords that are recognized by the particular MCI command. Variables are numbers or strings that apply to the MCI command or a flag.

Let's say you want to play a segment of audio or video. To do this you would use the play() command. This command uses the arguments "from position" and "to position" to indicate at what position to start and at what position to end playback. With command strings, you can list the flags used with a command in any order. When you use a flag that has a variable associated with it, you must supply a value for the variable. Unspecified (and optional) command arguments assume a default value.

We have translated the following example function from the Microsoft Multimedia help file (originally written in C) into Pascal. It sends the play() command with the "from" and "to" flags.

```
function PlayFromTo(lpstrAlias: LPSTR; dwFrom, dwTo: DWORD) : DWORD;
  Var
    achCommandBuff : array [0..127] of char;
begin
  // First create the command string.
    Fmtstr(achCommandBuff, 'play %s from %u to %u',
        lpstrAlias, dwFrom, dwTo);
  // Then send the command string; returning its result with the function
    return := mciSendString(achCommandBuff, NULL, 0, NULL);
end;
```

You can use the data types shown in Table 9-1 for the variables in a command string.

Table 9-1: Data types that can be used with variables in command strings

Data Type	Description
Strings	When used as part of a command string, string data types are delimited by leading and trailing white spaces and quotation marks. MCI removes single quotation marks from a string. To put a quotation mark in a string, use a set of two quotation marks where you want to embed your quotation mark. To use an empty string, use two quotation marks delimited by leading and trailing white spaces.
Signed long integers	These data types are delimited by leading and trailing white spaces. Unless otherwise specified, integers can be positive or negative. If you use negative integers, you should not separate the minus sign and the first digit with a space.
Rectangles	These data types are an ordered list of four signed short values that define x and y coordinates of a rectangle's upper-left and lower-right corners. White space delimits this data type and separates each integer in the list.

Command Messages

Having provided an overview of command strings, we'll next take a look at command messages. The command message interface is designed to be used by applications written in languages like C or Pascal. The command message interface provides the same capabilities in controlling multimedia devices as the command string interface. It uses a message passing paradigm to communicate with various MCI devices. To send a command you use the MciSendCommand() function. In addition to the MciSendCommand() function, Windows provides the MciGetError-String() function to return the error string that corresponds to a particular error number. Like the MciSendString() function, the MciSendCommand() function returns zero when successful. However, if the function fails, the low-order word of the return value contains an error code. You can pass this error code to MciGetErrorString() to get a text description of it.

MCI command messages have a similar structure to MCI command strings. Like the earlier system, they consist of the following three elements: 1) a constant message value; 2) a structure containing parameters for the command; and 3) a set of flags specifying options for the command and validating fields in the parameter block.

The following example (again based on the Windows help file) sends the MCI_PLAY command to the device identified by the device identifier, wDeviceID.

```
mciSendCommand(wDeviceID,                    // device identifier
               MCI_PLAY,                     // command message
               0,                            // flags
               DWORD(@mciPlayParms));        // parameter block
```

As with many of the previous multimedia functions we've seen, the device identifier given in the first parameter is retrieved when the device is opened using the MCI_OPEN command. Therefore, in an actual programming situation this command would be preceded by a command to open the device and followed by a command to close it. The last parameter is the address of an MCI_PLAY_PARMS structure, which might contain information about where to begin and end playback. Many MCI command messages use a record to contain parameters of this kind. The first field of each of these structures, dwCallback, identifies the window that receives an MM_MCINOTIFY message when the operation finishes.

Media Control Interface commands fall into the following general categories: system, required, basic, and extended. System commands are handled by the MCI directly, not by the driver. On the other hand, required commands are handled by the driver. All MCI drivers must support the required commands and flags. Basic commands (or optional commands) are used by some devices, but not others. If a device supports a basic command, it must support a defined set of flags for that command. Finally, extended commands are specific to a device type or driver. Extended commands include commands like the put (MCI_PUT) and the where (MCI_WHERE) commands for the digital video and overlay device types, and extensions to existing commands (like the STRETCH flag of the status (MCI_STATUS) command for the overlay device type).

While system and required commands are the minimum command set for any MCI driver, basic and extended commands are not supported by all drivers. You can always safely use system and required commands and their flags. However, if you need to use a basic or extended command or flag, you should first query the driver by using the capability (MCI_GETDEVCAPS) command. Tables 9-2 through 9-5 summarize the specific commands in each of these categories. A more detailed

9

Chapter

discussion of many of these commands is included at the end of this chapter after the explanation of the MCI functions.

Table 9-2: System commands

String	Command	Description
Break	MCI_BREAK	Sets a break key for an MCI device. MCI supports this command directly rather than passing it to the device.
Sysinfo	MCI_SYSINFO	Returns information about MCI devices. String information is returned in the application-supplied buffer pointed to by the lpstrReturn member of the structure identified by lpSysInfo. Numeric information is returned as a DWORD value placed in the application-supplied buffer. The dwRetSize member specifies the buffer's length.

Table 9-3: Required commands

String	Command	Description
Capability	MCI_GETDEVCAPS	Obtains the capabilities of a device.
Close	MCI_CLOSE	Closes the device.
Info	MCI_INFO	Obtains textual information from a device.
Open	MCI_OPEN	Initializes the device.
Status	MCI_STATUS	Obtains status information from the device. Some of this command's flags are not required, so it is also a basic command.

Table 9-4: Basic commands

String	Command	Description
Load	MCI_LOAD	Loads data from a file.
Pause	MCI_PAUSE	Stops playing. Playback or recording can be resumed at the current position.
Play	MCI_PLAY	Starts transmitting output data.
Record	MCI_RECORD	Starts recording input data.
Resume	MCI_RESUME	Resumes playing or recording on a paused device.
Save	MCI_SAVE	Saves data to a disk file.
Seek	MCI_SEEK	Seeks forward or backward.
Set	MCI_SET	Sets the operating state of the device.

String	Command	Description
Status	MCI_STATUS	Obtains status information about the device. This is also a required command; since some of its flags are not required, it is also listed here. (The optional items support devices that use linear media with identifiable positions.)
Stop	MCI_STOP	Stops playing.

We cannot provide an exhaustive list of extended commands since they vary from device to device; however, we can list some of these commands that are common to specific device types. As we said before, some MCI devices have additional commands, or they provide additional flags for existing commands. While some extended commands apply only to a specific device driver, most of them apply to all drivers of a particular device type. For example, the command set for the sequencer device type extends the set (MCI_SET) command to add time formats that are needed by MIDI sequencers.

As mentioned previously, you should not assume that a particular device supports the extended commands or flags. You can use the capability (MCI_GETDEVCAPS) command to determine whether a specific feature is supported, and your application should be ready to deal with "unsupported command" or "unsupported function" return values. Table 9-5 shows the extended commands that are available with specific device types.

Table 9-5: Extended commands available with specific device types

String	Command	Device Types	Description
Configure	MCI_CONFIGURE	digitalvideo	Displays a configuration dialog box.
Copy	MCI_COPY	digitalvideo	Copies data to the clipboard.
Cue	MCI_CUE	digitalvideo	Prepares for playing or recording.
Cut	MCI_CUT	digitalvideo	Removes data from the file and copies it to the clipboard.
Delete	MCI_DELETE	waveaudio	Deletes a data segment from the media file.
Escape	MCI_ESCAPE	videodisc	Sends custom information to a device.
Freeze	MCI_FREEZE	overlay	Disables video acquisition to the frame buffer.

9

Chapter

String	Command	Device Types	Description
Paste	MCI_PASTE	digitalvideo	Pastes data from the clipboard into a file.
Put	MCI_PUT	digitalvideo	Defines the source, overlay destination, and frame windows.
Realize	MCI_REALIZE	digitalvideo	Tells the device to select and realize its palette into a device context of the displayed window.
Setaudio	MCI_SETAUDIO	digitalvideo	Sets audio parameters for video.
Setvideo	MCI_SETVIDEO	digitalvideo	Sets video parameters.
Signal	MCI_SIGNAL	digitalvideo	Identifies a specified position with a signal.
Spin	MCI_SPIN	videodisc	Starts the disc spinning or stops the disc from spinning.
Step	MCI_STEP	digitalvideo	Steps the play one or more videodisc frames forward or reverse.
Unfreeze	MCI_UNFREEZE	overlay	Enables the frame buffer to acquire video data.
Update	MCI_UPDATE	digitalvideo	Repaints the current frame into the device context.
Where	MCI_WHERE	digitalvideo	Obtains the rectangle overlay specifying the source, destination, or frame area.
Window	MCI_WINDOW	digitalvideo	Controls the display window.

The Media Control Interface accomplishes its work through functions, macros, and messages. Most MCI applications use either or both of the two main functions we've been discussing, MciSendString() and/or MciSendCommand(), dozens of times. MCI provides other useful functions, but you'll find yourself using these less frequently. Each of these functions can use any of the large number of command strings or command messages we've been discussing.

Most MCI commands require a device identifier. To retrieve this identifier call, use the open command (MCI_OPEN). If you want to retrieve a device identifier (but not open the device) you should call the MciGetDeviceID() function. Among other things, you can query the device to learn its capabilities before completing another task. Another useful function, MciGetCreatorTask(), allows you to use a device identifier to retrieve a handle to the task that created that identifier.

You can use the MciGetYieldProc() and MciSetYieldProc() functions to assign and retrieve the address of the callback function associated with the "wait" (MCI_WAIT) flag.

The MciGetErrorString() function that we have discussed already retrieves a string that describes an MCI error value. Each string that MCI returns (data or an error description) is a maximum of 128 characters. Several general MCI types are defined in mmsystem.pas as follows:

```
type
  MCIERROR = DWORD;      { error return code, 0 means no error }
  MCIDEVICEID = UINT;   { MCI device ID type }
  TFNYieldProc = function(mciId: MCIDEVICEID; dwYieldData: DWORD): UINT
              stdcall;
```

Also, the various MCIERR return values (which are numbered up to 96 but are currently fewer in number) are defined in mmsystem.pas and shown in Table 9-6. Those messages with an asterisk (*) after their name apply only to the MciSendString() function, not to the MciSend-Command() function.

Table 9-6: MCI error messages and their meanings

Error Message	Meaning
MCIERR_INVALID_DEVICE_ID	Device ID is invalid; you must use the ID given to the device when the device was opened.
MCIERR_UNRECOGNIZED_KEYWORD*	An unknown command parameter was specified.
MCIERR_UNRECOGNIZED_COMMAND	The driver does not recognize the specified command.
MCIERR_HARDWARE	There is a problem with the specified device. Check that it is working correctly or contact the manufacturer.
MCIERR_INVALID_DEVICE_NAME	The device specified is not open and is not recognized.

9

Chapter

Error Message	Meaning
MCIERR_OUT_OF_MEMORY	The system does not have enough memory to perform the requested task. User must quit one or more applications to increase the available memory, then try to perform the task again.
MCIERR_DEVICE_OPEN	The device name is already being used as an alias by the application. Use a unique alias.
MCIERR_CANNOT_LOAD_DRIVER	The device driver specified will not load properly.
MCIERR_MISSING_COMMAND_STRING*	No command was specified.
MCIERR_PARAM_OVERFLOW*	The output string was not long enough.
MCIERR_MISSING_STRING_ARGUMENT*	A string value was missing from the command.
MCIERR_BAD_INTEGER*	An integer in the command string was invalid or missing.
MCIERR_PARSER_INTERNAL*	An internal parser error occurred.
MCIERR_DRIVER_INTERNAL	Problem with device driver; may need to obtain a new driver.
MCIERR_MISSING_PARAMETER	The command specified requires a parameter that is missing.
MCIERR_UNSUPPORTED_FUNCTION	The specified command is not supported by the MCI device driver the system is using.
MCIERR_FILE_NOT_FOUND	Requested file not found. Check that the path and filename are correct.
MCIERR_DEVICE_NOT_READY	The device driver is not ready.
MCIERR_INTERNAL	A problem occurred in initializing MCI. It may be necessary to restart Windows.
MCIERR_DRIVER	Problem with device driver; may need to obtain a new driver.
MCIERR_CANNOT_USE_ALL	The device name ALL is not allowed for this command.
MCIERR_MULTIPLE	Errors occurred in more than one device. Specify each command and device separately to identify the devices causing the errors.

Error Message	Meaning
MCIERR_EXTENSION_NOT_FOUND	The specified extension has no device type associated with it. Specify a device type.
MCIERR_OUTOFRANGE	The specified parameter value is out of range for the specified MCI command.
MCIERR_FLAGS_NOT_COMPATIBLE	The specified parameters cannot be used together.
MCIERR_FILE_NOT_SAVED	The file was not saved. Make sure your system has sufficient disk space or has a functioning network connection.
MCIERR_DEVICE_TYPE_REQUIRED	The specified device cannot be found on the system. Check that the device is installed and the device name is spelled correctly.
MCIERR_DEVICE_LOCKED	The device is in the process of being closed. Wait a few seconds, then try again.
MCIERR_DUPLICATE_ALIAS	The alias specified is already being used in the application. Use a unique alias.
MCIERR_BAD_CONSTANT*	The value specified for a parameter is unknown.
MCIERR_MUST_USE_SHAREABLE	The device driver is already in use. You must specify the "shareable" parameter with each open command to share the device.
MCIERR_MISSING_DEVICE_NAME*	No device name was specified.
MCIERR_BAD_TIME_FORMAT	The specified value for the time format is invalid.
MCIERR_NO_CLOSING_QUOTE*	A closing quotation mark is missing.
MCIERR_DUPLICATE_FLAGS*	A flag or other value was specified twice.
MCIERR_INVALID_FILE	The specified file cannot be played on the specified MCI device. The file may be corrupt or may use an incorrect file format.
MCIERR_NULL_PARAMETER_BLOCK	A null parameter block (structure) was passed to MCI.
MCIERR_UNNAMED_RESOURCE	You cannot store an unnamed file. Specify a filename.

9

Chapter

Error Message	Meaning
MCIERR_NEW_REQUIRES_ALIAS*	An alias must be used with the "new" device name.
MCIERR_NOTIFY_ON_AUTO_OPEN*	The NOTIFY flag is illegal with auto-open.
MCIERR_NO_ELEMENT_ALLOWED	The specified device does not use a filename.
MCIERR_NONAPPLICABLE_FUNCTION	The specified MCI command sequence cannot be performed in the given order. Correct the command sequence and try again.
MCIERR_ILLEGAL_FOR_AUTO_OPEN	MCI will not perform the specified command on an automatically opened device. Wait until the device is closed, then try to perform the command.
MCIERR_FILENAME_REQUIRED	The filename is invalid. Make sure the filename is no longer than eight characters, followed by a period and an extension.
MCIERR_EXTRA_CHARACTERS	You must enclose a string with quotation marks; characters following the closing quotation mark are not valid.
MCIERR_DEVICE_NOT_INSTALLED	The specified device is not installed on the system. Select the Drivers option from the Control Panel to install the device.
MCIERR_GET_CD	The requested file or MCI device was not found. Try changing directories or restarting your system.
MCIERR_SET_CD	The specified file or MCI device is inaccessible because the application cannot change directories.
MCIERR_SET_DRIVE	The specified file or MCI device is inaccessible because the application cannot change drives.
MCIERR_DEVICE_LENGTH	The device or driver name is too long. Specify a device or driver name that is less than 79 characters.
MCIERR_DEVICE_ORD_LENGTH	The device or driver name is too long. Specify a device or driver name that is less than 79 characters.

Error Message	Meaning
MCIERR_NO_INTEGER	The parameter for this MCI command must be an integer value.
MCIERR_WAVE_OUTPUTSINUSE	All waveform devices that can play files in the current format are in use. Wait until one of these devices is free and try again.
MCIERR_WAVE_SETOUTPUTINUSE	The current waveform device is in use. Wait until the device is free and try to set the device for playback.
MCIERR_WAVE_INPUTSINUSE	All waveform devices that can record files in the current format are in use. Wait until one of these devices is free and try again.
MCIERR_WAVE_SETINPUTINUSE	The current waveform device is in use. Wait until the device is free and try to set the device for recording.
MCIERR_WAVE_OUTPUTUNSPECIFIED	You can specify any compatible waveform playback device.
MCIERR_WAVE_INPUTUNSPECIFIED	You can specify any compatible waveform recording device.
MCIERR_WAVE_OUTPUTSUNSUITABLE	No installed waveform device can play files in the current format. Select the Drivers option from the Control Panel to install a suitable waveform device.
MCIERR_WAVE_SETOUTPUTUN- SUITABLE	The device you are using to play back a waveform cannot recognize the data format.
MCIERR_WAVE_INPUTSUNSUITABLE	No installed waveform device can record files in the current format. Select the Drivers option from the Control Panel to install a suitable waveform recording device.
MCIERR_WAVE_SETINPUTUNSUITABLE	The device you are trying to use to record a waveform cannot recognize the data format.
MCIERR_SEQ_DIV_INCOMPATIBLE	The time formats of the "song pointer" and SMPTE are singular. You cannot use them together.
MCIERR_SEQ_PORT_INUSE	The specified MIDI port is already in use. Wait until it is free and try again.

9

Chapter

Error Message	Meaning
MCIERR_SEQ_PORT_NONEXISTENT	The specified MIDI device is not installed on the system. Select the Drivers option from the Control Panel to install a MIDI device.
MCIERR_SEQ_PORT_MAPNODEVICE	The current MIDI mapper setup refers to a MIDI device that is not installed on the system. Use the MIDI mapper from the Control Panel to edit the setup.
MCIERR_SEQ_PORT_MISCERROR	An error occurred with specified port.
MCIERR_SEQ_TIMER	All multimedia timers are being used by other applications. Quit one of these applications and try again.
MCIERR_SEQ_PORTUNSPECIFIED	The system does not have a current MIDI port specified.
MCIERR_SEQ_NOMIDIPRESENT	This system has no installed MIDI devices. Select the Drivers option from the Control Panel to install a MIDI driver.
MCIERR_NO_WINDOW	There is no display window.
MCIERR_CREATEWINDOW	Could not create or use window.
MCIERR_FILE_READ	A read from the file failed. Make sure the file is present on your system or that your system has an intact network connection.
MCIERR_FILE_WRITE	A write to the file failed. Make sure your system has sufficient disk space or has an intact network connection.
MCIERR_NO_IDENTITY	Undefined MCI error.

We have briefly discussed MCI commands and error messages. But what about the MCI macros? These macros are used to create and disassemble values that specify time formats, which in turn are used in many of the MCI commands. The formats manipulated by these macros are hours/minutes/seconds (HMS), minutes/seconds/frames (MSF), and tracks/minutes/seconds/frames (TMSF). Table 9-7 lists the macros and their descriptions.

Table 9-7: MCI macros for time formats

Macro	Description
MCI_HMS_HOUR	Retrieves the hours component from an HMS value.
MCI_HMS_MINUTE	Retrieves the minutes component from an HMS value.
MCI_HMS_SECOND	Retrieves the seconds component from an HMS value.
MCI_MAKE_HMS	Creates an HMS value.
MCI_MAKE_MSF	Creates an MSF value.
MCI_MAKE_TMSF	Creates a TMSF value.
MCI_MSF_MINUTE	Retrieves the minutes component from an MSF value.
MCI_MSF_SECOND	Retrieves the seconds component from an MSF value.
MCI_MSF_FRAME	Retrieves the frames component from an MSF value.
MCI_TMSF_TRACK	Retrieves the tracks component from a TMSF value.
MCI_TMSF_MINUTE	Retrieves the minutes component from a TMSF value.
MCI_TMSF_SECOND	Retrieves the seconds component from a TMSF value.
MCI_TMSF_FRAME	Retrieves the frames component from a TMSF value.

MCI also provides two of its own messages: MM_MCINOTIFY and MM_MCISIGNAL. The MM_MCINOTIFY message notifies an application of the outcome of an MCI command whenever that command specifies the NOTIFY (MCI_NOTIFY) flag. The MM_MCISIGNAL message is specific to digital video devices; it notifies the application when a specified position is reached.

MCI Flags

As we have learned, most MCI commands include flags that modify the command. Two flags in particular, the WAIT flag (MCI_WAIT) and the NOTIFY flag (MCI_NOTIFY), are common to every MCI command. The

TEST flag (MCI_TEST) is available to digital video and VCR devices. Let's see how these three flags work.

In most cases, an MCI command will return immediately, even if the operation that it has initiated takes several minutes to complete. If for some reason you want the action to be completed before it returns control to the application, you can use the WAIT (MCI_WAIT) flag to direct the device to wait until the requested operation is finished. For example, by adding WAIT to the following play command, the operation will not return control to the application until the playback completes:

```
mciSendString('play mydevice from 0 to 100 wait',
    lpszReturnString, length(lpszReturnString), NULL);
```

The user can always cancel a wait operation by pressing a break key. By default, this key is Ctrl+Break. An application can redefine this key by using the Break (MCI_BREAK) command. (MCI_BREAK uses the MCI_BREAK_PARMS structure.) When a wait operation is canceled, MCI attempts to return control to the application without interrupting the command associated with the WAIT flag.

Another common flag, the NOTIFY flag (MCI_NOTIFY), directs the device to post an MM_MCINOTIFY message when it completes an action. Of course, an application must have established a window procedure to process the MM_MCINOTIFY message for such notification to have any effect. An MM_MCINOTIFY message indicates that the processing of a command has completed, but it does not indicate the status of that operation—whether the command completed successfully, failed, was superseded, or was aborted.

To use this flag, when the application issues a command it must specify the handle to the destination window for the message. In the command string interface, this handle is the last parameter of the MciSendString() function. In the command message interface, the handle is specified in the low-order word of the dwCallBack member of the structure sent with the command message. (Every structure associated with a command message contains this member.)

The TEST flag (MCI_TEST) queries the device to determine if it can execute the command; it simply returns control to the application without executing the command. The device returns an error if it cannot execute the command or returns no error if it can handle the command. This flag is supported by digital video and VCR devices for all commands except open (MCI_OPEN) and close (MCI_CLOSE).

MCI Shortcuts

The Media Control Interface also provides several shortcuts you can use when working with MCI commands. With these shortcuts, you can use a single identifier to refer to all the devices your application has opened. You can also open a device without explicitly issuing an open (MCI_OPEN) command.

One useful shortcut is the ALL specifier. You can specify ALL (MCI_ALL_DEVICE_ID) as a device identifier for any command that does not return information. When you do this, MCI sends the command sequentially to all devices opened by the current application. For example, the close ALL command closes all open devices and the play ALL command starts playing all devices opened by the application. Because MCI sequentially sends the commands to the MCI devices, there is an interval between when the first and last devices receive the command. While using ALL is a convenient way to broadcast a particular command to all your devices, you should not rely on it to synchronize devices; the timing between messages can vary.

Unlike some of the other APIs we've examined, when you issue a command to a device that is not yet open, MCI tries to open the device before implementing the command. Keep in mind the following restrictions that apply to automatically opening devices:

- The automatic open feature works only with the command string interface.
- The automatic open feature fails for commands that are specific to custom device drivers.
- Automatically opened devices do not respond to commands that use ALL as a device name.
- The automatic open feature does not let your application specify the TYPE flag. Without the device name, MCI determines the device name from the entries in the registry. To use a specific device, you can combine the device name with the filename by using the exclamation point, as described in the reference material for the open command.

Tip: If your application uses the automatic open feature to open a device, you should check the return value of every subsequent open command to verify that the device is still open.

MCI also automatically closes any device that it automatically opens and typically closes a device in the following situations:

■ The command is completed.

■ You abort the command.

■ You request notification in a subsequent command.

■ MCI detects a failure.

Working with MCI Devices and Drivers

What are the MCI devices and how can we manipulate them with MCI commands? We already have some idea of what the devices are from some of the earlier material we've examined. MCI recognizes a basic set of device types. An MCI device type is defined as a set of MCI drivers that share a common command set and are used to control similar multimedia devices or data files. Many MCI commands, such as open (MCI_OPEN), require that you specify a device type. Table 9-8 shows all of the device types currently defined. Device type names (given in the first column) are used with the command string interface; device type constants second column) are used with the command message interface.

Table 9-8: Device types used in MCI

Device Type	Constant	Description
Cdaudio	MCI_DEVTYPE_CD_AUDIOCD	Audio player
Dat	MCI_DEVTYPE_DAT	Digital audio tape player
Digitalvideo	MCI_DEVTYPE_DIGITAL_VIDEO	Digital video in a window (not GDI based)
Other	MCI_DEVTYPE_OTHER	Undefined MCI device
Overlay	MCI_DEVTYPE_OVERLAY	Overlay device (analog video in a window)
Scanner	MCI_DEVTYPE_SCANNER	Image scanner
Sequencer	MCI_DEVTYPE_SEQUENCERMIDI	Sequencer
Vcr	MCI_DEVTYPE_VCR	Video cassette recorder or player

Device Type	Constant	Description
Videodisc	MCI_DEVTYPE_VIDEODISC	Videodisc player
Waveaudio	MCI_DEVTYPE_WAVEFORM_AUDIO	Audio device that plays digitized waveform files

What if there's more than one device of a particular type on a machine? For any of the above device types, there might be several MCI drivers that share the same command set but operate on different data formats. To solve this potential problem, the Windows system uses device names that uniquely identify an MCI driver. Device names are identified either in the [mci] section of the SYSTEM.INI file or in the appropriate part of the Windows Registry. This information identifies all MCI drivers to Windows. The entries in the [mci] section use the following form:

```
device_name = driver_filename.extension
```

The following example shows the [mci] section from the author's SYSTEM.INI:

```
[mci]
cdaudio=mcicda.drv
sequencer=mciseq.drv
waveaudio=mciwave.drv
avivideo=mciavi.drv
MPEGVideo=mciqtz.drv
videodisc=mcipionr.drv
vcr=mcivisca.drv
Overlay=MCIK2V.DRV
AC3AUDIO=CCMT_AC3.DRV
CompVideo=SOFTPEG.DRV
```

There's also a naming issue if there's more than one device of a particular type installed. If an MCI driver is installed using a device name that already exists in SYSTEM.INI or the registry, the system appends an integer to the device name of the new driver, creating a unique device name. In the preceding example, if we were to install another driver using the cdaudio device name, Windows would assign cdaudio1 as the device name.

As with the Wave API, the MIDI API, and the other APIs we have discussed, in MCI it's the drivers that provide the functionality for the MCI commands. As we'll see, the system software performs some basic data management tasks. However, the multimedia tasks of playback,

9

Chapter

presentation, and recording are all handled by the individual MCI drivers. You can find these drivers in the registry under HKEY_LOCAL_MACHINE\System\CurrentControlSet\control\MediaResources.

Drivers vary in their support for MCI commands and command flags. Because multimedia devices can have widely varying capabilities, MCI is designed to let individual drivers extend or reduce the command sets to match the capabilities of the device with which they are associated. For example, the record (MCI_RECORD) command is part of the command set for MIDI sequencers. However, the MCISEQ driver included with Windows does not support this command. This demonstrates an important caveat: Just because devices of a particular type are supposed to recognize a certain command does not necessarily mean that all devices of that type support that command. Therefore, applications should use the capability command (MCI_GETDEVCAPS) to determine the capabilities of a particular device before issuing questionable commands.

In many situations, the MCI command specifications define the default values and behavior for drivers associated with a particular type of device. Multimedia devices can have a wide range of features, limitations, and requirements. For this reason there can be undefined areas of behavior. Also, drivers might handle exceptions differently, based on the capabilities of the device. See examples in the Windows Multimedia help file for specific instances of unusual behavior.

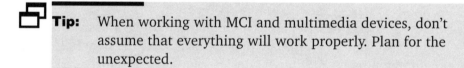

Tip: When working with MCI and multimedia devices, don't assume that everything will work properly. Plan for the unexpected.

Basic Tasks: Capabilities; Opening and Closing Devices; Playing, Recording, and Controlling Media

Often before you open a device, you need to determine its capabilities to make certain it can accomplish the task we have in mind. Every device responds to the capability (MCI_GETDEVCAPS), status (MCI_STATUS), and info (MCI_INFO) commands. These commands obtain information about the device. For example, this example from the Windows Multimedia help file returns TRUE if a cdaudio device can eject the disc:

```
mciSendString('capability cdaudio can eject',
    lpszReturnString, length(lpszReturnString), NULL);
```

The flags listed for the required and basic commands provide a minimum amount of information about a device. Many devices supplement the required and basic commands with extended flags to provide additional information about the device. We'll discuss this further when we take a detailed look at the MCI_GETDEVCAPS command.

What if you want to determine specific information about the multimedia capabilities of a particular machine? You can use the sysinfo (MCI_SYSINFO) command to obtain system information about MCI devices. Since this information is not specific to any device, MCI handles the command without sending it to any MCI device. For the command message interface, MCI returns the system information in the MCI_SYSINFO_PARMS structure. That structure is shown under the MCI_SYSINFO command.

You can use the sysinfo (MCI_SYSINFO) command to retrieve information such as the number of MCI devices on a system, the number of MCI devices of a particular type, the number of open MCI devices, and the names of those devices. Often this command must be called more than once to retrieve a particular piece of information. For example, you might retrieve the number of devices of a particular type in the first call and then enumerate the names of the devices in the next. Now we'll discuss opening a device, a rather complex topic.

As we discussed above, MCI can implicitly open a multimedia device, but often you want or need to explicitly open a device. Generally speaking, before you use a multimedia device, you must initialize it by using the Open (MCI_OPEN) command. This command loads the driver into memory (if it isn't already loaded) and retrieves the device identifier you will use to identify it in subsequent MCI commands. You should check the return value of the MciSendString() or MciSendCommand() function and make sure the function returned successfully (with a value of 0) before using a new device identifier. If the function did not return successfully, the identifier will not be valid. You can also retrieve a device identifier by using the MciGetDeviceID() function.

Like all MCI command messages, MCI_OPEN has an associated structure. These structures are sometimes called parameter blocks. The default structure for MCI_OPEN is MCI_OPEN_PARMS. Certain devices (such as

9

Chapter

376 ■ *Chapter Nine*

waveform and overlay) have extended structures (such as MCI_WAVE_
OPEN_PARMS and MCI_OVLY_OPEN_PARMS) to accommodate additional optional parameters. If you have no need to use these additional
parameters, you can simply use the MCI_OPEN_PARMS structure with
any MCI device. These three structures and their related structures are
defined in mmsystem.pas as follows:

```
type
  PMCI_Open_ParmsA = ^TMCI_Open_ParmsA;
  PMCI_Open_ParmsW = ^TMCI_Open_ParmsW;
  PMCI_Open_Parms = PMCI_Open_ParmsA;
  tagMCI_OPEN_PARMSA = record
    dwCallback: DWORD;
    wDeviceID: MCIDEVICEID;
    lpstrDeviceType: PAnsiChar;
    lpstrElementName: PAnsiChar;
    lpstrAlias: PAnsiChar;
  end;
  tagMCI_OPEN_PARMSW = record
    dwCallback: DWORD;
    wDeviceID: MCIDEVICEID;
    lpstrDeviceType: PWideChar;
    lpstrElementName: PWideChar;
    lpstrAlias: PWideChar;
  end;
  tagMCI_OPEN_PARMS = tagMCI_OPEN_PARMSA;
  TMCI_Open_ParmsA = tagMCI_OPEN_PARMSA;
  TMCI_Open_ParmsW = tagMCI_OPEN_PARMSW;
  TMCI_Open_Parms = TMCI_Open_ParmsA;
  MCI_OPEN_PARMSA = tagMCI_OPEN_PARMSA;
  MCI_OPEN_PARMSW = tagMCI_OPEN_PARMSW;
  MCI_OPEN_PARMS = MCI_OPEN_PARMSA;
type
  PMCI_Wave_Open_ParmsA = ^TMCI_Wave_Open_ParmsA;
  PMCI_Wave_Open_ParmsW = ^TMCI_Wave_Open_ParmsW;
  PMCI_Wave_Open_Parms = PMCI_Wave_Open_ParmsA;
  tagMCI_WAVE_OPEN_PARMSA = record
    dwCallback: DWORD;
    wDeviceID: MCIDEVICEID;
    lpstrDeviceType: PAnsiChar;
    lpstrElementName: PAnsiChar;
    lpstrAlias: PAnsiChar;
    dwBufferSeconds: DWORD;
  end;
  tagMCI_WAVE_OPEN_PARMSW = record
    dwCallback: DWORD;
```

```
    wDeviceID: MCIDEVICEID;
    lpstrDeviceType: PWideChar;
    lpstrElementName: PWideChar;
    lpstrAlias: PWideChar;
    dwBufferSeconds: DWORD;
  end;
  tagMCI_WAVE_OPEN_PARMS = tagMCI_WAVE_OPEN_PARMSA;
  TMCI_Wave_Open_ParmsA = tagMCI_WAVE_OPEN_PARMSA;
  TMCI_Wave_Open_ParmsW = tagMCI_WAVE_OPEN_PARMSW;
  TMCI_Wave_Open_Parms = TMCI_Wave_Open_ParmsA;
  MCI_WAVE_OPEN_PARMSA = tagMCI_WAVE_OPEN_PARMSA;
  MCI_WAVE_OPEN_PARMSW = tagMCI_WAVE_OPEN_PARMSW;
  MCI_WAVE_OPEN_PARMS = MCI_WAVE_OPEN_PARMSA;
type
  PMCI_Ovly_Open_ParmsA = ^TMCI_Ovly_Open_ParmsA;
  PMCI_Ovly_Open_ParmsW = ^TMCI_Ovly_Open_ParmsW;
  PMCI_Ovly_Open_Parms = PMCI_Ovly_Open_ParmsA;
  tagMCI_OVLY_OPEN_PARMSA = record
    dwCallback: DWORD;
    wDeviceID: MCIDEVICEID;
    lpstrDeviceType: PAnsiChar;
    lpstrElementName: PAnsiChar;
    lpstrAlias: PAnsiChar;
    dwStyle: DWORD;
    hWndParent: HWND;
  end;
  tagMCI_OVLY_OPEN_PARMSW = record
    dwCallback: DWORD;
    wDeviceID: MCIDEVICEID;
    lpstrDeviceType: PWideChar;
    lpstrElementName: PWideChar;
    lpstrAlias: PWideChar;
    dwStyle: DWORD;
    hWndParent: HWND;
  end;
  tagMCI_OVLY_OPEN_PARMS = tagMCI_OVLY_OPEN_PARMSA;
  TMCI_Ovly_Open_ParmsA = tagMCI_OVLY_OPEN_PARMSA;
  TMCI_Ovly_Open_ParmsW = tagMCI_OVLY_OPEN_PARMSW;
  TMCI_Ovly_Open_Parms = TMCI_Ovly_Open_ParmsA;
  MCI_OVLY_OPEN_PARMSA = tagMCI_OVLY_OPEN_PARMSA;
  MCI_OVLY_OPEN_PARMSW = tagMCI_OVLY_OPEN_PARMSW;
  MCI_OVLY_OPEN_PARMS = MCI_OVLY_OPEN_PARMSA;
```

9

Chapter

The number of devices you can have open is limited only by the amount of memory available on the machine. When you open a device, you can use the ALIAS flag to specify a device identifier for it. This flag lets you assign a short device identifier for compound devices with lengthy file-names. It also lets you open multiple instances of the same file or device. In the following example based on one from the Microsoft help file, a command string is used to assign the device identifier Birdcall to the lengthy filename C:\NABIRDS\SOUNDS\MOCKMTNG.WAV:

```
mciSendString(
    'open c:\nabirds\sounds\mockmtng.wav type waveaudio alias birdcall',
    lpszReturnString, length(lpszReturnString), NULL);
```

To accomplish the same task with the command message interface, you should specify an alias by using the lpstrAlias field of the MCI_OPEN_PARMS structure. Whenever you open a device, you can use the TYPE flag to refer to a particular device type, rather than to a specific device driver. The following example opens the waveform audio file C:\WINDOWS\CHIMES.WAV and assigns the alias Chimes. This example uses the TYPE flag to specify the waveaudio device type. In the command message interface, the functionality of the TYPE flag is supplied by the lpstrDeviceType member of the MCI_OPEN_PARMS structure.

```
mciSendString(
    'open c:\windows\chimes.wav type waveaudio alias chimes',
    lpszReturnString, length(lpszReturnString), NULL);
```

The Media Control Interface has two ways of classifying device drivers—compound or simple. Drivers for compound devices require the name of a data file for playback; drivers for simple devices do not. Simple devices include CD audio and videodisc devices. There are two ways to open a simple device: you can specify a pointer to a null-terminated string containing the device name from the registry or the SYSTEM.INI file or you can specify the actual name of the device driver.

The following example (again based on one in the Windows help file) opens a videodisc device by specifying a pointer to a null-terminated string containing the device name from the SYSTEM.INI file. In this case, videodisc is the device name from the [mci] section of SYSTEM.INI:

```
mciSendString("open videodisc", lpszReturnString,
    length(lpszReturnString), NULL);
```

If you open a device using the device driver filename, however, this makes the application device specific and can prevent it from running if the system configuration changes. If you use a filename, you do not need to specify the complete path or the filename extension; MCI assumes drivers are located in a system directory and have a .DRV extension.

Compound devices include wave audio and sequencer devices. The data for a compound device is sometimes called a device element, but we'll follow the convention established in the Windows Multimedia help file and call this data a file, even though in some cases the data might not be stored as a file. There are three ways to open a compound device: specifying only the device name, specifying only the filename, or specifying both the filename and the device name.

If you open a compound device specifying only the device name, you cannot associate that device with a particular filename. When opened in this manner, most compound devices process only the Capability (MCI_GETDEVCAPS) and Close (MCI_CLOSE) commands. If you specify only the filename, the device name will be determined from the associations in the registry. Finally, if you specify both the filename and the device name, MCI will ignore the entries in the registry and open the specified device.

If you want to associate a data file with a particular device, you can specify the filename and device name. For example, the following command opens the waveaudio device with the filename myvoice.snd:

```
mciSendString('open myvoice.snd type waveaudio', lpszReturnString,
    length(lpszReturnString), NULL);
```

If you're using the command string interface, you can abbreviate the device name specification by using the alternative exclamation point format. See the description of the open command below. If the Open (MCI_OPEN) command specifies only the filename, MCI uses the filename extension to select the appropriate device from the list in the registry or (according to the Windows Multimedia help file) the [mci extensions] section of the SYSTEM.INI file. However, the author found this section in the WIN.INI rather than the SYSTEM.INI file. The entries in the [mci extensions] section use the following form:

```
filename_extension=device_name
```

MCI implicitly uses device_name if the extension is found and if a device name has not been specified in the open command.

The following example shows the [mci extensions] section from the author's WIN.INI file:

```
[mci extensions]
mid=Sequencer
rmi=Sequencer
wav=waveaudio
avi=AVIVideo
mpeg=MPEGVideo
mpe=MPEGVideo
mpa=MPEGVideo
enc=MPEGVideo
mov=MPEGVideo
qt=MPEGVideo
au=MPEGVideo
snd=MPEGVideo
aif=MPEGVideo
aiff=MPEGVideo
aifc=MPEGVideo
AC3=AC3AUDIO
mpg=CompVideo
dat=CompVideo
m2p=CompVideo
mp2=CompVideo
mpv=CompVideo
m1v=CompVideo
```

Using these definitions, MCI opens the waveaudio device if the following command is issued:

```
mciSendString("open train.wav", lpszReturnString,
    length(lpszReturnString), NULL);
```

To create a new data file, you simply specify a blank filename. MCI does not save a new file until you save it by using the Save (MCI_SAVE) command. When creating a new file, you must include a device alias with the Open (MCI_OPEN) command. The following example from the Windows Multimedia help file opens a new waveaudio file, starts and stops recording, then saves and closes the file:

```
mciSendString('open new type waveaudio alias capture', lpszReturnString,
    length(lpszReturnString), NULL);
mciSendString('record capture', lpszReturnString,
    length(lpszReturnString), NULL);
mciSendString('stop capture', lpszReturnString,
    length(lpszReturnString), NULL);
mciSendString('save capture orca.wav', lpszReturnString,
    length(lpszReturnString), NULL);
```

```
mciSendString('close capture', lpszReturnString,
    length(lpszReturnString), NULL);
```

It is possible to share multimedia devices. By using the shareable
(MCI_OPEN_SHAREABLE) flag with the Open (MCI_OPEN) command,
you can enable multiple applications to access the same device (or file)
and device instance simultaneously. If your application opens a device or
file as shareable, other applications can also access it by opening it as
shareable. The shared device or file gives each application the ability to
change the parameters governing its operating state. Each time a device
or file is opened as shareable, MCI returns a unique device identifier,
even though the different identifiers actually refer to the same instance.

On the other hand, if your application opens a device or file without
using the shareable flag, no other application can access it until your
application closes it. Some devices do not support multiple open
instances. If a device supports only one open instance, the open command will fail if you specify the shareable flag. If your application opens
a device and specifies that it is shareable, it should not make any
assumptions about the state of that device. In some cases, your application might need to compensate for changes made by other applications
accessing the device.

Most compound files are not shareable; however, you can open multiple
files, or you can open a single file multiple times. If you open a single file
multiple times, MCI creates an independent instance for each, with each
instance having a unique operating status. If you open multiple instances
of a file, you must assign a unique device identifier to each. You can use
an alias to assign a unique name for each file. Once we have opened a
file or a device there are several things we can do: play, record, or
change position. We'll begin by discussing playback and positioning, then
discuss recording.

A number of MCI commands, such as play (MCI_PLAY), stop
(MCI_STOP), pause (MCI_PAUSE), resume (MCI_RESUME), and seek
(MCI_SEEK), affect the playback or positioning of a multimedia file. If an
MCI device receives a playback command while another playback com-
mand is in progress, it accepts the command and either stops or
supersedes the previous command.

Many MCI commands, such as set (MCI_SET), do not affect playback and
can be called when playback is taking place. A notification from one of

9

Chapter

these commands does not interfere with any pending playback or positioning command provided that the notifications are not performed from the same instance of the driver. For example, you can issue a set or status (MCI_STATUS) command while a device is performing a seek command without stopping or superseding the seek command.

Here's the caveat: There can be only one pending notification. For example, if an application requests a notification for play and follows that request with status "start position notify," the play notification will return "superseded" and the notification for the status command will return when it is finished. Interestingly, the play command will still succeed, even though the application did not receive the notification and nothing really happened.

Besides playing, recording is probably the second most important multimedia topic. While the general MCI specification supports recording with a variety of devices, only two device-types are currently supported: waveform audio and video cassette recorder (VCR) devices. Presumably, recording with digital video and MIDI sequencers will be added in the future.

You can insert or overwrite recorded information into an existing file or record into a new file. To record to an existing file, open a waveform audio device and file as you would normally. To record into a new file, when you open the device specify "new" as the device name if you are using the command string interface. If you are using the command message interface, specify a zero length filename.

When MCI creates a new file for recording, the data format is set to a default format specified by the device driver. To use a format other than the default format, you can use the set (MCI_SET) command. To begin recording, use the record command (or MCI_RECORD and the MCI_RECORD_PARMS structure). If you record in insert mode to an existing file, you can use the "from" (MCI_FROM) and "to" (MCI_TO) flags of the record command to specify starting and ending positions for recording. For example, if you record to a file that is 20 seconds long, and you begin recording at 5 seconds and end recording at 10 seconds, the resulting file will be 25 seconds long. The file will have a 5-second segment inserted 5 seconds into the original recording.

If you record with overwrite mode to an existing file, you can use the "from" and "to" flags to specify starting and ending locations of the section that is overwritten. For example, if you record to a file that is 20 seconds long, and you begin recording at 5 seconds and end recording at 10 seconds, you still have a recording 20 seconds long, but the section beginning at 5 seconds and ending at 10 seconds will have been replaced.

If you do not specify an ending location, recording continues until you send a Stop (MCI_STOP) command, or until the driver runs out of free disk space. If you record to a new file, you can omit the "from" flag or set it to zero to start recording at the beginning of a new file. You can specify an ending location to terminate recording when recording to a new file.

The record command is sometimes accurate to within only 1 second of the starting location, such as with VCR devices. To record more accurately, you should use the cue (MCI_CUE) command. This command is recognized by digital video, VCR, and waveform audio devices. For more information about recording with VCR devices, see the entry for the MCI_RECORD command.

When recording is complete, you need to save your work. Of course, if you close the device without saving, the recorded data will be lost. To preserve your work, use the save command (or MCI_SAVE and the MCI_SAVE_PARMS structure) before closing the device. The MCI_SAVE_PARMS structure and its related structures are shown under the MCI_SAVE command.

If you're recording on a PCM (pulse code modulation) waveform audio input device, you may want to check input levels. To get the level of the input signal before recording on such a device, use the status (MCI_STATUS) command. Specify the "level" flag (or the MCI_STATUS_ITEM flag and set the dwItem member of the MCI_STATUS_PARMS structure to MCI_WAVE_STATUS_LEVEL). The average input signal level will be returned. The left channel value is in the high-order word and the right or mono channel value is in the low-order word. The input level is represented as an unsigned value. For 8-bit samples, this value is in the range 0 through 127 (0x7F); for 16-bit samples, it is in the range 0 through 32,767 (0x7FFF).

Whether recording or playing back you may want to provide support for pausing or resuming a device. MCI provides these capabilities along with stopping a device completely. The Stop (MCI_STOP) command suspends the playing or recording of a device. Many devices also support the Pause (MCI_PAUSE) command. The difference between stop and pause depends on the device. Usually pause suspends operation but leaves the device ready to resume playing or recording immediately.

If you use the play (MCI_PLAY) or record (MCI_RECORD) command to restart a device, either command resets the locations specified with the "to" (MCI_TO) and "from" (MCI_FROM) flags before the device was paused or stopped. Without the "from" flag, these commands reset the starting location to the current position. Without the "to" flag, they reset the ending location to the end of the media. To continue playing or recording without resetting a previously specified stop position, use the play or record command's "to" flag to specify an ending position.

Some devices support the resume (MCI_RESUME) command to restart a paused device. This command does not change the "to" and "from" locations specified with the play or record command that preceded the pause command. We have one last topic to consider before we take a detailed look at the functions and commands: closing a device.

The close (MCI_CLOSE) command releases access to a device or file. MCI frees a device when all tasks using a device have closed it. To help MCI manage the devices, your application must close each device or file when it is finished using it. When you close an external MCI device that uses its own media instead of files (such as CD audio), the driver leaves the device in its current mode of operation. Thus, if you close a CD audio device that is playing, even though the device driver is released from memory, the CD audio device will continue to play until it reaches the end of its content. Keep in mind that closing an application that includes one or more open MCI devices can prevent other applications from using those devices until Windows is restarted.

MCI Functions

function MciSendCommand   *mmsystem.pas*

Syntax

```
function MciSendCommand(
  mciID: MCIDEVICEID;
  uMessage: UINT;
  dwParam1, dwParam2: DWORD
  ): MCIERROR; stdcall;
```

Description

This function sends a command message to the specified MCI device.

Parameters

mciID: An MCIDEVICEID identifying the MCI device to receive the command message. This parameter is not used with the MCI_OPEN command message.

uMessage: An integer (UINT) indicating the command message. For information about command messages, see the "Command Messages" section near the beginning of the chapter. Also, be sure to examine the many commands described in the "MCI Commands" section.

dwParam1: DWORD containing flags for the command message.

dwParam2: DWORD containing address of the structure that contains parameters for the command message.

Return Value

Returns zero if successful or an error otherwise. The low-order word of the returned DWORD value contains the error return value. If the error is device specific, the high-order word of the return value is the driver identifier; otherwise, the high-order word is zero. For a list of possible return values, see Table 9-6. To retrieve a text description of MciSendCommand() return values, pass the return value to the MciGetErrorString() function. Error values that are returned specifically when a device is being opened are listed under the discussion of the MCI_OPEN command message. The MCI_OPEN command is used to obtain the device identifier specified by the IDDevice parameter.

Example

Listing 9-1 shows how to play a sound using MciSendCommand().

Listing 9-1: Playing a sound using MciSendCommand()
```
procedure TForm1.btnPlaySoundwithCommandClick(Sender: TObject);
var
  AMCIResult : MCIError;
  OpenParams : MCI_OPEN_PARMS;
  PlayParams : MCI_PLAY_PARMS;
begin
  OpenParams.dwCallback := DWord(AHandle);
```

```
OpenParams.lpstrDeviceType := 'waveaudio';
OpenParams.lpstrElementName := 'd:\auxaudio\sample.wav';
AMCIResult := mciSendCommand(0, MCI_OPEN, (MCI_OPEN_TYPE or
              MCI_OPEN_ELEMENT), DWord(@OpenParams));
if AMCIResult<>0 then
  begin
    mciGetErrorString(AMCIResult, ErrMsg, MsgLen);
    ShowMessage(ErrMsg);
    Exit;
  end;
DeviceID := OpenParams.wDeviceID;
PlayParams.dwCallback := AHandle;
if MonitorYieldCalls then
  StartYieldProc;
AMCIResult := mciSendCommand(DeviceID, MCI_PLAY, MCI_NOTIFY,
              DWord(@PlayParams));
if MonitorYieldCalls then
  StopYieldProc;
end;
```

function MciSendString   *mmsystem.pas*

Syntax

```
function MciSendString(
  lpstrCommand, lpstrReturnString: PChar;
  uReturnLength: UINT;
  hWndCallback: HWND
  ): MCIERROR; stdcall;
```

Description

This function sends a command string to an MCI device. The device that the command is sent to is specified in the command string.

Parameters

lpstrCommand: A PChar containing the address of a null-terminated string that specifies an MCI command string. For more information about the command strings, see the discussion of command strings above.

lpstrReturnString: A PChar containing the address of a buffer that receives return information. If no return information is needed, this parameter can be NULL.

uReturnLength: An integer (UINT) indicating the size (in characters) of the return buffer specified by the lpszReturnString parameter. Use the Length() function to retrieve this value.

hWndCallback: The handle of a callback window if the NOTIFY flag was specified in the command string.

Return Value

Returns zero if successful or an error otherwise. The low-order word of the returned Double Word value contains the error return value. If the error is device specific, the high-order word of the return value is the driver identifier; otherwise, the high-order word is zero. For a list of possible return values, see Table 9-6. To retrieve a text description of MciSendCommand() return values, pass the return value to the MciGetErrorString() function.

Example

Listing 9-2 shows several examples of using the MciSendString() function to play a WAV file. There are a number of other examples of the use of this function in the first part of this chapter.

Listing 9-2: Using the MciSendString() function to play WAV files

```
procedure TForm1.btnPlaySoundWithStringClick(Sender: TObject);
begin
  // The following line is "hard-coded." Ideally, you would have a file
  // open dialog to select the wave file to play
  mciSendString('open C:\BookCode\Ch9_Code\sample.wav type waveaudio alias
        song', ErrMsg, MsgLen, AHandle);
  mciSendString('set song time format samples', ErrMsg, MsgLen, AHandle);
  mciSendString('play song from 1 wait', ErrMsg, MsgLen, AHandle);
  mciSendString('close song', ErrMsg, MsgLen, AHandle);
end;
```

function MciGetDeviceID   mmsystem.pas

Syntax

function MciGetDeviceID(
  pszDevice: PChar
): MCIDEVICEID; stdcall;

9

Chapter

388 ■ Chapter Nine

Description

This function retrieves the device identifier corresponding to the name of an open device.

Parameter

pszDevice: The address of a null-terminated string that specifies the device name or the alias name by which the device is known.

Return Value

If successful, returns the device identifier assigned to the device when it was opened. The identifier is used in the MciSendCommand() function. If the device name is not known, if the device is not open, or if there was not enough memory to complete the operation, the return value is zero.

Example

Listing 9-3 shows how to set up a Yield procedure. It uses the MciGetDeviceID() function and several other MCI functions.

Listing 9-3: Using MCI to yield

```
procedure TForm1.btnTestYieldProcClick(Sender: TObject);
var
  AMCIResult : MCIError;
  OpenParams : MCI_OPEN_PARMS;
  PlayParams : MCI_PLAY_PARMS;
begin
  OpenParams.dwCallback        := DWORD(Form1.Handle);
  OpenParams.lpstrDeviceType   := 'waveaudio';
  OpenParams.lpstrElementName  := 'd:\auxaudio\sample.wav';
  OpenParams.lpstrAlias        := 'song';
  AMCIResult :=mciSendCommand(0, MCI_OPEN,
                   MCI_OPEN_TYPE or MCI_OPEN_ELEMENT or MCI_OPEN_ALIAS,
                   DWORD(@OpenParams));
  if (AMCIResult<>0) then
    begin
      mciGetErrorString(AMCIResult, ErrMsg, MsgLen);
      ShowMessage(ErrMsg);
      mciSendCommand(MCI_ALL_DEVICE_ID, MCI_CLOSE,
                   MCI_WAIT, DWORD(NULL));
      exit;
    end;
  // setup stuff
  DeviceId := OpenParams.wDeviceID;
```

```
  if ( DeviceId <> mciGetDeviceID('song')) then
    begin
      ShowMessage('Device ID Mismatch; canceling operation');
      mciSendCommand(MCI_ALL_DEVICE_ID, MCI_CLOSE,
                     MCI_WAIT, DWORD(NULL));
      exit;
    end;
  PlayParams.dwCallback   := DWORD(Form1.Handle);
  Label2.Caption := 'Creator task handle: ' +
IntToStr(mciGetCreatorTask(DeviceId));
  // set yield process
  StartYieldProc;
  // Now do some playback
  AMCIResult := mciSendCommand(DeviceId,
                   MCI_PLAY,
                   MCI_WAIT,
                   DWORD(@PlayParams));
// And shut everything down
  mciSendCommand(DeviceId, MCI_CLOSE, 0, 0{DWORD(NULL)});
  StopYieldProc;
  Edit1.Text := IntToStr(YieldProcCalls);
end;
```

function MciGetErrorString   *mmsystem.pas*

Syntax

```
function MciGetErrorString(
  mcierr: MCIERROR;
  pszText: PChar;
  uLength: UINT
  ): BOOL; stdcall;
```

Description

This function returns a string that describes the specified MCI error code, mcierr. The error string is placed in the pszText parameter.

Parameters

mcierr: Error code returned by the MciSendCommand or MciSendString function.

pszText: A Char giving the address of a buffer that receives a null-terminated string describing the specified error.

uLength: An integer (UINT) indicating the size of the PChar buffer that holds the description of the error. A length of 128 should be sufficient for any of the message strings.

Return Value

Returns TRUE if successful or FALSE if the error code is not known.

Example

See Listing 9-3.

function MciSetYieldProc   *mmsystem.pas*

Syntax

```
function MciSetYieldProc(
  mciDevID: MCIDEVICEID;
  fpYieldProc: TFNYieldProc;
  dwYieldData: DWORD
  ): BOOL; stdcall;
```

Description

This function sets the address of a procedure to be called periodically when an MCI device is waiting for a command to finish because the WAIT (MCI_WAIT) flag was specified. This function overrides any previous yield procedure for this device.

Parameters

mciDevID: An integer identifying the device to assign a procedure to.

 Tip: In mmsystem.pas this first parameter is of type MCIERROR, which conflicts with the Windows documentation. It has been changed to the correct type here.

fpYieldProc: The address of the procedure to call when yielding for the specified device. If this parameter is NULL, the function disables any existing yield procedure.

dwYieldData: Data to be sent to the yield procedure when it is called for the specified device.

Return Value

Returns TRUE if successful, or FALSE otherwise.

Example

See Listing 9-3.

function MciGetCreatorTask   mmsystem.pas

Syntax

```
function MciGetCreatorTask(
  mciDevID: MCIDEVICEID
  ): HTASK; stdcall;
```

Description

This function retrieves a handle to the creator task for the specified
device.

Parameter

mciDevID: An integer identifying the device for which the creator task is
    returned.

Tip: In mmsystem.pas this first parameter is of type
MCIERROR, which conflicts with the Windows
documentation in this and the next function. We
have changed it to the correct type here.

Return Value

Returns the handle of the creator task responsible for opening the device,
if successful. If the device identifier is invalid, the return value is NULL.

Example

See Listing 9-3.

function McIGetYieldProc   *mmsystem.pas*

Syntax

```
function McIGetYieldProc(
  mciDevID: MCIDEVICEID;
  lpdwYieldData: PDWORD
  ): TFNYieldProc; stdcall;
```

Description

This function retrieves the address of the callback function associated with the WAIT (MCI_WAIT) flag. The callback function is called periodically while an MCI device waits for a command specified with the WAIT flag to finish.

Parameters

mciDevID: An iteger identifying the MCI device being monitored (the device performing an MCI command).

 Tip: In mmsystem.pas this first parameter is of type MCIERROR, which conflicts with the Windows documentation. It has been changed to the correct type here.

lpdwYieldData: The address of a buffer containing yield data to be passed to the callback function. This parameter can be NULL if there is no yield data.

Return Value

Returns the address of the current yield callback function if successful, or NULL if the device identifier is invalid.

Example

See Listing 9-4 for an example that uses this procedure and its companion, McISetYieldProc().

Listing 9-4: Starting the Yield procedure using McIGetYieldProc() and McISetYieldProc()

```
procedure TForm1.StartYieldProc;
var
```

```
    YieldProcSet : boolean;
begin
  YieldProcCalls := 0;
  Edit1.Text := '0';
  // First save existing YieldProc so we can re-establich it
  YieldProcedure := mciGetYieldProc(AHandle, 0);
  YieldProcSet := mciSetYieldProc(AHandle, @TestYieldProc, DWord(0));
  YieldProcTimer := SetTimer(AHandle, 1, 20, 0);
end;
```

MCI Commands

As explained in the section on MCI flags, most MCI commands include flags to modify the command. Two flags, MCI_WAIT and MCI_NOTIFY, are common to every command. MCI_TEST is used with digital video and VCR devices. Flags specific to certain commands will be described along with those commands.

command MCI_OPEN

Description

This command initializes a device or file. The MCI_OPEN_TYPE flag must be used whenever a device is specified in the MciSendCommand() function. If you open a device by specifying a device type constant, you must specify the MCI_OPEN_TYPE_ID flag in addition to MCI_OPEN_TYPE. If the MCI_OPEN_SHAREABLE flag is not specified when a device or file is initially opened, all subsequent MCI_OPEN commands to the device or file will fail. If the device or file is already open and this flag is not specified, the call will fail even if the first open command specified MCI_OPEN_SHAREABLE. Files opened for the MCISEQ.DRV and MCIWAVE.DRV devices are nonshareable. To use automatic type selection (via the entries in the registry), assign the filename and file extension to the lpstrElementName member of the structure identified by lpOpen, set the lpstrDeviceType member to NULL, and set the MCI_OPEN_ELEMENT flag.

Applies to

All devices recognize this command.

9

Chapter

Use

```
AMCIReturnValue := mciSendCommand(0, MCI_OPEN, FFlags, Longint(
                                      @AOpen_Parms_Struc));
```

Parameters (MciSendCommand):

lpOpen: For waveform audio devices, the lpOpen parameter points to an MCI_WAVE_OPEN_PARMS structure. Note that the MCIWAVE driver requires an asynchronous waveform audio device. For video overlay devices, the lpOpen parameter points to an MCI_OVLY_OPEN_ PARMS structure. For digital video devices, the lpOpen parameter points to an MCI_DGV_OPEN_PARMS structure. (All of these structures are outlined earlier in this chapter).

dwParam1: Additional flags for this parameter are given in Tables 9-9 through 9-13.

Table 9-9: Additional flags for the dwParaml parameter of MciSendCommand()

Flag	Meaning
MCI_OPEN_ALIAS	An alias is included in the lpstrAlias member of the structure identified by lpOpen.
MCI_OPEN_SHAREABLE	The device or file should be opened as shareable.
MCI_OPEN_TYPE	A device type name or constant is included in the lpstrDeviceType member of the structure identified by lpOpen.
MCI_OPEN_TYPE_ID	The low-order word of the lpstrDeviceType member of the structure identified by lpOpen contains a standard MCI device type identifier and the high-order word optionally contains the ordinal index for the device. Use this flag with the MCI_OPEN_TYPE flag.

Table 9-10: Additional flags for compound devices only

Flag	Meaning
MCI_OPEN_ELEMENT	Indicates that the lpstrElementName member of the structure identified by lpOpen is a filename.
MCI_OPEN_ELEMENT_ID	Indicates that the lpstrElementName member of the structure identified by lpOpen is interpreted as a DWORD value and has meaning internal to the device. Use this flag with the MCI_OPEN_ELEMENT flag.

Table 9-11: Additional flags for digital video devices only

Flag	Meaning
MCI_DGV_OPEN_NOSTATIC	Indicates that the device should reduce the number of static (system) colors in the palette. This increases the number of colors available for rendering the video stream. This flag applies only to devices that share a palette with Windows.
MCI_DGV_OPEN_PARENT	Indicates that the parent window handle is specified in the hWndParent member of the structure identified by lpOpen.
MCI_DGV_OPEN_WS	Indicates that a window style is specified in the dwStyle member of the structure identified by lpOpen.
MCI_DGV_OPEN_16BIT	Indicates a preference for 16-bit MCI device support.
MCI_DGV_OPEN_32BIT	Indicates a preference for 32-bit MCI device support.

Table 9-12: Additional flags for overlay devices only

Flag	Meaning
MCI_OVLY_OPEN_PARENT	Indicates that the parent window handle is specified in the hWndParent member of the structure identified by lpOpen.
MCI_OVLY_OPEN_WS	Indicates that a window style is specified in the dwStyle member of the structure identified by lpOpen. The dwStyle value specifies the style of the window that the driver will create and display if the application does not provide one. The style parameter takes an integer that defines the particular window style. These constants are the same as the standard window styles (such as WS_CHILD, WS_OVERLAPPEDWINDOW, or WS_POPUP).

Table 9-13: Additional flag for waveaudio devices only

Flag	Meaning
MCI_WAVE_OPEN_BUFFER	Indicates that a buffer length is specified in the dwBufferSeconds member of the structure identified by lpOpen.

9

Chapter

command MCI_CLOSE

Description

This command releases access to a device or file. As mentioned above, terminating an application without closing all MCI devices it has opened can leave those devices inaccessible until the computer is restarted. Your application should explicitly close each device or file when it is finished with it. MCI unloads the device when all instances of the device or all associated files are closed.

Applies to

All devices recognize this command.

Use

```
AMCIReturnValue := mciSendCommand(ADeviceID, MCI_CLOSE, FFlags, Longint(
                       @ATMCI_Gen_Parms_Struc));
```

Parameters (mciSendCommand):

lpClose: Final parameter is the address of an MCI_GENERIC_PARMS structure. (You can also use an MCI_CLOSE_PARMS structure.)

command MCI_ESCAPE

Description

This command sends a string (an escape sequence) directly to the device.

Applies to

Videodisc devices recognize this command.

Use

```
AMCIReturnValue := mciSendCommand(ADeviceID, MCI_ESCAPE, MCI_WAIT OR
                       MCI_NOTIFY OR MCI_VD_ESCAPE_STRING, Longint(
                       @AMCI_VD_ESCAPE_PARMS_Struc));
```

Parameters (mciSendCommand):

dwParam1: Additional flag, MCI_VD_ESCAPE_STRING, indicates that the MCI_VD_ESCAPE_PARMS structure contains a command string.

dwParam2: The address of an MCI_VD_ESCAPE_PARMS structure. The low-order word of the dwCallback field holds the window handle used for the MCI_NOTIFY flag. The lpstrCommand field holds the command to send to the device. When assigning data to the members of this structure, be sure to set the corresponding flags in the fdwCommand parameter of the MciSendCommand() function to validate the fields. This structure and its related structures are defined in mmsystem.pas as follows:

```
type
  PMCI_VD_Escape_ParmsA = ^TMCI_VD_Escape_ParmsA;
  PMCI_VD_Escape_ParmsW = ^TMCI_VD_Escape_ParmsW;
  PMCI_VD_Escape_Parms = PMCI_VD_Escape_ParmsA;
  tagMCI_VD_ESCAPE_PARMSA = record
    dwCallback: DWORD;
    lpstrCommand: PAnsiChar;
  end;
  tagMCI_VD_ESCAPE_PARMSW = record
    dwCallback: DWORD;
    lpstrCommand: PWideChar;
  end;
  tagMCI_VD_ESCAPE_PARMS = tagMCI_VD_ESCAPE_PARMSA;
  TMCI_VD_Escape_ParmsA = tagMCI_VD_ESCAPE_PARMSA;
  TMCI_VD_Escape_ParmsW = tagMCI_VD_ESCAPE_PARMSW;
  TMCI_VD_Escape_Parms = TMCI_VD_Escape_ParmsA;
  MCI_VD_ESCAPE_PARMSA = tagMCI_VD_ESCAPE_PARMSA;
  MCI_VD_ESCAPE_PARMSW = tagMCI_VD_ESCAPE_PARMSW;
  MCI_VD_ESCAPE_PARMS = MCI_VD_ESCAPE_PARMSA;
```

command MCI_PLAY

Description

This command signals the device to begin transmitting output data.

Applies to

CD audio, digital video, MIDI sequencer, videodisc, VCR, and waveform audio output devices recognize this command.

Use

```
AMCIReturnValue := mciSendCommand(ADeviceID, MCI_PLAY, FFlags, Longint(
                           @AMCI_Play_Parms_Struc);
```

Parameters (mciSendCommand):

dwParam1: The flags shown in Table 9-14 apply to all devices supporting MCI_PLAY; Tables 9-15 through 9-17 show flags for specific
devices including digital video, VCR, and videodisc devices.

dwParam2: The address of an MCI_PLAY_PARMS structure. (Devices
with extended command sets might replace this structure with a
device-specific structure.) For digital video devices, dwParam2
points to an MCI_DGV_PLAY_PARMS structure. For VCR devices,
dwParam2 points to an MCI_VCR_PLAY_PARMS structure. Neither
of these structures is included in mmsystem.pas. MCI_PLAY_PARMS
and its related structures are defined in mmsystem.pas as follows:

```
type
  PMCI_Play_Parms = ^TMCI_Play_Parms;
  tagMCI_PLAY_PARMS = record
    dwCallback: DWORD;
    dwFrom: DWORD;
    dwTo: DWORD;
  end;
  TMCI_Play_Parms = tagMCI_PLAY_PARMS;
  MCI_PLAY_PARMS = tagMCI_PLAY_PARMS;
```

Table 9-14: Flags for MCI_PLAY

Flag	Meaning
MCI_FROM	A starting location is included in the dwFrom member of the structure identified by lpPlay. The units assigned to the position values are specified with the MCI_SET_TIME_FORMAT flag of the MCI_SET command. If MCI_FROM is not specified, the starting location defaults to the current position.
MCI_TO	An ending location is included in the dwTo member of the structure identified by lpPlay. The units assigned to the position values are specified with the MCI_SET_TIME_FORMAT flag of MCI_SET. If MCI_TO is not specified, the ending location defaults to the end of the media.

Table 9-15: Flags for the digital video device type

Flag	Meaning
MCI_DGV_PLAY_REPEAT	Playback should start again at the beginning when the end of the content is reached.
MCI_DGV_PLAY_REVERSE	Playback should occur in reverse.

Flag	Meaning
MCI_MCIAVI_PLAY_WINDOW	Playback should occur in the window associated with a device instance (the default). (This flag is specific to MCIAVI.DRV.)
MCI_MCIAVI_PLAY_FULLSCREEN	Playback should use a fullscreen display. Use this flag only when playing compressed or 8-bit files.

Table 9-16: Flags for the VCR device type

Flag	Meaning
MCI_VCR_PLAY_AT	The dwAt member of the structure identified by dwParam2 contains a time when the entire command begins, or if the device is cued, when the device reaches the "from" position given by the MCI_CUE command.
MCI_VCR_PLAY_REVERSE	Playback should occur in reverse.
MCI_VCR_PLAY_SCAN	Playback should be as fast as possible while maintaining video output.

Table 9-17: Flags for the videodisc device type

Flag	Meaning
MCI_VD_PLAY_FAST	Play fast
MCI_VD_PLAY_REVERSE	Play in reverse
MCI_VD_PLAY_SCAN	Scan quickly
MCI_VD_PLAY_SLOW	Play slowly
MCI_VD_PLAY_SPEED	The playing speed is included in the dwSpeed member in the structure identified by dwParam2.

command MCI_SEEK

Description

This command changes the current position in the content as quickly as possible. Video and audio output are disabled during the seek. After the seek is complete, the device is stopped.

Applies to

CD audio, digital video, MIDI sequencer, VCR, videodisc, and waveform audio devices recognize this command.

9

Chapter

Use

```
AMCIReturnValue := mciSendCommand(ADeviceID, MCI_SEEK, FFlags, Longint(
                                  @AMCI_Seek_Parms_Struc);
```

Parameters (mciSendCommand):

dwParam1: The flags shown in Table 9-18 are generally ones that apply to all devices supporting MCI_SEEK. Tables 9-19 and 9-20 show additional flags used with specific devices such as the VCR and videodisc.

dwParam2: The address of an MCI_GENERIC_PARMS structure. (Devices with extended command sets might replace this structure with a device-specific structure.) For VCR devices, the dwParam2 parameter points to an MCI_VCR_SEEK_PARMS structure. This structure is not supported by the current implementation of mmsystem.pas.

Table 9-18: Flags used with the MCI_SEEK command

Flag	Meaning
MCI_SEEK_TO_END	Seek to the end of the content.
MCI_SEEK_TO_START	Seek to the beginning of the content.
MCI_TO	A particular position is included in the dwTo member of the structure identified by dwParam2. The units assigned to the position values are specified with the MCI_SET_TIME_FORMAT flag of the MCI_SET command. Do not use this flag with MCI_SEEK_TO_END or MCI_SEEK_TO_START.

Table 9-19: Flags used with VCR devices and the MCI_SEEK command

Flag	Meaning
MCI_VCR_SEEK_AT	The dwAt member of the structure identified by dwParam2 contains a time when the entire command begins.
MCI_VCR_SEEK_MARK	The dwMark member of the structure identified by dwParam2 contains the numbered mark for which to search.
MCI_VCR_SEEK_REVERSE	Seek direction is in reverse; this flag is used only with the MCI_VCR_SEEK_MARK flag.

Table 9-20: Flag used with videodisc and the MCI_SEEK command

Flag	Meaning
MCI_VD_SEEK_REVERSE	Seek direction is reverse.

command MCI_STOP

Description

This command stops all play and record sequences, unloads all play buffers, and ceases display of video images. The difference between the MCI_STOP and MCI_PAUSE commands depends on the device. If possible, MCI_PAUSE suspends device operation but leaves the device ready to resume play immediately. For the CD audio device, MCI_STOP resets the current track position to zero; in contrast, MCI_PAUSE maintains the current track position, anticipating that the device will resume playing.

Applies to

CD audio, digital video, MIDI sequencer, videodisc, VCR, and waveform audio devices recognize this command.

Use

```
AMCIReturnValue := mciSendCommand(ADeviceID, MCI_STOP, FFlags, Longint(
                                  @ATMCI_Gen_Parms_Struc);
```

Parameter (mciSendCommand):

dwParam2: The address of an MCI_GENERIC_PARMS structure. (Devices with extended command sets might replace this structure with a device-specific structure.) MCI_GENERIC_PARMS and its related structures are defined in mmsystem.pas as follows:

```
type
  PMCI_Generic_Parms = ^TMCI_Generic_Parms;
  tagMCI_GENERIC_PARMS = record
    dwCallback: DWORD;
  end;
  TMCI_Generic_Parms = tagMCI_GENERIC_PARMS;
  MCI_GENERIC_PARMS = tagMCI_GENERIC_PARMS;
```

9

Chapter

command MCI_PAUSE

Description

This command pauses the current action.

Applies to

CD audio, digital video, MIDI sequencer, VCR, videodisc, and waveform audio devices recognize this command.

Use

```
AMCIReturnValue := mciSendCommand(ADeviceID, MCI_PAUSE, FFlags, Longint(
                                  @ATMCI_Gen_Parms_Struc);
```

Parameter (mciSendCommand):

dwParam2: The address of an MCI_GENERIC_PARMS structure. (Devices with extended command sets might replace this structure with a device-specific structure.)

command MCI_INFO

Description

This command retrieves string information from a device. Information is returned in the lpstrReturn member of the structure identified by lpInfo. The dwRetSize member specifies the buffer length for the returned data.

Applies to

All devices recognize this command.

Use

```
AMCIReturnValue := mciSendCommand(ADeviceID, MCI_INFO, FFlags, Longint(
                                  @AMCI_Info_Parms_Struc);
```

Parameters (MciSendCommand):

dwParam1: Table 9-21 shows the standard, command-specific flag that applies to all devices supporting MCI_INFO. Device-specific flags for CD audio, digital video, sequencer devices, VCRs, overlay devices, and wave audio devices are described in Tables 9-22 through 9-27.

dwParam2: The address of an MCI_INFO_PARMS structure. (Devices with extended command sets might replace this structure with a device-specific structure.)

Table 9-21: Flag used with the MCI_INFO command

Flag	Meaning
MCI_INFO_PRODUCT	Obtains a description of the hardware associated with a device. Devices should supply a description that identifies both the driver and the hardware used.

Table 9-22: Flags used with CD audio and the MCI_INFO command

Flag	Meaning
MCI_INFO_MEDIA_IDENTITY	Produces a unique identifier for the audio CD currently loaded in the player being queried. This flag returns a string of 16 hexadecimal digits.
MCI_INFO_MEDIA_UPC	Produces the Universal Product Code (UPC) that is encoded on an audio CD. The UPC is a string of digits. It might not be available for all CDs.

Table 9-23: Flags used with videodisc and the MCI_INFO command

Flag	Meaning
MCI_DGV_INFO_ITEM	A constant indicating the information desired is included in the dwItem member of the structure identified by lpInfo. The constants in this table are defined for digital video devices.
MCI_DGV_INFO_AUDIO_ALG	Returns the name for the current audio compression algorithm.
MCI_DGV_INFO_AUDIO_QUALITY	Returns the name for the current audio quality descriptor.
MCI_DGV_INFO_STILL_ALG	Returns the name for the current still image compression algorithm.
MCI_DGV_INFO_STILL_QUALITY	Returns the name for the current still image quality descriptor.
MCI_DGV_INFO_USAGE	Returns a string describing usage restrictions that might be imposed by the owner of the visual or audible data in the workspace.
MCI_DGV_INFO_VIDEO_ALG	Returns the name for the current video compression algorithm.

9

Chapter

Flag	Meaning
MCI_DGV_INFO_VIDEO_QUALITY	Returns the name for the current video quality descriptor.
MCI_INFO_VERSION	Returns the release level of the device driver and hardware. Device driver developers must document the syntax of the returned string.
MCI_DGV_INFO_TEXT	Obtains the window caption.
MCI_INFO_FILE	Obtains the path and filename of the last file specified with the MCI_OPEN or MCI_LOAD command. If a file has not been specified, the device returns a null-terminated string. This flag is supported only by devices that return TRUE to the MCI_GETDEV-CAPS_USES_FILES flag of the MCI_GETDEVCAPS command. For digital video devices, lpInfo points to an MCI_DGV_INFO_PARMS structure.

Table 9-24: Flags used with sequencer devices and the MCI_INFO command

Flag	Meaning
MCI_INFO_COPYRIGHT	Obtains the copyright notice of a MIDI file from the copyright meta event.
MCI_INFO_FILE	Obtains the filename of the current file. NOTE: This flag is supported only by devices that return TRUE when they call the MCI_GETDEVCAPS command with the MCI_GETDEVCAPS_USES_FILES flag.
MCI_INFO_NAME	Obtains the sequence name from the sequence/track name meta event.

Table 9-25: Flag used with VCR devices and the MCI_INFO command

Flag	Meaning
MCI_VCR_INFO_VERSION	Sets the lpstrReturn member of the MCI_INFO_PARMS structure to point to the version number. Also sets the dwRetSize member equal to the length of the string pointed to.

Table 9-26: Flags used with overlay devices and the MCI_INFO command

Flag	Meaning
MCI_INFO_FILE	Obtains the filename of the current file. This flag is supported only by devices that return TRUE to the MCI_GETDEVCAPS_USES_FILES flag of the MCI_GETDEVCAPS command.
MCI_OVLY_INFO_TEXT	Obtains the caption of the window associated with the video overlay device.

Table 9-27: Flags used with wave audio devices and the MCI_INFO command

Flag	Meaning
MCI_INFO_FILE	Obtains the filename of the current file. This flag is supported by devices that return TRUE when you call the MCI_GETDEVCAPS command with the MCI_GETDEVCAPS_USES_FILES flag.
MCI_WAVE_INPUT	Obtains the product name of the current input.
MCI_WAVE_OUTPUT	Obtains the product name of the current output and its value is device specific.

command MCI_SPIN

Description

This command starts the device spinning up or down.

Applies to

Videodisc devices recognize this command.

Use

```
AMCIReturnValue := mciSendCommand(ADeviceID, MCI_SPIN, FFlags, Longint(
                                  @ATMCI_Gen_Parms_Struc);
```

Parameters (mciSendCommand):

dwParam1: The following additional flags apply to videodisc devices:

- ■ MCI_VD_SPIN_DOWN   Stops the disc spinning.
- ■ MCI_VD_SPIN_UP   Starts the disc spinning.

dwParam2: The address of an MCI_GENERIC_PARMS structure. (Devices with extended command sets might replace this structure with a device-specific structure.)

command MCI_SET

Description

This command sets device information.

Applies to

CD audio, digital video, MIDI sequencer, VCR, videodisc, video overlay, and waveform audio devices recognize this command.

Use

```
AMCIReturnValue := mciSendCommand(ADeviceID, MCI_SET, FFlags, Longint(
                                  @AMCI_Set_Parms_Struc);
```

Parameter (mciSendCommand):

dwParam2: The address of an MCI_SET_PARMS structure. (Devices with extended command sets might replace this structure with a device-specific structure.) MCI_SET_PARMS and its related structures are defined in mmsystem.pas as follows:

```
type
  PMCI_Set_Parms = ^TMCI_Set_Parms;
  tagMCI_SET_PARMS = record
    dwCallback: DWORD;
    dwTimeFormat: DWORD;
    dwAudio: DWORD;
  end;
  TMCI_Set_Parms = tagMCI_SET_PARMS;
  MCI_SET_PARMS = tagMCI_SET_PARMS;
```

command MCI_STEP

Description

This command steps the player one or more frames.

Applies to

Digital video, VCR, and CAV format videodisc devices recognize this command.

Use

```
AMCIReturnValue := mciSendCommand(ADeviceID, MCI_STEP, FFlags, Longint(
                                  @ATMCI_Gen_Parms_Struc);
```

Parameter (mciSendCommand):

dwParam2: The address of an MCI_GENERIC_PARMS structure. (Devices
with extended command sets might replace this structure with a
device-specific structure.)

command MCI_RECORD

Description

This command starts recording from the current position or from one
specified location to another specified location.

Applies to

VCR and waveform audio devices recognize this command. Although
digital video devices and MIDI sequencers also recognize this command,
the MCIAVI and MCISEQ drivers do not implement it.

Use

```
AMCIReturnValue := mciSendCommand(ADeviceID, MCI_RECORD, FFlags, Longint(
                                  @AMCI_Record_Parms_Struc);
```

Parameter (mciSendCommand):

dwParam2: The address of an MCI_RECORD_PARMS structure. (Devices
with extended command sets might replace this structure with a
device-specific structure.) This structure and its related structures
are defined in mmsystem.pas as follows:

```
type
  PMCI_Record_Parms = ^TMCI_Record_Parms;
  tagMCI_RECORD_PARMS = record
    dwCallback: DWORD;
    dwFrom: DWORD;
    dwTo: DWORD;
  end;
  TMCI_Record_Parms = tagMCI_RECORD_PARMS;
  MCI_RECORD_PARMS = tagMCI_RECORD_PARMS;
```

command MCI_SYSINFO

Description

This command retrieves information about MCI devices. MCI supports
this command directly rather than passing it to the device. Any MCI

application can use this command. String information is returned in the application-supplied buffer pointed to by the lpstrReturn member of the structure identified by dwParam2. Numeric information is returned as a Double Word value placed in the application-supplied buffer. The dwRetSize member specifies the buffer length. The wDeviceType member of the structure identified by dwParam2 is used to indicate the device type of the query. If the wDeviceID parameter is set to MCI_ALL_DEVICE_ID, it overrides the value of wDeviceType. Integer return values are Double Word values returned in the buffer pointed to by the lpstrReturn member of the structure identified by dwParam2. String return values are null-terminated strings returned in the buffer pointed to by the lpstrReturn member of the structure identified by dwParam2.

Applies to

Does not apply specifically to devices but to the system as a whole.

Use

```
AMCIReturnValue := mciSendCommand(ADeviceID, MCI_SYSINFO, FFlags, Longint(
                                  @AMCI_Sysinfo_Parms_Struc);
```

Parameters (MciSendCommand):

dwParam1: Table 9-28 shows the standard and command-specific flags, of which you can use one or more with this function.

dwParam2: The address of an MCI_SYSINFO_PARMS structure. This structure and its related structures are defined in mmsystem.pas as follows:

```
type
  PMCI_SysInfo_ParmsA = ^TMCI_SysInfo_ParmsA;
  PMCI_SysInfo_ParmsW = ^TMCI_SysInfo_ParmsW;
  PMCI_SysInfo_Parms = PMCI_SysInfo_ParmsA;
  tagMCI_SYSINFO_PARMSA = record
    dwCallback: DWORD;
    lpstrReturn: PAnsiChar;
    dwRetSize: DWORD;
    dwNumber: DWORD;
    wDeviceType: UINT;
  end;
  tagMCI_SYSINFO_PARMSW = record
    dwCallback: DWORD;
    lpstrReturn: PWideChar;
    dwRetSize: DWORD;
```

```
      dwNumber: DWORD;
      wDeviceType: UINT;
   end;
   tagMCI_SYSINFO_PARMS = tagMCI_SYSINFO_PARMSA;
   TMCI_SysInfo_ParmsA = tagMCI_SYSINFO_PARMSA;
   TMCI_SysInfo_ParmsW = tagMCI_SYSINFO_PARMSW;
   TMCI_SysInfo_Parms = TMCI_SysInfo_ParmsA;
   MCI_SYSINFO_PARMSA = tagMCI_SYSINFO_PARMSA;
   MCI_SYSINFO_PARMSW = tagMCI_SYSINFO_PARMSW;
   MCI_SYSINFO_PARMS = MCI_SYSINFO_PARMSA;
```

Table 9-28: Flags used with the MCI_SYSINFO command

Flag	Meaning
MCI_SYSINFO_INSTALLNAME	Obtains the name (listed in the registry or the SYSTEM.INI file) used to install the device.
MCI_SYSINFO_NAME	Obtains a device name corresponding to the device number specified in the dwNumber member of the structure identified by dwParam2. If the MCI_SYSINFO_OPEN flag is set, MCI returns the names of open devices.
MCI_SYSINFO_OPEN	Obtains the quantity or name of open devices.
MCI_SYSINFO_QUANTITY	Obtains the number of devices of the specified type that are listed in the registry or the [mci] section of the SYSTEM.INI file. If the MCI_SYSINFO_OPEN flag is set, the number of open devices is returned.

command MCI_BREAK

Description

This command sets a break key for an MCI device. MCI supports this command directly rather than passing it to the device. Be aware that you might have to press the break key multiple times to interrupt a wait operation. Pressing the break key after a device wait is canceled can send the break to an application. If an application has an action defined for the virtual key-code, then it can inadvertently respond to the break. For example, an application using VK_CANCEL for an accelerator key can respond to the default Ctrl+Break key if it is pressed after a wait is canceled.

Applies to

Any MCI application can use this command.

9

Chapter

Use

```
AMCIReturnValue := mciSendCommand(ADeviceID, MCI_BREAK, FFlags, Longint(
                                  @AMCI_Break_Parms_Struc);
```

Parameters (mciSendCommand):

dwParam1: Table 9-29 contains the flags used with the MCI_BREAK command.

dwParam2: Address of an MCI_BREAK_PARMS structure. This structure and its related structures are defined in mmsystem.pas as follows:

```
type
  PMCI_Break_Parms = ^TMCI_BReak_Parms;
  tagMCI_BREAK_PARMS = record
    dwCallback: DWORD;
    nVirtKey: Integer;
    hWndBreak: HWND;
  end;
  TMCI_BReak_Parms = tagMCI_BREAK_PARMS;
  MCI_BREAK_PARMS = tagMCI_BREAK_PARMS;
```

Table 9-29: Flags used with the MCI_BREAK command

Flag	Meaning
MCI_BREAK_HWND	The hwndBreak member of the structure identified by lpBreak contains a window handle that must be the current window in order to enable break detection for that MCI device. This is usually the application's main window. If omitted, MCI does not check the window handle of the current window.
MCI_BREAK_KEY	The nVirtKey member of the structure identified by lpBreak specifies the virtual key-code used for the break key. By default, MCI assigns Ctrl+Break as the break key. This flag is required if MCI_BREAK_OFF is not specified.
MCI_BREAK_OFF	Disables any existing break key for the indicated device.

command MCI_SAVE

Description

This command saves the current file. Devices that modify files should not destroy the original copy until they receive the save message.

Applies to

Video overlay and waveform audio devices recognize this command. Although digital video devices and MIDI sequencers also recognize this command, the MCIAVI and MCISEQ drivers do not implement it.

Use

```
AMCIReturnValue := mciSendCommand(ADeviceID, MCI_SAVE, FFlags, Longint(
                                  @AMCI_Save_Parms_Struc);
```

Parameters (mciSendCommand):

dwParam1: Tables 9-30 and 9-31 show the additional flags used with the digital video and overlay device types.

dwParam2: The address of an MCI_SAVE_PARMS structure. (Devices with additional parameters might replace this structure with a device-specific structure.) For digital video devices, the lpSave parameter points to an MCI_DGV_SAVE_PARMS structure. This structure is not currently supported in mmsystem.pas. For video overlay devices, the lpSave parameter points to an MCI_OVLY_SAVE_PARMS structure. The MCI_SAVE_PARMS structure, the MCI_OVLY_SAVE_PARMS structure, and their related structures are defined in mmsystem.pas as follows:

```
type
  PMCI_Save_ParmsA = ^TMCI_SaveParmsA;
  PMCI_Save_ParmsW = ^TMCI_SaveParmsW;
  PMCI_Save_Parms = PMCI_Save_ParmsA;
  TMCI_SaveParmsA = record
    dwCallback: DWORD;
    lpfilename: PAnsiChar;
  end;
  TMCI_SaveParmsW = record
    dwCallback: DWORD;
    lpfilename: PWideChar;
  end;
  TMCI_SAVE_PARMS = TMCI_SaveParmsA;

type
  PMCI_Ovly_Save_ParmsA = ^TMCI_Ovly_Save_ParmsA;
  PMCI_Ovly_Save_ParmsW = ^TMCI_Ovly_Save_ParmsW;
  PMCI_Ovly_Save_Parms = PMCI_Ovly_Save_ParmsA;
  tagMCI_OVLY_SAVE_PARMSA = record
    dwCallback: DWORD;
```

```
        lpfilename: PAnsiChar;
        rc: TRect;
     end;
     tagMCI_OVLY_SAVE_PARMSW = record
        dwCallback: DWORD;
        lpfilename: PWideChar;
        rc: TRect;
     end;
     tagMCI_OVLY_SAVE_PARMS = tagMCI_OVLY_SAVE_PARMSA;
     TMCI_Ovly_Save_ParmsA = tagMCI_OVLY_SAVE_PARMSA;
     TMCI_Ovly_Save_ParmsW = tagMCI_OVLY_SAVE_PARMSW;
     TMCI_Ovly_Save_Parms = TMCI_Ovly_Save_ParmsA;
     MCI_OVLY_SAVE_PARMSA = tagMCI_OVLY_SAVE_PARMSA;
     MCI_OVLY_SAVE_PARMSW = tagMCI_OVLY_SAVE_PARMSW;
     MCI_OVLY_SAVE_PARMS = MCI_OVLY_SAVE_PARMSA;
```

Table 9-30: Flags used with digital video devices and the MCI_SAVE command

Flag	Meaning
MCI_DGV_RECT	The rc member of the structure identified by lpSave contains a valid rectangle. The rectangle specifies a region of the frame buffer that will be saved to the specified file. The first pair of coordinates specifies the upper left corner of the rectangle; the second pair specifies the width and height. Digital video devices must use the MCI_CAPTURE command to capture the contents of the frame buffer. (Video overlay devices should also use MCI_CAPTURE.) This flag is for compatibility with the existing MCI video overlay command set.
MCI_DGV_SAVE_ABORT	Stops a save operation in progress. This must be the only flag present.
MCI_DGV_SAVE_KEEPRESERVE	Unused disk space left over from the original MCI_RESERVE command is not deallocated.

Table 9-31: Flag used with overlay devices and the MCI_SAVE command

Flag	Meaning
MCI_OVLY_RECT	The rc member of the structure identified by lpSave contains a valid display rectangle indicating the area of the video buffer to save.

command MCI_STATUS

Description

This command retrieves information about an MCI device. Information is returned in the dwReturn member of the structure identified by the dwParam2 parameter.

Applies to

All devices recognize this command.

Use

```
AMCIReturnValue := mciSendCommand(ADeviceID, MCI_STATUS, FFlags, Longint(
                                  @AMCI_Status_Parms_Struc);
```

Parameters (mciSendCommand):

dwParam1: Table 9-32 describes the standard and command-specific flags that apply to all devices supporting MCI_STATUS. Tables 9-33 through 9-47 describe device-specific flags.

dwParam2: The address of an MCI_STATUS_PARMS structure. (Devices with extended command sets might replace this structure with a device-specific structure.) For digital video devices, the lpStatus parameter points to an MCI_DGV_STATUS_PARMS structure. For VCR devices, the lpStatus parameter points to an MCI_VCR_STATUS_PARMS structure. Neither of these structures is included in the current version of mmsystem.pas. Using the MCI_STATUS_LENGTH flag to determine the length of the media always returns 2 hours for VCR devices, unless the length has been explicitly changed using the MCI_SET command. The MCI_STATUS_PARMS structure and its related structures are defined in mmsystem.pas as follows:

```
type
  PMCI_Status_Parms = ^TMCI_Status_Parms;
  tagMCI_STATUS_PARMS = record
    dwCallback: DWORD;
    dwReturn: DWORD;
    dwItem: DWORD;
    dwTrack: DWORD;
  end;
  TMCI_Status_Parms = tagMCI_STATUS_PARMS;
  MCI_STATUS_PARMS = tagMCI_STATUS_PARMS;
```

9

Chapter

Table 9-32: Flags used with the MCI_STATUS command

Flag	Meaning
MCI_STATUS_ITEM	Specifies that the dwItem member of the structure identified by lpStatus contains a constant specifying which status item to obtain. The remaining constants in this table define which status item to return in the dwReturn member of the structure.
MCI_STATUS_CURRENT_ TRACK	The dwReturn member is set to the current track number. MCI uses continuous track numbers.
MCI_STATUS_LENGTH	The dwReturn member is set to the total media length.
MCI_STATUS_MODE	The dwReturn member is set to the current mode of the device. The modes include the following: MCI_MODE_ NOT_READY, MCI_MODE_PAUSE, MCI_MODE_PLAY, MCI_MODE_STOP, MCI_MODE_OPEN, MCI_MODE_ RECORD, and MCI_MODE_SEEK.
MCI_STATUS_NUMBER_ OF_TRACKS	The dwReturn member is set to the total number of playable tracks.
MCI_STATUS_POSITION	The dwReturn member is set to the current position.
MCI_STATUS_READY	The dwReturn member is set to TRUE if the device is ready; it is set to FALSE otherwise.
MCI_STATUS_TIME_ FORMAT	The dwReturn member is set to the current time format of the device. The time formats include: MCI_FORMAT_BYTES, MCI_FORMAT_FRAMES, MCI_FORMAT_HMS, MCI_FORMAT_MILLISECONDS, MCI_FORMAT_MSF, MCI_FORMAT_SAMPLES, and MCI_FORMAT_TMSF.
MCI_STATUS_START	Obtains the starting position of the media. To get the starting position, combine this flag with MCI_STATUS_ ITEM and set the dwItem member of the structure identified by lpStatus to MCI_STATUS_POSITION.
MCI_TRACK	Indicates a status track parameter is included in the dwTrack member of the structure identified by lpStatus. You must use this flag with the MCI_STATUS_POSITION or MCI_STATUS_LENGTH constants. When used with MCI_STATUS_POSITION, MCI_TRACK obtains the starting position of the specified track. When used with MCI_STATUS_LENGTH, MCI_TRACK obtains the length of the specified track. MCI uses continuous track numbers.

The additional flags shown in Table 9-33 are used with the CD audio device type. These constants are used in the dwItem member of the structure pointed to by the lpStatus parameter when MCI_STATUS_ITEM is specified for the dwFlags parameter.

Table 9-33: Flags used with CD audio and the MCI_STATUS command

Flag	Meaning
MCI_CDA_STATUS_TYPE_TRACK	The dwReturn member is set to one of the following values: MCI_CDA_TRACK_AUDIO or MCI_CDA_TRACK_OTHER. To use this flag, the MCI_TRACK flag must be set, and the dwTrack member of the structure identified by lpStatus must contain a valid track number.
MCI_STATUS_MEDIA_PRESENT	The dwReturn member is set to TRUE if the media is inserted in the device; it is set to FALSE otherwise.

The additional flags shown in Table 9-34 are used with the digital video device type.

Table 9-34: Flags used with digital video and the MCI_STATUS command

Flag	Meaning
MCI_DGV_STATUS_DISKSPACE	The lpstrDrive member of the structure identified by lpStatus specifies a disk drive or, in some implementations, a path. The MCI_STATUS command returns the approximate amount of disk space that could be obtained by the MCI_RESERVE command in the dwReturn member of the structure identified by lpStatus. The disk space is measured in units of the current time format.
MCI_DGV_STATUS_INPUT	The constant specified by the dwItem member of the structure identified by lpStatus applies to the input.
MCI_DGV_STATUS_LEFT	The constant specified by the dwItem member of the structure identified by lpStatus applies to the left audio channel.
MCI_DGV_STATUS_NOMINAL	The constant specified by the dwItem member of the structure identified by lpStatus requests the nominal value rather than the current value.

9

Chapter

Flag	Meaning
MCI_DGV_STATUS_OUTPUT	The constant specified by the dwItem member of the structure identified by lpStatus applies to the output.
MCI_DGV_STATUS_RECORD	The frame rate returned for the MCI_DGV_STATUS_FRAME_RATE flag is the rate used for compression.
MCI_DGV_STATUS_REFERENCE	The dwReturn member of the structure identified by lpStatus returns the nearest key frame image that precedes the frame specified in the dwReference member.
MCI_DGV_STATUS_RIGHT	The constant specified by the dwItem member of the structure identified by lpStatus applies to the right audio channel.

The constants shown in Table 9-35 are used with the digital video device type in the dwItem member of the structure pointed to by the lpStatus parameter when MCI_STATUS_ITEM is specified for the dwFlags parameter.

Table 9-35: Flags used with digital video and the MCI_STATUS command

Flag	Meaning
MCI_AVI_STATUS_AUDIO_BREAKS	The dwReturn member returns the number of times the audio portion of the last AVI sequence broke up. The system counts an audio break whenever it attempts to write audio data to the device driver and discovers that the driver has already played all of the available data. This flag is recognized only by the MCIAVI digital video driver.
MCI_AVI_STATUS_FRAMES_SKIPPED	The dwReturn member returns the number of frames that were not drawn when the last AVI sequence was played. This flag is recognized only by the MCIAVI digital video driver
MCI_AVI_STATUS_LAST_PLAY_SPEED	The dwReturn member returns a value representing how closely the actual playing time of the last AVI sequence matched the target playing time. The value of 1000 indicates that the target time and the actual time were the same. A value of 2000, for example, would indicate that the AVI sequence took twice as long to play as it should have. This flag is recognized only by the MCIAVI digital video driver.

Flag	Meaning
MCI_DGV_STATUS_AUDIO	The dwReturn member returns MCI_ON or MCI_OFF depending on the most recent MCI_SET_AUDIO option for the MCI_SET command. It returns MCI_ON if either or both speakers are enabled, and MCI_OFF otherwise.
MCI_DGV_STATUS_AUDIO_ INPUT	The dwReturn member returns the approximate instantaneous audio level of the analog audio signal. A value greater than 1000 implies there is clipping distortion. Some devices can determine this value only while recording audio. This status value has no associated MCI_SET or MCI_SETAUDIO command. This value is related to, but normalized differently than the waveform audio command MCI_WAVE_STATUS_ LEVEL.
MCI_DGV_STATUS_AUDIO_ RECORD	The dwReturn member returns MCI_ON or MCI_OFF reflecting the state set by the MCI_DGV_SETAUDIO_ RECORD flag of the MCI_SETAUDIO command.
MCI_DGV_STATUS_AUDIO_ SOURCE	The dwReturn member returns the current audio digitizer source, one of the MCI_DGV_SETAUDIO_ constants described in Table 9-36.
MCI_DGV_STATUS_AUDIO_ STREAM	The dwReturn member returns the current audio stream number.
MCI_DGV_STATUS_ AVGBYTESPERSEC	The dwReturn member returns the average number of bytes per second used for recording.
MCI_DGV_STATUS_BASS	The dwReturn member returns the current audio bass level. Use MCI_DGV_STATUS_NOMINAL with this flag to obtain the nominal level.
MCI_DGV_STATUS_BITS PERPEL	The dwReturn member returns the number of bits per pixel used for saving captured or recorded data.
MCI_DGV_STATUS_BITSPER SAMPLE	The dwReturn member returns the number of bits per sample the device uses for recording. This applies only to devices supporting the PCM format.
MCI_DGV_STATUS_BLOCK ALIGN	The dwReturn member returns the alignment of data blocks relative to the start of the input waveform.
MCI_DGV_STATUS_ BRIGHTNESS	The dwReturn member returns the current video brightness level. Use MCI_DGV_STATUS_NOMINAL with this flag to obtain the nominal level.

9

Chapter

Flag	Meaning
MCI_DGV_STATUS_COLOR	The dwReturn member returns the current color level. Use MCI_DGV_STATUS_NOMINAL with this flag to obtain the nominal level.
MCI_DGV_STATUS_ CONTRAST	The dwReturn member returns the current contrast level. Use MCI_DGV_STATUS_NOMINAL with this flag to obtain the nominal level.
MCI_DGV_STATUS_FILE FORMAT	The dwReturn member returns the current file format for recording or saving.
MCI_DGV_STATUS_FILE_ MODE	The dwReturn member returns the state of the file operation, one of the file modes indicated by the MCI_DGV_FILE_MODE_ constants described in Table 9-37.
MCI_DGV_STATUS_FILE_ COMPLETION	The dwReturn member returns the estimated percentage a load, save, capture, cut, copy, delete, paste, or undo operation has progressed. (Applications can use this to provide a visual indicator of progress.) This flag is not supported by all digital video devices.
MCI_DGV_STATUS_ FORWARD	The dwReturn member returns TRUE if the device direction is forward or the device is not playing.
MCI_DGV_STATUS_FRAME_ RATE	The dwReturn member must be used with MCI_DGV_STATUS_NOMINAL, MCI_DGV_ STATUS_RECORD, or both. When used with MCI_DGV_STATUS_RECORD, the current frame rate used for recording is returned. When used with both MCI_DGV_STATUS_RECORD and MCI_DGV_ STATUS_NOMINAL, the nominal frame rate associated with the input video signal is returned. When used with MCI_DGV_STATUS_NOMINAL, the nominal frame rate associated with the file is returned. In all cases the units are in frames per second multiplied by 1000.
MCI_DGV_STATUS_GAMMA	The dwReturn member returns the current gamma value. Use MCI_DGV_STATUS_NOMINAL with this flag to obtain the nominal level.
MCI_DGV_STATUS_HPAL	The dwReturn member returns the ASCII decimal value for the current palette handle. The handle is contained in the low-order word of the returned value.

Flag	Meaning
MCI_DGV_STATUS_HWND	The dwReturn member returns the ASCII decimal value for the current explicit or default window handle associated with this device driver instance. The handle is contained in the low-order word of the returned value.
MCI_DGV_STATUS_KEY_COLOR	The dwReturn member returns the current key color value.
MCI_DGV_STATUS_KEY_INDEX	The dwReturn member returns the current key index value.
MCI_DGV_STATUS_MONITOR	The dwReturn member returns a constant indicating the source of the current presentation. The constants are defined in Table 9-38.
MCI_DGV_STATUS_PAUSE_MODE	The dwReturn member returns MCI_MODE_PLAY if the device was paused while playing and returns MCI_MODE_RECORD if the device was paused while recording. The command returns MCIERR_NON-APPLICABLE_FUNCTION as an error return if the device is not paused.
MCI_DGV_STATUS_SAMPLESPERSECOND	The dwReturn member returns the number of samples per second recorded.
MCI_DGV_STATUS_SEEK_EXACTLY	The dwReturn member returns TRUE or FALSE indicating whether or not the seek exactly format is set. (Applications can set this format by using the MCI_SET command with the MCI_DGV_SET_SEEK_EXACTLY flag.)
MCI_DGV_STATUS_SHARPNESS	The dwReturn member returns the current sharpness level. Use MCI_DGV_STATUS_NOMINAL with this flag to obtain the nominal level.
MCI_DGV_STATUS_SIZE	The dwReturn member returns the approximate playback duration of compressed data that the reserved workspace will hold. The duration units are in the current time format. It returns zero if there is no reserved disk space. The size returned is approximate since the precise disk space for compressed data cannot, in general, be predicted until after the data has been compressed.
MCI_DGV_STATUS_SMPTE	The dwReturn member returns the SMPTE time code associated with the current position in the workspace.

9

Chapter

Flag	Meaning
MCI_DGV_STATUS_SPEED	The dwReturn member returns the current playback speed.
MCI_DGV_STATUS_STILL_FILEFORMAT	The dwReturn member returns the current file format for the MCI_CAPTURE command.
MCI_DGV_STATUS_TINT	The dwReturn member returns the current video tint level. Use MCI_DGV_STATUS_NOMINAL with this flag to obtain the nominal level.
MCI_DGV_STATUS_TREBLE	The dwReturn member returns the current audio treble level. Use MCI_DGV_STATUS_NOMINAL with this flag to obtain the nominal level.
MCI_DGV_STATUS_UNSAVED	The dwReturn member returns TRUE if there is recorded data in the workspace that might be lost as a result of an MCI_CLOSE, MCI_LOAD, MCI_RECORD, MCI_RESERVE, MCI_CUT, MCI_DELETE, or MCI_PASTE command. The member returns FALSE otherwise.
MCI_DGV_STATUS_VIDEO	The dwReturn member returns MCI_ON if video is enabled or MCI_OFF if it is disabled.
MCI_DGV_STATUS_VIDEO_RECORD	The dwReturn member returns MCI_ON or MCI_OFF, reflecting the state set by the MCI_DGV_SETVIDEO_RECORD flag of the MCI_SETVIDEO command.
MCI_DGV_STATUS_VIDEO_SOURCE	The dwReturn member returns a constant indicating the type of video source set by the MCI_DGV_SETVIDEO_SOURCE flag of the MCI_SETVIDEO command.
MCI_DGV_STATUS_VIDEO_SRC_NUM	The dwReturn member returns the number within its type of the video input source currently active.
MCI_DGV_STATUS_VIDEO_STREAM	The dwReturn member returns the current video stream number.
MCI_DGV_STATUS_VOLUME	The dwReturn member returns the average of the volume to the left and right speakers. Use MCI_DGV_STATUS_NOMINAL with this flag to obtain the nominal level.
MCI_DGV_STATUS_WINDOW_VISIBLE	The dwReturn member returns TRUE if the window is not hidden.
MCI_DGV_STATUS_WINDOW_MINIMIZED	The dwReturn member returns TRUE if the window is minimized.

Flag	Meaning
MCI_DGV_STATUS_WINDOW_MAXIMIZED	The dwReturn member returns TRUE if the window is maximized.
MCI_STATUS_MEDIA_PRESENT	The dwReturn member returns TRUE.

Table 9-36: Flags used with the MCI_DGV_STATUS_AUDIO_RECORD flag of the MCI_STATUS command

Flag	Meaning
MCI_DGV_SETAUDIO_AVERAGE	Specifies the average of the left and right audio channels.
MCI_DGV_SETAUDIO_LEFT	Specifies the left audio channel.
MCI_DGV_SETAUDIO_RIGHT	Specifies the right audio channel.
MCI_DGV_SETAUDIO_STEREO	Specifies stereo.

Table 9-37: File mode flags used with the MCI_DGV_STATUS_FILE_MODE flag of the MCI_STATUS command

Flag	Meaning
MCI_DGV_FILE_MODE_EDITING	Returned during cut, copy, delete, paste, and undo operations.
MCI_DGV_FILE_MODE_IDLE	Returned when the file is ready for the next operation.
MCI_DGV_FILE_MODE_LOADING	Returned while the file is being loaded.
MCI_DGV_FILE_MODE_SAVING	Returned while the file is being saved.

Table 9-38: Monitoring mode flags used with the MCI_DGV_STATUS_MONITOR flag of the MCI_STATUS command

Flag	Meaning
MCI_DGV_MONITOR_FILE	A file is the source.
MCI_DGV_MONITOR_INPUT	The input is the source.
MCI_DGV_STATUS_MONITOR_METHOD	The dwReturn member returns a constant indicating the method used for input monitoring. The constants are defined in Table 9-39.

9

Chapter

Table 9-39: Monitoring mode flags used with the MCI_DGV_STATUS_MONITOR_METHOD flag of the MCI_STATUS command

Flag	Meaning
MCI_DGV_METHOD_DIRECT	Direct input monitoring
MCI_DGV_METHOD_POST	Post-input monitoring
MCI_DGV_METHOD_PRE	Pre-input monitoring

The following flags described in Table 9-40 are used with the sequencer device type. These constants are used in the dwItem member of the structure pointed to by the lpStatus parameter when MCI_STATUS_ITEM is specified for the dwFlags parameter.

Table 9-40: Flags used with sequencer devices and the MCI_STATUS command

Flag	Meaning
MCI_SEQ_STATUS_DIVTYPE	The dwReturn member is set to one of the following values indicating the current division type of a sequence: MCI_SEQ_DIV_PPQN, MCI_SEQ_DIV_SMPTE_24, MCI_SEQ_DIV_SMPTE_25, MCI_SEQ_DIV_SMPTE_30, or MCI_SEQ_DIV_SMPTE_30DROP.
MCI_SEQ_STATUS_MASTER	The dwReturn member is set to the synchronization type used for master operation.
MCI_SEQ_STATUS_OFFSET	The dwReturn member is set to the current SMPTE offset of a sequence.
MCI_SEQ_STATUS_PORT	The dwReturn member is set to the MIDI device identifier for the current port used by the sequence.
MCI_SEQ_STATUS_SLAVE	The dwReturn member is set to the synchronization type used for slave operation.
MCI_SEQ_STATUS_TEMPO	The dwReturn member is set to the current tempo of a MIDI sequence in beats per minute for PPQN files, or frames per second for SMPTE files.
MCI_STATUS_MEDIA_PRESENT	The dwReturn member is set to TRUE if the media is inserted in the device; it is set to FALSE otherwise.

The additional flags described in Table 9-41 are used with the VCR device type. These constants are used in the dwItem member of the structure pointed to by the lpStatus parameter when MCI_STATUS_ITEM is specified for the dwFlags parameter.

Table 9-41: Flags used with VCR devices and the MCI_STATUS command

Flag	Meaning
MCI_STATUS_MEDIA_ PRESENT	The dwReturn member is set to TRUE if the media is inserted in the device; it is set to FALSE otherwise.
MCI_VCR_STATUS_ ASSEMBLE_RECORD	The dwReturn member is set to TRUE if assemble mode is on; it is set to FALSE otherwise.
MCI_VCR_STATUS_AUDIO_ MONITOR	The dwReturn member is set to a constant, indicating the currently selected audio monitor type.
MCI_VCR_STATUS_AUDIO_ MONITOR_NUMBER	The dwReturn member is set to the number of the currently selected audio monitor type.
MCI_VCR_STATUS_AUDIO_ RECORD	The dwReturn member is set to TRUE if audio will be recorded when the next record command is given; it is set to FALSE otherwise. If you specify MCI_TRACK in the dwFlags parameter of this command, dwTrack contains the track to which this inquiry applies.
MCI_VCR_STATUS_AUDIO_ SOURCE	The dwReturn member is set to a constant, indicating the current audio source type.
MCI_VCR_STATUS_AUDIO_ SOURCE_NUMBER	The dwReturn member is set to the number of the currently selected audio source type.
MCI_VCR_STATUS_CLOCK	The dwReturn member is set to the current clock value, in total clock increments.
MCI_VCR_STATUS_CLOCK_ ID	The dwReturn member is set to a number that uniquely describes the clock in use.
MCI_VCR_STATUS_ COUNTER_FORMAT	The dwReturn member is set to a constant describing the current counter format. For more information, see the MCI_SET_TIME_FORMAT flag of the MCI_SET command.
MCI_VCR_STATUS_ COUNTER_RESOLUTION	The dwReturn member is set to a constant describing the resolution of the counter, and is one of the values shown in Table 9-42.
MCI_VCR_STATUS_ COUNTER_VALUE	The dwReturn member is set to the current counter reading, in the current counter time format.
MCI_VCR_STATUS_FRAME_ RATE	The dwReturn member is set to the current native frame rate of the device.

9

Chapter

Flag	Meaning
MCI_VCR_STATUS_INDEX	The dwReturn member is set to a constant, describing the current contents of the on-screen display, and is one of the following: MCI_VCR_INDEX_COUNTER, MCI_VCR_INDEX_DATE, MCI_VCR_INDEX_TIME, or MCI_VCR_INDEX_TIMECODE.
MCI_VCR_STATUS_INDEX_ON	The dwReturn member is set to TRUE if the on-screen display is on; it is set to FALSE otherwise.
MCI_VCR_STATUS_MEDIA_TYPE	The dwReturn member is set to one of the following: MCI_VCR_MEDIA_8MM, MCI_VCR_MEDIA_HI8, MCI_VCR_MEDIA_VHS, MCI_VCR_MEDIA_SVHS, MCI_VCR_MEDIA_BETA, MCI_VCR_MEDIA_EDBETA, or MCI_VCR_MEDIA_OTHER.
MCI_VCR_STATUS_NUMBER	The dwNumber member is set to the logical tuner number when you use this flag with the MCI_VCR_STATUS_TUNER_CHANNEL flag.
MCI_VCR_STATUS_NUMBER_OF_AUDIO_TRACKS	The dwReturn member is set to the number of audio tracks that are independently selectable.
MCI_VCR_STATUS_NUMBER_OF_VIDEO_TRACKS	The dwReturn member is set to the number of video tracks that are independently selectable.
MCI_VCR_STATUS_PAUSE_TIMEOUT	The dwReturn member is set to the maximum duration, in milliseconds, of a pause command. The return value of zero indicates that no time out will occur.
MCI_VCR_STATUS_PLAY_FORMAT	The dwReturn member is set to one of the following: MCI_VCR_FORMAT_EP, MCI_VCR_FORMAT_LP, MCI_VCR_FORMAT_OTHER, or MCI_VCR_FORMAT_SP.
MCI_VCR_STATUS_POSTROLL_DURATION	The dwReturn member is set to the length of the videotape that will play after the spot at which it was stopped, in the current time format. This is needed to brake the VCR tape transport from a stop or pause command.
MCI_VCR_STATUS_POWER_ON	The dwReturn member is set to TRUE if the power is on; it is set to FALSE otherwise.
MCI_VCR_STATUS_PREROLL_DURATION	The dwReturn member is set to the length of the videotape that will play before the spot at which it was started, in the current time format. This is needed to stabilize the VCR output.

Flag	Meaning
MCI_VCR_STATUS_RECORD _FORMAT	The dwReturn member is set to one of the following: MCI_VCR_FORMAT_EP, MCI_VCR_FORMAT_LP, MCI_VCR_FORMAT_OTHER, or MCI_VCR_ FORMAT_SP.
MCI_VCR_STATUS_SPEED	The dwReturn member is set to the current speed. For more information, see the MCI_VCR_SET_SPEED flag of the MCI_SET command.
MCI_VCR_STATUS_TIME_ MODE	The dwReturn member is set to one of the following: MCI_VCR_TIME_COUNTER, MCI_VCR_TIME_ DETECT, or MCI_VCR_TIME_TIMECODE. (For more information, see the reference for the MCI_VCR_SET_TIME_MODE flag of the MCI_SET command.)
MCI_VCR_STATUS_TIME_ TYPE	The dwReturn member is set to a constant describing the current time type in use (used by play, record, seek, and so on), and is one of the constants described in Table 9-43.
MCI_VCR_STATUS_ TIME_CODE_PRESENT	The dwReturn member is set to TRUE if the timecode is present at the current position in the content; it is set to FALSE otherwise.
MCI_VCR_STATUS_ TIME_CODE_RECORD	The dwReturn member is set to TRUE if the timecode will be recorded when the next record command is given; it is set to FALSE otherwise.
MCI_VCR_STATUS_ TIME_CODE_TYPE	The dwReturn member is set to a constant, describing the type of timecode that is directly supported by the device, and is one of the constants described in Table 9-44.
MCI_VCR_STATUS_TUNER_ CHANNEL	The dwReturn member is set to the current channel number. If you specify MCI_VCR_STATUS_NUMBER in the dwFlags parameter of this command, dwNumber contains the logical tuner number this command applies to.
MCI_VCR_STATUS_VIDEO_ MONITOR	The dwReturn member is set to a constant, indicating the currently selected video monitor type.
MCI_VCR_STATUS_VIDEO_ MONITOR_NUMBER	The dwReturn member is set to the number of the currently selected video monitor type.

9

Chapter

Flag	Meaning
MCI_VCR_STATUS_VIDEO_ RECORD	The dwReturn member is set to TRUE if video will be recorded when the next record command is given; it is set to FALSE otherwise. If you specify MCI_TRACK in the dwFlags parameter of this command, dwTrack contains the track to which this inquiry applies.
MCI_VCR_STATUS_VIDEO_ SOURCE	The dwReturn member is set to a constant indicating the currently selected video source type.
MCI_VCR_STATUS_VIDEO_ SOURCE_NUMBER	The dwReturn member is set to the number of the currently selected video source type.
MCI_VCR_STATUS_WRITE_ PROTECTED	The dwReturn member is set to TRUE if the media is write protected; it is set to FALSE otherwise.

Table 9-42: Flags used with the MCI_VCR_STATUS_COUNTER_RESOLUTION flag and the MCI_STATUS command

Flag	Meaning
MCI_VCR_COUNTER_RES_FRAMES	Counter has resolution of frames.
MCI_VCR_COUNTER_RES_SECONDS	Counter has resolution of seconds.

Table 9-43: Flags used with the MCI_VCR_STATUS_TIME_TYPE flag and the MCI_STATUS command

Flag	Meaning
MCI_VCR_TIME_COUNTER	Counter is in use.
MCI_VCR_TIME_TIMECODE	Timecode is in use.

Table 9-44: Flags used with the MCI_VCR_STATUS_TIMECODE_TYPE flag and the MCI_STATUS command

Flag	Meaning
MCI_VCR_TIMECODE_TYPE_NONE	This device does not use a timecode.
MCI_VCR_TIMECODE_TYPE_OTHER	This device uses an unspecified timecode.
MCI_VCR_TIMECODE_TYPE_SMPTE	This device uses SMPTE timecode.
MCI_VCR_TIMECODE_TYPE_SMPTE_ DROP	This device uses SMPTE drop timecode.

The additional flags shown in Table 9-45 are used with the overlay device type. These constants are used in the dwItem member of the structure pointed to by the lpStatus parameter when MCI_STATUS_ITEM is specified for the dwFlags parameter.

Table 9-45: Flags used with overlay device types and the MCI_STATUS command

Flag	Meaning
MCI_OVLY_STATUS_HWND	The dwReturn member is set to the handle of the window associated with the video overlay device.
MCI_OVLY_STATUS_STRETCH	The dwReturn member is set to TRUE if stretching is enabled; it is set to FALSE otherwise.
MCI_STATUS_MEDIA_PRESENT	The dwReturn member is set to TRUE if the media is inserted in the device; it is set to FALSE otherwise.

The additional flags described in Table 9-46 are used with the videodisc device type. These constants are used in the dwItem member of the structure pointed to by the lpStatus parameter when MCI_STATUS_ITEM is specified for the dwFlags parameter.

Table 9-46: Flags used with videodisc device types and the MCI_STATUS command

Flag	Meaning
MCI_STATUS_MEDIA_PRESENT	The dwReturn member is set to TRUE if the media is inserted in the device; it is set to FALSE otherwise.
MCI_STATUS_MODE	The dwReturn member is set to the current mode of the device. Videodisc devices can return the MCI_VD_MODE_PARK constant, in addition to the constants any device can return, as documented with the dwFlags parameter.
MCI_VD_STATUS_DISC_SIZE	The dwReturn member is set to the size of the loaded disc in inches (8 or 12).
MCI_VD_STATUS_FORWARD	The dwReturn member is set to TRUE if playing forward; it is set to FALSE otherwise. The MCI videodisc device does not support this flag.
MCI_VD_STATUS_MEDIA_TYPE	The dwReturn member is set to the media type of the inserted media. The following media types can be returned: MCI_VD_MEDIA_CAV, MCI_VD_MEDIA_CLV, or MCI_VD_MEDIA_OTHER.
MCI_VD_STATUS_SIDE	The dwReturn member is set to 1 or 2 to indicate which side of the disc is loaded. Not all videodisc devices support this flag.

9

Chapter

Flag	Meaning
MCI_VD_STATUS_SPEED	The dwReturn member is set to the play speed in frames per second. The MCIPIONR.DRV device driver returns MCIERR_UNSUPPORTED_ FUNCTION.

The additional flags described in Table 9-47 are used with the wave audio device type. These constants are used in the dwItem member of the structure pointed to by the lpStatus parameter when MCI_STATUS_ ITEM is specified for the dwFlags parameter.

Table 9-47: Flags used with wave audio device types and the MCI_STATUS command

Flag	Meaning
MCI_WAVE_FORMATTAG	The dwReturn member is set to the current format tag used for playing, recording, and saving.
MCI_WAVE_INPUT	The dwReturn member is set to the wave input device used for recording. If no device is in use and no device has been explicitly set, then the error return is MCIERR_WAVE_INPUTUNSPECIFIED.
MCI_WAVE_OUTPUT	The dwReturn member is set to the wave output device used for playing. If no device is in use and no device has been explicitly set, then the error return is MCIERR_WAVE_OUTPUTUNSPECIFIED.
MCI_WAVE_STATUS_ AVGBYTESPERSEC	The dwReturn member is set to the current bytes per second used for playing, recording, and saving.
MCI_WAVE_STATUS_ BITSPERSAMPLE	The dwReturn member is set to the current bits per sample used for playing, recording, and saving PCM formatted data.
MCI_WAVE_STATUS_ BLOCKALIGN	The dwReturn member is set to the current block alignment used for playing, recording, and saving.
MCI_WAVE_STATUS_ CHANNELS	The dwReturn member is set to the current channel count used for playing, recording, and saving.
MCI_WAVE_STATUS_LEVEL	The dwReturn member is set to the current record or playback level of PCM formatted data. The value is returned as an 8- or 16-bit value, depending on the sample size used. The right or mono channel level is returned in the low-order word. The left channel level is returned in the high-order word.

Flag	Meaning
MCI_WAVE_STATUS_ SAMPLESPERSEC	The dwReturn member is set to the current samples per second used for playing, recording, and saving.

command MCI_CUE

Description

This command cues a device so that playback or recording begins with minimum delay. When cuing for playback by using the MCI_CUE command with the MCI_VCR_CUE_OUTPUT flag, you can cancel MCI_CUE by issuing the MCI_PLAY command with MCI_FROM, MCI_TO, or MCI_VCR_PLAY_REVERSE. When cuing for recording by using MCI_CUE with the MCI_VCR_CUE_INPUT flag, you can cancel MCI_CUE by issuing the MCI_RECORD command with MCI_FROM, MCI_TO, or MCI_VCR_RECORD_INITIALIZE.

Applies to

Digital video, VCR, and waveform audio devices recognize this command.

Use

```
AMCIReturnValue := mciSendCommand(ADeviceID, MCI_CUE, FFlags, Longint(
                                    @AMCI_Gen_Parms_Struc);
```

Parameters (mciSendCommand):

dwParam1: The additional flags described in Tables 9-48 through 9-50 are used with the digital video, VCR, and waveform audio device types.

dwParam2: The address of an MCI_GENERIC_PARMS structure. (Devices with extended command sets might replace this structure with a device-specific structure.) For digital video devices, this parameter points to an MCI_DGV_CUE_PARMS structure. For VCR devices, this parameter points to an MCI_VCR_CUE_PARMS structure.

9

Chapter

Table 9-48: Flags used with digital video device types and the MCI_CUE command

Flag	Meaning
MCI_DGV_CUE_INPUT	A digital video instance should prepare for recording. If the application has not reserved disk space, the device reserves the disk space using its default parameters. The application can omit this flag if the current presentation source is already the external input. (This flag has no effect on selecting the presentation source.)
MCI_DGV_CUE_NOSHOW	A digital video instance should prepare for playing the frame specified with the command without displaying it. When this flag is specified, the display continues to show the image in the frame buffer even though its corresponding frame is not the current position. For example, if the frame buffer contains the image from frame 7, the device continues to show frame 7 when this flag is used to cue the device to any other position. A subsequent cue command without this flag and without the MCI_TO flag displays the current frame.
MCI_DGV_CUE_OUTPUT	A digital video instance should prepare for playing. If the workspace is paused, no positioning occurs. If the workspace is stopped, the position might change to a previous key frame image. The application can omit this flag if the current presentation source is already the workspace.
MCI_TO	A workspace position is included in the dwTo member of the structure identified by dwParam2. The units assigned to position values are specified using the MCI_SET_TIME_FORMAT flag of the MCI_SET command. This is equivalent to seeking to a position, except the device is paused after the command.

Table 9-49: Flags used with VCR device types and the MCI_CUE command

Flag	Meaning
MCI_FROM	The dwFrom member of the structure pointed to by dwParam2 contains the starting location specified in the current time format.
MCI_TO	The dwTo member of the structure pointed to by dwParam2 contains the ending (pausing) location specified in the current time format.
MCI_VCR_CUE_INPUT	Prepare for recording.

Flag	Meaning
MCI_VCR_CUE_OUTPUT	Prepare for playing. If neither MCI_VCR_CUE_INPUT nor MCI_VCR_CUE_OUTPUT is specified, MCI_VCR_CUE_OUTPUT is assumed.
MCI_VCR_CUE_PREROLL	Cue the device to the current position, or the dwFrom position, minus the pre-roll duration. This will allow the device to prepare itself before entering record or playback mode.
MCI_VCR_CUE_REVERSE	The direction of the next play or record command is reverse.

Table 9-50: Flags used with waveform audio device types and the MCI_CUE command

Flag	Meaning
MCI_WAVE_INPUT	A waveform audio input device should be cued.
MCI_WAVE_OUTPUT	A waveform audio output device should be cued. This is the default flag if a flag is not specified.

command MCI_REALIZE

Description

This command causes a graphic device to realize its palette into a device context (DC). You should use this command when your application receives the WM_QUERYNEWPALETTE message.

Applies to

Digital video devices recognize this command.

Use

```
AMCIReturnValue := mciSendCommand(ADeviceID, MCI_REALIZE, FFlags, Longint(
                                  @AMCI_Gen_Parms_Struc);
```

Parameters (mciSendCommand):

dwParam1: The additional flags described in Table 9-51 are used with the digital video device type.

dwParam2: The address of an MCI_GENERIC_PARMS structure. (Devices with extended command sets might replace this structure with a device-specific structure.) For digital video devices, the lpRealize parameter points to an MCI_REALIZE_PARMS structure. For more information, see comments in the MCI_GENERIC_PARMS structure.

Table 9-5l: Flags used with digital video device types and the MCI_REALIZE command

Flag	Meaning
MCI_DGV_REALIZE_BKGD	Realizes the palette as a background palette.
MCI_DGV_REALIZE_NORM	Realizes the palette normally. This is the default.

command MCI_WINDOW

Description

This command specifies the window and the window characteristics for graphic devices. Graphic devices should create a default window when a device is opened but should not display it until they receive the MCI_PLAY command. The MCI_WINDOW command is used to supply an application-created window to the device and to change the display characteristics of an application-defined or default display window. If the application supplies the display window, it should be prepared to update an invalid rectangle on the window.

Applies to

Digital video and video overlay devices recognize this command.

Use

```
AMCIReturnValue := mciSendCommand(ADeviceID, MCI_WINDOW, FFlags, Longint(
                                  @AMCI_Gen_Parms_Struc);
```

Parameters (mciSendCommand):

dwParam1: Tables 9-52 and 9-53 describe the additional flags used with the digital video and video overlay device types.

dwParam2: The address of an MCI_GENERIC_PARMS structure. (Devices with extended command sets might replace this structure with a device-specific structure.) For digital video devices, this parameter points to an MCI_DGV_WINDOW_PARMS structure. This structure is not currently supported in mmsystem.pas. For video overlay devices, this parameter points to an MCI_OVLY_WINDOW_PARMS structure. The MCI_OVLY_WINDOW_PARMS structure and its related structures are defined in mmsystem.pas as follows:

```
type
  PMCI_Ovly_Window_ParmsA = ^TMCI_Ovly_Window_ParmsA;
  PMCI_Ovly_Window_ParmsW = ^TMCI_Ovly_Window_ParmsW;
  PMCI_Ovly_Window_Parms = PMCI_Ovly_Window_ParmsA;
  tagMCI_OVLY_WINDOW_PARMSA = record
    dwCallback: DWORD;
    WHandle: HWND; { formerly "hWnd"}
    nCmdShow: UINT;
    lpstrText: PAnsiChar;
  end;
  tagMCI_OVLY_WINDOW_PARMSW = record
    dwCallback: DWORD;
    WHandle: HWND; { formerly "hWnd"}
    nCmdShow: UINT;
    lpstrText: PWideChar;
  end;
  tagMCI_OVLY_WINDOW_PARMS = tagMCI_OVLY_WINDOW_PARMSA;
  TMCI_Ovly_Window_ParmsA = tagMCI_OVLY_WINDOW_PARMSA;
  TMCI_Ovly_Window_ParmsW = tagMCI_OVLY_WINDOW_PARMSW;
  TMCI_Ovly_Window_Parms = TMCI_Ovly_Window_ParmsA;
  MCI_OVLY_WINDOW_PARMSA = tagMCI_OVLY_WINDOW_PARMSA;
  MCI_OVLY_WINDOW_PARMSW = tagMCI_OVLY_WINDOW_PARMSW;
  MCI_OVLY_WINDOW_PARMS = MCI_OVLY_WINDOW_PARMSA;
```

Table 9-52: Flags used with digital video devices and the MCI_WINDOW command

Flag	Meaning
MCI_DGV_WINDOW_HWND	The handle of the window needed for use as the destination is included in the hWnd member of the structure identified by dwParam2.
MCI_DGV_WINDOW_STATE	The nCmdShow member of the structure identified by dwParam2 contains parameters for setting the window state.
MCI_DGV_WINDOW_TEXT	The lpstrText member of the structure identified by dwParam2 contains an address of a buffer containing the caption used in the window title bar.

9

Chapter

Table 9-53: Flags used with overlay devices and the MCI_WINDOW command

Flag	Meaning
MCI_OVLY_WINDOW_DISABLE_STRETCH	Disables stretching of the image.
MCI_OVLY_WINDOW_ENABLE_STRETCH	Enables stretching of the image.
MCI_OVLY_WINDOW_HWND	The handle of the window used for the destination is included in the hWnd member of the structure identified by dwParam2. Set this flag to MCI_OVLY_WINDOW_DEFAULT to return to the default window.
MCI_OVLY_WINDOW_STATE	The nCmdShow member of the dwParam2 structure contains parameters for setting the window state. This flag is equivalent to calling ShowWindow with the state parameter. The constants are the same as those defined in Windows.pas (such as SW_HIDE, SW_MINIMIZE, or SW_SHOWNORMAL).
MCI_OVLY_WINDOW_TEXT	The lpstrText member of the structure identified by dwParam2 contains an address of a buffer containing the caption used for the window.

command MCI_PUT

Description

This command sets the source, destination, and frame rectangles.

Applies to

Digital video and video overlay devices recognize this command.

Use

```
AMCIReturnValue := mciSendCommand(ADeviceID, MCI_PUT, FFlags, Longint(
                                  @AMCI_Gen_Parms_Struc);
```

Parameters (mciSendCommand):

dwParam1: Tables 9-54 and 9-55 describe the additional flags that are used with the digital video and overlay device types.

dwParam2: The address of an MCI_GENERIC_PARMS structure. (Devices with extended command sets might replace this structure with a device-specific structure.) For digital video devices, dwParam2 points to an MCI_DGV_PUT_PARMS structure. For video overlay devices, dwParam2 points to an MCI_OVLY_RECT_PARMS structure.

Table 9-54: Flags used with digital video devices and the MCI_PUT command

Flag	Meaning
MCI_DGV_PUT_CLIENT	The rectangle defined for MCI_DGV_RECT applies to the position of the client window. The rectangle specified is relative to the parent window of the display window. MCI_DGV_PUT_WINDOW must be set concurrently with this flag.
MCI_DGV_PUT_DESTINATION	The rectangle defined for MCI_DGV_RECT specifies a destination rectangle. The destination rectangle specifies the portion of the client window associated with this device driver instance that shows the image or video.
MCI_DGV_PUT_FRAME	The rectangle defined for MCI_DGV_RECT applies to the frame rectangle. The frame rectangle specifies the portion of the frame buffer used as the destination of the video images obtained from the video rectangle. The video should be scaled to fit within the frame buffer rectangle. The rectangle is specified in frame buffer coordinates. The default rectangle is the full frame buffer. Specifying this rectangle lets the device scale the image as it digitizes the data. Devices that cannot scale the image reject this command with MCIERR_UNSUPPORTED_FUNCTION. You can use the MCI_GETDEVCAPS_CAN_STRETCH flag with the MCI_GETDEVCAPS command to determine if a device scales the image. A device returns FALSE if it cannot scale the image.
MCI_DGV_PUT_SOURCE	The rectangle defined for MCI_DGV_RECT specifies a source rectangle. The source rectangle specifies which portion of the frame buffer is to be scaled to fit into the destination rectangle.
MCI_DGV_PUT_VIDEO	The rectangle defined for MCI_DGV_RECT applies to the video rectangle. The video rectangle specifies which portion of the current presentation source is stored in the frame buffer. The rectangle is specified using the natural coordinates of the presentation source. It allows the specification of cropping that occurs prior to storing

Flag	Meaning
MCI_DGV_PUT_VIDEO (cont.)	images and video in the frame buffer. The default rectangle is the full active scan area or the full decompressed images and video.
MCI_DGV_PUT_WINDOW	The rectangle defined for MCI_DGV_RECT applies to the display window. This rectangle is relative to the parent window of the display window (usually the desktop). If the window is not specified, it defaults to the initial window size and position.
MCI_DGV_RECT	The rc member of the structure identified by dwParam2 contains a valid rectangle.

Table 9-55: Flags used with overlay devices and the MCI_PUT command

Flag	Meaning
MCI_OVLY_PUT_DESTINATION	The rectangle defined for MCI_OVLY_RECT specifies the area of the client window used to display an image. The rectangle contains the offset and visible extent of the image relative to the window origin. If the frame is being stretched, the source is stretched to the destination rectangle.
MCI_OVLY_PUT_FRAME	The rectangle defined for MCI_OVLY_RECT specifies the area of the video buffer used to receive the video image. The rectangle contains the offset and extent of the buffer area relative to the video buffer origin.
MCI_OVLY_PUT_SOURCE	The rectangle defined for MCI_OVLY_RECT specifies the area of the video buffer used as the source of the digital image. The rectangle contains the offset and extent of the clipping rectangle for the video buffer relative to its origin.
MCI_OVLY_PUT_VIDEO	The rectangle defined for MCI_OVLY_RECT specifies the area of the video source capture by the video buffer. The rectangle contains the offset and extent of the clipping rectangle for the video source relative to its origin.
MCI_OVLY_RECT	The rc member of the structure identified by lpDest contains a valid display rectangle. If this flag is not specified, the default rectangle matches the coordinates of the video buffer or window being clipped.

command MCI_WHERE

Description

This command obtains the clipping rectangle for the video device. The top and left members of the returned RECT contain the origin of the clipping rectangle, and the right and bottom members contain the width and height of the clipping rectangle. (This is not the standard use of the right and bottom members.)

Applies to

Digital video and video overlay devices recognize this command.

Use

```
AMCIReturnValue := mciSendCommand(ADeviceID, MCI_WHERE, FFlags, Longint(
                                  @AMCI_Gen_Parms_Struc);
```

Parameters (mciSendCommand):

dwParam1: Tables 9-56 and 9-57 describe the additional flags that are used with the digital video and overlay device types.

dwParam2: The address of an MCI_GENERIC_PARMS structure. (Devices with extended command sets might replace this structure with a device-specific structure.) For digital video devices, this parameter points to an MCI_DGV_WHERE_PARMS structure. The MCI_DGV_WHERE_PARMS structure is identical to the MCI_DGV_RECT_PARMS structure. For video overlay devices, the lpQuery parameter points to an MCI_OVLY_RECT_PARMS structure.

Table 9-56: Flags used with digital video devices and the MCI_WHERE command

Flag	Meaning
MCI_DGV_WHERE_DESTINATION	Obtains a description of the rectangular region used to display video and images in the client area of the current window.
MCI_DGV_WHERE_FRAME	Obtains a description of the rectangular region of the frame buffer into which images from the video rectangle are scaled. The rectangle coordinates are placed in the rc member of the structure identified by lpQuery.

Flag	Meaning
MCI_DGV_WHERE_MAX	When used with MCI_DGV_WHERE_DES-TINATION or MCI_DGV_WHERE_SOURCE, the rectangle returned indicates the maximum width and height of the specified region. When used with MCI_DGV_WHERE_WINDOW, the rectangle returned indicates the size of the entire display.
MCI_DGV_WHERE_SOURCE	Obtains a description of the rectangular region (cropped from the frame buffer) that is stretched to fit the destination rectangle on the display.
MCI_DGV_WHERE_VIDEO	Obtains a description of the rectangular region cropped from the presentation source to fill the frame rectangle in the frame buffer. The rectangle coordinates are placed in the rc member of the structure identified by dwParam2.
MCI_DGV_WHERE_WINDOW	Obtains a description of the display window frame.

Table 9-57: Flags used with overlay devices and the MCI_WHERE command

Flag	Meaning
MCI_OVLY_WHERE_DESTINATION	Obtains the destination display rectangle. The rectangle coordinates are placed in the rc member of the structure identified by dwParam2.
MCI_OVLY_WHERE_FRAME	Obtains the overlay frame rectangle. The rectangle coordinates are placed in the rc member of the structure identified by dwParam2.
MCI_OVLY_WHERE_SOURCE	Obtains the source rectangle. The rectangle coordinates are placed in the rc member of the structure identified by dwParam2.
MCI_OVLY_WHERE_VIDEO	Obtains the video rectangle. The rectangle coordinates are placed in the rc member of the structure identified by dwParam2.

command MCI_FREEZE

Description

This command freezes motion on the display.

Applies to

Digital video, video overlay, and VCR devices recognize this command.

Use

```
AMCIReturnValue := mciSendCommand(ADeviceID, MCI_FREEZE, FFlags, Longint(
                                  @AMCI_Gen_Parms_Struc);
```

Parameters (mciSendCommand):

dwParam1: Tables 9-58 and 9-59 describe the additional flags that are used with the VCR and overlay device types.

dwParam2: The address of an MCI_GENERIC_PARMS structure. (Devices with additional parameters might replace this structure with a device-specific structure.) For digital video devices, this parameter points to an MCI_DGV_FREEZE_PARMS structure. For VCR devices, this parameter points to an MCI_GENERIC_PARMS structure. For video overlay devices, this parameter points to an MCI_OVLY_RECT_PARMS structure.

Table 9-58: Flags used with VCR devices and the MCI_FREEZE command

Flag	Meaning
MCI_VCR_FREEZE_FIELD	Freeze only one member of the current frame.
MCI_VCR_FREEZE_FRAME	Freeze both fields of the current frame.
MCI_VCR_FREEZE_INPUT	Freeze the current frame on the screen (used for recording).
MCI_VCR_FREEZE_OUTPUT	Freeze the current frame from the VCR (used with frame capture).

Table 9-59: Flag used with overlay devices and the MCI_FREEZE command

Flag	Meaning
MCI_OVLY_RECT	The rc member of the structure identified by dwParam2 contains a valid rectangle. If this flag is not specified, the device driver will freeze the entire frame.

9

Chapter

command *MCI_UNFREEZE*

Description

This command restores motion to an area of the video buffer frozen with the MCI_FREEZE command.

Applies to

Digital video, VCR, and video overlay devices recognize this command.

Use

```
AMCIReturnValue := mciSendCommand(ADeviceID, MCI_UNFREEZE, FFlags,
                                  Longint(@AMCI_Gen_Parms_Struc);
```

Parameters (mciSendCommand):

dwParam1: Tables 60 through 62 describe the additional flags that are used with the digital video, VCR, and overlay device types.

dwParam2: The address of an MCI_GENERIC_PARMS structure. (Devices with extended command sets might replace this structure with a device-specific structure.) For digital video devices, this parameter points to an MCI_DGV_UNFREEZE_PARMS structure. For video overlay devices, this parameter points to an MCI_OVLY_RECT_PARMS structure. That structure and its related structures are given below. The MCI_DGV_RECT_PARMS structure is not currently supported in mmsystem.pas.

```
type
  PMCI_Ovly_Rect_Parms = ^ TMCI_Ovly_Rect_Parms;
  tagMCI_OVLY_RECT_PARMS = record
    dwCallback: DWORD;
    rc: TRect;
  end;
  TMCI_Ovly_Rect_Parms = tagMCI_OVLY_RECT_PARMS;
  MCI_OVLY_RECT_PARMS = tagMCI_OVLY_RECT_PARMS;
```

Table 9-60: Flag used with digital video devices and the MCI_UNFREEZE command

Flag	Meaning
MCI_DGV_RECT	The rc member of the structure identified by dwParam2 contains a valid display rectangle. The rectangle specifies a region within the frame buffer whose pixels should have their lock mask bit turned off. Rectangular regions are specified as described for the MCI_PUT command. If omitted, the rectangle defaults to the entire frame buffer. By using a sequence of freeze and unfreeze commands with different rectangles, arbitrary patterns of lock mask bits can be described.

Table 9-61: Flags used with VCR devices and the MCI_UNFREEZE command

Flag	Meaning
MCI_VCR_UNFREEZE_INPUT	Unfreeze the input
MCI_VCR_UNFREEZE_OUTPUT	Unfreeze the output

Table 9-62: Flag used with overlay devices and the MCI_UNFREEZE command

Flag	Meaning
MCI_OVLY_RECT	The rc member of the structure identified by dwParam2 contains a valid display rectangle. This is a required parameter.

command MCI_LOAD

Description

This command loads a file.

Applies to

Digital video and video overlay devices recognize this command.

Use

```
AMCIReturnValue := mciSendCommand(ADeviceID, MCI_LOAD, FFlags, Longint(
                                  @AMCI_Load_Parms_Struc);
```

Parameters (mciSendCommand):

dwParam1: Table 9-63 shows the additional flags used with all devices supporting MCI_LOAD. Table 9-64 shows the additional flag used with overlay devices.

9

Chapter

dwParam2: The address of an MCI_LOAD_PARMS structure. (Devices with additional parameters might replace this structure with a device-specific structure. For digital video devices, the lpLoad parameter points to an MCI_DGV_LOAD_PARMS structure.) For video overlay devices, this parameter points to an MCI_OVLY_LOAD_PARMS structure. This structure and its related structures are defined in mmsystem.pas as follows:

```
type
  PMCI_Ovly_Load_ParmsA = ^TMCI_Ovly_Load_ParmsA;
  PMCI_Ovly_Load_ParmsW = ^TMCI_Ovly_Load_ParmsW;
  PMCI_Ovly_Load_Parms = PMCI_Ovly_Load_ParmsA;
  tagMCI_OVLY_LOAD_PARMSA = record
    dwCallback: DWORD;
    lpfilename: PAnsiChar;
    rc: TRect;
  end;
  tagMCI_OVLY_LOAD_PARMSW = record
    dwCallback: DWORD;
    lpfilename: PWideChar;
    rc: TRect;
  end;
  tagMCI_OVLY_LOAD_PARMS = tagMCI_OVLY_LOAD_PARMSA;
  TMCI_Ovly_Load_ParmsA = tagMCI_OVLY_LOAD_PARMSA;
  TMCI_Ovly_Load_ParmsW = tagMCI_OVLY_LOAD_PARMSW;
  TMCI_Ovly_Load_Parms = TMCI_Ovly_Load_ParmsA;
  MCI_OVLY_LOAD_PARMSA = tagMCI_OVLY_LOAD_PARMSA;
  MCI_OVLY_LOAD_PARMSW = tagMCI_OVLY_LOAD_PARMSW;
  MCI_OVLY_LOAD_PARMS = MCI_OVLY_LOAD_PARMSA;
```

Table 9-63: Flag used with the MCI_LOAD command

Flag	Meaning
MCI_LOAD_FILE	The lpfilename member of the structure identified by lpLoad contains an address of a buffer containing the filename.

Table 9-64: Flag used with overlay device types and the MCI_LOAD command

Flag	Meaning
MCI_OVLY_RECT	The rc member of the structure identified by lpLoad contains a valid display rectangle that identifies the area of the video buffer to update.

command MCI_CUT

Description

This command removes data from the file and copies it to the clipboard.

Applies to

Digital video devices recognize this command.

Use

```
AMCIReturnValue := mciSendCommand(ADeviceID, MCI_CUT, FFlags, Longint(
                                  @AMCI_DGV_CUT_Parms_Struc);
```

Parameters (mciSendCommand):

dwParam1: Table 9-65 lists the additional flags that apply to digital video devices.

dwParam2: The address of an MCI_DGV_CUT_PARMS structure. This structure is not currently supported in mmsystem.pas.

Table 9-65: Flags used with digital video devices and the MCI_CUT command

Flag	Meaning
MCI_DGV_CUT_AT	A rectangle is included in the rc member of the structure identified by lpCut. The rectangle specifies the portion of each frame to cut. If the flag is omitted, MCI_CUT cuts the entire frame.
MCI_DGV_CUT_AUDIO_STREAM	An audio stream number is included in the dwAudioStream member of the structure identified by lpCut. If you use this flag and also want to cut video, you must also use the MCI_DGV_CUT_VIDEO_STREAM flag. (If neither flag is specified, data from all audio and video streams is cut.)
MCI_DGV_CUT_VIDEO_STREAM	A video stream number is included in the dwVideoStream member of the structure identified by lpCut. If you use this flag and also want to cut audio, you must also use the MCI_DGV_CUT_AUDIO_STREAM flag. (If neither flag is specified, data from all audio and video streams is cut.)
MCI_FROM	A starting location is included in the dwFrom member of the structure identified by lpCut. The units assigned to the position values are specified with the MCI_SET_TIME_FORMAT flag of the MCI_SET command.

9 Chapter

Flag	Meaning
MCI_TO	An ending location is included in the dwTo member of the structure identified by lpCut. The units assigned to the position values are specified with the MCI_SET_TIME_FORMAT flag of MCI_SET.

command MCI_COPY

Description

This command copies data to the clipboard.

Applies to

Digital video devices recognize this command.

Use

```
AMCIReturnValue := mciSendCommand(ADeviceID, MCI_COPY, FFlags, Longint(
                              @AMCI_DGV_COPY_Parms_Struc);
```

Parameters (mciSendCommand):

dwParam1: Table 9-66 describes the additional flags that apply to digital video devices.

dwParam2: The address of an MCI_DGV_COPY_PARMS structure. This structure is not currently supported in mmsystem.pas.

Table 9-66: Flag used with digital video devices and the MCI_COPY command

Flag	Meaning
MCI_DGV_COPY_AT	A rectangle is included in the rc member of the structure identified by lpCopy. The rectangle specifies the portion of each frame to copy. If the flag is omitted, MCI_COPY copies the entire frame.
MCI_DGV_COPY_AUDIO_STREAM	An audio stream number is included in the dwAudioStream member of the structure identified by lpCopy. If you use this flag and also want to copy video, you must also use the MCI_DGV_COPY_VIDEO_STREAM flag. (If neither flag is specified, data from all audio and video streams is copied.)

Flag	Meaning
MCI_DGV_COPY_VIDEO_STREAM	A video stream number is included in the dwVideoStream member of the structure identified by lpCopy. If you use this flag and also want to copy audio, you must also use the MCI_DGV_COPY_AUDIO_STREAM flag. (If neither flag is specified, data from all audio and video streams is copied.)
MCI_FROM	A starting location is included in the dwFrom member of the structure identified by lpCopy. The units assigned to the position values are specified with the MCI_SET_TIME_FORMAT flag of the MCI_SET command.
MCI_TO	An ending location is included in the dwTo member of the structure identified by lpCopy. The units assigned to the position values are specified with the MCI_SET_TIME_FORMAT flag of the MCI_SET command.

command MCI_PASTE

Description

This command pastes data from the clipboard into a file.

Applies to

Digital video devices recognize this command.

Use

```
AMCIReturnValue := mciSendCommand(ADeviceID, MCI_PASTE, FFlags, Longint(
                                  @ATMCI_DGV_PASTE_Parms_Struc);
```

Parameters (mciSendCommand):

dwParam1: Table 9-67 describes the additional flags that apply to digital video devices.

dwParam2: The address of an MCI_DGV_PASTE_PARMS structure. This structure is not currently supported in mmsystem.pas.

9

Chapter

Table 9-67: Flags used with digital video devices and the MCI_PASTE command

Flag	Meaning
MCI_DGV_PASTE_AT	A rectangle is included in the rc member of the structure identified by dwParam2. The first two values of the rectangle specify the point within the frame to place the clipboard information. If the rectangle height and width are nonzero, the clipboard contents are scaled to those dimensions when they are pasted in the frame. If the flag is omitted, MCI_PASTE defaults to the entire frame rectangle.
MCI_DGV_PASTE_AUDIO_STREAM	An audio stream number is included in the dwAudioStream member of the structure identified by dwParam2. If only one audio stream exists on the clipboard, the audio data is pasted into the designated stream. If more than one audio stream exists on the clipboard, the stream indicates the starting number for the stream sequences. If you use this flag and also want to paste video, you must also use the MCI_DGV_PASTE_VIDEO_STREAM flag. (If neither flag is specified, all audio and video streams are pasted starting with the first audio and video stream. Each pasted stream retains its original stream number.)
MCI_DGV_PASTE_INSERT	Clipboard data should be inserted in the existing workspace at the position specified by the MCI_TO flag. Any existing data after the insertion point is moved in the workspace to make room. This is the default.
MCI_DGV_PASTE_OVERWRITE	Clipboard data should replace data already present in the workspace. The workspace data replaced follows the insertion point.
MCI_DGV_PASTE_VIDEO_STREAM	A video stream number is included in the dwVideoStream member of the structure identified by dwParam2. If only one video stream exists on the clipboard, the video data is pasted into the designated stream. If more than one video stream exists on the clipboard, the stream indicates the starting number for the stream sequences. If you use this flag and also want to paste audio, you must also use the MCI_DGV_PASTE_AUDIO_STREAM flag. (If neither flag is specified, all audio and video streams are pasted starting with the first audio and video stream. Each pasted stream retains its original stream number.)

Flag	Meaning
MCI_TO	A position value is included in the dwTo member of the structure identified by dwParam2. The position value specifies the position to begin pasting data into the workspace. If this flag is omitted, the position defaults to the current position.

command MCI_UPDATE

Description

This command updates the display rectangle.

Applies to

Digital video devices recognize this command.

Use

```
AMCIReturnValue := mciSendCommand(ADeviceID, MCI_UPDATE, FFlags, Longint(
                                  @AMCI_Gen_Parms_Struc);
```

Parameters (mciSendCommand):

dwParam1: Table 9-68 describes the additional flags used with the digital video device type.

dwParam2: The address of an MCI_GENERIC_PARMS structure. (Devices with extended command sets might replace this structure with a device-specific structure.) For digital video devices, the lpDest parameter points to an MCI_DGV_UPDATE_PARMS structure. This structure is not currently supported in mmsystem.pas.

Table 9-68: Flag used with digital video devices and the MCI_UPDATE command

Flag	Meaning
MCI_DGV_UPDATE_HDC	The hDC member of the structure identified by lpDest contains a valid window of the DC to paint. This flag is required.
MCI_DGV_RECT	The rc member of the structure identified by lpUnfreeze contains a valid display rectangle. The rectangle specifies the clipping rectangle relative to the client rectangle.

Flag	Meaning
MCI_DGV_UPDATE_PAINT	An application uses this flag when it receives a WM_PAINT message that is intended for a display DC. A frame buffer device usually paints the key color. If the display device does not have a frame buffer, it might ignore the MCI_UPDATE command when the MCI_DGV_UPDATE_PAINT flag is used because the display will be repainted during the playback operation.

command MCI_RESUME

Description

This command causes a paused device to resume the paused operation. It resumes playing and recording without changing the current track position set with MCI_PLAY or MCI_RECORD.

Applies to

Digital video, VCR, and waveform audio devices recognize this command. Although CD audio, MIDI sequencer, and videodisc devices also recognize this command, the MCICDA, MCISEQ, and MCIPIONR device drivers do not support it.

Use

```
AMCIReturnValue := mciSendCommand(ADeviceID, MCI_RESUME, FFlags, Longint(
                                  @AMCI_Gen_Parms_Struc);
```

Parameter (mciSendCommand):

dwParam2: The address of an MCI_GENERIC_PARMS structure. (Devices with extended command sets might replace this structure with a device-specific structure.)

command MCI_DELETE

Description

This command removes data from the file.

Applies to

Digital video and waveform audio devices recognize this command.

Use

```
AMCIReturnValue := mciSendCommand(ADeviceID, MCI_DELETE, FFlags, Longint(
                                  @AMCI_Gen_Parms_Struc);
```

Parameters (mciSendCommand):

dwParam1: Tables 9-69 and 9-70 describe the additional flags that apply to the digital video and waveform audio device types.

dwParam2: The address of an MCI_GENERIC_PARMS structure. (Devices with extended command sets might replace this structure with a device-specific structure.) For digital video devices, the lpDelete parameter points to an MCI_DGV_DELETE_PARMS structure. This structure is not currently supported in mmsystem.pas. For waveform audio devices, the lpDelete parameter points to an MCI_WAVE_ DELETE_PARMS structure. This structure and its related structures are defined in mmsystem.pas as follows:

```
type
    PMCI_Wave_Delete_Parms = ^TMCI_Wave_Delete_Parms;
    tagMCI_WAVE_DELETE_PARMS = record
      dwCallback: DWORD;
      dwFrom: DWORD;
      dwTo: DWORD;
    end;
    TMCI_Wave_Delete_Parms = tagMCI_WAVE_DELETE_PARMS;
    MCI_WAVE_DELETE_PARMS = tagMCI_WAVE_DELETE_PARMS;
```

Table 9-69: Flags used with digital video devices and the MCI_DELETE command

Flag	Meaning
MCI_DGV_DELETE_AT	A rectangle is included in the rc member of the structure identified by lpDelete. The rectangle specifies the portion of each frame to delete. When this flag is used, the frame is retained in the workspace and the area specified by the rectangle becomes black. If the flag is omitted, MCI_DELETE defaults to the entire frame and removes the frame from the workspace.

Flag	Meaning
MCI_DGV_DELETE_AUDIO_STREAM	An audio stream number is included in the dwAudioStream member of the structure identified by lpDelete. If you use this flag and also want to delete video, you must also use the MCI_DGV_DELETE_VIDEO_STREAM flag. (If neither flag is specified, data from all audio and video streams is deleted.)
MCI_DGV_DELETE_VIDEO_STREAM	A video stream number is included in the dwVideoStream member of the structure identified by lpDelete. If you use this flag and also want to delete audio, you must also use the MCI_DGV_DELETE_AUDIO_STREAM flag. (If neither flag is specified, data from all audio and video streams is deleted.)
MCI_FROM	A starting location is included in the dwFrom member of the structure identified by lpDelete. The units assigned to the position values are specified with the MCI_SET_TIME_FORMAT flag of the MCI_SET command.
MCI_TO	An ending location is included in the dwTo member of the structure identified by lpDelete. The units assigned to the position values are specified with the MCI_SET_TIME_FORMAT flag of MCI_SET.

Table 9-70: Flags used with waveform audio devices and the MCI_DELETE command

Flag	Meaning
MCI_FROM	A starting location is included in the dwFrom member of the structure identified by lpDelete. The units assigned to the position values are specified with the MCI_SET_TIME_FORMAT flag of MCI_SET.
MCI_TO	An ending location is included in the dwTo member of the structure identified by lpDelete. The units assigned to the position values are specified with the MCI_SET_TIME_FORMAT flag of MCI_SET.

Other Structures for the dwParam2 parameter of Various Commands

While mmsystem.pas does not currently support all of the structures discussed above (particularly those for digital video devices), it does include the following additional structures that may be used with the indicated commands.

MCI_SEEK_PARMS Structure

The following parameter block, defined in mmsystem.pas, can be used with the MCI_SEEK command message.

```
type
  PMCI_Seek_Parms = ^TMCI_Seek_Parms;
  tagMCI_SEEK_PARMS = record
    dwCallback: DWORD;
    dwTo: DWORD;
  end;
  TMCI_Seek_Parms = tagMCI_SEEK_PARMS;
  MCI_SEEK_PARMS = tagMCI_SEEK_PARMS;
```

MCI_INFO_PARMS and Related Structures

The following parameter block, defined in mmsystem.pas, can be used with the MCI_STATUS command message:

```
{ parameter block for MCI_INFO command message }
type
  PMCI_Info_ParmsA = ^TMCI_Info_ParmsA;
  PMCI_Info_ParmsW = ^TMCI_Info_ParmsW;
  PMCI_Info_Parms = PMCI_Info_ParmsA;
  tagMCI_INFO_PARMSA = record
    dwCallback: DWORD;
    lpstrReturn: PAnsiChar;
    dwRetSize: DWORD;
  end;
  tagMCI_INFO_PARMSW = record
    dwCallback: DWORD;
    lpstrReturn: PWideChar;
    dwRetSize: DWORD;
  end;
  tagMCI_INFO_PARMS = tagMCI_INFO_PARMSA;
  TMCI_Info_ParmsA = tagMCI_INFO_PARMSA;
  TMCI_Info_ParmsW = tagMCI_INFO_PARMSW;
  TMCI_Info_Parms = TMCI_Info_ParmsA;
```

Chapter **9**

```
MCI_INFO_PARMSA = tagMCI_INFO_PARMSA;
MCI_INFO_PARMSW = tagMCI_INFO_PARMSW;
MCI_INFO_PARMS = MCI_INFO_PARMSA;
```

MCI_GETDEVCAPS_PARMS and Related Structure

The following parameter block, defined in mmsystem.pas, can be used with the MCI_GETDEVCAPS command message:

```
type
  PMCI_GetDevCaps_Parms = ^TMCI_GetDevCaps_Parms;
  tagMCI_GETDEVCAPS_PARMS = record
    dwCallback: DWORD;
    dwReturn: DWORD;
    dwItem: DWORD;
  end;
  TMCI_GetDevCaps_Parms = tagMCI_GETDEVCAPS_PARMS;
  MCI_GETDEVCAPS_PARMS = tagMCI_GETDEVCAPS_PARMS;
```

MCI_SOUND_PARMS and Related Structures

The following parameter block, defined in mmsystem.pas, can be used with the MCI_SOUND command message:

```
type
  PMCI_Sound_Parms = ^TMCI_Sound_Parms;
  TMCI_Sound_Parms = record
    dwCallback: Longint;
    lpstrSoundName: PChar;
  end;
```

MCI_LOAD_PARMS and Related Structures

The following parameter block, defined in mmsystem.pas, can be used with the MCI_LOAD command message:

```
type
  PMCI_Load_ParmsA = ^TMCI_Load_ParmsA;
  PMCI_Load_ParmsW = ^TMCI_Load_ParmsW;
  PMCI_Load_Parms = PMCI_Load_ParmsA;
  tagMCI_LOAD_PARMSA = record
    dwCallback: DWORD;
    lpfilename: PAnsiChar;
  end;
  tagMCI_LOAD_PARMSW = record
    dwCallback: DWORD;
    lpfilename: PWideChar;
  end;
```

```
tagMCI_LOAD_PARMS = tagMCI_LOAD_PARMSA;
TMCI_Load_ParmsA = tagMCI_LOAD_PARMSA;
TMCI_Load_ParmsW = tagMCI_LOAD_PARMSW;
TMCI_Load_Parms = TMCI_Load_ParmsA;
MCI_LOAD_PARMSA = tagMCI_LOAD_PARMSA;
MCI_LOAD_PARMSW = tagMCI_LOAD_PARMSW;
MCI_LOAD_PARMS = MCI_LOAD_PARMSA;
```

MCI_VD_PLAY_PARMS and Related Structures

The following parameter block, defined in mmsystem.pas, can be used
with the MCI_PLAY command message:

```
type
  PMCI_VD_Play_Parms = ^TMCI_VD_Play_Parms;
  tagMCI_VD_PLAY_PARMS = record
    dwCallback: DWORD;
    dwFrom: DWORD;
    dwTo: DWORD;
    dwSpeed: DWORD;
  end;
  TMCI_VD_Play_Parms = tagMCI_VD_PLAY_PARMS;
  MCI_VD_PLAY_PARMS = tagMCI_VD_PLAY_PARMS;
```

MCI_VD_STEP_PARMS and Related Structures

The following parameter block, defined in mmsystem.pas, can be used
with the MCI_STEP command message:

```
type
  PMCI_VD_Step_Parms = ^TMCI_VD_Step_Parms;
  tagMCI_VD_STEP_PARMS = record
    dwCallback: DWORD;
    dwFrames: DWORD;
  end;
  TMCI_VD_Step_Parms = tagMCI_VD_STEP_PARMS;
  MCI_VD_STEP_PARMS = tagMCI_VD_STEP_PARMS;
```

MCI_WAVE_SET_PARMS and Related Structures

The following parameter block, defined in mmsystem.pas, can be used
with the MCI_SET command message:

```
type
  PMCI_Wave_Set_Parms = ^TMCI_Wave_Set_Parms;
  tagMCI_WAVE_SET_PARMS = record
    dwCallback: DWORD;
    dwTimeFormat: DWORD;
```

```
    dwAudio: DWORD;
    wInput: UINT;
    wOutput: UINT;
    wFormatTag: Word;
    wReserved2: Word;
    nChannels: Word;
    wReserved3: Word;
    nSamplesPerSec: DWORD;
    nAvgBytesPerSec: DWORD;
    nBlockAlign: Word;
    wReserved4: Word;
    wBitsPerSample: Word;
    wReserved5: Word;
  end;
  TMCI_Wave_Set_Parms = tagMCI_WAVE_SET_PARMS;
  MCI_WAVE_SET_PARMS = tagMCI_WAVE_SET_PARMS;
```

MCI_SEQ_SET_PARMS and Related Structures

The following parameter block, defined in mmsystem.pas, can be used with the MCI_SET command message:

```
type
  PMCI_Seq_Set_Parms = ^TMCI_Seq_Set_Parms;
  tagMCI_SEQ_SET_PARMS = record
    dwCallback: DWORD;
    dwTimeFormat: DWORD;
    dwAudio: DWORD;
    dwTempo: DWORD;
    dwPort: DWORD;
    dwSlave: DWORD;
    dwMaster: DWORD;
    dwOffset: DWORD;
  end;
  TMCI_Seq_Set_Parms = tagMCI_SEQ_SET_PARMS;
  MCI_SEQ_SET_PARMS = tagMCI_SEQ_SET_PARMS;
```

MCI_ANIM_OPEN_PARMS and Related Structures

The following parameter block, defined in mmsystem.pas, can be used with the MCI_OPEN command message:

```
type
  PMCI_Anim_Open_ParmsA = ^TMCI_Anim_Open_ParmsA;
  PMCI_Anim_Open_ParmsW = ^TMCI_Anim_Open_ParmsW;
  PMCI_Anim_Open_Parms = PMCI_Anim_Open_ParmsA;
  tagMCI_ANIM_OPEN_PARMSA = record
    dwCallback: DWORD;
```

```
  wDeviceID: MCIDEVICEID;
  lpstrDeviceType: PAnsiChar;
  lpstrElementName: PAnsiChar;
  lpstrAlias: PAnsiChar;
  dwStyle: DWORD;
  hWndParent: HWND;
end;
tagMCI_ANIM_OPEN_PARMSW = record
  dwCallback: DWORD;
  wDeviceID: MCIDEVICEID;
  lpstrDeviceType: PWideChar;
  lpstrElementName: PWideChar;
  lpstrAlias: PWideChar;
  dwStyle: DWORD;
  hWndParent: HWND;
end;
tagMCI_ANIM_OPEN_PARMS = tagMCI_ANIM_OPEN_PARMSA;
TMCI_Anim_Open_ParmsA = tagMCI_ANIM_OPEN_PARMSA;
TMCI_Anim_Open_ParmsW = tagMCI_ANIM_OPEN_PARMSW;
TMCI_Anim_Open_Parms = TMCI_Anim_Open_ParmsA;
MCI_ANIM_OPEN_PARMSA = tagMCI_ANIM_OPEN_PARMSA;
MCI_ANIM_OPEN_PARMSW = tagMCI_ANIM_OPEN_PARMSW;
MCI_ANIM_OPEN_PARMS = MCI_ANIM_OPEN_PARMSA;
```

MCI_ANIM_PLAY_PARMS and Related Structures

The following parameter block, defined in mmsystem.pas, can be used
with the MCI_PLAY command message:

```
type
  PMCI_Anim_Play_Parms = ^TMCI_Anim_Play_Parms;
  tagMCI_ANIM_PLAY_PARMS = record
    dwCallback: DWORD;
    dwFrom: DWORD;
    dwTo: DWORD;
    dwSpeed: DWORD;
  end;
  TMCI_Anim_Play_Parms = tagMCI_ANIM_PLAY_PARMS;
  MCI_ANIM_PLAY_PARMS = tagMCI_ANIM_PLAY_PARMS;
```

MCI_ANIM_STEP_PARMS and Related Structures

The following parameter block, defined in mmsystem.pas, can be used
with the MCI_STEP command message:

```
type
  PMCI_Anim_Step_Parms = ^TMCI_Anim_Step_Parms;
  tagMCI_ANIM_STEP_PARMS = record
```

9

Chapter

```
    dwCallback: DWORD;
    dwFrames: DWORD;
  end;
  TMCI_Anim_Step_Parms = tagMCI_ANIM_STEP_PARMS;
  MCI_ANIM_STEP_PARMS = tagMCI_ANIM_STEP_PARMS;
```

MCI_ANIM_WINDOW_PARMS and Related Structures

The following parameter block, defined in mmsystem.pas, can be used
with the MCI_WINDOW command message:

```
type
  PMCI_Anim_Window_ParmsA = ^TMCI_Anim_Window_ParmsA;
  PMCI_Anim_Window_ParmsW = ^TMCI_Anim_Window_ParmsW;
  PMCI_Anim_Window_Parms = PMCI_Anim_Window_ParmsA;
  tagMCI_ANIM_WINDOW_PARMSA = record
    dwCallback: DWORD;
    Wnd: HWND;  { formerly "hWnd" }
    nCmdShow: UINT;
    lpstrText: PAnsiChar;
  end;
  tagMCI_ANIM_WINDOW_PARMSW = record
    dwCallback: DWORD;
    Wnd: HWND;  { formerly "hWnd" }
    nCmdShow: UINT;
    lpstrText: PWideChar;
  end;
  tagMCI_ANIM_WINDOW_PARMS = tagMCI_ANIM_WINDOW_PARMSA;
  TMCI_Anim_Window_ParmsA = tagMCI_ANIM_WINDOW_PARMSA;
  TMCI_Anim_Window_ParmsW = tagMCI_ANIM_WINDOW_PARMSW;
  TMCI_Anim_Window_Parms = TMCI_Anim_Window_ParmsA;
  MCI_ANIM_WINDOW_PARMSA = tagMCI_ANIM_WINDOW_PARMSA;
  MCI_ANIM_WINDOW_PARMSW = tagMCI_ANIM_WINDOW_PARMSW;
  MCI_ANIM_WINDOW_PARMS = MCI_ANIM_WINDOW_PARMSA;
```

MCI_ANIM_RECT_PARMS and Related Structures

The following parameter block, defined in mmsystem.pas, can be used
with the MCI_PUT, MCI_UPDATE, and MCI_WHERE command messages:

```
type
  PMCI_Anim_Rect_Parms = ^ TMCI_Anim_Rect_Parms;
  tagMCI_ANIM_RECT_PARMS = record
    dwCallback: DWORD;
    rc: TRect;
  end;
  TMCI_Anim_Rect_Parms = tagMCI_ANIM_RECT_PARMS;
  MCI_ANIM_RECT_PARMS = tagMCI_ANIM_RECT_PARMS;
```

MCI_ANIM_UPDATE_PARMS and Related Structures

The following parameter block, defined in mmsystem.pas, can be used with the MCI_UPDATE PARMS:

```
type
  PMCI_Anim_Update_Parms = ^TMCI_Anim_Update_Parms;
  tagMCI_ANIM_UPDATE_PARMS = record
    dwCallback: DWORD;
    rc: TRect;
    hDC: HDC;
  end;
  TMCI_Anim_Update_Parms = tagMCI_ANIM_UPDATE_PARMS;
  MCI_ANIM_UPDATE_PARMS = tagMCI_ANIM_UPDATE_PARMS;
```

Having discussed the last structure of the final multimedia API, the MCI API, we've reached the end of our journey. If you have thoroughly examined all of the author's code and example programs, be sure to check out the other freeware and shareware examples included on the CD-ROM to further enhance your understanding.

A Primer on Delphi Experts

In Chapter 2, we built a Delphi expert to generate the series of components we used to create our multimedia database application. While we touched on a few of the details of writing experts there, we saved most of them to discuss in this appendix. We could divide the task of building any Delphi expert into three basic steps as follows:

■ Creating the Delphi expert interface

■ Creating the user interface

■ Carrying out the work of the expert

You may recall that in Chapter 2, we discussed steps two and three in some detail. Each is closely related to sound-producing issues we discussed in that chapter. Here we'll concentrate on the expert-specific issues. We'll begin with an overview of the various types of experts. Then we'll take a detailed look at the two types of experts we built in Chapter 2, standard experts and add-in experts. In that latter discussion we'll explore using Tool Services to access information about components installed in the Visual Component Library.

A Wealth of Delphi Experts

There are several types of Delphi experts. In Delphi 1, there are three types: form experts, project experts, and standard experts. With the addition of add-in experts (starting with Delphi 2), there are four in each of the 32-bit versions. Form and project experts create new forms and new projects. A form expert generally adds its new form to the project that is currently open in Delphi. A project expert can add one or more new forms to the projects it creates.

Form and project experts were included in Delphi 1. However, their implementation is different in the 32-bit versions of Delphi. In Delphi 1, form and project experts are placed in the Form Gallery and Project Gallery, respectively. In Delphi's 32-bit versions, they are placed in the Object Repository. In the expert we built in Chapter 2, we used a standard expert for Delphi 1 and an add-in expert for the 32-bit versions. We'll concentrate on those two expert types in this appendix.

The three original types share four methods: Execute(), GetIDString(), GetName(), and GetStyle(). Form and project experts share two more (four in 32-bit versions) which are GetComment(), and GetGlyph(). Standard experts include two unique methods, GetMenuText() and GetState(). All of these methods are implemented in Listing A-1.

Managing Different Expert Types Using Conditional Defines

Not only are there different types of experts, there are different ways of implementing an expert—within the Delphi IDE as a DLL expert or independent of Delphi as an EXE expert. A DLL expert, which runs in the Delphi environment, has the advantage of allowing you to perform other tasks in that environment; if you're generating component code as we did in Chapter 2, you can install your new component. The disadvantage is the extra overhead in terms of memory. And in Delphi 1, you may not want your Help menu to get cluttered with a bunch of additional standard experts.

A stand-alone expert has the advantage of always being available whether Delphi is running or not. If the computer you are using has memory constraints (rare these days), this approach might make sense. A disadvantage with a code-generating expert is that you still need to run Delphi to do anything useful with it. Also, some experts must be run within the Delphi environment because they depend upon information that is only available when Delphi is running or they enhance the Delphi environment in some way.

You can manage different types of experts and different implementations of experts using the same source code if you use conditional defines. Such defines look like old-style Pascal comments with curly braces, but include a dollar sign ($) after the initial brace.

In the expert we built in Chapter 2, we used both an EXE expert for debugging and a DLL one to install and use. Below is the code (explained in Chapter 2) that controls the compilation of the expert. This code is from the main unit, SndExp1.pas. The first step is to include the line that defines the DEBUG condition as in this code from that file:

```
(* To run this as an *.EXE with the ExpTest project, un-comment next line *)
(* {$DEFINE DEBUG}  *)
```

When you do that, Delphi produces an EXE file that can run outside of Delphi but that does not have access to any of the RTTI capabilities we'll be discussing later. The next example shows a use of the conditional define, DEBUG, later in the unit:

```
procedure ExecuteExpert( ToolServices: TIToolServices );
begin
  {$IFNDEF DEBUG}
  iTools := ToolServices; { Keep a local copy of the Tools API instance }
  {$ENDIF}
```

The {$IFNDEF DEBUG} block allows you to run the expert as an *.exe rather than a *.dll during modification/testing phases of development. Of course, you cannot use the Tool Services if Delphi isn't running and we're not using a resident *.dll expert. However, entering some of the data manually during testing is not that much of a hardship!

You can also use conditional defines to build either a standard expert or an add-in expert. The main difference between the two is where they are located in Delphi's menu system. Standard experts are always listed under the Help menu; add-in experts can be installed anywhere in Delphi's menu structure. One of the things you must always do if your expert will be run in the Delphi IDE is to tell Delphi what kind of expert you are installing. The Delphi expert interface ensures that Delphi knows about the expert (usually a DLL) and is able to load it, execute it, and unload it when Delphi is finished. While this hasn't been well documented in Delphi in the past, it is not terribly complicated. Once you get the hang of it, you can create a basic framework for a new Delphi expert with little difficulty. Here is the code fragment from the obligatory GetStyle() method we use to accomplish this:

```
{$ifndef Ver80}
  Result := esAddIn;
{$else}
  Result := esStandard;
```

```
{$endif}
```

Ver80 is Delphi 1. Since add-in experts are not available under Delphi 1 (and since the expert is not intended to produce new forms or projects), the logical type is Standard (esStandard). For the 32-bit version there are more options. In this case, we place the sound component creating expert under the Component menu, the logical place for all processes that create or manipulate components. Listing A-1 shows the expert project (library) that builds the DLL.

Listing A-l: An expert project (library) for building a DLL

```
library SNDEXPRT;

uses
{$IFNDEF VER80}
  ShareMem,
{$ENDIF}
  Forms,
  WinTypes,
  ExptIntf,
  ToolIntf,
  VirtIntf,
  SysUtils,
  WinProcs,
  Compgen1 in 'COMPGEN1.PAS' {CodeGenForm},
  Sndtypes in 'SNDTYPES.PAS',
  OptDlg in 'OptDlg.pas' {SoundPlayingOptions},
  sndexp1 in 'sndexp1.pas'; {Global Types}

type  {Expert Class for a Standard Expert}
  TSoundExpert = class( TIExpert )
    function GetName: String; override;
    function GetComment: String; override;
    function GetStyle: TExpertStyle; override;
    function GetState: TExpertState; override;
    function GetMenuText: String; override;
    function GetIDString: String; override;
    {$ifndef Ver80}
    function GetAuthor: string; override;
    procedure RunSoundExpert(Sender: TIMenuItemIntf);
    constructor Create;
    destructor Destroy; override;
    {$endif}
    procedure Execute; override;
  private
```

```
    NewMenuItem: TIMenuItemIntf;
  end;


{ Expert Methods }
{$ifndef Ver80}
constructor TSoundExpert.Create;
var
  MainMenu : TIMainMenuIntf;
  MainMenuItems, ComponentMenu : TIMenuItemIntf;
begin
  inherited Create;
  MainMenu := Nil;
  MainMenuItems := Nil;
  ComponentMenu := Nil;
  NewMenuItem := Nil;
  try
    try
      MainMenu := ToolServices.GetMainMenu;
      MainMenuItems := MainMenu.GetMenuItems;
      ComponentMenu := MainMenuItems.GetItem(6);
      NewMenuItem := ComponentMenu.InsertItem(0, 'S&ound',
                    'TSoundComponentExpert' , '', 0, 0,
                    0, [mfVisible, mfEnabled], RunSoundExpert);
    finally
      ComponentMenu.Free;
      MainMenuItems.Free;
      MainMenu.Free;
    end;
    Except
      ToolServices.RaiseException(ReleaseException);
    end;
end;

procedure HandleException;   {Exceptions must be handeled this way}
begin
  ToolServices.RaiseException( ReleaseException );
end;

procedure TSoundExpert.RunSoundExpert;
begin
  try
    ExecuteExpert(ToolServices);
  except
    ToolServices.RaiseException(ReleaseException);
  end;
end;
```

```
destructor TSoundExpert.Destroy;
begin
  NewMenuItem.Free;
  inherited Destroy;
end;

function TSoundExpert.GetAuthor: string;
begin
  try
  result := 'Alan C. Moore';
  except
    HandleException;
  end;
end;
{$endif}

function TSoundExpert.GetName: String;
begin
  try     {try/except blocks needed for each expert method}
    Result := 'Sound Component Delphi Expert';
  except
    HandleException;
  end;
end;

function TSoundExpert.GetComment: String;
begin
  try
    Result := 'A Delphi Expert to add Sound to a Component';
  except
    HandleException;
  end;
end;

function TSoundExpert.GetStyle: TExpertStyle;   {All experts have this
                                                 method}
begin
  try
  {$ifndef Ver80}
    Result := esAddIn;
  {$else}
    Result := esStandard;
  {$endif}
  except
    HandleException;
  end;
```

```
end;

function TSoundExpert.GetState: TExpertState;   {Possible states of menu
                                                 item}
begin
  try
    Result := [esEnabled];
  except
    HandleException;
  end;
end;

function TSoundExpert.GetMenuText: String;
begin
  try
    Result := 'Sound Component';   {Text that will appear in help menu}
  except
    HandleException;
  end;
end;

function TSoundExpert.GetIdString: String;
begin
  try
    Result := 'TSoundExpert';   {Unique ID string for our new expert}
  except
    HandleException;
  end;
end;

procedure TsoundExpert.Execute; {executes our DLL in main form unit}
begin
  try
    ExecuteExpert( ToolServices );   {in unit, sndexp1.pas}
  except
    HandleException;
  end;
end;

procedure DoneExpert; export; {Cleanup code, if needed}
begin
 { Exit code here if needed }
end;

{Delphi 2/3/4 and Delphi 1-specific ways of accessing TIToolServices}
{$IFDEF WIN32}
```

```
function InitExpert( ToolServices:   TIToolServices;
                     RegisterProc:   TExpertRegisterProc;
                     var Terminate: TExpertTerminateProc ): Boolean;
stdcall; export;
{$ELSE}
function InitExpert( ToolServices:   TIToolServices;
                     RegisterProc:   TExpertRegisterProc;
                     var Terminate: TExpertTerminateProc ): Boolean;
export;
{$ENDIF}
begin

  {Make sure this is the first and only instance of these services }
  Result := ExptIntf.ToolServices = nil;
  if not Result then Exit;

  ExptIntf.ToolServices := ToolServices;
  if ToolServices <> nil then
    Application.Handle := ToolServices.GetParentHandle;

  Terminate := DoneExpert;   {We know where to exit}

  RegisterProc( TSoundExpert.Create );

end;
{$IFDEF WIN32}
{$ELSE}

function FaultHandler( FaultID: Word; FaultAddr: Pointer ):
                       TFaultResponse; export;
begin
  DefaultExceptHandler( FaultID, FaultAddr );
end;
{$ENDIF}

exports
{$IFNDEF WIN32}
  FaultHandler name FaultHandlerSignature resident,
{$ELSE}
{$ENDIF}
  InitExpert   name ExpertEntryPoint resident;

begin

end.
```

Delphi's Expert Interface

The code in Listing A-1 shows how to create a Delphi interface. Here are the details. In any expert you need to be sure that certain files are included in the Uses clause: Forms, WinTypes, ExptIntf, ToolIntf, VirtIntf, SysUtils, WinProcs, and any additional files your expert uses. If you use Pascal strings in a Delphi 32-bit expert, you need to include ShareMem as the first unit; this little omission cost me quite a few hours of needless debugging when I first wrote the Sound Component Expert! Note the Uses clause in Listing A-1. Then you must define your expert class, overriding the appropriate methods. In this case, the declaration (as shown in Listing A-1) is:

```
TSoundExpert = class( TIExpert )
  function GetName: String; override;
  function GetComment: String; override;
  function GetStyle: TExpertStyle; override;
  function GetState: TExpertState; override;
  function GetMenuText: String; override;
  function GetIDString: String; override;
  procedure Execute; override;
end;
```

We discussed the last method, Execute, in Chapter 2. The other functions are extremely simple, consisting of a single Result statement enclosed within the required Try/Except block. Study the code in Listing A-1 to confirm this for yourself. The basic information (result types and contents) is described in Table A-1.

Table A-I: Result types

Function	Result Type	Result Contents
GetName()	string	Unique identifier name
GetComment()	string	Short description
GetStyle()	TExpertStyle	[esStandard, esForm, or esProject]
GetState()	TExpertState	[esChecked or esEnabled]
GetMenuText()	string	Text for Help menu item
GetIDString()	string	Unique expert identifier

Using Tool Services to Access Installed Components

Earlier we mentioned Delphi's Tool Services. But what are these Tool Services? In all versions (and extended in Delphi's 32-bit versions), the Tool Services provide access to the inner working of the Delphi Integrated Development Environment (IDE). So, for example, if you're developing a project expert you have CloseFile(), CloseProject(), and many other similar methods available. You can also query the Tool Services for information on components in the Visual Controls Library (VCL), as we'll demonstrate later.

To use Tool Services you must first initialize them. You accomplish this task with the InitExpert() function, which is not part of our expert class definition. Note that it has a slightly different format in each Delphi version (see Listing A-1). Within this function we register our new expert with Delphi using the RegisterProc() method. If you need to free any memory or perform other cleanup (which we don't in this instance), you also need a DoneExpert() procedure, which is included just for your reference. For Delphi 1 only, a FaultHandler() function also needs to be included.

In the expert we discussed in Chapter 2, we kept a local copy of Tool Services so that we could use it to help us populate the combo box with the names of all of the components in the VCL. Here is the method (from SndExp1.pas) that accomplishes this:

```
procedure TSoundCompForm.PopulateComboBox;
var
  NumComps,
  CurrentComp,
  NumMods,
  CurrentMod : Integer;
begin
{$IFNDEF DEBUG}
  try
  NumMods := iTools.GetModuleCount;
  For CurrentMod := 0 to NumMods-1 do
    begin
      NumComps := iTools.GetComponentCount(CurrentMod);
      If NumComps>0 then For CurrentComp := 0 to NumComps-1 do
        begin
          ComboBox1.Items.Add(iTools.GetComponentName(CurrentMod,
            CurrentComp));
        end;      {inner loop}
```

```
    end;  {outer loop}
  finally
  end;
{$ELSE}
ComboBox1.Items.Add('TBitBtn');
ComboBox1.Items.Add('TListBox');
ComboBox1.Items.Add('TPanel');
{$ENDIF}

end;
```

This example provides at least a superficial idea of how Delphi's Tool Services can be useful in writing experts. Beyond this, these services can also provide a good deal of information about what is going on in the background. The Tool Services functions used here include GetModule-Count (which returns the number of files that register components), GetComponentCount (which returns the number of components registered in a registration unit), and GetComponentName (which returns the name of a particular component). With these three functions you can traverse the entire Visual Component Library and retrieve the name of each component.

However, you can do much more than that. For example, you can find out the number of forms or units used in a project with GetFormCount() and GetUnitCount() respectively. You can retrieve the names of forms and units with GetFormName() and GetUnitName(), respectively. You can also perform useful actions like opening a project (OpenProject), opening a file (OpenFile), saving a project (SaveProject), or saving a file (SaveFile), all from within an expert you write!

There are four special methods in the Tool Services related specifically to components installed in the VCL. These are the methods that are used in this expert. Table A-2 lists and briefly describes each.

Table A-2: Tool Services methods

Method Name	Use of Method
GetComponentCount(X)	This method returns the number of components registered in a module with X being the index number of a module.
GetComponentName(X,Y)	This method returns the name of a component in which X is the index number of a module and Y is the index number of a component registered in that module.

Method Name	Use of Method
GetModuleCount()	This method returns the number of registration modules (not component units) in the VCL.
GetModuleName(X)	This method returns the name of a module where X is the index number of a module.

In both 16- and 32-bit versions of this expert we used all but the last method. Take a look at the TSoundCompForm.PopulateComboBox method above to see how they are used. Within a Try/Finally block we used two loops. The outer loop iterated through all of the installed modules (For CurrentMod := 0 to NumMods 1 do begin) and the inner loop iterated through the components registered in each module (If NumComps>0 then For CurrentComp := 0 to NumComps 1 do begin) if there are any.

This appendix provides the basic information on writing experts and should help you get started. Be sure to read the parts of Chapter 2 that explain building the user interface and the expert engine. An excellent source of information on creating experts is Ray Lischner's early works, *Secrets of Delphi 2* and *Hidden Paths of Delphi 3*.

Appendix B

Other Sources of Information

General Multimedia Programming Books

Advanced Multimedia Programming by Steve Rimmer (Wincrest/McGraw-Hill; ISBN: 0-07-911897-6) is a useful, C-oriented programming book covering a wide range of multimedia topics. As you would expect, there are sections on WAV files and MIDI. In addition to audio topics, this work deals with other techniques often associated with multimedia including animation. Finally, it includes sections on programming joysticks and *.avi video files.

Maximum MIDI by Paul Messick (Manning; ISBN: 1-884777-44-9) is a seminal work on programming MIDI. If you plan to do much work with MIDI you should definitely examine this book. It includes a number of tools that you could easily incorporate into your applications. These include a library of MIDI routines with source code included. This work also provides a comprehensive overview of MIDI.

A Programmer's Guide to Sound by Tim Kientzle (Addison-Wesley; ISBN: 0-201-41972-6) is an excellent work. If you are working with multimedia on multiple platforms (particularly Windows, Macintosh, and/or UNIX), this book is essential. If you have a background in C++, you'll appreciate Kientzle's object-oriented approach. The coverage of audio topics is quite comprehensive. There is an excellent introduction to programming sound including important topics like acoustics and psycho-acoustics. Of course, there are equally excellent sections on waveform audio and MIDI.

Windows 95 Multimedia and ODBC API Bible by Richard J. Simon (Waite Group Press; ISBN: 1-57169-011-5) presents a thorough overview of Windows' current support for multimedia, telephony, and Open Database

Connectivity (ODBC). The multimedia chapters comprise nearly half of the book and provide a comprehensive exposition of all of the constants, structures, and functions in the Windows Multimedia APIs. This book was one of the main resources I used in writing this work. The explanations are clear and concise, and the C examples provided excellent models for much of the code in this book.

Delphi Programming Books

Delphi 2 Multimedia Adventure Set by Scott Jarol, Dan Haygood, and Chris Coppola (Coriolis Group Books; ISBN: 1-883577-64-0) is the "classic" Delphi book on multimedia. One of the interesting features of this book is the HTML application (web browser and hypertext engine) that constitutes one of its major threads. This aspect has been a bit controversial. I know some developers who love it and others who do not feel that HTML should be a part of a book on multimedia. Personally, I found the sections on the multimedia APIs very helpful. These include excellent (though incomplete) introductions to the WAVE API, the MIDI API, and MCI (Media Control Interface). These chapters are particularly helpful in providing a context in which to use the functions in mmsystem.pas.

Developing Custom Delphi 3 Components by Ray Konopka (Coriolis Group Books, ISBN: 1-57610-112-6) is the generally accepted classic in writing Delphi components. If you plan to create your own components (multimedia or otherwise), you cannot find a better introduction to the topic than this work. All of the essential component-creation topics are included. You'll be learning this useful discipline from one of the acknowledged masters of Delphi component writing.

Hidden Paths of Delphi 3 by Ray Lischner (Informant Press, ISBN: 0-9657366-0-1) is the most complete work on writing Delphi experts. While there is no specific information on multimedia topics per se, the coverage of advanced expert writing topics is indispensable for anyone who plans to write Delphi experts. And don't be concerned with Delphi 3 in the title; all of the material is applicable to the 32-bit Delphi versions released since Delphi 3. Furthermore, the author has provided updates to each subsequent Delphi version on his web site.

Secrets of Delphi 2 by Ray Lischner (Waite Group Press, ISBN: 1-57169-026-3) is one of the best sources of information on building Delphi experts. While there is very little information on multimedia topics per se, the coverage of advanced topics will be extremely helpful to anyone writing Delphi experts or components. And don't be put off by Delphi 2 in the title; just about all of the material is applicable to every 32-bit Delphi version. Furthermore, the author has provided updates to each subsequent Delphi version on his web site.

The Tomes of Delphi 3: Win32 Core API by John Ayers, et al. (Wordware Publishing, Inc. ISBN: 1-55622-556-3) was the book that inspired me to write the current volume. As most in the Delphi community would acknowledge, there is simply no better introduction to API-level programming. As much as possible, I have tried to follow the conventions of this first work in this exploration of the multimedia APIs. There is a small amount of overlap between the two works since the first volume also deals with joysticks and timers, but in a somewhat different manner.

General Multimedia Sites

The Audio File Format FAQ (http://home.sprynet.com/~cbagwell/audio.html) has up-to-date information on many audio file formats as well as links to some interesting articles (including one on audio effects algorithms).

Audio Lab's Audio and Acoustic Links (http://audiolab.uwaterloo.ca/aa_links.html) provides links to many audio and acoustic sites containing useful technical information.

The EDN Access site (htpp://www.ednmag.com/reg/1995/110995/) has articles on various technologies including a very detailed one from 1995 entitled "Multimedia Codecs Move beyond Basic Conversion."

The Midi Farm (http://www.midifarm.com/) has information on commercial products and a large collection of MIDI files and resources.

The MidiWeb (http://www.midiweb.com/programming/index.shtml) includes a section on programming (C/C++ and Visual Basic) and MIDI file downloads.

Online Communicator's (http://www.communicator.com/audio1.html) audio section has a number of useful links to audio technology sites including some related to MPEG audio. Check out the "Channel 1" File Library. This is a very good source for shareware and freeware programs and utilities, including several hundred multimedia items.

The Sampling Zone (http://www.synthzone.com/sampling.htm) is devoted to audio samples and sampling resources. It includes a large list of links to sites where you can find tools and sound resources.

32bit.com (http://www.32bit.com/software/listings/Multimedia/) contains a large multimedia section. This site is well-organized and easy to navigate. There are a large number of utilities (but without source code).

Delphi Multimedia Sites

Athena's Place (http://www.bhnet.com.br/~simonet/hotoprojs.htm) includes eight Delphi how-to projects with full source code. Most of these projects are related to multimedia. If you're just getting started in multimedia and prefer to "do it yourself" rather than use preexisting components, I think you'll find Alex Simonetti's cool site worth visiting. The particular projects include the following tasks:

- Creating and saving a WAVE file to your own custom format
- Saving a WAVE file to a BLOB field
- Creating high-resolution timers using the multimedia services
- Detecting multimedia devices and setting their volumes
- Creating and using resource-only DLLs that can be used with multimedia data
- Extracting version information from DLLs, EXEs, and VXDs

Colin Wilson's (http://www.wilsonc.demon.co.uk/delphi.htm) site features a large collection of freeware multimedia components and demonstration applications with full source code that include the following:

- "Mixer Demo" encapsulating the master volume control along with balance, mute, bass and treble, MIDI volume, balance, and mute controls
- "Mixer Explorer" that displays the mixer components supported on a particular system in a tree view
- "MIDI Controls and Sequencer," a particularly feature-rich application
- "MIDI Controls Demo," an application that plays MIDI files and displays MIDI events in piano roll style

- "MIDI Jukebox," an application that uses the MIDI controls and the mixer components
- "Multimedia Level Data and Meter," an application that includes an LED Ladder control and a Multimedia Meter Data control. All of these applications include full source code. There are also a number of NT-specific routines among many others. Indeed, this is a very rich site well worth visiting.

Dave's MIDI Software (http://www.netcomuk.co.uk/~dave.ch/midisoft.html) is one of the major Delphi MIDI sites, with links to many other sites. You should find his freeware collection, MidiComp, particularly valuable. It includes MIDI input and output components for Delphi and demonstration applications that use these components. I have tried some of these components and recommend them for your consideration.

Delphi Multimedia (http://www.kobira.co.jp/sakura/d_Multi.htm) is a Japanese Delphi site with some nice downloads including David Taylor's Sweepgen application, which I discuss in Chapter 3.

Swift Software (http://www.swiftsoft.de/) provides a full line of professional multimedia Delphi components for manipulating wave data, working with mixers, and handling AVI files. There are unusual components that filter sounds, create sound effects, and work with the newer technologies including DirectSound (3D) and MPEG. (I have not yet tested these so I cannot comment on their quality.) There are also some freeware Delphi tools and components on this site. All of these tools and components include source code.

Appendix C

A Glossary of Audio and Multimedia Terms

aliasing – Audio distortion in digital recording or analog to digital conversion. This can occur when the sampling rate is too slow and noises that were not present in the original sound are introduced.

amplitude – The strength of an electronic signal; in audio, this is generally the same as the loudness of a sound. See also amplitude modulation.

amplitude modulation (AM) – The process of electronically changing the amplitude of a particular sound in a particular (usually regular) manner over a period of time. Corresponds to the musical effect called tremolo. See also amplitude and frequency modulation.

band-pass filter – A filter that passes only frequencies in a certain band width, eliminating frequencies above or below. See also filter, high-pass filter, and low-pass filter, and notch filter.

compression – A technique using a mathematical algorithm that stores data in a more efficient (compressed) format, thus saving disk space and speeding up downloading time. Commonly applied to audio and movie files.

chorusing – Creating the effect of a musical chorus through combining a sound with a delayed and modulated version of the sound itself.

clip – A discrete segment of audio or video data generally stored in a separate file.

clipping – A type of distortion that occurs when the amplitude of a sound is above a certain maximum allowed level.

cutoff frequency – In filtering, the frequency at which the signal begins to fall off rapidly.

decibel (DB) – The acoustical unit (expressed as a ratio) for measuring amplitude or loudness.

dithering – Adding additional noise to a signal to cover quantization noise. See also quantization.

equalization – The process of raising or lowering the amplitude of particular frequency ranges in a sound file. Useful in emphasizing certain instruments or voices in a musical file. See also filtering.

filter – An electronic device that removes or decreases the amplitude of sounds within a certain frequency range. See also filtering, band-pass filter, high-pass filter, low-pass filter, and notch filter.

filtering – The process of removing or decreasing the amplitude of sounds within a certain frequency range. See also filter, band-pass filter, high-pass filter, low-pass filter, and notch filter.

frequency – The number of vibrations or cycles per second (hertz) of a periodic sound. In musical terms, the highness or lowness of a pitch or tone. See also frequency modulation and hertz.

frequency modulation – The process of modifying one frequency (within the audible range) with another frequency (usually below the audible range). The musical effect produced is called vibrato, which is a regular fluctuation in pitch. See also frequency and amplitude modulation.

hertz (hZ) – Acoustical term for measurement of frequency; cycles per second (cps).

high pass filter – A filter that passes through frequencies above a certain point and removes those below that frequency (called the cut-off frequency). See also filter, band-pass filter, low-pass filter, and notch filter.

low pass filter – A filter that passes through frequencies below a certain point and removes those above that frequency (called the cutoff frequency). See also filter, band-pass filter, high-pass filter, and notch filter.

mix (mixer, mixing) – The combination of two or more discrete independent sounds or sound files into a new sound file. A mixer is a device that performs this task; mixing is the task itself. The Mixer API is one of the multimedia APIs discussed in this book.

Musical Instrument Device Interface (MIDI) – Standard asynchronous (serial) communications protocol for sending sound data between various sound devices such as synthesizers, electronic keyboards, and computer sound cards. One of the multimedia APIs discussed in this book.

noise – Sometimes refers to unwanted or extraneous sounds that are introduced. In electronic music, it can refer to complex sounds created through combining a large number of frequencies. White noise is the combination of all audible frequencies together.

notch filter – A filter that passes only frequencies above or below a certain band, or range of frequencies; opposite of band-pass filter. See also filter, band-pass filter, high-pass filter, and low-pass filter.

quantization – The process of rounding off certain values during the analog to digital conversion processing, often resulting in the introduction of additional noise.

reverberation (reverb) – An echo-like effect similar to the way sound behaves in many natural environments where it bounces off a surface and is heard a moment later but at a reduced volume.

Resource Interchange File Format (RIFF) – A general file format developed by Microsoft that is used a great deal with multimedia files.

sample – A "snapshot" of a digital sound, often used in synthesized music to mimic the sound quality of a particular instrument.

signal to noise ratio (SNR) – The ratio between a recorded sound and any background noise that may be present. The higher the SNR the better the quality of the recording.

synthesizer – An electronic music device that can combine various sound waves to simulate the timbre of musical instruments or create new ones. Most multimedia computers have a built-in synthesizer.

timbre – Tone quality; what makes it possible to differentiate between different instruments in the same pitch range (clarinet, oboe, violin, etc.).

waveform – The native sound format used by Microsoft Windows. (One of the multimedia APIs discussed in this book.) Also, a visual representation of a sound, particularly a periodic sound that would be perceived as a pitch (single tone).

Index

Page numbers for function and command syntax blocks are printed in bold.

I don't have time for learning curves.

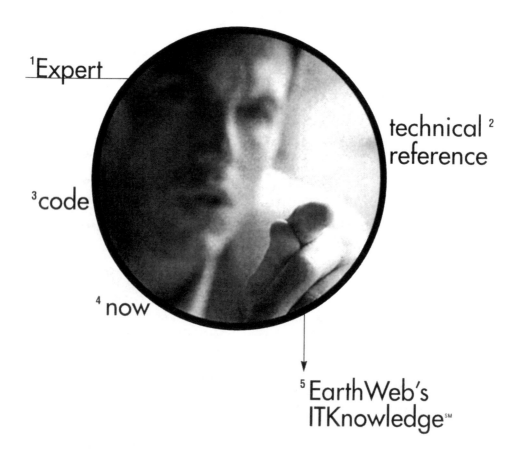

¹Expert

technical ²
reference

³code

⁴ now

⁵ EarthWeb's
ITKnowledge℠

They rely on you to be the ❶ expert on tough development challenges. There's no time for learning curves, so you go online for ❷ technical references from the experts who wrote the books. Find answers fast simply by clicking on our search engine. Access hundreds of online books, tutorials and even source ❸ code samples ❹ now. Go to ❺ EarthWeb's ITKnowledge, get immediate answers, and get down to it.

Get your FREE ITKnowledge trial subscription today at itkgo.com.
Use code number 026.

EARTHWEB
Go further *faster*